The
Thousand Year
Reign of Christ

The Classic Work on the Millennium

"To whom do we owe it that the Evangelical Church of today no longer, after the fashion of the old Dogmatics, brands, as a heterodoxy, the Chiliastic view of the End-Time, but has taken it up into her deepest and innermost life, so that today, a believing Christian can scarcely be found who does not enjoy it? To whom do we owe it that the Church of to-day believes in a glorious future for Israel, and sees, in Old Testament History, a Pre-history and forelight of Israel's End-history, and in Old Testament Prophecy a far-sight, not merely of the glory of the Gentile Church, but of Israel in a literal sense? To whom do we owe it that the Church, in recognition of the sensuous reality in which the super-sensuous salvation is clothed, has again reinstated Old Testament History in its right, and conceived the spiritual and corporeal in their organic relations, and limitations? We owe it to none other than Bengel. He it was who emptied out the last dregs of an Anti-Chiliastic Theology, disposed to Heresy-Mania, under the appearance of Orthodoxy, and, even yet more, led, to a better view, the Moravian Brethren who thought they realized, in their own fellowship, the glorious future of the Church, the so-called Philadelphian Period. He burst asunder the chains of a binding traditionalism of interpretation, deemed, in his day, almost unassailable, vindicated the mother-right of Exegesis to control Dogmatics, and showed, to the Church, the Castalian Fount, in the Scriptures, from which she must ever renew her youth."

—Delitzsch

The Thousand Year Reign of Christ

The Classic Work on the Millennium

NATHANIEL WEST

kregel
PUBLICATIONS

Grand Rapids, MI 49501

The Thousand Year Reign of Christ by Nathaniel West.

Copyright © 1993 by Kregel Publications.

Published in 1993 by Kregel Publications, a division of Kregel, Inc., P.O. Box 2607, Grand Rapids, MI 49501.

Cover Design: Alan G. Hartman

Library of Congress Cataloging-in-Publication Data
West, Nathaniel, 1826-1906.
   [Studies in eschatology]
   The thousand year reign of Christ / Nathaniel West.
     p.   cm.
   Originally published: Studies in eschatology, 1899.
   1. Millennium. 2. Eschatology. I. Title.
BT890.W52   1993   236'.9—dc20   93-4549
                                            CIP

ISBN 0-8254-4000-9 (paperback)

1 2 3 4 5 Printing / Year 97 96 95 94 93

Printed in the United States of America

FOREWORD

Of the many widely-read students of prophecy in our country in the latter part of the nineteenth century, I would say that there were five who could be called outstanding, scholars of unquestioned ability and deep insight into the Word of God. These would be Dr. Samuel H. Kellogg (1839-1899), for some years Professor at Western Theological Seminary, Allegheny, Pennsylvania; and then Dr. James H. Brookes (1830-1897), of St. Louis; Dr. E. R. Craven, who wrote the exceedingly rich notes on the Book of Revelation in the American Edition of the Lange Series of Commentaries, pastor for many years of the Third Presbyterian Church of Newark, New Jersey; the Reverend George N. H. Peters (1825-?) of the Evangelical Lutheran Church, and for most of his life living in Springfield, Ohio; and Dr. Nathanael West, the author of the learned volume for which this stands as a Preface. Of these five men, all but Mr. Peters were members of the Presbyterian Church. Such students of prophecy, of such depth of learning and insight into the Holy Scriptures cannot be found, I regret to say, in America today.

Dr. Nathanael West was one of those who, like Peters and Craven, never made any of the more important American Biographical Dictionaries. As far as I know, not even a sketch of Dr. Nathanael West has ever been attempted before for any printed volume. For many of the details of his various pastorates, which I am about to name, I am deeply indebted to my friend, Miss Helen Harris, of Princeton, New Jersey, who very kindly traced the pastorates of Dr. West, from the beginning of his ministry until his retirement, in the rich Presbyterian historical material available in the Library of Princeton Theological Seminary.

Nathanael West was born in Sunderland, England, in 1826. The time of his coming to America is not indicated in any of the sources that have been at my disposal, but twenty years later, in 1846, Mr. West graduated from the University of Michigan, with the degree of B.A. In 1850 the University of Michigan conferred on him the degree of M.A. From 1847 to 1850, Mr. West was a student in the Allegheny Seminary. What happened to postpone his ordination in the Presbytery of Pittsburgh until 1855 is not recorded. In fact, he became the Pastor of the Fifth Church of Pittsburgh before ordination had taken place, for the years 1853 and 1854, and immediately following ordination he became pastor of the Central Church of Cincinnati, Ohio, where he remained for nearly five years, 1855-1859. It may well be that between the time of his graduation from Allegheny Seminary, until his pastorate in Pittsburgh, he was engaged upon the exhausting work of a volume which Scribner's published for him in 1853, *A Complete Analysis of the Holy Bible*, a work of over 1,000 pages, which went through many, many reprintings, and became a standard reference work for multitudes of ministers and professors throughout our country. If he did devote two or three years of unremitting labor to this work, without a definite pastorate, unless Scribner's at that time advanced him a considerable sum of money to be applied to and paid back with future contemplated royalties, Mr. West must have had some independent means, and this is what one would judge from the later history of this distinguished scholar.

Mr. West's pastoral history is not one which could be called ideal in one area, and that is, that he held eight different pastorates within a period of thirty-three years, six of them within a period of eighteen years. He was pastor of the Second Presbyterian Church of Brooklyn, New York, 1860-1868, and then became a Professor in the Danville Theological Seminary, teaching there from 1869-1875. This latter would have seemed to be the ideal labor for one of his gifts for research and investigation, but he returned to the pastorate in 1875, ministering for not much more than a year in the Lincoln Park Presbyterian Church of Cincinnati. I have no record of where he was or what he was doing from 1876-1883, practically eight blank years. In 1883, for a pastorate of not much more than a year, he was the stated supply at the Westminster Church of Detroit. For less than a year, 1884, he was the stated supply of the Central Church of Louisville, Kentucky, and then pastor of the First Presbyterian Church of St. Paul, in 1886. This was, I believe, the last pastorate which he held, though he was only at this time sixty years of age. The minutes of the General Assembly for this period list him as a Minister Without Charge, from 1887 to 1904. Though his membership remained in the St. Paul Presbytery, from 1900 he was a resident of Clifton Springs, New York. Mr. West passed away in Washington, D.C., July 7, 1906, at the age of eighty.

There is one more item about the personal domestic and professional life of Dr. West that will be of great interest to many who know anything about the history of Princeton University during the early part of our century. There was born to Mr. and Mrs. West, while they were living in Allegheny (in the year 1853), a son whom they named Andrew Fleming. Now Andrew Fleming West became one of the most noted classical scholars, and defenders of a classical education, in the entire University sphere of American education in the latter part of the nineteenth and the beginning of the twientieth centuries. Professor West was the Professor of Latin in Princeton University from 1883-1928, that is, from the age of thirty to the age of seventy-five; remarkable that he should be allowed to continue at least ten more years teaching Latin after the age of sixty-five. But more than that, it was this Dr. West who so vigorously contended for the establishment of a graduate school at Princeton University, against the bitter and constant opposition of Mr. Woodrow Wilson during his presidency of Princeton University. Dean West, as he was then called, won this long drawn-out battle and not only saw the graduate school erected, but was himself appointed the Dean of the Graduate School in 1901, a position that he retained until 1928. Dean West died in 1943. I have often wondered what happened to the great prophetic library of Nathanael West, and if Dean. West of the Graduate School of Princeton was well taught in the great prophetic tradition of the Holy Scriptures. But this will probably never be known.

Now may we turn to a brief consideration of the part Nathanael West played in the development of prophetic study in our own country in the last half of the nineteenth century. Mr. West became active in early Prophetic Conferences, and

took a very important part in the one held in New York City
October 30, and 31, and November 1, 1878. The messages delivered at this time were reprinted, first in an extra edition of
the *New York Tribune,* fifty thousand copies of which were
sold before the edition was exhausted! Much of this material
then was reprinted in a large volume, which Revell published
in 1879, with the title, *Premillennial Essays of the Prophetic
Conference held in the Church of the Holy Trinity in New
York City.* This work was not only edited by Dr. Nathanael
West but in this volume, one will find the most important
history of Premillennialism that exists in the literature of that
generation, entitled, "History of the Premillennial Doctrine,"
pages 313-404 written by Dr. West. At the end of this volume is
an Appendix of some forty pages, with extracts from many works
published on the continent supporting the premillennial position,
and the literal first resurrection, many of them being outstanding
scholars of a world-wide reputation at that time, much of this
material never appearing in any other volume in English. Here
one finds what is discovered in all the later writings of our author,
and that is, a knowledge of the whole vast literature of prophetic study and interpretation, not only of the early church
and the Middle Ages, but especially all the major works of
German and French theologians and exegetes of the nineteenth
century, with translations of and quotations from scores and
scores of these volumes, many of which could not even be
found in the libraries of our larger theological seminaries today.
    As an illustration of the vast extent of Dr. West's knowledge
of the prophetic literature of the Continent, one might point
to his reference to a work by Dr. Christian August Crusius, *De
caelo per Adventum Christi cammoto,* published in 1757. Kant
characterized Crusius as "the clearest philosopher, and second
to none in the promotion of philosophy in our age." Yet, as
far as I have been able to discover, there is not a copy of this
work by Crusius in any library in America.
    The volume of which this forms a Preface is a very difficult
work to read, and at the same time, in many ways, the most
learned work on this aspect of Biblical prophecy ever to appear
in the English language, i.e., on the subject of the Millennium
and the symbolic significance of Biblican numbers. I think one
would do well, if I may make a suggestion here, to begin possibly with the second part, and then go on into the book as far

as one wishes, possibly skipping for the time being, Part Three, then resuming one's reading of Part Four, and continuing down until Part Eleven, and then go back and read, I would say, Part One and the other chapters one has skipped. If one wishes to read continuously, then he must decide to give very serious consideration to every single sentence of the earlier pages, so as not to be lost in the rich material and profound arguments which Mr. West develops. I need say nothing more about the volume itself.

The last work which our learned author published was a volume now very rarely come upon, *Daniel's Great Prophecy, the Eastern Question of the Kingdom.* This was published in New York in 1898 by the Hope of Israel movement, of which no less a person than Dr. A. G. Gaebelein was superintendent. In other words, by this time Mr. West, then past sixty, was working in cooperation with another great student of prophecy, soon to produce even more works with wider circulation than Mr. West was able to accomplish, Mr. West, being seventy-two and Dr. Gaebelein being thirty-seven years of age. There is an extended Appendix, not listed in the Table of Contents, extending to some sixty pages in which we have chapters on Prophetic Numbers, Daniel the Father of Universal History, the Relation of Daniel's Prophecy to the Olivet Discourse, and the Apocalypse, Gog and Antichrist, and a searching criticism of Canon Farrar's very liberal work on Daniel in the *Expositor's Bible.*

One does not have to agree with all of the author's interpretations in recognizing this work as a major contribution to the understanding of some of the deeper aspects of Biblical prophecy.

Wilbur M. Smith

San Marino, California.

PREFACE

A profound interest in the word of divine prophecy has become general in our day, among a vast multitude of God's children, and is the necessary result not only of the great principle of free investigation set in motion by the Reformation of the 16th century, but of a special prediction that, "in the Time of the End," it should be so, Dan. xii:4, and of the fact that the End of our Age is fast approaching, Matt. xxiv:32–40. Eschatological questions have stepped to the front, in connection with apologetics and polemics in defence of Christianity, and this character of the first Age of Christianity repeats itself. Among these questions, are the deepening apostasy of Christendom from the pure truth and the ancient faith, the rapid extension of missions, restoration and conversion of Israel, the Antichrist, the coming of the Lord from heaven, the judgment of the church and the world, the resurrection from among the dead, the binding of Satan, and the millennial reign. Educated men, as well as devout souls of humbler pretension, begin to see, as never before, that not only "the testimony of Jesus is the Spirit of prophecy," Rev. xix:10, but that the prophetic page is a word "more sure" than ocular demonstration, or audible voice from heaven; "a lamp shining in a dark place, whereunto they do well to take heed, until the Day dawn, and the Day-Star,"—the phosphor of millennial glory,—"arise upon their hearts." II Pet. i:19. The nearer the End of the present Age, the more are their eyes directed to those facts of the Scripture where the "Last Things" are the theme, and the more do their hearts begin to breathe the prayer, "Come, Lord Jesus!" There is an unusual "searching" after the "what time and the what manner of time, the Spirit of Christ, who was in the prophets, did point to when foretestifying the sufferings of Christ, and the glories after these." I Pet. i:11. Hence the almost fabulous increase of

prophetic and apocalyptic literature, in our day, and deep exegetical investigation in reference to the " Last Things," new
volumes daily pouring from the press, in an uninterrupted
stream. It is one of the predicted "Signs of the Times."
Dan. xii:4.

It is not to be denied that a large part of the professing
church, swayed by its teachers, is indifferent to these themes,
and to this phenomenon, and regard the word of prophecy as
unprofitable, and its unfulfilled part as unintelligible. This
also is a " Sign of the Times," Isa. xxix:9–12, even as the
concurrence of these two contradictory facts, the increase of
apostasy and extension of missions, constitute another "Sign."
Matt. xxiv:10–14. A false spiritualizing, allegorizing, and
idealizing, interpretation has contributed to rob the predictions
concerning Israel of their realistic value, _failing to discriminate
between what is common to Jew and Gentile alike, in the one
spiritual salvation which comes to all_, and where " there is _no_
distinction," Acts xv:9; Rom. iii:23, and what is _peculiar to
literal Israel, as the people bringing salvation to the world, and
ordained in the future, as in the past, to a distinguished place in
the kingdom of God._ As a result of this false lure, " blindness
in part " has happened to the Gentiles until Israel is saved, a
blindness that affects all eschatological questions, and has
brought the Church, in many places, to regard the doctrine of
the pre-millennial coming of Israel's Messiah as a " Jewish
fable" not to be believed. Eschatology is assigned to a back
seat, and the Voice from heaven that summons all to " hear
what the Spirit saith to the churches," and commands a blessing on " him who readeth and them who hear the words of
this prophecy,"—the preacher and his congregation,—is dis-
regarded. Rev. i:3; ii:7. The Church does not understand the
present age, nor its relation to the coming age, nor Israel's
relation to both, and to the Nations, and to the Church herself. And this blindness will continue until the false systems
of interpretation, by which it has been caused, are rejected.
Until the glamour of this enchantment has been dissolved, it
is impossible to understand either the organic structure of
prophecy, the mission of the Church, the position of our
present Age, Israel's place in history, the Antichrist, the Ages
and the Ends, the difference between the Kingdom and the
Church, or the time of Christ's appearing. The Anti-Semitism
of our modern times, with its hatred of the Jew,—a thing dis-
graceful to Christendom, and so unlike the Philo-Israelism of

the apostolic days,—is due, in no small degree, to these false systems of interpretation.

These pages re-assert, upon the ground of God's word alone,—redundant with its justifying proof,—that Doctrine of *the Pre-Millennial Coming of Christ,* which, in the apostolic and old-Catholic Church, was, for 300 years, "the test of orthodoxy," and formed a chief article of faith and hope. They profess to demonstrate the revelation and the designation of *"the* 1000 *years,"* in the Old as well as in the New Testament, and more repeatedly in the former than in the latter. Hence the title of the book: *" The Thousand Years in both Testaments."* Two " Parts " are devoted to this theme. The *" Supplementary Discussions"* in their separate and more numerous " Parts," are auxiliary to this main purpose, sweeping the wide compass of Scripture from Moses to John, discussing the great question of symbolical numbers, exhibiting the vital organism of all prophecy, and illustrating the perfect unity of the whole word of God. The writer ventures to hope that the severe, and hitherto perplexing problem of the 70 Weeks of Daniel and which, when understood, displays a complete scheme of prophecy, divine purpose, course of history, and relation of Israel to the Nations and to the Church, from the Exile down to the Second Coming of Christ, has at length reached a satisfactory solution. Where Greek and Hebrew terms appear, the English letter has been used, solely for the sake of the ordinary reader. The discussion is wholly exegetical and critical, for the reason that the writer desired to give to many earnest seekers after truth, a biblical foundation in the terms of the Holy Ghost Himself, for a precious doctrine which, with some, is more a matter of sentiment than of knowledge. The views of distinguished men are freely reviewed, and distinctly approved or condemned. It is one of the virtues which characterizes all great investigators, like Augustine, Hengstenberg, Keil, and Kliefoth, that the very *clearness* of their utterances, serves only to *expose* the fundamental error which vitiates their otherwise matchless and meritorious work.

Should any one, reading these pages, dream that the writer, by adhering to the literal and realistic interpretation, i. e. the grammatical and historical, as opposed to the false systems just named, has robbed the *" Church "* of her inheritance in the promises of God, it is enough to answer, *Man! thine hour is not yet come!* " Salvation is *from* the Jews."

The Old Covenant at Sinai, and the New Covenant at Jerusalem, were, both, made with the literal Israel, with Jews, and not with Gentiles. Heb. viii:8–13. *Christian Israel,* according to the flesh, was the historic and organic Root and Basis of the Church, at the first coming of Messiah. *Christian Israel,* according to the flesh, and *as a Nation,* will be the historic and organic Root and Basis of the Kingdom, at Messiah's second coming. It is the uniform doctrine of the Bible. Only after the conversion of Israel as a Nation, at the second coming of Messiah, will the *"veil"* be taken from the Nations, as from Israel, and a national Christianity exist in the glorified Kingdom of Christ on earth. The Gentile proselyte engrafted into the Old Covenant took Israel's name. The Gentile convert, engrafted into the New Covenant, acquires a privilege no less. *But only in a spiritual sense.* The incorporation does not annihilate the tree, nor abolish the *standing distinction,* or *national contrast,* everywhere seen from Moses to John, between the native and the wild branches, or *"Israel"* and the *" Gentiles."* Spiritually, *" in Christ"* there is " neither Jew nor Greek," and for the same reason, " neither male nor female." But he needs instruction in "the first principles of the oracles of God," who builds on this the unscriptural doctrine that, externally, neither in the " Church," nor in the " Kingdom," are Jew and Gentile, male and female, to be discovered. The Church is not Christ. The Kingdom is not Christ. All nations, and both sexes, are found in both. In the spiritual relation, all distinctions disappear. *" In Christ,"* there is neither parent nor child, husband nor wife. To use the sweet words of Tertullian, when speaking of the Christian husband and wife, *" ambo fratres," " both are brethren."* In the economical or dispensational relation, nationalities, and sex, both abide, save in the case of the risen saints. The *antithesis* between Israel and the Nations endures, not only in the Millennial Age, but on the New Earth.

These are preliminary thoughts. Our present Age, occupied with evangelizing the Nations, belongs to the " Times of the Gentiles," when Israel is under foot, and will be followed by another in which Christ's Kingdom will be Israel's Kingdom, Gentile supremacy over Israel having passed away, and Israel once more placed in their historical position and relation to the Nations, as a converted people, holy to the Lord. In Abraham's seed, *collectively,* all Nations shall bless themselves. Such is the realistic interpretation concerning Israel and the Kingdom of the 1000 years.

These truths are enforced, in these pages, by constant textual reference, and also by ample quotations from men of eminent scholarship and piety, than whom the Church enjoys none greater. The quotations could have been multiplied a hundred fold. Their presence is meant to refute the foolish statement, so often made by persons of superficial attainment, or improper bias, that the learning of the Age is opposed to the pre-millennial view. Nothing is more seriously erroneous. The reader will judge whether he can name, as scholars, anywhere, men superior in learning, authority, influence or true devotion to the cause of Christ, or worthier to be trusted than the shining lights hereinafter cited. The appeal must, however, be made, in the last as well as the first instance, to the written Word of God.

How imperfectly so vast and difficult a theme as " *The* 1000 *years in both Testaments*," has been handled, in these pages, the writer is painfully aware. The problems involved are among the most intricate. It is a comfort to know that, as the evening of our Age approaches, " there shall be light," and " the wise shall understand." God will raise up faithful men to add still better demonstrations of His truth, until the time arrives when, as the great Bengel said, not only Old Testament prophecy, but the Apocalypse, will become so clear, that both will be taught to children as " parts of their juvenile instruction." If the time bestowed upon these pages, and the use made of the toil of other men, shall enable any of God's children to catch a glimpse of the glory of His word, and the grandeur of His way, or confirm their faith and hope in the literal realities of the Sacred Prophecies, and lead them to look beyond themselves, to the Coming Kingdom, and its bright rewards, and to work, do, suffer, wait, watch and pray for its approach, neither the hours nor the labor will have been in vain.

To my dear brethren in the ministry, and others, noble men and women, all " one in Christ," who have assisted to bear the burden of publishing these pages, and but for whose counsel and encouragement the pen had many times dropped, not to be relifted, and especially to my brothers Dr. L. W. Munhall of Germantown, Pa., and Professor Dr. W. G. Morehead of Xenia, O., I desire, here and openly, to express my sincere and grateful acknowledgments. In the day of recompense, their service will not be forgotten ! Nor will the deep interest of my dear brethren Drs. Brookes of St. Louis, A. T. Pierson,

Philadelphia, Pa., Erdmann of Asheville, Erdmann of Morris-
town, Duffield of Princeton, S. H. Kellogg and Parsons of
Toronto, W. Parlane, Esq. of Collingwood, S. P. Harbison
and Joseph Albree of Pittsburgh, Pa., Hon. J. W. Baldwin of
Columbus, O., and Benjamin Douglass, Esq of Chicago, fail
of its reward. To my faithful friend Hon. Henry Hastings
Sibley, L.L.D. of St. Paul, Minn., thanks are due which I
know not how to express. More than all, to Him who has
given me "songs in the night," and a love for His dear Son
that is quenchless, and whose blessed Spirit is the source of
all light, an eternal self-sacrifice is due.

I commit this work to the providence of God,—for whose
glory it is written,—casting my little loaf upon the waters,
expecting to find,—perhaps not "after *many* days,"—that it
has contributed to instruct, strengthen and cheer, some of
God's dear children in their journey Kingdomward. May His
blessing go with it, pardoning whatever is amiss in conception,
argument or expression, and opening the hearts of some to
receive whatever is according to His will. In the hour of
affliction we learn more of God's word, and God's way, than in
a whole age of sunshine and prosperity, and it is well to remember that the prophecies were spoken first in that moment when
Israel's night was the darkest. Paradoxical indeed, it was then
the light was the brightest, the promise the sweetest, and the
devotion the deepest. So will it be again. Israel will be able
to say, when emerging from the last great tribulation, as when
returning from Exile to build the Temple·

> " *The Lord hath chastened me sore,*
> *But not abandoned me to death.*
> *The Lord is God. He hath given us light;*
> *Bind the sacrifice with cords,*
> EVEN TO THE HORNS OF THE ALTAR!"

Affliction, Lignt, and Consecration, these are the best hand-
maids of a true interpretation.

NATHANIEL WEST

St. Paul, Minnesota, June 1, 1889

CONTENTS

The Thousand Years
in Both Testaments

PART 1

Part 2

Supplementary Discussions

Part 1
SYMBOLIC NUMBERS

Part 2
THE 1,260 DAYS, OR 3 ½ YEARS

Part 3
THE CAUSE OF ERROR IN DETERMINING THE 70 SEVENS

Part 4
THE 144,000

Part 5
THE 1,000 YEARS

Part 6
CHARACTERISTICS OF THE 1,000 YEARS

Part 7
IDEAL THEORY OF NUMBERS

Part 8
THE TESTIMONY OF THE SYNAGOGUE

Part 9

THE APOCALYPSE OF JOHN

Part 10

THE 1,000 YEARS IN EZEKIEL

Part 11
OUR PRESENT AGE— THE CHRISTIAN STATE

POSTSCRIPT TO PART 11

DIAGRAM.

LITERAL INTERPRETATION.

Appendix

POST-MILLENNIALISM

EXTRACTS FROM EMINENT AUTHORS.

SOLI DEO GLORIA

Part 1

THE THOUSAND YEARS
IN BOTH TESTAMENTS

It is a very common opinion, widely spread throughout Christendom, and in most cases believed to be true, that "the thousand years" of which John speaks in the Apocalypse, Rev. xx:1-7, are mentioned nowhere else in the sacred Scriptures. The doctrine of a millennial kingdom on earth, introduced by the advent of Christ in His glory, is a Jewish fable without support from the word of God. A deeper study of the sacred volume dissipates this false prejudice and reveals the fact that, not only are "the thousand years" of which John speaks found everywhere in both Testaments, but that next to the eternal state, the millennial blessedness of God's people on earth, and of the nations, is the one high point in all prophecy, from Moses to John, the bright, broad tableland of all eschatology. The prejudice against the study of a theme so sublime and far-reaching, and occupying so much space in the revelation God has been pleased to give us, is as remarkable in our age, as

1

it is inexcusable, although by no means surprising. To use the words of Prof. Van Oosterzee, "We cannot be surprised that the inner discrepancy between the modern theological philosophy and the prophetic and apostolic Scriptures should perhaps, on no point come forth so clearly, and apparently so irreconcilably, as precisely in reference to the doctrine of the '*Last Things*'—*Eschatology:* Here, especially are the terms, ' Jewish conception,' 'oriental garb,' 'poetic imagery,' 'accommodation to the narrow ideas of the age,' etc., etc., the order of the day, and the doctrine of the consummation of the ages is ordinarily regarded as a moderately insignificant appendix to some philosophico-dogmatic system. In Scripture, on the contrary, it is distinctly presented in the foreground, and for the believer it attains, with every year and every century, increased significance, so that what for a time seems to be an appendix, becomes eventually the *main question !*" *

Every faithful student of the Scriptures, unbiased by false theories of interpretation, will attest these words as true. What we find in the New Testament as its outcome in respect to the ages and the kingdom, has already lain in the bosom of the Old Testament from the beginning. The closing part of the New Testament is but the full flower of which the opening part of the Old Testament was the precious seed, the kingdom one and the same, in essence, all the way. Nothing appears in the later revelation that was not hid in the earlier, nothing in John that was not in Moses. This is what Augustine meant by his golden maxim, "Novum Testamentum in Vetere *latet*, Vetus in Novo *patet*." "In the

---

* Person and work of the Redeemer, 450.

Old Testament the New is *concealed;* in the New the Old is *revealed.*" We shall find "the thousand years" in many places of God's word, long before the Rabbis ever had a being or a name.

We shall be obliged in this investigation to make use of what men call "technical" terms, in order to save circumlocution. We speak of the "Last Things." The Greek term for this is *"Eschata,"* and by these are meant what should "come to pass," not in the *"latter,"* as oftentimes King James' version has it, but in the *" last"* days, as Moses, Joel, Isaiah, Ezekiel, Daniel, Peter, Paul and John, preferred to have it. If we study the eschatology of the Old Testament, we will find the *Eschata* there identical with the *Eschata* of the New Testament, and the Eschatology of both Testaments the same, only the New is more developed than the Old. Such is the organic and genetic character of revelation and of prophecy that if "the thousand years" are not in Moses, the Psalms, and the Prophets, they have no right to be in John. To understand the prophets it is necessary, however, to understand the Apocalypse, and to understand the Apocalypse it is necessary to understand the prophets. The one is a light to the other, and reciprocally. In order to attain a clear conception of Old Testament prophecy and its fulfilment, we must *combine* both Advents of Messiah, remembering that the first only brought a *partial* fulfilment of the prophetic word which yet awaits the second in order to secure its *plenary* accomplishment.

Joel's prophecy as to the outpouring of the Spirit in the last days, and of the great and notable day of the Lord, with all its terrestrial and celestial phenomena, the final redemption of Israel, and the transfiguration of the Holy Land, was only incipiently and partly ful-

filled to a few, an election out of Israel, at the first coming of Christ, and awaits a far larger fulfilment at His
second appearing. So the prediction of Amos, in reference to the dispersion and sifting of Israel the "Sinful
Kingdom," and God's visitation of the Gentiles, "after
this," to take out of them a people for His name, met a
partial and precursive fulfilment in the first calling of
the Gentiles to the knowledge of Christ, in the days of
the apostles, as James in the first council at Jerusalem
assures us. We see that by comparing Acts xv:13-18
with Amos ix:8-12. But there is to be a grander fulfilment still in coming days, when, now that a Second Dispersion and Sifting of Israel has occurred, since James
spoke, there shall be a fulness of the Gentiles "after
this," also, and finally the fallen Booth of David, or
Israel's proper Kingdom, as the prophets picture it,
will be re-erected with the fulness of Israel converted
to God, and the glorious millennial age heave into view.
So it is with reference to Isaiah's Redeemer coming to
Zion, and Hosea's Israel abiding alone for many days,
and Micah's halting daughter of Zion to whom, at
length, comes the "former dominion." Whatever occurred to Israel graciously, at the first coming of Christ,
was only a preliminary fulfilment to be exhaustively
completed for Israel, at His second coming. Such is
the law of prophecy and the law of fulfilment, and it
will save us from many an error, if only we are careful
to remember it.

A.   THE KINGDOM AND PROPHECY

From first to last, the Kingdom of God on earth, its
inception, progress, conduct, and consummation in
glory, is the one theme of Old Testament prophecy.
To this end were the covenants with Christ, Adam

Noah, Abraham, Israel and David. To this end was the choice of the one national "Israel," the "choice forever," as a prophetic, priestly, kingly nation, a messianic and mediatorial nation, the one national "Servant of Jehovah," and national Son of God, standing between God and mankind, and bringing salvation to a lost world; a people from whom should come the one personal "Israel," Prophet, Priest and King, the one Mediator and true Messiah, Seed of the woman, Seed of Abraham, Seed of David, Son of Man and Son of God, in whom all nations should bless themselves—*Jesus Christ.* Identified with Him, individually, and called by His name, stands Israel collectively, in His whole Messianic work and kingdom. Neither acts without the other. The Pentateuch prophecies refer chiefly to the people. The Messianic Psalms emphasize the King, the Kingdom, and the Priest. Isaiah dwells upon the prophetic character of Israel; Ezekiel displays the priestly; Daniel reveals the kingly; Zechariah blends all in one. *Old Testament prophecy knows no other subjects of discourse than these, Israel, Messiah, and the Nations.* As to the kingdom, Israel had it, under the Old Testament, in its outward form; the Gentiles have it under the New Testament, in its inward form; in the age to come, Jews and Gentiles together, shall have it, both forms in one, one kingdom of Messiah, spiritual, visible and glorious, with Israel still the central people, the prelude of the New Jerusalem and the nations walking in its light forever.

The division of the Davidic kingdom into two, laid the ground for all the prophecies concerning the "Kingdom of *Israel*" and the "Kingdom of *Judah*," i. e., the ten-tribed Israel, called "Ephraim," and the two-tribed Israel, called "Judah," as distinguished from "all

Israel," or the twelve-tribed Israel, an election from whose children shall one day form the national nucleus of the millennial kingdom.

The catastrophe that brought destruction to Jerusalem and captivity to Judah under the Chaldean King, forms the ground of the common distribution of the canonical prophets into their present classification. The Babylonian exile is the middle point   If we study the prophecies that speak of the Kingdom of Messiah, Israel's Kingdom, the Millennial Kingdom, and the relation of the nations to each,—all as parts of the Kingdom of God on earth,—we shall take in all the prophets.   If we group these around the several great epochs of Israel's history, they will fall into three main divisions, (1), pre-exile prophets (2), exile prophets (3), post-exile prophets.   Or, to be still more specific, they will fall into five chief divisions: (1) The pre-Assyrian, viz., Obadiah, Joel, Jonah ; *i. e.*, the prophets of the period prior to the Assyrian invasion and captivity of Israel ; (2), The Assyrian, viz., Amos, Hosea, Isaiah, Micah, Nahum ; (3) The transition prophets, viz., Zephaniah and Habbakuk ; (4) The prophets of the Chaldean period, viz., Jeremiah, Ezekiel, Daniel ; (5) the Persian period, or period of the Restoration down to the close of prophecy, viz., Haggai, Zechariah, Malachi.   Sixteen in all; all speaking of the Kingdom of God and its development through Israel in relation to the nations, amid conflicts and victories, judgment and mercy, apostasy and recovery, until the whole world becomes subject to Israel and Israel's king.

As a further help to our investigation, it is necessary we should know that *the Kingdom of God, in its development, though one, exists in different forms, and runs through various ends and ages.*   Essentially, it is one.

Phenomenally, it is many. It is singular and plural, both. It is an everlasting kingdom in its essence. It is a temporal kingdom in its forms. It exists forever. The Dispensations pass away. The Kingdom still abides. New forms emerge along the ages until the endless age arrives, and the final form appears. And yet more. With the outer historic development of prophecy as well as of history, an inner genetic development runs parallel. The original prophetic germ, found in the first promise in the garden, true to scientific law, parts itself into law and gospel, divides, expands, and assumes more ample and concrete forms. What is at first most general, becomes particular. What is obscure becomes more clear. The ages and the ends are evolved according to the same law of "becoming," which obtains in the natural world, viz., by division and integration. The result from all is that, as prophecy advances, what is folded up darkly, at first, is opened out in clearer and distincter statement later on. The ages and the ends become more definite. The later predictions explain the earlier ones. And, along this line of divine evolution, as there is no "spontaneous generation" in the kingdom of God, so there is no "transmutation of species." God alone creates. Israel, the created people of God, abides Israel, and *the history of Israel is not a mere frame in which to hang pictures of the New Testament Gentile church.* The kingdom is ever the kingdom, one sided for Israel alone in time past, one sided for the Gentiles alone now, outward in the one case, inward in the other, but both sided for both in one, hereafter, Israel evermore the root, the center, organic basis, and ground, of all. By observation of this, we learn the characteristic differences between pre-exile prophecy on the one hand, and exile with post-exile prophecy on

the other. It is precisely along this line of development we detect the evolution of the ages in prophecy
itself, and are obliged to hold that Prophecy as well as
History is an *"organism,"* as is Nature, the Kingdom and
the Church—the one a parable of the other—" natural
law in the spiritual world ;" and " spiritual law in the
natural world," in short, as Newton showed, a system
of universal and identical laws producing analogous
phenomena in different spheres. Where there is life
there is law. It is precisely along this line of study
of the Word of God, we discover not only a description
of the Millennial Kingdom yet to be, but are able
to detect the relative location of the millennial age
itself, even in Old Testament prophecy, and find it
exactly as the Apostle John has pictured and located
it—its character, its name, its measure, and the events
by which it is opened and closed. The existence of
" the 1,000 years " in the Old Testament is a matter
of scientific demonstration, as truly as the existence of
any geological age in the history of the planet, and is
supported by an exegesis, grounded in the organic
unity and continuity of prophecy in both Testaments,
that is unassailable. It is another proof of the truth of
the golden saying of Augustine, " The New Testament
lies *concealed* in the Old, the Old stands *revealed* in the
New."

The six pre-exile prophets form a connected chain
ending with Nahum. Of these, Isaiah is the chief, his
radius of vision spanning all horizons, near, remote,
and between and losing itself in the breast of eternal
glory. He sees all things, however, in one divine perspective, one divine light, one divine picture, Messiah
the center of all, Israel around Him, the Nations around
both. The ends and ages are all confounded in the

first end, and the age following. All is a composite photography, the events standing cheek to cheek, which only later prophecy can separate. On the earlier prophets, the exile and post-exile prophets rest as on sure ground, the spirit of prophecy being one. Their office is not to transcend, but develop, the earlier. What Isaiah was to the earlier, Daniel was to the later. He bequeaths to them, and to us, the great problem of the Millennial Age, whose epoch Isaiah, Micah, and Ezekiel, have fixed, the problem of Israel's final future and relation to the nations, with Israel's history between the return from exile, and Israel's final redemption in the glory of the Kingdom at Messiah's second coming. Its solution is given, also, in the various visions of the four empires, four beasts, and seventy weeks, whose last week is rent off from the rest in fulfilment, the Roman times of the Gentiles lying between—a seventieth week wholly eschatological, the basis of the seals trumpets and vials in John's Apocalypse. The same problem appears in another form in the night visions of Zechariah, Haggai's shaking of the nations, and Malachi's burning day, whose close is crowned with healing from the sun of righteousness. The solution of the great problem of Israel's future, sprung from the breach in David's Kingdom, is the solution of the problem of the Millennial Kingdom, and comes with Israel's future acceptance of David's Son as their Lord, the closing up of the ancient breach in David's Kingdom, the union of Israel and Judah in one nation, on the mountains of the fatherland forever;—in short, Israel a converted people and nation, acknowledged by Christ in person, the nations applauding. With that consummation, after judgments and mercies unknown before, and the revelation of Christ Himself

in His glory, dawns the Millennial Age. Search where
we may, through all the prophets, this is the one
theme, the redemption of Israel, and of the nations
through Israel, after judgment has fallen on both,
Christ the glory of all. It is the time of the " Kingdom restored to Israel." Search where we may, we
shall nowhere find unveiled the mystery of the New
Testament "Church." See Rom. xvi:25. I Cor. ii:7, 8.
Eph. iii:8, 9. Col. i:24-27. Nor does the disclosure of
this, in the New Testament, avail to destroy the prophetic word of the Old in reference to Israel, or abolish
the *standing contrast* in the Old between Israel and the
Nations, or in the New between Israel, the Nations,
and the Church.

It is among the " *Eschata*," or "*Last Things*," the
things to "come to pass in the last days," or " End-
Time," that we find the Millennial Age. It lies, as we
shall see, between the "*Yom Yehovah*," or " Day of the
Lord," which, in the New Testament, is called "The
Apocalypse of Jesus Christ," and the endless age of the
" New Jerusalem " in the final " New heaven and
earth." It is bounded by two distinct judgments, one
at the opening, one at the close of the Millennial Age,
the opening judgment being that of the Nations, and of
all powers, terrestrial and super-terrestrial, opposed to
Christ and His reign, as also by a judgment upon Israel
and Jerusalem, ending in the redemption of both. The
" Yom Yehovah " everywhere *precedes* the Millennial
Age, which is the age of Israel's glory in the Kingdom, and comprehends in itself most of the *Eschata* of
the Old Testament. The judgment that closes the Millennial Age is represented as a judgment on Gog and
Magog, which extends itself to a " visitation " of final
doom upon all the wicked, after which Israel rests eter-

nally secure in their glorified land, the nations of the saved walking in the light of the Holy City, the Lord Himself dwelling forever among His people. Such, in general, is the Old Testament representation.

To understand this, however, it is necessary to know first, the manner in which the prophets divided the whole course of time, and the way in which the ages and ends are represented in prophecy, as also the relation in which the *Eschata* stand to these ends and ages, first in pre-exile prophecy, and next in exile and post-exile prophecy.

B.   GENERAL DISTRIBUTION OF TIME, PRE-EXILE PROPHECY

And first, as to the division of time, in pre-exile prophecy. The whole course of time, from the creation of the heaven and earth to the re-creation of the same, is divided into *two great ages,* the bisecting epoch between which is called the "*End.*" In this End is placed the "Yom Yehovah," during which the personal self-revelation of Jehovah in glory, for the deliverance of Israel, and the destruction of His and their enemies, is also placed, and for the establishment of His kingdom in glory on earth. To this "Day of the Lord" belong all the Eschata, or Last Things, that precede the age of glory on earth, and are connected with the Advent of Messiah. To this one End all prophecy constantly looks, in every picture of the future, from Joel to Malachi. The first of these two ages is the pre-Messianic age, or Jewish age, with all the time preceding, and is called in Hebrew theology, "*Olam Hazzeh,*" "this present world." The second of these ages is the Messianic age, and is called "*Olam Habba,*" or "the world to come." The New Testament employs

these divisions of time, and they are ever in the mouth
of our Lord and His Apostles, as "*Aion ho houtos,*"
"this present world," and "*Aion ho mellon,*" "the
world to come," i. e. "this age," and the "coming age."
These terms have no reference to individual life here,
or the life of the disembodied spirit, after death. The
bisecting point between them is not death, but the End
of the first age. They relate wholly to the course of
earthly history, and the development of the kingdom
of God on earth. In pre-exile prophecy in general,
there is but one End, and that between the two ages,
the last of which is endless; *One* End, *One* Day of the
Lord, *One* Judgment, *One* Advent of Messiah in glory;
an End all-comprehensive and undeveloped with but
One age succeeding, the Messianic Age, the age of
Israel in the kingdom and the glory, an End that "does
not discriminate between the Parousia in humility and
the Parousia in glory, but beholds the whole work of
Messiah as complete." (Delitzsch.) Therefore does
Isaiah's page shine the more intensely, for into that one
age the whole grace and glory of Messiah's work is
concentrated. All the sufferings of the "Servant of
Jehovah," all the splendor of His Reward, all there is
for Jew, and all for Gentile, focalize themselves in that
one End and radiate out to that one succeeding age.
It is the uniform view of all pre-exile prophecy. In the
"Yom Yehovah,"—day of judgment, day of wonders,—
day of wrath and day of mercy,—day of reeling for
earth and shaking for heaven,—of tumult, storm, and
fire,—of dissolution and reconstruction,—the nations
are judged, the Gentile powers are smitten, Antichrist
is destroyed, the wicked are swept away, the dragon is
bound, Satan and his hosts are imprisoned in the pit,
and Israel's faithful dead are raised. We see it all in

the "Little Apocalypse of Isaiah,"—Chapters XXIV—
XXVII. Israel's times begin. In the proverb of the
Rabbis, " Esau is the end of *Olam Hazzeh,* Jacob is the
beginning of *Olam Habba.*" It is the view of the
prophetic portions of the Pentateuch, the Historical
books, the Messianic Psalms, and of all the prophets
prior to the exile.

The character of this Messianic age is painted in
colors the most gorgeous and brilliant in the prophets,
even as it is sung in strains the most inspiring, in the
Psalms. When the Lord has come and brought salvation with His own right arm, and Jacob's tribulation is
past, everything puts on a new appearance. Under
the New Covenant, sin is pardoned through Messiah's
death, the gospel is preached, the Gentiles are gathered,
the Spirit is poured from on high, and streams of knowledge, holiness and life, perpetually overflow. Showers
of blessing continually fall. The people are all righteous, and the righteous shine. The City of Jerusalem
is transformed, made glorious not alone by the boundless wealth of nations then tributary to it, but by the
new-creating presence of the Lord Himself. The
Temple is rebuilt in glory unsurpassed. The Land
itself is transfigured to an Eden. Jerusalem is Jehovah's
throne. Zion is His dwelling place. The very desert
blooms like Sharon. Unwonted fruitfulness appears.
All nature is at peace, and man in harmony therewith.
Idolatry and War and Crime, exist no more. Sin is
restrained and death is checked, because Satan is bound
The curse is gone, longevity returns, and Israel's risen
saints enjoy a deathless life, fresh and beauteous, as the
flower on which the morning dew still rests, and the
morning light still shines. In a new heaven and earth,

the Holy City is crowned with light, and the nations walk in that light. A painless, tearless, sorrowless state, the reproach taken from the Jew, the veil taken from the nations, and death swallowed up in victory, the Bridegroom rejoicing over His Bride, Messiah reigning on David's throne, a festive jubilee, Jehovah dwelling with His people, both in perfect fellowship and blessedness, is what we see, Eternal splendors streaming everywhere. And just because all future ages are here inclosed in this one age, therefore, is it, for Isaiah, the "everlasting" age, and all things are everlasting that belong to it. Not indeed that it has but one form, and this one form eternal, but that its facts are so, be they of grace which is glory begun, or of glory which is grace made perfect. All is everlasting, with Isaiah; an everlasting Kingdom, an everlasting Throne, an everlasting Covenant, an everlasting Nation, an everlasting Name, an everlasting Righteousness, an everlasting Joy, an everlasting Song, an everlasting Peace, an everlasting Holiness, an everlasting Life, an everlasting Dwelling, an everlasting Rock, an everlasting Redeemer, an everlasting Salvation, an everlasting God. All, is olamic, æonian, eternal, forever! All eschatologies are mingled here in one, all ends in the one End in which Messiah comes, all ages in the one Age which follows that one appearing. The Rabbis call it the "Immortal Age," and say of the righteous raised from their graves, that they "sit with crowns on their head and behold the splendor of God;" and that "All the good the prophets have spoken concerning Israel belongs to *Olam Habba*," the "world to come."

If we represent, in schematic form, the manner

and ends as seen, in general, in pre-exile prophecy, the
diagram will stand thus:

	Advent.	
Pre-Messianic	$\mathbf{O}$	Messianic
Age.	End.	Age.

That is, two ages and one end between, the last age the
everlasting one, or age that has no end.

C. EXILE PROPHECY

Let us come now to speak of exile prophecy.   Here
we find a marked difference from all preceding prophecy, in respect to the ages and the ends, and the disposition of the Eschata.   Events that stood together in
one picture, in the earlier prophets, begin to be parted
here.   The hints in Hosea, Isaiah, and Micah, of such a
possible development, and of which we shall speak later
on, receive now their true significance.   We learn how
the great epochs of Israel's history are the great epochs
of prophecy, and that the development of both runs
parallel.   Our attention is attracted to the partition of
the one end, and the development of the one age following.   Two Ends instead of one appear.   Two
Advents instead of one.   Two Judgments instead
of one.   Two Resurrections instead of one.   Two Ages
following the ends instead of one, the endless age,
of course, the last.   The whole cast and character of the future seem changed, as if some strange
fatality on the part of the people, still unprepared to
receive their promised Messiah at His first coming,
had served to postpone the promised redemption.   This
much is clear, that national Israel has not profited as it
should by the catastrophe of the exile, for prophecy
now speaks of a second destruction of rebuilt Jerusalem
as the result of Israel's impenitence, even after the

return from Babylon; a second dispersion, another
long period of desolation, a curse for rejecting Messiah
Himself. And yet it pictures a second coming of Messiah, and Israel redeemed at last, triumphant in the
promised kingdom and glory.

Something new has occurred. The synthesis of
ends and ages in pre-exile prophecy gives place to
their analysis in post-exile prophecy. The one end
parts into two, each part closing itself up again, the
space between becoming that of an intermediate age,
though still foreshortened, the age that is endless lying
behind the last of these ends. Instead of two ages
and one end, as in pre-exile prophecy, we have three
ages and two ends, schematized thus:

Jewish Age.	1st. Advent. ⊙ End.	Christian Age.	2d. Advent. ⊙ End.	Millennial Age.

At the end of the pre-Messianic or Jewish Age Messiah comes, but not in glory. He is "cut off," and there
is "nothing for Him"—no kingdom in the form predicted, no crown. He is rooted out by a violent death,
and Israel is, moreover, rejected. The Messianic Age is
now divided into two, during the first of which the risen
Messiah, ascended to Heaven, remains concealed and
unseen throughout the whole period of Israel's rejection, while the news of His name and His great salvation goes to the Gentiles. It is the Church-historical
period between the first and second Advents, a period
closed up to Daniel, or at most, only briefly alluded to,
even though its termini, the two Advents, are given. It
is the period when Israel's national history is a blank before God. As the end of the intermediate age, which is
the end of His concealment in Heaven, He comes again
and appears "in the clouds of Heaven," and comes to

Israel penitent and believing, in the crisis of Israel's last tribulation, and comes to " restore the kingdom to Israel." At His first coming He was rejected by Israel, and Israel was rejected by Him. At His second coming He is accepted by Israel, and Israel is accepted by Him. Then, there was "nothing for Him." Now there is everything for Him. Then, also, there was nothing for Israel as a nation. Now, there is all. The kingdom and the glory are for both, " under the whole heaven." *Olam Habba*, or the world to come, has become two worlds, of which the first, being an intermediate age, shares the nature of both, and while being the " world to come," or *Olam Habba*, with respect to the age preceding, is yet " this present world," or *Olam Hazzeh*, with respect to the age still following. It is our Christian Dispensation. The *Yom Yehovah*, with its unaccomplished *Eschata*, still lies beyond. Such is the picture Daniel gives us: Two ends, two ages, two advents, for the one end, one age, one advent, of pre-exile prophecy. Messiah comes at the beginning of the fourth Empire. He comes also at its close.

But this is not all. Ezekiel develops the ends and ages still more than Daniel does. He has nothing to say of the first Advent, as Daniel has, and nothing of the Antichrist. He has nothing to say of the missionary proclamation of the Gospel, or Israel's prophetic calling, as Isaiah has. He leaves to Isaiah the prophetic, to Daniel the kingly, and presents almost exclusively the priestly side of Israel in the kingdom. He speaks in his earlier prophecies of the judgments of God on Jerusalem and the nations, but, his later visions are of Israel's deliverance and the splendor of their land, city and temple, in the day of the personal manifestation of the "glory " to His people. He speaks not

only of Israel's spiritual regeneration by means of the
" New Covenant," which Hosea, Isaiah, and Jeremiah
have celebrated, but also of Israel's final restoration as
a people, their political reunion and national conversion, and independence, their blessedness and glory
in the land promised to their fathers, God's sanctuary
in their midst, God their God, and David their Shep-
herd-Prince forevermore.   Instead of the Valley of
Dry Bones with the Colossus towering over them,
what we see is a resurrected people, standing up as a
great army, and instinct with the " Spirit of Life from
God."   It is new-born-Israel of the end-time, coming
to their inheritance and priestly royalty, re-established
in their land forever.   All this we get in what is called
" Ezekiel's Apocalypse," embracing chapters 37-48. His
vision of the land, the city and the temple, chapters
40-48, is but a further expansion of what is foretold in
chapter 37, and presents the priestly side of the same
kingdom whose royal greatness Daniel had predicted.
Great in majesty it was to Daniel.   Glorious in holiness it is to Ezekiel.   And, as to Daniel, it came with
the coming of the " Son of Man " in the clouds of
Heaven, in all its kingly grandeur, so, to Ezekiel, does
it come in all its priestly ornament and holy beauty,
with the entrance of the "glory" in the temple.   With
the personal appearing of the "glory" the cosmical
transfiguration begins, the temple waters flow.

But the peculiarity of Ezekiel is this, that even to
this coming age of Israel's blessedness in the kingdom,
he sees an "end;" not an end to the *kingdom*, but an
end to the *age*.   Another end heaves into sight, the
transition point between the Millennial Age and the age
that is endless; an end beyond the second end already
seen in Daniel; a third end followed by the age with-

out end. The event that marks this new end is the predicted war-march and judgment of Gog and Magog, at the end of Israel's "many days" in the kingdom. Just as in exile prophecy the one pre-exile end is developed into two, so, once again, these two ends are developed into three. In Ezekiel, the second end expands itself to two. Just as, in Daniel, the judgment on Antichrist and Israel's restoration in the kingdom, marks the opening of the age that lies beyond the second coming, so, in Ezekiel, does the judgment of Gog and Magog, which appears as the last judgment, mark the close of that age. With that judgment, which, as we shall see, extends itself to the resurrection of the wicked and their final doom, in John's Apocalypse, Ezekiel's vision ceases. What we have now, instead of two ends and three ages, are three ends and four ages, covering all time, from the exile down to the final new heaven and earth of which Isaiah speaks, viz.: The Jewish Age and the end of it, the Christian Age and the end of it, the Millennial Age and the end of it, and the Endless Age of the New Jerusalem. If we schematize the conception the diagram will stand thus:

Jewish Age.	ıst. Advent O End.	Christian Age.	2d. Advent O End.	Millennial Age.	White Throne O End.	Endless. Age.

What to us is now the "world to come," will be to its own inhabitants "the present world," even as our present age was the world to come, to pre-Christian Judaism. As time wears away, and the future comes to make the present, then glides into the past, *Olam Habba* becomes *Olam Hazzeh*, even on the other side of the second Advent. In other words, the Messianic or everlasting age, which, in pre-exile prophecy, was

but one age following Messiah's one Advent, and
which in Daniel became two ages, by reason of the
clear separation of the comings, has, in Ezekiel, become
three ages by reason of the new end introduced; so
making four in all, if we begin with the Jewish Age,
viz.: (1) The period of Old Testament times; (2) the
Church-historical period; (3) the Millennial Age of
Israel in the kingdom; and (4) the Eternal State or
New Jerusalem in the "New Heaven and Earth."
The end of the Jewish Age brought resurrection,
judgment, and a new age succeeding. The end of our
present age will do the same. The end of the Millennial Age will do the same. In each case the kingdom
receives a re-establishment in new form. There is a
re-creation. A personal advent of Messiah marks the
close of each age, save the Millennial. No third Advent at the judgment on Gog or Magog is intimated
in Ezekiel's nor even in John's Apocalypse, for the
final resurrection and the judgment of the wicked, into
which the judgment on Gog extends itself, for the
reason that no second departure of Christ from His
people is revealed. As in the Old Testament, so in
the New, the last judgment is perspectively covered
and connected with the judgment at the second coming of the Son of Man.

Such is the entire development of the ages and the
ends in prophecy,—the Biblical Æonology and Teleology—from Genesis to Regenesis; the whole time
prior to the first coming being regarded as the pre-
Messianic Age. Our own age is a parenthetic one.
The age next beyond that of our own is that of Israel
in the kingdom. The last age is what we call "Eternity;" time rolling on unto "ages of ages," in the
illimitable future, "world without end."

D.   THE SUB-DISTRIBUTION OF TIME

The Scriptures give us not only the ages and the ends, but also a sub-distribution of prophetic and historic time, from the period of the exile or blotting out of the visible kingdom of God on earth, down to its re-establishment, *i. e.*, from the time of Israel's subjection to the Gentile power to the time of Israel's redemption from the same; or until the "mystery of God" concerning Israel's blindness and rejection, and Israel's new sight and recovery, is "finished," under the sounding of the seventh trumpet.   Beyond that we find no sub-distribution, save the judgment on Gog already mentioned, and which, in connection with Isaiah xxiv:22 and Isaiah lxv:17, extends itself to the final resurrection and judgment, and the New Heaven and Earth.   The sub-distribution we refer to is found, first of all, in the vision of the great metallic image, or Monarchy-Colossus, Nebuchadnezzar saw in his dream (B. C. 604) eighteen years before the destruction of Jerusalem (B. C. 586), that image being a symbol of the Gentile power standing on Israel's prostrate body ; or, if we combine the visions in Daniel with those in Ezekiel, then the Colossus stands erect in the midst of Israel's national graveyard—"*Habbikah Meleah Atsamoth*"—"the valley full of bones, and very dry,"—and remains standing, while national Israel remains dead, until that image is overthrown.   In short, that Colossus represents a series of four Gentile empires, appearing and disappearing in successional order,—four different forms or phases of the one God-opposed world-power, as it comes in contact with Israel ; from the time of the Babylonian Empire down to the Cloud-Comer from Heaven to overthrow the world-power, erect His kingdom on its ruins, and restore the lost sovereignty

to Israel.   The vision of the four-empired image and
its fate was given to humiliate the monarch's pride and
inspire afresh the sinking hope of Israel.   To the same
end was the vision of the Valley of Dry Bones reanimated by the word of prophecy, and the blowing of
God's Spirit in the last days, given to Ezekiel at the
Gola, when the news reached him of Jerusalem's fall
(Oct. B. C. 586).   The one vision shows the Colossus
falling down, the other Israel rising up ; the one, man's
kingdoms passing away; the other, Messiah's kingdom
come forever, with Israel in the front.

Again, the same distribution of the period of Israel's
national sepulture and corruption, the high Colossus
standing as the tombstone, with a " *hic jacet Israel,*" as
it were, upon its breast, is given to Daniel in a new
vision of four beasts (B. C. 541) forty-five years after
Jerusalem's fall,—a vision parts of which were ex-
panded two years later (B. C. 539) under the symbols
of the Ram and Goat.   The design of the beast vision
was not merely to show how differently from men God
looks upon the phases of the world power, they regarding the world-kingdoms as the concentration of
all material wealth, splendor, and might.   He regarding
them as predacious beasts, but also to allow a *further
development* from the symbol of the ten horns which
would have been unnatural in the ten toes.   Careering
on through Babylonian, Medo-Persian, Greek and Roman Empires, down to the last outcome of the Roman
power, divided, lost, and yet revived and reappearing
in the " Little Horn," Gentile power shall wend its
way—Israel still underneath its feet,—until the Mountain-Stone strikes the Image in its toes, and the Cloud-
Comer smites the Horn on its head, the one sent whirl-
ing like the chaff to the wind, the other tossed, living,

to the flame, while Israel, resurgent from the grave, appears a mighty host, and wields the empire of the world. The radius of prophetic vision reaches to the Second Coming of the Son of Man. Till then Israel, as a nation, is dead, the people scattered, and the Holy City trodden under Gentile feet. But then, "at that time," Israel, as a nation, revives. And here we meet a strange phenomenon. As it is with Israel and the Nations Daniel has to do, and not with the New Testament Church; as his mission is to prophesy of the world kingdoms and Israel's relation thereto, and the fall of these kingdoms when Israel's "Basileia" comes; so we find that both in the vision of the Colossus (Chap. II) and that of the four beasts (Chap. VII), the whole period between the rise of the fourth beast and the final ten horns out of which the last Antichrist comes (Israel's last oppressor)—the entire period between the First and Second Comings of Christ—is overleaped. Or, better, the period itself lies hid without any sign of the First Advent, in the legs and feet of the Colossus. The *terminus a quo* is not given. It has two aspects, viz.: That of the Church-dispensation, and that of Israel's national prostration, both running parallel during the same period. With the Church Daniel has nothing to do. It is Israel and the Colossus that absorb his attention; and neither in the Colossus, nor in the Beasts, is the First Advent marked anywhere. The period of the Gentile domination runs on continuous to the end. Only in the 70 Weeks, does the First Advent appear, and the interval between the two comings begin to be opened out; as we shall see.

Once more. Still another sub-distribution of the same stretch of time is given in the celebrated prophecy of the "Seventy Weeks" (Chap. IX), the last week of which is eschatological, since it follows the interval that follows the Roman or second destruction of Jerusalem, consequent upon the national rejection of Messiah "cut off" by the Jews,—a week divided into two equal periods of three and one-half years, or forty-two months, or 1,260 days each, during which we have the rise, reign and ruin of the last Antichrist, the "prince that shall come" (*Nagid Habba*), the "Desolator" (*Meshomem*), who perishes beneath the outpoured vials of divine wrath. It is of supreme importance to recognize this fact. The 70th of Daniel's seventy weeks is *not* immediately sequent upon the 69th week at whose close Messiah was "cut off." The Jews nailed the "King of the Jews" to the cross, and while at the First Advent the kingdom came in its *spiritual inward power* on the day of Pentecost—a "tasting of the powers of the world to come," — it was postponed in its *outward, visible and glorious part*, as a polity and public sovereignty, until Messiah's Second Coming; and this because of Israel's unbelief. This is the sun-clear statement of prophecy. The 70th week stands in the midst of the *Yom Yehovah*, or Day of the Lord. It *precedes* the Second Advent, the destruction of Antichrist, the Resurrection, and Israel's glory in the kingdom restored to Israel. The Church Fathers saw this: Irenæus, Cyprian, Primasius, Hippolytus, Appolinaris, and others. Modern eschatologists see it and victoriously defend it,—Delitzsch, Hofmann, Luthardt, Godet, Koch, Christiani, Rinck, Baur, Weiss, Nägelsbach, Karsten, Ebrard, Van Oosterzee, Kliefoth, and how many more! More than a hundred living expositors maintain it. The interval, however, between the First and Second Advents—our Church-Historical period—twinkles into light. The same interval that lies *concealed* in the image and four beasts, between the rise of the fourth empire proper and the final ten horns, or (what is the same thing) the final Antichrist, is here *revealed* as lying between the 69th and 70th of the "seventy weeks," the period of the Roman "times of the Gentiles," from Cæsar onward. At the close of the 69th week Messiah comes and is "cut off," and there is "nothing for Him," no Messianic kingdom as predicted. He is despised, and rejected, and crucified, as the "King of the Jews." For this the nation is despised, rejected, slaughtered, and entombed by Gentile hands "until He come." The histories of Israel and Christ are analogous, as sin-bearers and salvation-bringers. The 70th week resumes God's gracious dealings with the Jewish people, "as a people." The prophetic formula, including the 70 years' captivity, viz.: 70 plus 7 plus 62 plus (interval) plus 1, represents the whole stretch of time measured by the height of the Colossus, from head to feet, which is also the whole stretch of time measured by the life of the four beasts, in all reaching to the Second Advent. The *termini a quo* and *ad quem* are the same for all. In pre-exile prophecy, the return from exile retreats into the background, and the entire period from the exile to the final gathering of Israel is viewed as one continuous two-day dispersion and subjection. It is true that the final redemption of Israel seems to come, in pre-exile prophecy, with the return from Babylonian exile itself. But that is due to the law of prophetic representation. Two horizons, the near and remote, the time-historical and the eschatological, are blended into one. The present is thrown into the future. The future is attracted to the present. All things are seen in the light of the "end." Hence prophecy is "complex and apotelesmatic." The same law works in exile and post-exile prophecy, but modified because of the later stand-point, and the progress of both prophecy and history. It is here the law of "perspective" comes in. A First Advent is specifically marked in Daniel, and in Zechariah, yet only to emphasize the fact of Israel's rejection of Messiah, and rejection by Messiah, then leap at once to paint the time of Israel's final struggle and redemption, at Messiah's Second Coming. Until then Israel's history, as a nation, is a blank before God. All gracious covenant relations between God and that people, as such, are *suspended*, on account of Israel's apostasy. This strange phenomenon, as to the "over-leaping" of the intervals, or what Delitzsch calls the "deep silence" of the prophets in their "concealment of the mystery of the church," has its true ground in what Hofmann calls the "organic structure of Old Testament Prophecy in relation to Israel." And herein, Auberlen, following Baumgarten, has stated clearly the solution of the riddle. "Israel, after having rejected salvation, ceased to be the subject of sacred history, and became that of profane history alone. The intervening period between the two Messianic epochs—between the time the kingdom of God is taken from Israel and given to the Gentiles until the Second Coming of Christ, *i. e.*, between the destruction of Jerusalem and the conversion of 'All Israel' and which forms for the people of the covenant a great parenthesis—is veiled from Daniel, in much obscurity, on account of his Old Testament and Israelitish standpoint." *

Thus do the visions of the empires, beasts, and

---

*Auberlen Der Prophet Daniel, 141.

seventy weeks, concur harmoniously and, with their corresponding intervals, span the course of ages from the Babylonian time down to the second Advent. All, without exception, overleap the interval of Israel's national rejection, and locate the point when Israel's blessedness begins at Christ's second appearing. Here enter those times of " Return," "Reviving," "Refreshing," " Restitution," "Regeneration," " Resurrection" and "Redemption," foretold for Israel, and the result- ant blessing, after judgment, for the nations; millennial times described in terms so glowing and so wonderful. The pre-condition of them all is the second Advent, itself pre-conditioned by the witness of the gospel to all nations, and Israel's begun repentance and return to Christ. Nowhere, in all prophecy, is the Millennial Age located in the " Times of the Gentiles," the Church-Historical Period, the time of Israel's national death and resting in the grave. Impossible! Nowhere is the word of God guilty of the nameless folly of con- founding the " Times of the Gentiles" with "the 1,000 years." It would make all prophecy a contradiction of itself. These never come before the fall of the Colossus, nor before the overthrow of Antichrist, nor before the end of Gentile power, nor before the resurrection of the faithful dead; none of which events occur before Messiah's coming in the clouds of heaven, descending to alight "on Olivet," "come to Zion," and cause His voice to "roar from Jerusalem." (Zech. xiv:3; Isa. lix: 20; Dan. vii:9, 22; xii:2; Joel iii:16). No figurative exposition and no spiritualizing interpretation, such as we find in Hengstenberg, Fairbairn, Keil, Brown, Milligan, Glasgow, and others of the same school, can avail to break the oracles of God, or transmute Israel into the New Testament Church, Canaan into Christendom, or the times *after* Christ's second Coming into the times *before* it.   It is impossible upon the ground of Old Testament prophecy, or of New, in their common distribution of the ages, to locate the Millennium between the First and Second Advents, for the simple reason that, between these Advents, Israel lies nationally dead, and the Millennial Age begins with Israel's national resurrection.   (Ezek. xxxvii: 1–28) ; and also for the simple reason that between these Advents the Gentile Colossus still remains standing and the Millennial Age begins when the Colossus is struck and blown away like chaff. (Dan. ii:35.)   And that this was not a fact at the first Advent, and is not a fact now, is proved by the further fact that Gentile politics and power still rule, and Israel, as a nation, is still unrisen from the dead.

The contrary view which makes a "figure" of the Second Advent, would break down the whole Apocalypse of John which is built up, line for line, on Old Testament prophecy, and the words of our Lord in His Olivet discourse, and puts the crown and consummation on Israel's hope.   Impossible—forever impossible—that the prophetic pictures of Israel's future, so brilliant and glowing, should belong to that period of time when, in God's account, Israel is a blank, their nation non-existent, the woful Gentile times ; an age in history when Jerusalem lies trodden in the dust with Gentile chains on her neck, and the proud Colossus tramples on the bones of Israel still bleaching in the valley, and Israel's faithful dead still slumber in the grave ; an age when Israel remains outcast, dispersed, rejected, still enthralled and unredeemed ! Impossible ! Impossible ! As impossible as that the Covenant of God should break, or the "Strength of Israel" should lie ! It cannot be ! To evade, by dogmatic prepossession or

false hermeneutics, or ignorant prejudice, or indifference, the clear revelation of God herein, and insist
that the "Jewish people," "Daniel's people," "Ezekiel's and Isaiah's people," "the whole House of
Israel," mean "the totality of believers in all ages of the
world," or "The New Testament Church," and that
"the land" means Spain, Italy, Germany, France, Great
Britain, the United States, "the Territories of Christendom" (Keil), is to do more than trifle with God's
Word. "It is to distort and negate it." (Delitzsch).
To plead "difficulty of conception" is to bid for the
rejection of every well-established doctrine. By such
a method of exposition, all the *Eschata* of both Testaments are dislocated, fact is evaporated, development in
prophecy ignored, our present age misunderstood, no
time or history beyond the Second Advent allowed,
Israel's future destiny and mission denied, the unity
and continuity of prophecy left unheeded, and *our* conceptions substituted for the thought and will of *God*.

If we sum up, therefore, the result of our study, the
whole subject will shine out with a clearness equal to
the brilliance of the noonday. What we have is the
development, in prophecy, of God's kingdom on earth,
by means of Israel the Messianic people. The history
of Israel prior to the Prophetic Age, it has not been
necessary to discuss. It is enough that we began with
the blotting out of God's visible kingdom on earth, by
means of Israel's subjection to Gentile politics and
power. From that time onward, the prophets look to
the time of the restoration of the kingdom to Israel at
Messiah's Coming in the clouds of heaven, and even to
the eternal glory beyond. We get the whole range of
their visions in the expressions "Until," "Unto," "After
two days," which bring us to the Second Coming, even

as the sixty-nine weeks bring us to the First Coming.
Then we have the "Third Day" which is a "Multitude
of Days," "Many Days," "His Days," "the one thousand years," which bring us down to Gog's destruction, the last resurrection and judgment and the final
new Heaven and Earth. We have swept the ages and
the ends, and also the intervals in prophecy; all con-
structed and revealed with special reference to Israel;
the Jewish or Mosaic Age down to the rejection of
Israel's Messiah. Then the interval concealed in
prophecy, viz., the Church-Historical Period, covered
simply by "and unto," in Dan. ix:27. Then comes
Israel to the front again, when the times of the Gentiles
are ended at the Second Coming of Messiah to reclaim
His people, and we enter upon the interval of Gentile
subjection to Israel's supremacy, the tables being
turned in an age of Millennial Glory. Then, after this,
Israel and the nations, in the New Jerusalem under a
new heaven and on a new earth, Jew, Gentile, and the
Church of God, all one, their distinctions still remaining, their unity eternal, and God all in all. If we put
the whole Old Testament Chronological Prophecy together, concerning Israel, after David's kingdom was
broken, we shall get the *formula* of the combined 70
years' Captivity, and the Seventy Year-Weeks, including the Great Interval between the 69th and 70th
week, thus: 70 years, plus 483 years, or 69 weeks, plus
the interval of our present age, plus the closing or seventieth week of years, *i. e.*, seven years ; or, in a briefer
form, the formula will be 70 plus 7 plus 62 plus our interval plus 1, a formula that covers the whole time from
the Babylonish captivity down to the Second Coming of
Christ. If we now annex to this the *Yammim Rabbim*,
or "Many Days" of Ezekiel, *i. e.*, the Millennial Age

for Israel restored, at the close of which is Gog's destruction and the new heaven and earth predicted by Isaiah, then the formula will be 70 plus 7 plus 62 plus our interval plus 1 plus the "many days," plus "Gog's little season" followed by the final judgment and the new heaven and earth. We get the total æonology and teleology of both Old and New Testament prophecy with respect to Israel, the Church and the Nations; and in all we see how Israel, God's "choice forever," stands out, in rejection and in their calling, mission, death and resurrection, as the Bringer, nationally, of Salvation to mankind. It is God's plan, and full, as Paul tells us, of the "unsearchable wisdom of God." Rom. xi:33. "Salvation is from the Jews." John iv:22.

E. Post-Exile Prophecy

A word here must suffice. Haggai sees the final glory of the Messianic kingdom and connects it immediately with the Second Temple reared by Zerubbabel, and into which the "glory" comes and fills the house. To him, this consummation is in the near future. Once, already, Israel's God has overthrown proud Babylon and brought a partial redemption, though poor, to His people. "Yet once more, it is a little while!" "How short a time!" and Israel's God will not only shake one nation but "all nations," and "not only earth, but heaven also, sea and dry land" together, and all "the precious things of the nations" shall be made tributary to the structure of the Temple, and into it the "glory" will enter personally, and "fill the House" with His splendor. The Temple shall thus become the constant dwelling of Jehovah, the bond of union, and the center of all light to surviving na-

tions, in a kingdom that cannot be shaken.   Haggai ii:6-
9, 21-23.   While this oracle was, in part, fulfilled by the
personal appearing of Christ in the Temple, whose
Advent was preceded by the overthrow of the Persian
and the Greek monarchies and Rome's Republic, and the
subjugation of the world by Roman arms,we have Paul's
apotelesmatic word for it that it looks to the Second
Coming of Christ, and that the catastrophe it pictures,
more appalling than the scenes at Sinai, at Marathon,
or Salamis, or Philippi, is a universal world-catas-
trophe, such as we see in John's Apocalypse under the
sixth seal, and only after which the "Basileia Asaleutos,"
or " Immovable Kingdom" comes.   Heb. xii:26-29.
"Marathon" and "Maranatha" are in the same perspective! This is Haggai's peculiarity, one Advent, the
Second, and one age following, and yet implying a
previous Advent of the " Glory " and to be connected
with the Second Temple.   At any rate, the promised
kingdom cannot come until after the " Day of the
Lord " in which heaven, earth, sea, dry land, and all
nations are shaken.   So says Isaiah ii:10-22 ; xxiv:1-23.

In the clearest manner Zechariah distinguishes
Two Advents, two Ends, and the Millennial Age following the second, but without Gog and Magog at its
termination.   He sees Zion's king coming meek and
lowly riding on a colt, ix:9, then pierced with cruel
hands, Jehovah's Fellow smitten by the sword of justice, xiii:7 ; xii:10.   As a result of this, he sees the *Suspension of the Covenant with Israel*, not God's Covenant
of Grace, which is eternal, but the " *Suspension of the
National Covenant of God with Israel as a People*," (Delitzsch, Hofmann, Köhler, Auberlen, Luthardt, Godet,
Wright, Pember, Anderson, Seiss,) by the breaking of
the two staves of " *Beauty and Bands*," Zech. xi:7-10,

Israel's existence as a covenant Nation forfeited, because of Israel's rejection of Messiah, until the time of Israel's penitence, travail, reunion, and resurrection, Micah v.1-3. Ezekiel xxxvii.1-28. He sees Him again descending on the Mount of Olives in His Majesty, with all His "holy ones" for Israel's deliverance, and the erection of the kingdom in its universal glory. The scene is that of the "Yom Yehovah" replete with terrestrial and super-terrestrial phenomena, a day unique—nocturnal day and solar night. It is a day preceded by the outpouring of the Spirit upon Israel, attended by the reappearing of their wounded shepherd to them, their national, domestic, personal and universal, penitence and tears; beyond the tears "at Hadadrimmon in the valley of Megiddo," where young Josiah fell. At first, Judah is seen in deep apostasy. But, as in the case of Paul, so here, a sudden change occurs; and Judah fights with superhuman power to raise the siege against Jerusalem. Miraculous is Israel's deliverance, even by Messiah's own appearing, xii:1-14; xiii:1-9, xiv:1-7. Then follows the Messianic Age of glory, the Millennial day, when Israel's land is transfigured, Jerusalem inhabited forever, and the theocracy becomes a universal empire with Messiah as the universal king. The holiness of Israel is universal also. All nations are obedient to Israel's king. Jerusalem has seen a Jewish Christian Passover, and a Jewish Christian Pentecost, in which some Gentiles shared. She sees a Jewish Christian "Feast of Tabernacles" now, in which all nations blend their harvest jubilee. Two Advents, two Ends, two Ages, the Millennial Age still following the Second Advent as in all the other prophets; this is Zechariah's painted page, a page among the very brightest and the richest in all Old Testament prediction.

We come to Malachi, the last of the prophets. As
he stands nearest the First Coming of Christ, and in the
midst of deepening apostasy, the "Glory" retreats into
the background, night comes on with the storm attending, and the picture of Israel's near future is dark indeed. The sun has gone down. Malachi predicts two
Advents, between which Israel is rejected and the Gentiles do homage to Messiah, yet after which Israel is redeemed through judgment and returns to the faith of
their fathers. The promise that Messiah's name should
be "great among the Gentiles," etc., i:3, is really a
threatening against apostate Israel, foreboding the rejection of the nation, the passing of the Gospel to the
Gentiles, and the substitution of a spiritual worship
for the ancient ritual, "in every place." This plainly
looks into the "times of the Gentiles," or Church-Historical period, following the first Advent and Israel's
national rejection. Nevertheless, Israel shall be saved
by means of judgment, in the burning "Day of the
Lord," and by a return to the spiritual essence of the
ancient faith, under the prophetic testimony of Elias
sent to restore them, and to herald the Advent of the
"Angel of the Covenant," iii:1-3 ; iv:4-6. After purga-
tion by judgment, and an outpoured Spirit, Israel's
worship shall be pleasant to Jehovah, their "land become fruitful," and "all nations call them blessed,"
iii:1-4, 10-12. After the storm, comes the sunshine.
Upon all who fear Jehovah's name, "the Sun of
Righteousness will rise with healing in His beams,"
and Israel, redeemed, shall gambol in the glory like
calves that frisk and play upon the sunlit pasture when
loosened from their stalls, iv:2, 3.

Part 2

The 1,260 Days, or 3 ½ Years

A. It remains now to speak definitely of the different *names* given to the Millennial Age in the Old Testament, and point out the passages where John found his " 1,000 years." In this we shall admire still more the unity of both Testaments, and learn that John understood the prophets better than do most of his expositors. It will fasten upon us the conviction that the New Testament "Apocalypse of Jesus Christ" is but the Old Testament *Yom Yehovah*, in which the Lord reveals Himself for the redemption of His people, and that the *Esehata* in that Apocalypse are only what we elsewhere find in Old Testament predictions, in the words of Christ Himself, and in the utterances of His Apostles; and that in all these *Eschata* Israel still holds his place, as in all the prophets, and still awaits the promised glory in the Millennial Kingdom.

While what we have said concerning pre-exile prophecy is true, there are yet not wanting intimations, or, if we may so call them, "germs" of the later development of the ages and ends we find in exile and post-exile prophecy. These belong to the organic nature of prophecy, and in them we find the *names* of the age which John describes as "the 1,000 years." Apoc. xx:1-7. There is a text in what is known among scholars as the "little Apocalypse of Isaiah," a section consisting of chapters xxiv-xxvii. It is found in Isaiah xxiv:21-23. Referring to the *Yom Yehovah*, or Day of the Lord, in which Messiah comes to hold judgment and restore the kingdom to Israel, the prophet says, It shall come to pass, in that day, that the Lord shall visit upon (*punish*) the Host of the High Ones on high, and the kings of the earth on the earth. And they shall be gathered together as prisoners are gathered in the pit, and shall be shut up in prison. And after a multitude of days—*Rov Yammim*—they shall be visited (released for final judgment). "Then shall the moon be confounded and the sun ashamed, when the Lord of Hosts shall reign in Mount Zion, and glory shall be in presence of His ancient ones." The "Day of the Lord" is, as already seen, that which closes our present age, the day of the Second Coming of Christ. The judgment predicted in the preceding context is that of the proud nations, and Israel's land, to which is added the dissolution of the present cosmic order; xxiv:1-20. With this is connected the judgment upon the *terrestrial powers of evil*, "the Kings of the Earth on the Earth," or the Anti-christian hosts, and the judgment at the same time, of the *aerial powers of evil*, "the Host of the High Ones on High," *i. e.*, "the principalities and powers and world-rulers of darkness, the spiritual hosts of wickedness in the heavenlies," Eph. vi:12, "the prince of the power of the air," Eph. ii:2, "the dragon and his angels," Rev. xii:7-9; xx:1-3,—in short, Satan and his legions, who are cast down from their height to be shut up in the abyss, as prisoners are chained in a dungeon, restrained from public activity, and reserved for future release and final judgment.

The *time* when this dejection of Satan and his legions occurs is said to be " in that day," the time when Michael stands up to fight for Israel, Dan. xii:1 ; Rev. xii:7, the time when, in the vision of John, " the angel, having the key of the abyss, and a great chain in his hand, laid hold of the dragon, the Old Serpent, which is the Devil and Satan, and bound him for a thousand years, and cast him into the abyss, and shut and sealed it over him that he should deceive the nations no more, until the thousand years should be finished, after which he must be loosed for a little season." Rev. xx:1-3.

The time of this casting down of Satan and his hosts from their ærial mansions to earth, is that mentioned also in Rev. xii:7, 8, 12, 13, when the dragon, in great rage, having but "short time" to work upon earth before he is sent to the abyss, "makes war with the woman, and with the remnant of her seed who keep the commandments of God, and have the testimony of Jesus." That is, it is the time of Israel's conversion, Rev. xii:7-11, the time of the close of the testimony of the two witnesses, the end of the first three and a half years (1,260 days) of Daniel's 70th week ; in short, the beginning of the great tribulation, Rev. xi:7, xiii:12, at whose end Satan is imprisoned in the abyss, Rev. xx:1-3. And this time of the judgment upon "the Host of the High Ones on High," is the time of the judgment of the " kings of the earth on the earth," or Antichrist and his armies, who are destroyed at the close of the last three and a half years (1,260 days) at the Second Coming of Christ from " Heaven

opened," Rev. xix:11-21. There is nothing clearer than
that the visions of John, in the text referred to, are the
companion pieces of the prophecy of Isaiah just quoted.
The judgments upon Antichrist and his armies, and
upon Satan and his hosts, are identical in Isaiah and
John, and occur " in that day," the day of the Second
Coming of Christ.

But this is not all. The imprisonment of Satan and
his demoniac powers is not their final judgment. The
prophet speaks of a reckoning "after" this. He fixes
the duration of the imprisonment at whose close the
reckoning comes. He defines the length of that duration as a "multitude of days," *Rov Yamim.* He says
that "after" this long period which follows Antichrist's
overthrow and Satan's captivity, the final reckoning
shall come. "After a multitude of days they shall be
visited," or as the verb here properly means, "they shall
be looked after for final retribution." This implies, as
is admitted, their future unchaining and letting loose
again. "They do not escape from prison, but are released, or let out, to meet their final award." In this,
all scholars agree. To this, corresponds the account in
John's Apocalypse, Rev. xx:1-7, where we read that
"After the thousand years are finished, Satan shall be
loosed out of his prison" to play his old game. As,
after his casting down from the heavenlies, and before
his imprisonment in the abyss, the "short time" of 1,260
days was allowed him to assail the saints, so between
his release from prison and his final casting into the
lake of fire, he is allowed "a little time" in which to
muster the nations, and make his last effort against the
Kingdom of God. This we read in the Apocalypse of
John who *separates* the events Isaiah *combines* in one
general expression. The demonstration is inductively

complete that the indefinite period of time called *Rov Yamim*, by Isaiah, or the "Multitude of Days," is identical with the period called *Chilia Ete*, or "the thousand years" by John. The judgments which *precede* this period are the same. The "First Resurrection" which occurs at the same time is the same, also; the resurrection of the faithful dead, as is clear from Deut. xxxii:39 Ps. xlix:14; Hos. xiii:14; Isa. xxv:8; xxvi:14, 19; Ezek. xxxvii:12; Dan. xii:1-3; I Cor. xv:54, 55; Rev. xi:18; xx:5. And the time of these judgments and this resurrection is the *Yom Yehovah* or "the Day of the Lord,"in which the "Lord Himself" visibly reveals His person to effect these events. The succeeding long period of the "Multitude of Days," or "The Thousand Years" is the same. And the judgments at the close of this period are the same. What confirms this all the more is the fact that unless the "visiting" of the imprisoned Anti-christian hosts, at the end of the "Multitude of Days" involves their resurrection—the resurrection of the wicked unto final judgment—there is no text in the Old Testament that does. Isa. xxiv:21, 22, is the *only* passage; since Dan. xii:2, properly translated, speaks only of the resurrection of the righteous.

But that Isaiah xxiv:22 does involve the resurrection of the wicked, at the close of the "Multitude of Days," is clear from this, that John interprets Isaiah's prophecy by his own vision of the resurrection of the wicked at the *close* of "the thousand years" which, we have seen, are identical with the "Multitude of Days." It stands exegetically fast, that John's Millennial Age is Isaiah's "Multitude of Days," dating from the Second Advent; that epoch of time which runs into the age following; the epoch when Israel is redeemed, and nationally restored; when Jerusalem,

the "beloved city" becomes the middle point of the
Millennial Kingdom during "the thousand years," Rev.
xx:9, and "the Lord of Hosts shall reign in Mount
Zion, even in Jerusalem, and glory shall be in presence
of His ancient ones." Isa. xxiv:23.

It is the time when, as the context in Isaiah shows,
the sleeping saints of God are raised, the veil is taken
off the nations, and Israel's rebuke and long reproach
exist no more. Isa. xxv:8, 9.

It will perhaps, assist our understanding, to see how
this exegesis of the passage in Isaiah, so little understood by many, is supported by a scholarship than
which none better can be found. " The binding of
Satan," says Auberlen, "is, like the thousand years,
peculiar to the Apocalypse, although, strictly speaking,
Isaiah prophesies the same thing in chap. xxiv:21-23."*
Better still are the words of Nägelsbach upon the
passage: " The prophet's eye here sees what will take
place at the end of the world. The invincible extra-
mundane heads of the worldly powers, as well as
their earthly visible organs, will, according to the
prophet, be collected as prisoners in the pit, and shut
up in it. But not merely the binding of these angelic
and worldly powers, but their being let loose for a
time, is also announced. Only by a brief obscure
word, perhaps not seen through by the prophet himself,
does the prophet intimate this. We would not,
perhaps, have understood this word, if the New
Testament revelation, which is nearer the time of the
fulfillment, did not throw light on this dark point. It
declares expressly that, after a thousand years, Satan
should be loosed from his prison. Rev. xx:7. Isaiah

---

* Der Prophet Daniel, p. 330.

uses here an indefinite announcement of time, 'After a multitude of days,' and an indefinite verb, '*pakad*,' stands here as in Isa. xxiii:17, of a 'visiting' which consists in a looking again after some one who, long time, has remained neglected. Jer. xxvii:22. The word is here taken in the sense of a visitation for judgment, as is seen in the place in the revelation by John.

"The letting loose of Satan is only the prelude to his total destruction, Rev. xx: 10. Then follows the last, highest, and grandest revelation of God. The earth becomes now what it ought originally to have been, but was hindered from being by the sin of man, the common dwelling place of God and men. The heavenly Jerusalem, the Tabernacle in which God dwells with men, Rev. xxi:3, descends upon the renovated earth, and here Jehovah reigns as king. This city needs no sun and no moon any more, for the Lord Himself is its light." *

And even better still is the comment of Weber on the passage. After showing that in the context the prophet predicts (1) the judgment on the earth, and plagues on men in general, in the end time, to which the sixth seal in the Apocalypse refers; (2) the judgment on the world-city or Babylon of the future; (3) the final judgment on Jerusalem and all who deal treacherously with Israel's remnant, he continues thus: " The Lord will hold ' in that day,' another judgment. He will ' visit the Host of the High Ones in the height, and the kings of the earth on the earth.' The earthly and heavenly powers, who have deceived mankind into apostasy, shall receive their punishment. They shall both be visited on that same day. The host of

---

* Dr. C. W. E. Nagelsbach, in Lange, on Isa. xxiv:11-23.

the high ones on high includes the angels of the nations
and kingdoms of which Daniel speaks, x:13, 21 ; xii:1,
and John, Rev. xii:7.   They have exercised over the
nations a God-opposing influence, and shall be judged
with them.   What the punishment of these ærial powers
is we are told.   They shall be thrust into a pit, as prisoners are into a dungeon, and 'after a multitude of
days,' shall be visited.   A time comes when once more
they shall be released and allowed to begin their earlier
practice of deception.   But it shall not continue long ;
for, after a brief last conflict, the kingdom of Jehovah
will begin in that full revelation of its glory on earth,
before which the light of the sun and moon shall fade,
and the God-opposed spirits of evil sink eternally in
the lake of fire.   In that day Jehovah of Hosts shall
rule royally upon Mount Zion, even in Jerusalem, and
in presence of the ancients shall be glory.   The intention of the prophet here is to unveil the future as it
will be at that great turning point of things in the
development of the kingdom on earth when Israel,
restored, shall turn the nations to the obedience of God.
This is achieved through a judgment of the nations, and
of the wicked spirits who deceived them.   This judgment is universal, and fulfils itself in a series of severest
plagues wherein God's hand must be confessed.   Only
a remnant of mankind will survive.   As Israel, through
judgment, comes to renovation, so it is with the nations.
As the sifting of Israel will not be in vain, so it will be
with the nations.   A remnant is converted and survives
the judgment.   Upon the ruins of the world-power a
new kingdom shall arise in which the Lord will reveal
Himself to all the earth.   This is the great announcement of the prophet.   What a lesson it teaches us in
reference to our own times !   How are we compelled

to confess that the great breach between Christendom and the laws, and ordinances, and covenant of God, is a present fact, and that with swift steps we are nearing the approaching judgment of the end! The age following this world judgment, and the judgment of ærial evil powers is that Millennial Age pictured in Isaiah xxv:6-9, in which upon Mount Zion the Lord will prepare a feast to all peoples, and destroy the veil spread over all nations, and swallow up death in victory, and take away the reproach of His people forever. There is so much likeness, and difference, between the millennial and eternal states of glory that here we may regard the description of both as one, and yet must again separate the one from the other, the one a prelude to the other. 'This mountain' (Zion) shall be the middle point of the Kingdom of God on Earth. No sickness, no dying, no weeping, a Sabbath-peace, the commencement of the renovation of the earth, of which the Holy Land redeemed will be the pledge. No place shall be found where God's people shall be ashamed or blasphemed. The Kingdom of God will have now its polity not merely in Heaven but on Earth. And this will continue until the wicked spirits, released once more, gain opportunity to introduce the final judgment, the transition act between time and eternity. In that day of Jehovah's self-manifestation and millennial blessedness, Israel shall sing, 'Lo, this is our God, we have waited for Him. He will save us. This is the Lord. We have waited for Him, and we will be glad and rejoice in His salvation.'"* Such the splendid comment of a loved and devoted man whom Delitzsch has honored as "one of the first Hebrew scholars of Europe."

---

*Dr. J. W. Weber, Der Prophet Jesaia, pp. 216, 223.

These extracts might suffice to show the meaning
of the prophet, and vindicate the Apostle John from
the empty charge made so often, that he was indebted
to the Apocryphal legends and literature of the Rabbis for his conception of "the thousand years!" But
there is a testimony yet more sublime than all the
rest, which ought here to be reproduced. It is the
comment of that childlike, deeply devout, and gifted
man, Dr. Christian August Crusius, Professor of
Theology in Leipsic forty years during the last century
(the successful antagonist of Leibnitz), a man of whom
Bahrdt said, " He is the greatest philosopher and richest thinker of our times," and of whom Kant said he
felt it an honor to be allowed to testify that " he is the
clearest philosopher, and second to none in the promotion of philosophy, in our age." In his work, " *De
cœlo per Adventum Christi commoto*," A. D. 1757, he
says, " With the gradual development of the Kingdom
of God on earth, since the incarnation, the great historical events in the spiritual world run parallel. Not
only earth but heaven also is shaken. The powers of
evil in the height are in commotion. Under the lead
of Satan they oppose every step of the development of
the Kingdom of God. It was so at the incarnation of
Christ. It was so at His death. It was so at His
resurrection and ascension. The prince of this world
was even then judged and cast out, and yet not so cast
out as that all access to ærial regions was forbidden
him. The final shaking of the heavens was not accomplished, nor will be, until the final *lucta ecclesiæ cum
Satana*." It is still permitted him to be the " Prince of
the power of the air," and "god of this world," to
tempt, accuse and plague the Church of Christ, which
like her Head, must pass through suffering to victory.

Once more, in the progress of the judgment on Satan, parallel with the progress of the heavenly kingdom, Satan shall be cast down from heaven to earth, amid the shaking of the powers of heaven, the earth, and the nations. Then, as John in his Apocalypse assures us, " No more place will be found for him or his angels in Heaven." Rev. xii:7. Knowing this, then, that his "time is short," Rev. xii:12, he makes use of it to introduce the Antichrist, Rev. xiii:1, after whose destruction he is cast out from the earth itself, chained and shut up in the abyss, in a weary long captivity of a thousand years, after which, a short period of liberation being allowed him,—and then eternal judgment, he closes his career in the lake of fire. Rev. xx:1-3, 7-10. Both these events, the tossing out of Satan from heaven to earth, and the overthrow of Antichrist, are accompanied by powerful shaking of the heavens. Other shakings had previously occurred, but this one, the mightiest of all, and of which both Haggai and Paul speak as the final one—the *apotelesma*—is connected with the Second Coming of the Son of Man and His appearing in glory. At the sound of the trumpet, more terrible than at Sinai, the powers of heaven shall be shaken, and the light of the sun shall be obscured before the splendor of the throne of Majesty. Then, in place of the things that are shaken, will come the *Basileia Asaleutos*, the kingdom that cannot be shaken. Heb. xii:26-29. Then Israel, converted to the Lord, shall receive the promise, and Jerusalem the seat of the first Christian Church from which the gospel—the Zionite law—went forth, shall be made glorious as the mother church and mother city of the Kingdom of God ; and then all nations shall come and worship before the Lord because His judgments are made manifest." *

From the latest commentary on Isaiah, we venture to quote the following admirable words by Prof. Von Orelli of Basle—words that will be welcomed by all: "Not the angelic host ministering to Jehovah is here intended," says Orelli, "but the host of the spirit world accountable to Jehovah, and which like the possessors of earthly power, is subject to His judgment. The figure is that of the arrest of State criminals who at first, without regard to the extent of their demerit, are thrown into prison, then afterward, at the day of judgment, are dealt with according to the measure of their guilt." "The world-judgment here presented, is pictured as a cosmical catastrophe, like the deluge, which once swept away mankind, but yet more fruitful of good. The earth shall altogether lose its hold, and be broken under the weight of its sin. The judgment shall not merely strike the rulers of the earth, but shall reach the super-earthly powers, also, who are not blameless before God. Between these, and the sinful world-powers there is a close connection, as the book of Daniel shows, and which is here asserted through the fact that they both are judged together. As common criminals, these highest rulers shall be ignominiously arrested and imprisoned in order that, *after a long time*, they may receive their sentence which shall be prononnced by the Lord enthroned on Mount Zion, and His glorious judgment host there assembled. Sun and moon shall lose their splendor in token of His great indignation against the world, while His people, redeemed on Mount Zion, dwell in the clearest light,

---

* Rev. xv:4.   (Quoted by Delitzsch Bibl. Proph. Theologie, pp. 123-138.)

their elders deemed worthy to behold the glory of God; so that, according to chap. iv:5, 6, and far more gloriously than in Moses' time, Ex. xxiv:9, 10, they shall be permitted to enjoy, permanently, the protection of the Shekinah-Cloud as the residence of the Lord who has now taken to Himself the sovereignty of the world."

"After this world-judgment, in which Antichrist and his hosts are destroyed, as also Satan and his legions judged, and both imprisoned in the abyss, and Israel is redeemed and delivered, comes the blessed time of the "Multitude of days," the Millennial Age, on which Orelli remarks, "Then following this judgment, comes the *Triumphlied* of the redeemed, chap. xxv, as at chap. xii, an exalted echo of Israel's song at the Red Sea, Ex. chap. xv. To all nations who do homage to the Lord in the end of the days, and undulate like swelling billows to the holy mountain to worship there, the Lord Himself will prepare a wondrous feast of joy. It shall be to them a divine surprise when now He takes away the covering which, long enough already, has veiled the eyes of the nations. They shall behold Him as the Dispenser of all life and grace, and taste how good He is to those who bend before His majesty.

"By a second act of almighty love and power, not less miraculous, He will abolish death with all the woe that wrung from man uncounted tears, and lift the curse which, from the beginning, has weighed so heavily upon the human race. Here is, indeed, the end of the ways of God with men, of which the New Covenant in Christ, the Risen One, has unveiled the aim. As the remnant of Israel, so also the remainder of mankind, spared through the judgment on the nations, shall be destined to unexpected blessedness by Him the All-Merciful

One, and this shall be, of itself, the most beautiful apology for Israel, while the pride of Gentile power, the odious rival of God's people, shall be crushed forever."

And, in conclusion, on chapter xxvi, the last of the "Little Apocalypse of Isaiah," he gives us this: "The songs of victory which first we heard far off in xxiv:14, and were next intoned from Zion to the nearing nations, v. 15, have now no end. The redeemed hymn a new song wherein, in glowing words, they justify the ways of God. Zion is now a city indestructible whose bulwark and defence are God's salvation. To all the righteous who trust in Him, the Rock of Ages, her gates are open. And she extols that righteousness. While the enemies of God fall into death remediless, v. 14, God's people find an increase of their numbers and a widening of their boundaries. All human birth-pains, for a better future, have been vain. No living soul has come from them; no increase has been born, v. 17, 18. But Jehovah brings such increase, in an unexpected way, as the sudden exclamation, interrupting Israel's moan, announces, ' Thy dead ones shall live! My dead body (Israel) shall arise! Awake! Sing! ye dwellers in the dust, for the dew of lights is thy dew, and the earth shall bring forth the dead!' V. 19. Not only shall Israel's ranks no more be thinned by death, but even the faithful who, in the bitter tribulation, have succumbed to death, shall come to life again; God's dead ones whom we never may forget, nor be without. These and the living church shall meet in life again! *Here is something new under the sun!* The unyielding under-world shall, through the power of heavenly dew, be fructified, and the departed rise and bloom in light and life again. Then, in that day, the Lord binds the Dragon, and Israel takes root, and fills the world with fruit, xxvii:1-6." *

Such the exposition of the contents, in part, of the "Little Apocalypse" of Isaiah, by Orelli—a picture of the World Judgment at the Second Advent and of the Millennial Age, the "Multitude of Days," the "long time" following that judgment; a period of blessedness opened by the restoration of Israel, the Judgment on Antichrist and Satan, the resurrection of the faithful dead, and the revelation of the glory of Christ to the nations, the companion piece to John's Apocalypse, chapters xix and xx. It is not possible to place the Millennial Age before the coming of Christ, except by an open contradiction of the Word of God.

B. EZEKIEL 38

An exile passage also claims our attention, in proof that "the thousand years" of John's Apocalypse are found in the Old Testament itself. It is the strangely introduced yet significant prediction concerning "Gog and Magog," in Ezek. xxxviii:8. It comes upon the reader suddenly, as an independent prediction of judgment due to Gog "after many days," and stands isolated, as it were, in the text. It seems to be a paren_thetic expression. It is a brief oracle, and yet it is the one word on which John's whole representation of the order of the *Eschata* is pivoted, in the twentieth chapter of his Apocalypse. "After many days—*Rabbim Yamim* —thou shalt be visited." The verb (*tippakedh*) its tense form and import are the same as in Isa. xxiv:22 ; xxix: 6, not merely a testing by divine judgment, but a destruction. Smend's rendering " Thou shalt be *mustered*," and the rendering " Thou shalt be *commissioned*,"

---

* Orelli, in Strack-Zöckler's Kurtz Komm, Der Proph. Jesaia, pp. 86, 89-93.

are insufficient. The verb imports here judicial visitation for destruction. What the prophet here predicts
is Satan's last attempt, through Gog and Magog, in
the latter years, against the Kingdom of Messiah, after
Israel has been long time restored, and dwelling safely
in their fatherland as a reunited and converted people,
and the final judgment on Gog and his armies.

This prediction occurs in the Apocalypse of Ezekiel, chaps. xxxvii-xlviii, where we find (1) Ezekiel's
vision of the Valley of Dry Bones reanimated, or the
final religious and political rehabilitation of the "whole
house of Israel," in their fatherland, for "many days,"
even "forever;" one flock under one shepherd, one
nation under one king, xxxvii:1-28. (2) Ezekiel's prophecy of the war-march of Gog and his conglomerate
swarm against Israel long time restored, and the judgment on Gog, xxxviii:1-23 ; xxxix:1-29. (3) Ezekiel's
vision of the glory of the temple, city, and land, during
these "many days," a further expansion of what is
foretold in xxxvii:1-28, when the Lord has poured His
Spirit out upon the people, revived their nationality,
awaked their faithful dead, and planted them forever
in their own inheritance.

The *time* of the visitation on Gog is said to be *"after"*
these "many days," which belong to "the latter years."
(1) The *terminus a quo* of these "many years" is Israel's
restoration, conversion to Christ as a people and a
nation, and the repossession of their land ; the epoch
of the resurrection of their faithful dead, an event
included in the promise made xxxvii:12, as is proved
by Deut. xxxii:39; Ps. xvii:15 ; xlix:14, 15 ; Hos. xiii:14;
Isa. xxv;6-9; xxvi:14, 19 ; Dan. xii:1-3, all of which passages refer directly to this same epoch, and forean-
nounce the literal resurrection of Israel's faithful dead,

and non-resurrection of the wicked "at that time," and
"in that day." All this we have in chapter xxxvii. It
is the *terminus a quo*. It is the same epoch, also, of the
judgment upon Antichrist and his armies, and upon Satan and his angels, that we find in Isa. xxiv:21, 22; Dan.
xii:1; Rev. xii:7-9; xx:1-3. (2) The period, or age, that
follows this *terminus a quo* is plainly the *Rabbim Yamim*
or "many days," whose glory, peace and blessedness
are described in chapters xl-xlviii, which are the expansion of xxxvii:1-28, and of what Isaiah has predicted; Isa. ii:2-5; xi:6-9; xxiv:23; xxv:6-9; lx:1-22;
lxi:4-11; lxii:2-12; lxv:17-25; lxvi:20-23. They are the
period "after" Israel has been "gathered out from
many nations," "brought back from the sword," is
"dwelling safely, and at rest, in unwalled villages having neither bars nor gates,"—God alone their protection,—abundant in wealth and all possessions. Ezek.
xxxviii:8-12, 14. They are the period of the new in-
dwelling glory in New Israel, chapters xl-xliii; of the
New Service following the entrance of the Glory in
the Temple, which He makes the place of His throne
and of the soles of His feet, xliv-xlvi; of the life and
healing to the land from the flowing of the Temple
waters; and of the splendor to the city whose name is
Jehovah Shammah, "The Lord is there!" xlvii-xlviii.
(3) The *terminus ad quem* of these "many days" is
expressly said to be the judgment on Gog, precisely as
John makes the judgment on Gog to be the close of
"the thousand years." Rev. xx:7. "After many days
thou shalt be visited." The *termini* in Isa. xxiv:22, and
Ezek. xxxviii:8, are, therefore, identical. The passages
are parallel, supplementary, and mutually explanatory.
The character of the "visitation" at the end of the
"many days" is the same in both. The parties "vis-

ited" are different, but this is due to the fact that Ezekiel's prophecy is an advance upon Isaiah's word, and
brings to light new things occurring at the same time
with those of which Isaiah speaks. In Isaiah, the parties visited after "many days" are Satan and his angels
let loose from their imprisonment, and the Anti-christian wicked raised from their graves for the last judgment. In Ezekiel, they are the living nations outlying
on the extreme borders of the glorified kingdom of
Israel, whose center is Jerusalem restored and glorified, and who, as we learn from John, have been deceived again by Satan let loose. Each prophet is given
his own work to do, and vision to see, "by the same
Spirit who divides, severally, to every man as He will."
I Cor. xii:11. Isaiah says nothing of Gog. Ezekiel
says nothing of Antichrist. Both say much of Israel's
final redemption, at the coming and appearing of the
"Glory." Both speak of Israel's long blessedness after
restoration to their land and conversion to Messiah.
Both announce a "visitation" at the end of the "many
days" of that blessedness. What is undeveloped in the
one, is developed in the other. In the combination of
both we find the total picture of the end as seen by the
Old Testament prophets, whose work it was reserved
for John, in Patmos, to complete and crown by a development of prophecy and further revelation, the last
and brightest God has given.

If we turn to John's Apocalypse we shall find his
Eschata concerning Israel and the Millennial Kingdom
precisely what they are in the Old Testament, but only
more developed. We learn the organism and the
unity, the structure and the continuity, of all prophecy, its persistence, progress, and perfection. Interpretation is simply its own self-revelation, the shining
of its own face, self-evident, infallible.

Amid the vast variety in the unveiling of the word and plan of God, the unity remains the same from age to age. The ends and ages are the same in the New as in the Old Testaments. The Advents there are the Advents here. Israel there is Israel here. Antichrist there is Antichrist here. Gog there is Gog here. The judgments there are the judgments here. The resurrections there are the resurrections here. The power, the kingdom, and the glory there are the power, the kingdom, and the glory here. And the times of the Gentiles first, and the times of Israel next, in the last unfolding of the Kingdom of God, are the same there and here. In short, the relation of Israel to the nations, in the outcome of the Kingdom of God, is precisely what the prophets, to whom the "mystery" of Israel's blindness, rejection and recovery, was revealed, say it shall be; a mystery finished under the sounding echoes of the seventh trumpet.

In John, we have the period of "the 1,000 years." Their commencing date, or *terminus a quo*, is identical with that in Isa. xxiv:22, and Ezekiel xxxviii:8. The *Eschata* that open "the 1,000 years," prove this. We have (1) the gathering, sealing, conversion, and restoration of Israel to their own land and city, in the midst of tribulation and judgment. Rev. vii:1-8; x:7; xi:1; xii:1-6; xiv:1-5; xv:2-4; xx:9.

Chapters x, xi, and part of xii, introduce us to Ezekiel's Valley of Dry Bones, just when the voice begins to thunder, the witnesses to prophesy, the Spirit to come from the four winds, and the earthquake's shock to attend the resurrection from the dead. The whole riddle of Ezekiel's Apocalypse, *i. e,*, chapters xxxvii-xlviii, finds its solution in John's Apocalypse, chapters x-xx:7. (2) We have the personal visible and

glorious advent and appearing of Messiah, for the redemption of His people, destruction of His enemies,
and erection of His Kingdom. Rev. i:7; vi:16, 17;
x:1; xi:3, 17; xiv:1; xvi:15; xix:11-16. We have (3)
the judgment and imprisonment of Satan and His
angels. Rev. xii:7-9; xx:1-3. We have (4) the judgment of Antichrist and his armies. Rev. xiv:18-20;
xvi:16; xix:11-21. We have (5) the resurrection of the
faithful dead, and their reign with Christ in His kingdom of glory on the earth. Rev. v:10; xi:11, 18; xx:
4-6. And these events are precisely what Moses, David, Hosea, Isaiah, Ezekiel, Daniel, Zechariah, all say
precede the final glory of Israel, and stand in front of
and attend the "many days." And as to the *terminus
ad quem* of "the thousand years," the *Eschata* here are
(1) the loosing of Satan and his demonic powers,
Rev. xx:7, 8; (2) the war march of Gog and the nations
deceived by Satanic influence against Israel's land and
city, Rev. xx:9; (3) the judgment of Gog by fire, Rev.
xx:9; (4) the resurrection and judgment of the wicked,
Rev. xx:12; (5) the judgment of Satan, and his final
doom, Rev. xx:11; (6) the final and total destruction of
death, Rev. xx:13; (7) the final New Heaven and
Earth, Rev. xxi:1. And all these events are precisely
what Isaiah and Ezekiel declare and imply shall occur
at the close of, or *"after,"* the "many days." To him
who declines to accept that spiritualizing and allegorizing system of interpretation which negates and
destroys so much of the prophetic word itself, the conclusion is both necessary and irresistible that the *Rov
Yamim* of Isaiah and the *Rabbim Yamim* of Ezekiel, are
indeed the *Chilia Ete* of John; the "multitude of days"
and "many days," the same as the "thousand years."
In these two Old Testament Apocalypses of Isaiah,

chapters xxiv-xxxvii, and Ezekiel, chapters xxxvii-xlviii, where the period of Israel's blessedness is defined by these two equivalent terms of time just named, the *Eschata* that bound the opening of this period on the one side, and those which bound the close of it on the other side, are the same as those we find, respectively, in John's Apocalypse, as bounding the two extremes of the Millennial Age. And, for the opening of this period, the Apocalypses of Daniel and Zechariah, as the prophecies of the other prophets, Joel, Amos, Hosea, Micah, Zephaniah, Jeremiah, Haggai, when *combined*, show the same events, occurring in the *Yom Yehovah*, during which Messiah comes in glory and in judgment, to destroy His enemies, redeem His people, and erect His kingdom on the ruins of the Gentile powers and on the overthrow of Satan's empire; and if, in reference to the closing of this period, new characters emerge, or what was but obscure before becomes full formed and clear, it is because of the progress of prophecy itself, which, like its fulfilment, has a " springing and germinant accomplishment," its light increasing more and more unto the perfect day. And if, in earlier pre-exile prophecy, where but one end, one advent, and one judgment, with one age following, are found, we find a mother-source, or *general ground*, notably in Joel, for *both* great judgments, that on Antichrist and that on Gog; and if again in Isaiah, the ground is laid not only for these, but for *both* resurrections as well, with an interval between; and if, in exile prophecy, in addition to this, we find, notably in Ezekiel, the ground laid for the still clearer, farther, and closing revelations of John, in whose Apocalypse the remoter *Eschata stand out*, in all their brightness, or their gloom, distinct and uncon-

founded; it is because, from first to last, the word of
prophecy is one continuous genetic movement, struggling ever to *e*volve in its conclusion what was first
*in*volved in its beginning. The prophets all supplement each other, and John is the all-embracing consummation of them all. His light illuminates the rest.

From what has been said it must be clear that the
Millennial Kingdom is the time of blessedness on earth
for Israel restored to God, for Israel reclaimed to
Christ, and lies beyond His Second Coming, beyond
the resurrection from the dead. This cannot be successfully denied. Even post millennialists confess as
much, in contradiction of their own theory. "The binding of Satan," says Schroeder, on Ezekiel, in Lange, is
the necessary preliminary of the millennial kingdom,
If he is not to deceive the nations during this time but
after it, does so again, then it is clear even from that *to*
which he afterward deceives them, that his imprisonment means, above all, the cessation of war and violence,
and of violent combating of the church of God, inasmuch as the following vision of witnesses unto blood
seems to point particularly in the same direction."
"Gog and Magog both *follow* the resurrection (Ezek.
xxxvii), as in John's revelation (Rev. xx:4-6), and he who
is constrained to recognize, in Ezekiel, chap. xxxvii.
Israel's requickening as a nation, will not, thereby, be
hindered from conceding that it will be followed by the
requickening from their graves, of "all who are Christ's,"
as Paul expresses it. Moreover, the repeated "forever"—"*Leolam*"—(in Ezekiel, chapter xxxvii)—can
here be interpreted by the *Chilia Ete* there (in Rev.
xx:1-7.)*   Again: "After many days" denotes the

---

*Schroeder on Ezekiel, in Lange, 376, 350.

expiration of a long time, and supposed to be the last time, which is not only the consummation of the Kingdom of God, but of the world generally. The words "Days" and "Years" interchange harmoniously in the verse. " After many days" "in the latter years." That which appears in the single event as "many days," is, "for the eye of the Apocalyptic seer that ranges over the whole, the summation of what is still outstanding in years, or time generally. Both these phrases denote the Messianic age." *

So Schroeder speaks. And we add that, if indeed, as is the fact, the binding of Satan *precedes* the judgment on Gog; if it occurs at the Second Coming of Christ when the resurrection from the dead takes place; if Israel's political resurrection precedes this personal one; if " *Leolam*," " forever," is used in its qualified sense as equivalent to "the thousand years" of John, the "long time" or "outstanding" period, next preceding the consummation of the kingdom and the world; if all this is conceded, then it is hard to see how any who accept these conclusions could find relief from their force, by resort to the allegorical, spiritual, or symbolical theories of interpretation. The *relations* of the events must, at least, remain the same, and the "Many Days" must come in *between* the Second Coming of Christ and the judgment on Gog. If, moreover, we allegorize one event, to be consistent we must allegorize all. This wrecks the whole prediction, and denies the vast body of literal Scripture elsewhere with which it stands connected.

Riehm, as an exegete, though seeking to avoid the literal interpretation of prophecy in reference to Israel's

* Ibid 362.

future, yet finds it impossible to evade the clear representation of Ezekiel himself. He says, "In Ezekiel, we
certainly read of imminent danger to the Kingdom of
God in the 'End of the days' *after* its restoration. The
victory of Jehovah divides itself into two acts *rather
widely separated from each other.* The judgments
which bring deliverance to Israel, first of all, fall upon
the neighboring nations already in conflict with the
people of God. '*After*' Israel's deliverance, there is a
time of security and peace, Ezek. xxxviii:8, 11, 12, yet
still the distant nations have not learned to know Jehovah's power, and at the ' End of the Days' they assemble, under Gog, to fight against Israel, but the Lord
destroys them, and consumes their country with fire,
xxxix:6. Only after this is the kingdom assured against
further attack, xxxviii:29." "Most remarkable indeed,
are the words of Ezekiel in xxviii:25, 26. *After* the
first judgments securing Israel against surrounding nations, the kingdom is established in the Holy Land, and
for a long time the people enjoy undisturbed repose,
xxxviii:8, 11, 12. At the 'End of the Days,' Gog and
Magog make their final attack, after whose destruction
Israel remains forever secure against their foes."
"In *Micah*, the Messianic king has ascended the
throne *before the final attack* of the distant nations ; and
as in the Apocalypse of John, the Kingdom of Christ
has stood a thousand years before Satan is let loose to
lead the hosts of Gog and Magog against it, so also in
Ezekiel, Israel enjoys *for a long time* the blessing of
complete communion with Him before they are finally
assured of their safe possession of the blessing."*

Clearly, then, even according to Riehm's view, the

---

* Riehm, Messianic Proph. 110, 111, 210.

"many days" in Ezekiel, are the period of Israel's blessedness in the Messianic kingdom on earth, and are bounded at their opening, by the "first judgments" which bring deliverance to Israel and the establishment of Israel in the Messianic kingdom on earth, and at their close are bounded by the "destruction of Gog." The period *between* these different and separated judgments, which stand apart "rather widely," is a "long time," even "a thousand years," and Micah, Ezekiel and John, herein agree. The millennium announced by John is only what the prophets, pre-exile and exile, have foretold, and the duration of which they measure by the "many days" between Israel's introduction, by means of the Messianic judgment, into the kingdom established in the Holy Land, and the final overthrow of Gog. Micah, as well as Isaiah, forecasts "the thousand years" of John. Not before, but only after the future and final restoration of Israel, does the predicted kingdom come ; and not before, but only "after the thousand years," when Gog is judged, is the ultimate glory of the kingdom. In other words, the view of the *total End-Time*, in its widest and most comprehensive scope, as seen by the prophets, and embracing the perfect victory of Messiah for Israel's complete deliverance and complete establishment of the kingdom of glory on earth, in the latter days, is represented as that of two great acts or phases of judgment between which lie the "many days" of Ezekiel which are "the thousand years" of John. In other words again, the "End of the Days" of which Ezekiel and Isaiah speak, in the texts already referred to, is the end of "the thousand years," the "end" which Paul has in view, in I Cor. xv:24, when Messiah's victory is complete, and, all rule, authority and power being put down, and

death itself destroyed, the kingdom is surrendered
to the Father, and God is all in all, I Cor. xv:24-26.
The harmony and unity of Isaiah, Micah, Ezekiel,
Paul and John, herein, are both demonstrable and indestructible.   Their testimony to the location of the
Millennial Kingdom the other side of the Second
Coming of Christ, is final.   Pastor Koch, therefore, in
his admirable work on "The Thousand Years' Kingdom," eminent not less for its logic than for its critical
ability and thorough knowledge of the Scriptures, is
right when, discussing Ezekiel's "Many Days," he says:
"This period of Israel's peace and blessedness can be no
other than the thousand years' kingdom treated of in
Rev. xx:7-9.   The oppression of Israel and the Holy
Land, by the hosts of Antichrist, precedes it, and Zechariah speaks of this in chapter xiv, as John does in
Rev. xix:11-21.   *Between* the overthrow of Antichrist
and Gog's march lies the period in Rev. xx:1-6 which
is nothing else than "The Thousand Years." The
march of Gog follows only "after the thousand years
are finished." *

C.   *LEOLAM*— "FOREVER"

In the extract from Schroeder, quoted above, it was
said that the term *"Leolam,"* "forever," Ezek. xxxvii:
25, 26, 28, applied to the duration of the times of Israel
in the kingdom, in future days, "can be interpreted by
the *Chilia Ete*, or 'Thousand Years,' in Rev. xx:1-7."
This is as exegetically true as it is theologically important, and rests upon the Biblical use of the term itself.
It refutes the vain charge that Chiliasm denies the
"everlasting" character of Messiah's kingdom, because
it asserts its temporal form in a Millennial Age.

---

* Das tausendjährige Reich, p. 65.

A better knowledge of the *usus loquendi*, and of the term "forever," would render this, like many other similar objections, impossible. The kingdom of Messiah is, as the Scriptures everywhere declare, everlasting in its essence and existence. It has "no end." Isa. ix:7.; Heb. i:8-12. Messiah's throne is "forever." Ps. lxxxix:4, 29, 36; xlv:6; Heb. i:8; lxxii:77. Throughout its several forms or dispensations, it is an everlasting kingdom also, but yet to *each* of these forms there is an "end." Matt. xxiv:14; Heb. ix:26; I Cor. xv:24. It is olamic, æonian in both, but in a different sense; in the first, absolutely so; in the second, relatively so; unlimited as to its essence, limited as to its forms. As to its essence, no external event can limit it. As to its form, external events do limit it. Viewed in its essence it is eternal only. Viewed in its essence and form, together, it is both temporal and eternal, yet called eternal in its relative sense, that is, " age-abiding." Essentially it is one, and endures forever in an absolute sense. Circumstantially, or dispensationally, it is many, its forms evanescent, though each is age-abiding. This rests upon the nature of the case, and the Biblical expression is accommodated to the fact. The wise man tells us God has set " Olam," " Eternity," in the heart of man, and he knows "that whatsoever God doeth it should be Leolam, forever." Eccl. iii:11,14. No man can find, out the work of God from its beginning, or in its end, for no man can conceive an absolute beginning or an absolute end, because " God has set *Olam* in the heart of man." Eternity transcends human thought, and yet is the innermost core of man's spiritual constitution, writes vanity on all things perishable, and bespeaks man's immortality. In spite of the world's fading fashion which attracts and

lures his eyes, and with which he seeks to satisfy his
longings, "Olam" presides at the center of his soul,
pointing to an endless future, and an endless work of
God in which the soul finds its only satisfaction and
enjoyment. In man's deep consciousness of what still
lies before him, all temporal limits are annihilated. In
this sense, the kingdom of Messiah as a work of God
is absolutely everlasting. In this sense, it is established
forever. In this sense, God promises that His Spirit
shall rest upon converted Israel forever, and His words
abide in their mouth, the mouth of their seed, and the
mouth of their seed's seed from henceforth even forever; nor will He hide His face from them any more.
Isa. lix:21. Ezek. xxxix:29.

But on the other hand, there is another sense of
Olam, equally important—a shorter sense applied to the
forms of the kingdom, the age-forms or dispensations.

The Patriarchal, Jewish, Christian, and Millennial
Ages are but Stadia of definite duration and various
fashion in the one development of the Kingdom of God,
of which Messiah's kingdom is a part; itself of more
than one form. Each of these has its "end," yet each
is called "the kingdom." Each is an "Olam," and limited. Each is "Forever," yet only in the sense of "age-
abiding," not absolutely endless. And all these successive forms, these various ages, these *Olammin* are but
the great World-Æons, of which "the thousand years"
is only one. The Old Testament institutions, the
Aaronic priesthood, the Davidic royalty, the bloody
sacrifices, and the whole administration, are declared in
the Old Testament to be "forever," but which, as Paul
assures us, means only "till the time of reformation,"
Heb. ix:10.

While, therefore, on the one hand, the earlier

prophets contemplate the work of God as one, and see but one age following the one end they saw, and call it "everlasting" in form as well as essence, the later prophets, on the other hand, to whom two ages, then three, were revealed, distinguish between the forms of these ages, pointing to a time when, under the "New Covenant," the Leviticus shall pass away and a pure, spiritual worship supplant the ritual ; and, again, to a state still further on when an age of victory and glory shall crown an age of conflict and of grace. This, Peter himself plainly shows when he says that the prophets all "searched" not only the "what," but also the "what manner of time," the Spirit of prophecy meant when He testified beforehand the sufferings of Christ, and the glories after these." I Peter i:11. And Paul declares that "once for all, in the end of the ages, Christ appeared to put away sin by the sacrifice of Himself," and that "a second time He will appear to them that look for Him, apart from sin," and inaugurate the glories of the "world to come." Heb. ix:26-28 ; i:6; ii:5 ; iii:14 ; x:37 ; xii:26-29.

And yet, while limited in form, each dispensation is called " olamic," or " forever." Heb. i:10-13. The events of the end time for each, while limiting the form, do not limit the kingdom itself. The kingdom still goes on. It is everlasting still. And such is the case with respect to "the thousand years," or millennial form of the Kingdom of Christ. Beyond "the thousand years" it still endures, even after it has been surrendered to the Father. Through all eternity, the Son still rules His people even after He Himself has become "subjected to Him that did subject all things unto Him." I Cor. xv:28. That is the sounding note of the seventh trumpet. Rev. xi:15. But the *form* of the kingdom,

in the eternal state, will differ as greatly from its previous *form* in the millennial state, as that millennial
form will differ from our present *form*, and as ours
again differs from the old Mosaic, or as that did from
the patriarchal tent.

Schroeder is right, therefore, as are Kliefoth,
Oehler, Küper, and many others, when saying that
Ezekiel's *Leolam, Forever*, in xxxvii:25, 26, 28, is the
equivalent of John's *Chilia Ete*, or "one thousand
years," in Rev. xx:1-7. Isaiah's everlasting age concealed in its bosom all the relative ages of the great development, and their *termini*, even as Joel's prophecy
was "generic" and contained the two judgments of the
double end, the judgment on Antichrist and the nations, and the judgment on Gog. And in the whole
development, all things are connected with temporal
and terrestrial relations. From first to last, even in the
New Testament, the ages and the kingdom of the
heavens are associated with our planet. Nowhere in
the Old Testament, as nowhere in the New, can our
popular idea of "an end to the world," as the *terminus*
where Time and Eternity meet, or Time passes into
Eternity, and "our planet is no more," be found.
Such conceptions are unbiblical, Manichean, Orige-
nistic, Shakesperean and pessimistic. The "hills of
Olam" abide forever and forever. Materiality is glorified, not annihilated, in God's Kingdom. The creation
is re-created. A new heaven and earth supplant the
old, and this *begins* with the "many days," "the one
thousand years."

D. Hosea 3:4

Another expression, similar to those already noted,
is found in Hosea when predicting God's watchful
care over Israel in their dispersion and loneliness;—

the time of *Lo Ammi* and *Lo Ruhamah*—" Not my people," and " Not my beloved ;" the time when harlot
Israel, divorced from God, yet separated from idolatry, is still in desolation and concealment and provi-
dentially preserved for God. Hos. i:6, 9, 10; ii:20-23.
The words of punishment and grace are alike remarkable. " Thou shalt abide for me many days—*Yamim
Rabbim.* Thou shalt not play the harlot. Thou shalt
not be any man's wife. So will I also be for thee!"
God's pledge to the sinful Jewish Church, to apostate
Israel! To divorced *Lo Ammi* and *Lo Ruhamah!* This
is grace amazing. It tells the topmost mercy, boundless love, and bottomless compassion of God. This is
surely immeasurable. " For the children of Israel
shall abide (dwell, *yeshbhu*) many days,—*Yamim Rabbim,*—no king and no prince, and no sacrifice, and no
obelisk, and no ephod and teraphim. Afterward (*achar*)
shall the children of Israel return (convert, *yashubhu*)
and seek the Lord their God and David their King,
and shall come with fear to the Lord and His good-
ness, in the afterness of the days." Hos. iii:3-5. If we
ask what are these "many days" of Israel's loneliness
and isolation, and strangely-pledged preservation for
God, we can only answer promptly, with Delitzsch,
" The many days here are the long period of the exile,
the condition in which the Jewish people is, even now ;
—a people, but not a State with a King ;—a still worshiping congregation, but with no sacrifices, a people
so radically alienated from polytheism that it regards
itself as the pillar of monotheism ;—a people who, at
length, shall be seized with a repentant desire for Jehovah, and David its King, that is, as the Targum
translates, 'for Messiah the Son of David,' the King
David of the final period. Jer. xxx:9. Ezek. xxxiv:23-

31; xxxvii:24-28;" and then he adds: "The entire Old
Testament can exhibit no brighter prophecy respecting
the conversion of Israel than this companion-piece to
Rom. xi:25, and which received its full spiritual signifi-
cation, first of all, in the light of the New."* It is a
photograph of the condition of Israel to-day, and as
certain a prediction of what their end will be, as a
people, in a few short years. But this is not all.
There is another aspect of this period. Contrary to
Pusey's inadequate comment, the "many days" here
are gathered into *two great days, two historic days*, covering the whole time of Israel's national decease and rest,
as a nation, in the grave; the whole time of the existence of the Valley of Dry Bones; at the expiration of
which returning Israel's resurrection shall take place,
i. e., on the *third* historic day. "Come, and let us return unto the Lord, for He hath torn and will heal us;
He hath smitten and will bind us up. *After two days,
—Miyyomayim,*—He will requicken us. *On the third
day,—Bayom Hashshelishi,*—He will raise us up, and we
shall live in His sight," *i. e.*, "before Him." Hos. vi:1,
2. Then follows the age of perpetual sunshine and
spiritual showers, v. 3, the summer for the just, the
resurrection glory.

If we ask what these two historic days are, we can
only say again, with Delitzsch, "The prophecy refers
to the people, after the second day of whose death a
resurrection day follows." Rom. xi:15. The two days
of their death are, in the history of fulfilment, the Assyrian and Babylonian exile, and the Roman exile, in
which the Jewish people still are."† That is, the first
day of Israel's national death is the Old Testament

---

* Messianic Prophecies, p. 61.
† Ibid, p. 62.

period of Israel's destruction as a nation, the people carried captive, Jerusalem destroyed, the Temple gone, the land depopulated, and the outward kingdom blotted out; the second day is the New Testament period, with the like catastrophe repeated, the first day reaching to the First Coming of Christ, beginning with a new dispensation, the Roman or second day reaching to the Second Coming, the total period being the time of Israel, as a nation, in the Valley of Dry Bones, the Monarchy-Colossus still standing unstruck.

Then comes the "third," the resurrection day, in whose "morning" Israel arises, the time of Israel's repentance and home-coming, the time when the Colossus falls, and the Dry Bones stand up erect, reanimated, clothed with flesh, a host exceeding great! What we have here is a spiritual resurrection first, Ezek. xxxvi:25; a national and political resurrection next, Ezek. xxxvii:1-28; a literal corporeal resurrection of the faithful dead of Israel last, Ps. xlix;14, 15; Isa. xxvi:19; Dan. xii:1-3. The Apostle Paul quotes the words of Hos. xiii:14, "I will ransom them from the power of the grave; I will redeem them from death. O death, where are thy plagues? O grave, where is thy destruction?" in proof of a literal destruction of the body, I Cor. xv:55, and, in his letter to the Romans, tells us that this time of Israel's conversion and re-establishment will bring no less an event than "life out from the dead." Rom. xi:15.

What Hosea gives us here, at the beginning of the third day, is precisely what Moses gives us, Deut, xxxii:39; and David gives us, Ps. xlix:14, 15; and Isaiah gives us, xxv:8; xxvi:19; and Daniel gives us, xii:1-3; and Ezekiel gives us, xxxvii:1-28; and John's Apocalypse gives us, xi:11, 18: xii:5; x:11; 20:4-6.

Then, after these mighty events that mark the end of
our present age, or end of Israel's second day of national death, comes the Millennial Age of Israel's
blessedness, pictured beautifully, as the times of perennial reviving and refreshing, the age of Israel's
Dew, and Blossoming, and Lily growth, and deepening
roots like the Cedar tree, and spreading branches like
the Olive tree ; the age of blessing to the Nations, when
they, too, dwelling under Israel's shadow, shall revive
as the corn, and bloom as the vine, and be fragrant as
the wine of Lebanon ; and Israel, all holy to the Lord,
will have no more to do with idols, but, unwithering,
like the fir tree, bear holy fruit to God.   Hos. xiv:4-8.
    The demonstration, then, is clear, inductively.
Hosea's "many days" reach from the Assyrian captivity down to the Second Advent of Christ. During
this whole period Israel as a nation lies buried in the
grave with the Colossus on its breast. Israel's resurrection as a nation is on the " morning " of the " third
day." " In the history of Christ the history of Israel
is recapitulated." (Delitzsch.) " Israel must die as a
nation in order to live. From death to life is the path
for Israel to the kingdom." (Orelli.) Equally clear is
it that the "multitude of days" in Isa. xxiv:22, and
" Many Days " in Ezek. xxxviii:8, are identical with
"the Thousand Years" in John, Rev. xx:1-7, and reach
from the Second Coming of Christ to the destruction
of Gog.
    These two vast periods, taken together, cover, there
fore, the whole time from the Assyrian captivity to the
Last Judgment and the final New Heaven and Earth.
The age next before us is that of the " Third Day," the
" Sabbatism " of the world. Not at the First Coming of
Christ was Hosea's prediction fulfilled, as is clear

from John's Apocalypse, where, under the sixth vial, the Euphrates, beyond which the ten tribes roved into concealment among the nations, is "dried up" to make way for the return of Israel, under the care of "the princes from the sun rising. Rev. xvi:12. II Kings xvii:6. Isa. xi:16; xxiv:16; lxvi:19, 20; xli:2, 25. Zeph. iii:10. It is true that the terms "Afterward" and the "Last Days" are standing eschatological formulæ for the whole Messianic time covered by Isaiah's everlasting age, as well as for the time next preceding the "*Yom Yehovah*," or "Day of the Lord;" and that, as is clear from Joel and Peter, they include the first as well as second appearing of Messiah. Isa. ii:2. Joel ii:28. Acts ii:17; the outpouring of the spirit on the day of Pentecost, as well as the still future outpouring predicted by Paul. Rom. xi:27, and parallels; Isa. lix:21. Ezek. xxxvi:24, 25; and both which are wrapped up in Zechariah's oracle, Zech xii:10-14; xiii:1, 6. Compare Rev. i:7. But it is equally true that whatever conversion of Jews occurred on the day of Pentecost, or of any Israelites since, is only the initial, not the final, redemption of that people, since. Israel, as a nation, is still cast away, not gathered, their house desolate, and their land still trodden under Gentile feet. The "afterness of the days" is the end-time at the second coming of Christ. It refers to the epoch of Israel's entrance into the kingdom restored, the time when Israel seeks and welcomes Christ as King. Luke xiii:34, 35. Rev. xv:3; and also to those supernatural days of Messiah, called "his days," in Psalm lxxii:7, when Israel's "handful of corn," or saved remnant, "shall shake like Lebanon," and "they of the city shall flourish like grass of the earth," lxxii:16; the time when those words, so bitter and sad, "*Lo Ammi*"

and "*Lo Ruhamah,*" shall no more be spoken. Down
to this very hour Israel has remained pure from the
sin of " Idolatry" since the day their national exile
began, and, as a people, will so abide, reserved for the
Kingdom of Christ at His Coming. The same race,
punished for sin, is the race reclaimed by grace.
Nationally, as well as personally, God deals with the
Jewish people.

Israel's identity abides through all the ages. From
the genesis of Israel in Abraham to the regenesis of
Israel in Christ, Israel "abides," Israel, untransmuted,
and, from Sennacherib down to the last Antichrist, will
so ' abide," kept for that day when the " Branch of Jehovah shall become an ornament and glory, and He the
Fruit of the Land be a pride and a boast for the escaped of Israel." Isa. iv:2. So sing the prophetic
Blessing of Judah, the Oracles of Balaam, the Dying
Song of Moses, and the Words of David, preluding
the fortunes of the chosen people down to, and into,
the "Last Days." So sing Hosea and Amos, two
prophets of the ten tribes, in concert with all the rest.
In God's strange providence Israel "abides" for *Him*,
and not another, unobelisked and unteraphimed, and He
is "toward *them*," and will yet " have mercy on them."
Then, in that day of Israel's home-coming, the Jewish
Church of the end time will be revived. The Lord
will renew the Covenant of His love with "*Lo Ruhamah,*" take away ambiguous "*Baali*" from her mouth,
and put the loving "*Ishi*" there. He will betroth her
Himself in righteousness and judgment, in loving kindness and in mercies, even in faithfulness forevermore.
In her final tribulation He will allure her to the wilderness, as John's Apocalypse also shows us. Rev. xii:
6, 14 ; and nourish her, and tenderly repeat His "*Ammi*"

to her heart, and breathe *"Ruhamah!"* He will accept her penitence and tears, and give her again " the Valley of Trouble" for a door of hope, and make her sing her old Egyptian song. There will not only be a Wedding Day, but a Day of Victory. When David's fallen Booth is re-erected, in more than ancient splendor, Israel and Judah, reunited, as "one nation," and marching under "One Head," shall "come up from the land," victorious, across the plain of Megiddo, where Barak fought and Deborah sang, and "Great will be the Day of Jezreel!" Hos. i:11.

E.   Moses and the *Sheba*

But Moses demands a hearing. The Propnets nave said nothing on this great matter that even Moses had not already said before them. Let it be enough, just here, to say that Moses himself defines the time during which Israel shall be nationally cast away, and at whose close Israel shall be nationally restored, and made glorious in their fatherland. If we turn to Leviticus xxvii:18, 21, 24, 28, we shall hear God saying what He will do to Israel in case of their apostasy.. " If ye will not hearken unto me, but will walk contrary to me, then I will add to smite you Seven Times (*Sheba'*) upon your sins." When, however, in the *Acharith Hayyamin*, or *Last Days*, Israel repents, accepting the justice of their punishment, nationally, then, says God, " I will for their sakes *remember the covenant* of their ancestors, my covenant I made with Abraham, with Isaac, and with Jacob, *and I will remember the land*." Lev. xxvi;42, 45. Who cannot see that the *Sheba'* or Seven Times of Israel's national punishment are the whole stretch of time in Israel's chastisement, from the smiting of Israel and Judah, as kingdoms, down to the

"*Last Days*" when Israel nationally repents, *i. e.*, down to the Second Coming of Christ? They are the measure of the duration of Israel in the lion's den, and furnace of affliction, seven times hot, the whole period of the "Times of the Gentiles," the period of the Colossus standing erect on Israel's grave; the "Many Days" of Hosea, his "Two Days," at whose close Israel's resurrection and redemption occur, and the Millennial Age begins.

Listen to the "Song of Moses," Deut. xxxii:39-43. It predicts Israel's apostasy, and final recovery, as a nation, in the *Acharith` Hayyamin* or *Last Days*, the "*End of the Days*," still future to us. The fulfilment of that oracle, in Moses, has never yet taken place. Its radius of vision reaches to the Second Advent, as all successive prophecy shows, and all history confirms. Both Testaments conspire to prove this. It points, in clearest terms, to the Great Tribulation, the interposition of Christ, and the "making alive" of Israel's faithful dead by Him who "kills" Israel's adversaries. To spiritualize this into a subjective redemption of all God's people, or of the New Testament Church, is to mock the Scriptures. He who, in Moses, swears, as He lifts His hand, "I AM HE, I kill and I make alive, I live forever," and vows to "avenge the blood" of His martyred ones, and calls the nations to "rejoice with His people" (the Jews) in that crisis, is He who in John, Rev. x:7, lifts His hand and swears that, with the seventh trumpet, the Tribulation shall come to an end, the Antichrist be destroyed, Israel be delivered, as not only Moses, but Daniel also predicted (Dan. xii:1-3) and the righteous dead be restored to life. Such is the organic unity of all prophecy from Moses to John. Then the "mystery of God" *foreshown to the prophets,* "shall be finished" and the kingdom come. John is only repeating and filling out Moses and the Prophets!* Look at Deut. xxxi:28, 29; xxxii-39-43; Rev. vi:10; x;7; xv:3, 4; xix:11-21; xx:1-7. Sunlight is not clearer than that the Age of Israel's glory in the kingdom is placed, by Moses, *after* the Seven Times of punishment which reach down to the very *"End of the Days,"* or *" Acharith Hayyamin "* in their utmost development, that is, *after* Hosea's "two days." In other words, Moses puts it precisely where Hosea's "third day" stands, and John's 1,000 years belong. It *follows* Israel's national conversion to Christ. Deut. xxx:1-4. And he who studies Paul, will find him teaching the same truth when discussing the " Jewish Problem," as men call it. In Rom. x:6-10; xi:25-29, he puts Israel's conversion, as a people, even as Isaiah does, Isa. lix:16-21, and Peter does, Acts iii:19-21, at the Second Coming of Christ.

---

*. "Ani-Hu" (I am He) is a covenant name of Christ, in the Old Testament, Deut. xxxii:39; Isa. xliii:10; xlvi:3-5; xlviii:12. It is the name of the Second Person of the Trinity (I) making Himself equal in Essence with God (HE), while yet asserting a distinct Personality. It is the consubstantiality of the Son with the Father, of the Word with God, and is the ground of John's Logos doctrine. John i:1. He who here speaks, to Moses, is the personal "Word of God," who appears as the diademed Rider on the White Horse, Rev. xix:11, and as the Angel of the Covenant, or *Maleach Habberith*, coming, the second time to Israel, to wake His people out of the Valley of Dry Bones, and appearing with solar-face, rainbow-crown, His shoulders in cloud, and His feet in pillars of fire, Rev. x:1, and swearing the same words to John that He swore to Moses. It was Ani-Hu who dwelt in the Pillar of Cloud by day, and Fire by night. It was Ani-Hu who spoke to Moses in the "Bush." It was Ani-Hu who said to the Jews "Except ye believe that I am He, ye shall die in your sins." John viii:24,28, 58. The name is combined, sometimes, with a participle, as Ani-Hu Hammiddabber, I am He, the *Speaking One*, a motto Stier has taken for his "Words of Jesus." It is a name asserting the deity, eternity, personality, majesty, and real presence and glory of Christ, in Old Testament History. Ani-Hu is the "Alpha and Omega" in the Apocalypse, Isaiah's Immanu-El" or "With-us-God." The Christ who talked to John in Patmos, about Israel's future, is the same Christ who talked to Moses upon the same subject, and in reference to the same time.

F. THE PSALTER

Nor is the Psalter silent. All the sweet singers of Israel, from David to Ezra, pre-celebrate the same future for Israel. They sing in concert with Moses. The "Set Time" to favor Zion, as it stands in the prophetic outlook, Psalm cii:13-22, is demonstrably the "End-Time" when the Angel of Jehovah, the Lord Himself, throned on the "Clouds," comes with His holy "Angels" to "appear in His glory and build up Zion," to "judge the people, the world, the earth, in righteousness," to give the righteous "dominion in the morning," to cause them to "wake in His likeness," to "send the rod of His strength out of Zion," "rule in the midst of His enemies," "smite kings in the day of His wrath," "redeem Israel," "make known His salvation in the eyes of all nations," and "fill the earth with His glory." It is all eschatological. Those marvelous Psalms, cii, xcvii, xviii, xcvi, xlix, cx, lxxii, show this at once. The expression " *His Days*" in Psalm lxxii:7, denotes plainly the days of Messianic or Millennial glory on earth, foretold by the prophets, and as following the "Seven Times" of Moses. These "Days" are the "Third Day" of Hosea, the "Many Days" of Isaiah and Ezekiel, and the "Thousand Years of John." Moses, the Psalms, and the Prophets, all sing the same thing concerning Israel and Messiah, both as to their sufferings and glory, all idealizing critics to the contrary notwithstanding. A pre-advent Millennium is unknown to the Psalter. That bright constellation of five Psalms closing with the 100th Psalm, is a chorus of Second Advent songs. Delitzsch calls them "Apocalyptic Psalms." Prof. Binnie of·Aberdeen styles them "Songs of the Millennium." Herder named them a "Group of Millennial Psalms." Tholuck adorned them with the title " Millennial Anthems." What is it they celebrate ? The glorious kingdom of the Messiah, the kingdom restored to Israel, *after* the Second Coming, or personal Self-Revelation of Jehovah, to judge the world. Like so many others, they teach as the Prophets do, the pre-millennial Advent of Christ, and the " Shower Seasons," or " Times of Reviving" following, when "He shall come down like rain upon the mown grass, and as showers that water the earth;" the very "times of refreshing" of which Peter spoke, when the First Christian Pentecost, their pledge, was fully come. Paul tells the Hebrews in his first chapter that the 97th Psalm relates to the Second Advent when the First-Born Heir of all things is publicly installed in His inheritance amid the homage of all angels. The Old Hundredth Psalm is simply an anticipation of the Millennial Age when " All people that on earth do dwell" unite to praise the Lord. What is the 45th Psalm but an " Advent Hymn" as the great Crusius called it, "celebrating the victories of the Bridegroom-Warrior coming to His kingdom ?"

What is the 97th Psalm but a catalogue of the nations whose individuals are put on the burgess roll as born citizens of metropolitan Zion when God establishes her in universal empire? That the 37th Psalm refers to the Millennial Age, when " the meek shall inherit the earth," is our Lord's own teaching. The 68th Psalm is a "Great War-Hymn of the Conqueror of the World-Power." The 50th Psalm opens with the "Advent of Christ to judgment." The Hebrew Poets are all Pre-millennialists, as are the Hebrew Prophets, and the Psalter has to do with "the 1,000 years" as plainly as has the Apostle John.

G. SUMMARY

If we sum up the results of our investigation, we shall find that the Spirit of Prophecy has furnished us various time-designations which span the whole development of the Kingdom of God on earth from the Assyrian captivity down to the final New Heaven and Earth. Israel's fate is the measure of all history. Of these designations two cover the whole period from the Assyrian Exile down to the Second Coming of Christ, viz., the "Many Days" in Hosea iii:4, 5, during which Israel "abides," waiting for Jehovah, and which in Hosea vi:2, are summed up in " Two Days" the two great historic periods of national death for Israel, viz., (1) the Old Testament Day of Assyrian and Babylonian captivity and dispersion, and (2) the New Testament Day of Roman captivity and dispersion, these two days reaching down to the time of Israel's predicted return, resurrection, and national rehabilitation in their fatherland, at the Second Coming of Christ or in the morning of Hosea's "Third Day," Hosea vi:2; the history of "Israel" the national Messiah, and "Israel" the personal Messiah, being modeled on the same divine plan. What we further find is that the Messianic Kingdom and Glory on earth, *i. e.*, the Millennial Age, this side the final Regenesis of all things, is defined, in the Scriptures, by no less than six different equivalent expressions, viz.:

1. *Rov Yamim.* Multitude of Days. Isa. xxiv:22.
2. *Rabbim Yamim.* Many Days. Ezek. xxxviii:8.
3. *Yom Hashshelishi.* Third Day. Hos. iii:4, 5.
4. His Days. Psa. lxxii:7.
5. *Leolam.* Forever. Ezek. xxxvii:25, 26, 28.
6. *Chilia Ete.* Thousand Years. Rev. xx:1-7.

all descriptive of the same period of time, bounded

on each side by the same events, the period *between* the Second Advent and the Destruction of Gog, or *between* the binding and loosing of Satan. It is important to observe that the "Many Days" of Hosea, are a very different period from the "Many Days" of Ezekiel, and "Multitude of Days" of Isaiah. The former are the "Times of the Gentiles," the times of the Colossus, the Four Beasts, Israel's Graveyard, 69 weeks, with at least 1890 years of the Interval following the period of Israel's national Rejection and Death. The latter are the Mil‑ lennial Age itself, introduced by the Second Advent, the gathering and judgment of the nations, the downfall of the Colossus, the destruction of the Antichrist, the 70th week, and the resurrection of Israel. What we further find is that the 70th of Daniel's 70 weeks is divided into twice 3½ years or twice 1260 days for the Rise, Reign, and Ruin, of Antichrist, and that the formula, 70 years, *plus* 7 year-weeks, *plus* 62 year-weeks, *plus* our Interval, *plus* 1 year-week, all of which make the "Two Days" of Hosea, spans the whole time from the Destruction of the visible kingdom of God on earth to its setting up again; that the "Many Days" of Hosea, which are his "Third Day," span "the 1,000 years" of John; and that all, taken together, exhaust the whole prophetic calen‑ dar if we add, hereto, Gog's "little season," at the close of the Millennial Age. The formula of the total Æonology is 70 years *plus* 69 year-weeks, *plus* our In‑ terval, *plus* 1 year-week, *plus* the 1,000 years, *plus* Gog's little season.

And what we find further, is that no prophet of the Old Testament gives a complete, but only a partial pic‑ ture of the End-Time, even as neither Christ, nor any Apostle does, but that the work of John, under the guidance of the Spirit of Prophecy, was to *combine* the

Eschata of Joel, Amos, Hosea, Micah, Isaiah, Ezekiel,
Daniel, Zechariah ; in short, the Eschata of all the
prophets, *and arrange them in their temporal order and suc-*
cession, snpplementing by one prophet the partial picture of
the End drawn by another, until all the Eschata fall into
their places, as they shall occur in history, so furnishing to
us one grand tableau of the End-Time. This is what the
Holy Ghost did with the seer in the "Isle that is called
Patmos." Nothing is clearer than that "the 1,000 years"
of John are found in the Old Testament prophets, and
are Hosea's "Third Day," Isaiah's "Multitude of Days,"
Ezekiel's "Many Days," bounded by two resurrections,
two conflagrations, and two judgments, each distinguished from the other, and *between* which the Millennial
Kingdom lies. The New Testament Apocalypse answers herein, to the Old, as face answers to face
in water, and it belongs to the shame and reproach
due to the superficial knowledge of so many in
our day, who pretend to greater things, that they have
not recognized this fact, in their study of the Scriptures,
but still keep harping on the old and tuneless string
that "the Millennium is found in *only one passage* of the
Bible, and that in a very obscure book called the Apocalypse !" a boast and a blindness which have happened
in part to many Gentile interpreters who inform us
that the Israel of Old Testament Prophecy, *"Daniel's*
People" brought out of Egypt, and to whom a future so
glorious is reserved, after a punishment so great, means
believers in Christ, the Old and New Testament
"Church," from the "first man Adam," down to the
·" Second Adam, the Lord from heaven," a grand
spiritual company gathered not only from Parthians,
Medes, Elamites, and dwellers in Mesopotamia, but from
Greeks, Turks, Germans, Saxons, Romans, **Arabs,**

Frenchmen, Esquimaux and Indians. What a perversion, or as Delitzsch calls it, a "destruction and negation of the prophetic word," has the spiritualizing interpretation of the prophecies not effected! Or what is more humiliating to a scholar than the allegorizing "Anglo-Israelism" of some in our times! On the contrary, if we only let God speak for Himself—allowing Israel to " *abide*" Israel, till the Lord comes, that "*Genea*" not passing away, how bright the unclouded Apocalypses of Moses, Isaiah, Ezekiel, Daniel, Zechariah and John! How clear the Millennial Age following the Advent! How false the common view entertained by the Church, and blindly advocated by so many of her teachers!

I. It does seem strange that any student of God's word should doubt, for one moment, the truth that blazes everywhere so clearly in the Old as well as New Testaments, viz,, that the Second Coming of Christ *precedes* the Millennium. And it does seem criminal that such an unreasoning prejudice should exist in the minds of any against the use of a term as Scriptural as are the terms " *Baptism,*" " *Baptist,*" " *Episcopalian,*" "*Presbyterian ;*" words which the objectors themselves have chosen to consecrate as the names of their several denominations, and in which they glory. How unreasonable is man's opposition, even to God's own word! "Man would," as Bengel says, "take the very words of God out of His own mouth!" We coin the word "Millennialist," in Latin, from the words "*mille*" and "*annos,*" which are simply the Roman equivalents for the Greek "*Chilia Ete*" of John in Rev. xx:1-7, the English translation of which is a "*Thousand Years.*" It is Scriptural. We coin the word " *Chiliast* " from these same inspired words. It is as Scriptural a term, as is "Baptist," "Pres-

byterian," or "Episcopalian," or "Christian," and as
"orthodox" as any of these! It means that he who
wears it believes that the "Day of the Lord" in which
Christ comes, *precedes* the Millennium. The Advent is
before the Millennium. That is, he is a " *Pre-Millen-
nialist.*" It denies what the Scriptures everywhere
deny, viz., the fiction of a *pre-advent Millennium.* With
equal justice, we might coin the word *Ravyamist* from
the Hebrew terms *"Rov Yamim"* and *"Rabbim Yamim,"*
in Hosea, Isaiah, and Ezekiel, there used to denote the
same truth. Every prophet was a Ravyamist. He
believed in a period of time, *"after"* Messiah's Coming
to judge the Nations, in which Israel, regathered,
redeemed, restored, renewed, resurrected, and re-
nationalized, should enjoy the Messianic glory in the
kingdom on earth—a period of time called *"Many Days,"*
or as John has it, a *"thousand years,"* and prior to the
Last Judgment and the final New Heaven and Earth.
And Christ Himself was a "Ravyamist," or, as Auberlen somewhere truly says, " *Jesus was a Chiliast.*" All
the Apostles were the same. All the early Apologists
for Christianity were the same. Can we imagine when
we hear such a man as Delitzsch say, *"I am a Chiliast,"*
and "Chiliasm was the faith of the early Church," and
when also we hear the greatest modern patristic
scholar, Harnack, say, "Chiliasm is inseparably associated with the gospel, and this is its defense," that
these men are either heretics or foolish? On the
contrary, that great martyr and scholar, "Irenæus the
Great, "like "Justin the most learned man of his time,"
catalogued and held as "promoters of heresy," and
even of "blasphemy," all who denied the Chiliastic faith
which, in their day, was the " test of an orthodox
church," It is a proposition no honest critic dare deny

that, if the early church, having such teachers as Irenæus, Justin, and others of the same apostolic faith and influence, and knowing what Hosea, Isaiah, Micah, Daniel, Ezekiel, Zechariah, John, our Lord, and His Apostles, had taught, had *not* been Chiliastic in her creed, she *ought* to have been so, and her failure to have been so would have convicted her as recreant to what Moses and the Prophets, and Christ and His Apostles, had revealed of the course of history, and the outcome of God's kingdom on earth. It was impossible, however, that, standing next to Christ and His Apostles, and with the Psalms and Prophets in her hand, the Jew nationally cast away yet only for a time, and the Gentile erect on Israel's grave, and even persecuting the church itself, she could have been anything else than she was in her creed, and the proof is perfect, and increases more and more, with every fresh investigation of the early history of the church, that, only by means of apostasy from the Word of God, did she surrender for the sake of opulence and power, money and prosperity, extension in the empire, and freedom from fagot and flame, that blessed truth whose defense from Moses to John, God has made the mark of a faithful, a suffering. and a witnessing church. And, surely, if the pious Hebrew held the Hope of Christ's Coming to judge the nations, restore Israel, and set up His Kingdom on earth, as the only Hope for the world's redemption, the only way by which Gentile politics and power could be overthrown, the Antichrist destroyed, and the faithful dead awakened to share the promise of the kingdom, much more ought it to be our Hope, bound up as it is with our own deliverance, as well as the deliverance of Israel, and the final glory of the world. What a stupendous absurdity, in flat contradiction to every prophet, that the Millennial Age will come *prior* to the "Yom Yehovah," or " Day of the Lord," in which Messiah appears for Israel's final recovery ! Such an idea simply inverts, perverts and distorts, Moses and the Prophets, Christ and the Apostles. The whole testimony of prophecy, pre-exile, exile, and post-exile, is against it. The entire New Testament is against it. Never, till the Colossus comes down by means of judgment, and the Bones of Israel awake in the Valley, and the Antichrist is destroyed, and Satan is bound, and God's sleeping saints are raised, and heaven, earth, sea, dry land, and the nations are shaken, can the kingdom come, as predicted. And that none of these marvels can occur apart from the Second Coming of Christ, the merest tyro in Biblical knowledge must recognize as a first principle and truth in the interpretation of prophecy.

J.   A closing word is demanded as to Israel in the Apocalypse. That wonderful Book is capable of many "applications," but only of one organic "interpretation," based upon the entire unity, analogy, and identity of prophecy. We *may* "apply" its symbols to the times of early Pagan persecution, and also to later Papal persecutions. This is the figurative "application" based upon the equation of " Israel " with the "Christian Church." The Apocalypse was a book of comfort to the early church. It was a comfort, also, to the witnesses of Christ in the Middle Age, and during the Reformation. But as surely as Israel "abides" Israel, and Daniel's " people" are not the "Church," so surely is Israel the key for the true and final interpretation of the closing prophecy of the New Testament. It sums up in itself all the unfulfilled predictions respecting that chosen and predestined race. We meet

Israel everywhere. The very announcement of the *Theme* of the book, viz., the Lord's Second Coming. refers us to Israel. "Behold He *cometh with clouds*, and every eye shall see Him; *they also who pierced Him*," Rev. i:7, *i. e.* the Jewish nation, as Zechariah assures us. The text is a combination of two passages, one from Zechariah, the other from Daniel, both in strict textual connection, in the prophets, with Israel's deliverance at the Second Advent of Messiah. We encounter Israel again in the promise made to the Philadelphian Church, Rev. iii:7-11, by Him who is the "Lion of Judah's tribe," and has "the Key of David." Israel shall be converted in the last time, and in connection with the coming of Christ. Again, we find Israel in the sealing of the 144,000 out of all their tribes, Rev. vii:1-8, just before the Trumpet Judgments occur, and the Tribulation begins. Again, we see Israel in chapters x, xi and xii, chapters that place us in the very midst of Ezekiel's Valley of Dry Bones, and show us the prophet's word, and the Spirit of Life from God, with attending earthquake, beginning that work of spiritual, personal and national, conversion and resurrection foretold by the prophets. The oath-taking Angel of the Covenant, Solar-faced, and Rainbow-crowned, whose shoulders are robed in cloud and feet like pillars of fire, reminds us of the Pillar of Cloud in the Wilderness, and Him who dwelt in it coming to His people again. The "little book" is the matter of the testimony of the "two witnesses." Their 1260 days of witness is the first half of Daniel's 70th week. The slaughter of the witnesses is in the middle of that week, and is the first public persecuting act of the last Antichrist. The succeeding 1260 days is the second half of that week, the time of the tribulation. The "Worshipers," xi:1, the sun-clothed woman, or

Daughter of Zion, xii:1, the "Our Brethren," xii:10, the "Woman" fled to the wilderness, are all the same, the Jewish Christian Church of the End-Time, or 70th week of Daniel. The "Remnant of her seed, who keep the commandments of God, and have the testimony of Jesus," and whom Satan, through the Antichrist, persecutes 1260 days, xii:17, xiii:1, 5, 7, are either Gentile believers, or the remainder of Israel returning from the East under the care of Eastern princes, doubtless both, xvi:12. The 144,000 in xiv:1-5 are Israel again, secure with Messiah returned to Zion, after the Trumpet judgments are over. Again, Israel stands triumphant, in xv:3, 4, singing "the song of Moses the servant of God, and the song of the Lamb," blending their first and last deliverances in one, and declaring that the time for national Christianity on earth has come, now that Israel is victorious, and is a nation converted to Christ. What we see in xiv:20 and xix:11-21, is the Armageddon conflict, closed out, in the valley of Jehoshaphat, outside Jerusalem, the Lord Himself descending from "Heaven Opened" to destroy the Antichrist, bind Satan, raise the faithful dead, and begin the "thousand years" blessed kingdom of glory on earth, Rev. xx:1-7. And what shines before us in Rev. xx:9, is the "Beloved City," Jerusalem restored, the home of the Daughter of Zion, which, for a "thousand years" has enjoyed the uninterrupted peace and glory, foretold by the prophets. He who cannot see *"Israel"* here, in this book as distinct from the *"Church"* and the *"Nations,"* will see nothing. Wonderful is the regularity of Israel's recurrence ! After the 6th verse of the 1st chapter ; in the 6th of the seven Epistles to the Churches ; between the 6th and 7th seals ; between the 6th and 7th trumpets ; between the 6th and 7th vials ; in the Wilderness here; on Mount Zion there; a worshiping part in the city now; a multitude pressing into the land from the East; a shelter, a victory, a triumph, a glory, an effect on the nations, and all at the Second Coming of Christ! He who cannot see this will see nothing! It is the Eschatology of all the prophets. It is the Eschatology of Christ. Is is the Eschatology of the Apostles,—one eschatology, from first to last, built and based on the one eternal plan and purpose of God with respect to Israel, an interpretation grounded in the unity, continuity, organic structure, and genetic development of all prophecy, divine, infallible, sure, a light forever.

A glance is enough to confirm us. John has nothing here the prophets have not. He has nothing Christ has not, for the Apocalypse was given Him of God, and does not mean a literary production, or book, but the "Revelation of Jesus Christ" (Rev. i:1), as He comes the second time, in the clouds of heaven (Rev. i:7), and to His Covenant people, Israel of Old Testament Prophecy, to fulfil the word of His promise to them, to deliver them, restore their state, and give them the kingdom. He comes, indeed, to judge the professing Church and the world, but He comes to Israel as the " *Malakh Habberith*" or " *Angel of the Covenant*" the "*Lord Himself;*" and "who may abide the Day of His Coming, or stand when He appeareth?" (Rev. vi:17 ; vii:1-8, Malachi iii:2-4). John has nothing, the Apostles have not. His Eschatology is the same as that of Peter and Paul. Peter binds Israel's national repentance and the Second Coming of Christ together, Acts iii:19-21. He tells of scoffers in the last days, of the World-Judgment, the day of the Lord, the resurrection and glory, the visible kingdom, and the New Heaven and Earth.

He sees the judgment at the beginning and at the End of the Millennium in one, and overleaps the Millennial Age as a " Day," in order to speak of the final New Heaven and Earth. The whole future was before him in one view, and is couched in one all-comprehending expression. The Conflagration blazes in front, the Glory shines beyond. Paul also takes up each escha. tological point, and discusses it separately. In II Thess. ii:8, we have the Antichrist and Second Coming of the Lord, but nothing is said to Israel. In Romans, chapter xi, we have Israel's conversion and the Second Coming, but nothing is said about Antichrist, In I Cor. xv: 12-57, we hear him discussing the first resurrection at the Second Coming, but not a word about either Israel or Antichrist. In Rom. viii:17-23, we find him dilating upon the glorified inheritance on earth, to be received at the redemption of the body from the grave, when Christ comes, but nothing about any of the other points.

If we combine all these in one picture, what we shall get as a result is Antichrist destroyed, Israel redeemed, the Saints raised, the Inheritance glorified, all at the Second Coming of Christ, and the Millennial Interval *between* that Coming of Christ to *assume* the kingdom and the remote End when He shall have *surrendered* the Kingdom of God, even the Father, having abolished all rule, and all authority and power, and annihilated Hades and Death, "that God may be all in all." I Cor. xv:24-28. In short, we get precisely what John has given us in the Apocalypse, with this difference, that, whereas Peter and Paul discuss the points separately, John discusses nothing, but combines all in a total tableau of the End-Time, glowing under the highest light of the inspiration of the Holy Ghost. And so will every student of God's Word find it, if only he comes to that word with an humble heart, free from prejudice, and false theories of interpretation, and prays that God will open his eyes to see light in God's light alone, accounting all other light as but darkness. Blessed book is the Bible, the living word of the living God, one word from beginning to end, the work of one infinite mind, full of the wonders of wisdom, love and power! And from Moses to John, the Eschatology is one, because God's plan is one, the *"Thousand Years"* in John, following the Second Advent, and preceding the Last Judgment, being the very Interval Paul himself has acknowledged in I Cor. xv:24, and none other than that period of time, called by Hosea, the "Third Day," by Isaiah a "Multitude of Days," and by Ezekiel "Many Days"—in every case, in both Old and New Testaments, associated with the Glory of Israel in the Kingdom, and the Redemption of the Nations, accomplished at the Second Coming of Christ. The holy penmen mutually supplement each other. The Lord open the eyes of His Church to see it, love it, and teach it, and to Him be the glory forever.

SUPPLEMENTARY DISCUSSIONS

" Whoever is familiar with the writings of the prophets, and has devoted himself with loving attention to the same, will soon discover the right road along which he can safely pass through all the apparent labyrinths of the Apocalypse. If we renounce our own thoughts and imaginations, we shall have no difficulty in finding the meaning of God. The way of simplicity is the way of Truth. And if we do not forget that Jesus Christ is not only the confession of our faith and love, but also of our hope, so shall He be to us the Key of all prophecy. The testimony of Jesus is the Spirit of prophecy."

LUTHARDT.

SUPPLEMENTARY DISCUSSIONS

Part 1

SYMBOLIC NUMBERS

I have said in Part 1 of the previous discussion that "The Thousand Years," in John, are a *measure of time*, and that the formula 70 years plus 70 weeks of years, plus the Interval between the 69th and 70th weeks, plus the Thousand Years, plus Gog's "little season," spans all prophetic chronology, from the Assyrian captivity and Judah's exile, down to the final New Heaven and Earth.

A. THE OBJECTION

I desire, now, to consider the objection made to the above view, in modern times, and to-day so popular with our spiritualizing and idealizing expositors, an objection which forms the last refuge of post-millennialism, already driven from the field by exegesis, viz., that prophetic numbers are purely and only symbolical,

ideal, and void of all chronological value. They are
neither mathematical, nor arithmetical, but wholly
schematic and symbolical, belonging to the outward ideal
form of the prophecy, but not to its inward, real, essential content.   In this way, the thousand years are either
dissolved or identified with the "ideas of eternity and
ecumenicity."   To calculate even the 70 years of
Jeremiah, or the 70 weeks of Daniel, is a "folly," since
these numbers represent no particular measures of time
but only abstract ideas and relations applicable to all
times. So Bunsen, in his *"Hippolytus,"* saying, "What has
the Holy Ghost to do with counting years, and months,
and days?"* To the same purpose Dr. Kliefoth in his
recent *"Christian Eschatology,"* speaks. His maxim is
"Symbolical numbers don't count"—and " The number
1,000 (equal to 10×10×10) as the potentiated ten
number, expresses the idea of absolute, all-embracing
ecumenicity, and we should remember that the Scripture repeatedly denotes by this number, a thousand
years which are as one day, and one day as a thousand
years, before God." †   In like manner, Prof. Milligan
of Aberdeen in his work on *" The Revelation of St.
John,"* and following Augustine and Kliefoth, remarks, " If we interpret the thousand years literally, it
will be a solitary example of a literal use of numbers in
the Apocalypse, and this objection alone is fatal." ‡
Once more, Prof. Briggs, holding the same view, says,
"We claim that all prophetic numbers are symbolical,
and that none of them are to be taken as exact or
literal.   The efforts of interpreters to determine from
the numbers of Daniel the interval to the First Advent,

---

* Hippolytus II.   286.
† Christliche Eschatologie.   246.
‡Revelation of St. John.   202.

have ignominiously failed. Their efforts to measure
the times of the Apocalypse, and indicate the time of
the Second Advent, are worse than ridiculous. Those
who indulge in such follies are blindly laboring to undermine and destroy Hebrew prophecy and the Bible
itself, of which it is an essential part. *"

B.   General Remarks

In general, and on the whole subject, it must be
said, first of all, that this idealizing view—even granting
all that may be justly said against the well meant but
mistaken reckonings of many of the ablest and most
devoted servants of God—men like Luther, Bengel,
Newton, Elliott, who gave their lives to defend and
not undermine Hebrew prophecy—is *not* the view entertained by ninety-nine out of a hundred scholars who
have written on the subject. The theory that divests
prophetic numbers of their chronological exactness,
and makes them mere signs, or counters, of "abstract
ideas and proportions," is repelled by the overwhelming
majority of writers on prophecy, in our own time. It
sprang from the Augustinian view of the thousand
years, which, as a spiritualizing and allegorizing protest
against a gross, crass, Chiliasm, swung its reacting
pendulum to the opposite extreme, interpreting "Israel"
as the "New Testament Church," the "Church" as the
"Kingdom," and the thousand years as "all the years of
our Christian dispensation."† Just there was the *fons
et origo* of this hermenentical delusion, a view repudiated by all expositors—save the allegorizers and idealizers who follow Augustine—ever since it received its

---

* Messianic Prophecy I.   53.
† De Civitate Dei. xx:7.   " *Mille annos pro annis omnibus hujus
sæculi*"—"*a thousand years for all the years of this present age*," *i. e.*, from
the First to the Second Advent.

death blow in that famous critical conclusion of Vitringa, viz., "Nothing remains, therefore, but to date
the commencement of this Millennium from those times
in which the empire of the Beast terminates,"* *i. e.* at
the *Parousia,* or *Second Advent* of Christ. The only
possible escape from this is to spiritualize the "Parousia" itself, and make it mean an invisible Advent of
the Holy Ghost in showers of reviving upon the
Church, after the manner of Whitby, so inventing a
spiritual Parousia a thousand years before the literal
Parousia, that is, a millennium *before* Christ returns
to judge the world, redeem Israel, raise His saints,
and assume the Kingdom. Yet, even here, the thousand years are held to be *a measure of time,* although
indefinite, and placed wrongly *this side* the Second
Coming of Christ.

On the whole subject, then, and in general, it must
be replied that, even granting that prophetic numbers are symbolic and schematic, *it does not follow* that
they have no temporal value. The fact that they represent an "*idea*"—and no one denies this—does not
prove that they do not represent "*time*" also. Grant
that the thousand years are either "more or less than
ten centuries," still they are *a measure of literal historic time.* To conclude that, because they are not
just ten centuries "*exactly,*" therefore they have
"no chronological value," is, first of all, an illicit assumption, and, next, an illicit conclusion, insufferable
even in ordinary reasoning. It is as intolerable to
infer that, because they are not "*exact,*" therefore, they
are not "*literal*" as it is to assume, at the start, that

---

* Anakrisis Apoc. 884: "*Ergo, nihil superest aliud quam Millennii
Hujus initium in iis figendum esse temporibus in quibus Imperium Bestiæ
terminatur.*"

they are *"not"* exact. The framework is a part of the building, and not mere abstract form. These numbers, moreover, represent not only time, but quantity or magnitude, and character or quality. *Symbolism* is, indeed, the representation of great ideas or truths in sensuous concrete forms; as, for instance, in the opening Christophany of the Apocalypse, the Seven-Sealed-Scroll, the Seals, Trumpets, Vials, the Smoke-Altar, the Censer, the Swallowed Book, the Sun-Clothed Woman, Harlot, Ten-Horned Beast, Cithara-Players on the Glassy Sea, etc., etc. Yet, notwithstanding this, the very *forms* in which the truths here signified, are clothed, are realistic, denote historic fact, and are a part of the essential contents of the prophecy itself,

Still more. *Schematism* is different from *Symbolism*. *That* represents the general, or abstract ideal, in sensuous concrete forms, *This* represents, not the general, or abstract ideal, in any sense, but the *concrete real itself* in individualized, precise, and definite form. Here the ideal and the real are one. The Symbolism and the Schematism are the same. The form and reality, the sign and thing signified, are inseparable. Such are the Locusts in Joel and John's Apocalypse, the Two Witnesses, the Little Horn or Eighth Head, the Dragon, that Old Serpent, the diademed Rider on the White Horse, etc., etc. Here belong, also, the prophetic numbers which are both schematic and symbolic, and therefore literal as well as ideal; the 70 years of Jeremiah, 70 weeks of Daniel, "time, times, and a half," or three and a half years twice taken, the two halves of the one week in Dan. ix:27, the 1260 days, the 42 months, the 10 days, 5 months of locust torture, the $\frac{1}{4}$ part killed under the Seals, the $\frac{1}{3}$ part under the trumpets, the $\frac{1}{10}$ part of the city fallen, the 7,000 perished

the 144,000 sealed out of Israel, the 1,600 furlongs, the
monogram of Antichrist, 666. All these are schematic
and symbolic indeed ; but to infer that they are not
measures of historic time or locality, or import no literal
character or quality, is to accuse the Spirit of Prophecy
of the "folly" charged on its interpreters.   On their face
these numbers denote, not only ideas, but time, and we
are told that holy men of old "investigated what the
manner of the time here signified was."   I Pet. i:11.

The Holy Ghost might have schematized by *lines*
geometrically, as well as by *numbers* arithmetically,
had He chosen so to represent the ages and the ends,
the seasons and the times.   In any case, His numbers
or His lines, while representing "ideas," represent also
literal realities in time and space, historic entities, and
must so be taken.   We are not to explain the symbol
symbolically !   The *figure of a figure* is not *interpretation !*

PROPHECY A CHRONOMETER

Biblical prophecy is itself, and by necessity, a divine
measurer of time, is organically bound to history, and
connected with a calendar by which the Times and
Seasons, the ages and the ends, have been regulated in
the past, are so now, and will be in the future.   It
serves the Watchman of the night as the starry heavens serve the astronomer, or the traveler familiar with
their aspect and their motion.   It shines as " a light in
a dark place."   He who has learned to read the prophetic Dial may yet not see distinctly, nor tell precisely,
what o'clock it is in the Kingdom of God, "to-day" or
"to-morrow."   But he *can* know if it is midnight, or
the cock crowing.   He *can* tell if he is nearing sunrise, and "the morning cometh."   The Baptist and our
Lord Himself, thought so when they cried, "The Time

is fulfiiled.   Repent.   The Kingdom of Heaven is at
hand !"

The divine chronometer that ticks God's ages on
the face of prophecy may indeed express, in Pythago-
rean way, "abstract ideas," but it also measures off the
"ages and ends," the "seasons and times," the "time
and the manner of time," in the progress of the Kingdom
of God.   It has a wondrous Calendar attached, and, if we
take the figures of the Virgin, the Lion, the Lamb, the
Leopard, the Bear, the Ram, the He-Goat, the Ten-
Horned Beast, the Dragon, the Two-Horned Prophet,
it has a curious Zodiac as well.   At any rate, it explains
the past, the present, and all coming time.   The prophetic numbers are all grounded, as Leyrer and Crusius
both discerned, in "the cyclical relations of a higher order
of things than we yet see," but the laws of which work
on a greater or smaller scale, yet always in the same
analogous proportion.   Plato knew that God geome-
trizes.   Daniel knew that God chronologizes.   In like
manner, He ponderizes.   Science is but his many-col-
ored mantle.   History is but His footsteps.   He works
everywhere, and does all things " by number, measure,
and weight."   Somehow or other, with all their symbolism, the 6 days of creation and the 7th of rest, lie at
the basis of all history, are made the types and measures of literal time, and even of days of 24 hours, each.
And this, just because they were literal periods of time
themselves, and *equal* periods, if we may judge by the
record.

The entire visible world has its roots in the invisible.   The unseen is the source of all realities, and the
mind of God is behind all.   The trouble is not with
God's chronology, but with our " ideas" of it.   Because
we have made to ourselves 300 different chronologies,

we conclude that "all prophetic numbers are symbolical," and a "symbolical number don't count!" Stephen knew enough to tell the Sanhedrim that the 400
years of Israel's bondage in Egypt were prophetic
numbers, and so far from dwelling on any symbolic
meaning they had, he took them as " exact and literal,"
and as proof of the truth of God's predictive word.
Acts vii:6, 7; Gen. xv:13, 14. No otherwise did Daniel
regard the 70 years predicted by Jeremiah, full as they
were of symbolism. For both prophets these were
" exact and literal." Dan. ix:2 ; Jer. xxv:11, 12; xxix:10.
And when Hosea says, " After two *Yamim*, He will
revive us (Acts iii:19-21) in the third *Yom* we shall live
in his sight (Isa. xxvi:19; Eph. xxxvii:12; Dan. xii:2),"
Paul understands him to mean two great measures of
time, followed by a third *Yom*, whose morning is introduced by the Appearing of Jehovah Himself, bringing
outcast Israel's " reception" and " life from the dead."
Rom. xi:15. And this, notwithstanding all symbolism
hid in the terms and the mystic relation of Israel to
Christ. Since a " Nation" is a " Person" before God,
and dealt with as such, and Israel's history is molded on
that of Christ, the proof is clear that the conclusion,
that " because prophetic numbers are symbolical, *therefore* they don't count," is as erroneous in fact as it is
vicious in logic.

On the contrary, the prophetic numbers are symbolical only because, first of all, they are literal. The four
hundred years *did* begin and end. The seventy years
did begin and end. The one thousand years *shall* begin
and end. All are spoken of in the same way. The
seven weeks, and sixty-two weeks, *did* begin and end,
and so much of Daniel's prophecy is completed. Messiah *did* come " after threescore and two weeks," and

"seven weeks." "After," "until," "unto," in answer
to the question, "How long?" and "O my Lord,
When?" *are* chronological, although Professor Milligan thinks that "the word *'after'* is not to be used in a
chronological sense, but rather with the force of subordi-
nating the secondary to the primary effect (!)*" just as
Professor Fairbairn thought the word "*first*" in the
"First Resurrection," had "no temporal significance,"but
only meant the "greatest,"—or the "most important!"
Four is symbolical only because it is literal—the four
corners of the earth. Three is symbolical only because
it is literal,—the three persons of the Trinity. Ten is
the same, only because it is literal,—completion only
because the 9 digits are exhausted. And Twelve is
symbolical only because God gave to Jacob 12 sons to
become the heads of the 12 tribes, the chosen people.
So are the 6 and 7 symbolical only because God worked
six days and rested the seventh. The entire Calendar
is the same. The *law of the Sabbath underlies it all.*

C.   THE NUMBER SIX

Prophetic Numbers are indeed symbolical. No one
denies this. We know that the sacred 7 is so, and lies
at the basis of the Sacred Calendar of the Jews, and
also the Civil Calendar of the Christians. It points to
the "Rest," the "*Sabbath*" of God. It symbolizes that
Rest to which all believers come, even now, first in
their souls by faith ; a Rest to which they shall yet
come, soul and body together, and the "sign" of both
which is the 7th day rest of the Christian Sabbath,
now. The 6 is no less symbolical, just because literal.
It is a secular number grounded in the 6 days' work of
creation which preceded the 7th of rest, the 6 days

---

* Revelation of John 212.

commanded of God for man's toil, but in which the
unbelieving and ungodly, still secular in soul, and
pressed with worldly care, abide without a Sabbath.
They remember not the 7th to keep it holy. They have
no peace, no rest. Their souls have never ceased from
their work, as God did from His. The 6 can never
give the 7. The World can never bring, or give, God's
rest. If the Kingdom of God and His Christ has 7
as its holy signature, the Kingdom of Satan and Antichrist has 6 as its signature; an earthly kingdom, carnal, restless, and unsabbatized; the rule of worldly-
minded men, without a sign of sanctity, or covenant
between themselves and God; a Godless, Christless
kingdom, and a Godless, Christless nation, wherever
found. It is the atheist's mark. It is the apostate's.
sign. It is the seal of anti-Christianity, in league with
civil power; the 10-horned " Beast," who would blot
the *Heptad* from the Calendar and put the *Decade* there,
profane the 7 and consecrate the 6 and 10. We see the
symbolism of it in Dan. iii:1, where the Golden Image
of the Babylonian King was reared upon the plains of
Dura, " 66 cubits high."

" Ideas," indeed, are here, but literal numbers too,
and literal measures also. If the number 6 denotes the
compass of the World-*Time*, the number 66 denotes
the breadth and height of the World-*Power* in the Babylonian's day; 6 multiplied by 10; the number and the
symbol of a secular completeness. It is all the world
wants. It expresses all. It means negation; no God,
no Sabbath, no religion, save the world's religion; no
Rest for man or beast; no heaven; no hope; no immortality. It was the symbol of the Babylonian monarch's
empire over the then civilized and cultured world; an
empire with its feet on Israel's breast. Dan. iii:1-30;

ii:37, 38. In like manner the number "666," the monogram of Antichrist, denotes the topmost summit and the widest breadth of the anti-Christian World-Power, symbolized by the " Beast," the " Little Horn," at the end of our present age. It is a power that will abolish the Sabbath Day, and substitute its own Calendar for God's, with sounding honors to its heroes, with concourse, music and procession, "cornet and flute, sackbut and harp, dulcimer and psaltery," upon the plains of modern Dura, and "woe" to him who fails to worship it. Rev. xiii:1-8 ; Dan. iii:11. Secular, and only secular, it is, and full of culture, education, atheism, persecution, blasphemy and lust ; full of gold and silver, all that Science, Art, Philosophy and Power can bring. Already in our modern revolutions, in the Comtist Calendar, in the Communism and Socialism of our day, and in the swamp-sounding frog-like *"croak"* of its daily platform, and its press, against religion, we have the presage of its coming. Rev. xvi:13. It is the God-opposed World-Power in league with the God-opposed World-Wisdom, the gospel of the flesh, æsthetic and unclean, with spirit–forms and scientific wonders, as its aids, preparing Christendom for AntiChrist, the " Lawless" one. It is 666, and only 6 ; 6 *units* to reflect the secular days, 6 *tens* to represent attainment of its power, 6 *hundreds*, the symbol of its ecumenical, its universal, sway. It is no false democracy, or red republic, but the fruit of these, a Scarlet-Cæsarism, the last development, for which the others are a preparation.* It is headed up in a personal enormity. Its number is the "number of the *Beast*" the "number of his *Name*," the "number of a *Man*," and

---

* See Martensen. Christian Ethics, 352—356.

" ascending from the *Pit!*" Wisdom here is wanted. Let him who has it " *count.*" Permission is accorded, Rev. xiii:17, 18. To " *count*" implies the literality. It means a " Man" that is a " Beast ;" a Beast that is a " Devil ;" a Devil that is a " God." This is what our boasted progress, culture, and civilization are coming to, the outcome of post millennialism with its church leaven for the masses, its conventions to arrest the tide of crime in Christendom, and its proud, self-adulant statistics ! " 666" will not down at church bidding which has so much of "666" in its own character and constitution ! *Symbolical* indeed ! but *literal* too ! And only when the Antichrist is overthrown, and the future temple built to Christ from all " the precious things of all the nations," will the whole world's wealth,—the spoils redeemed from anti-Christianity,—the treasure of the world, its " 666 talents of the gold of Ophir" be consecrated to His service. I Kings x:14 ; II Chron. ix:13 ; Isa. lx:17, 10, 13 ; Hagg. ii:7 (*Revised Version.*) There is something more than mere abstract ideals here.*

D. THE SEVENTY WEEKS

That tne 70 Weeks of Daniel are measures of defi-

---

* Note on " 666." Irenæus found 666 in the word *Lateinos* written Greekly. The Benedictines saw it in *Romiith*, the Roman written Hebrewly. The Protestants found it in *Vicar of the Son of God*, written Latinly, *Vicarius Fillii Dei*, on the Pope's tiara. The Catholics found it in the word *Luther*, and both Catholics and Protestants found it in the name *Mahomet*, while Pagans see it in the word *Messias*, Messiah. Modern critics find it in the words *Nero Cæsar* written Hebrewly, although it is known John wrote in Greek. Some Germans see it in *Gallos Kaiser*, the Gallic Cæsar, *i. e. Napoleon*, while some Frenchmen see it in *Bismarck*, the German autocrat. Ebrard sees, in 6, the number of the *Roman* World-Power, *i. e.* the 6th head of the Beast. Rösch sees the 6 as the sign of the secular 6 days. Hengstenberg, after Vitringa, sees an allusion to the 666 sons of *Adenikam*, Ezra ii:13,—the self-exalting Lord ! But better than all, Hofmann, Auberlen, etc., hold that the future alone will reveal it. Constantine had his Labarum, and his Monogram. Antichrist will have his parliament, his number and his banner too! The world will know its " 666!"

nite literal time, and not mere symbols of ideas, cannot be successfully denied. Ever since God rested
from His creative work, the number 7 has not only
borne a sacred Sabbatic value, but has been a measure of exact time, and the septennial division of time
has been the peculiar characteristic of sacred history
and prophecy, alike, and continues repeating itself
down to the sounding of the 7tu trumpet. Whatever
chronology men may devise, its supreme test in relation to all the events of Israel's history, and to all prophecy concerning Israel's future, must be the Sacred Calendar of Sabbatic Years and Jubilees, established
through Moses, by divine authority. All Hebrew chronology resolves itself into Cycles of Sevens, great or
small, and Daniel's prediction conforms itself, of set
purpose, to this " law of the Week," " law of Seven,"
" law of the Sabbath," and " law of Jubilee." That
law determines not only the whole period of the 70
Sevens, or Weeks, but the formal subdivision into 7
plus 62 plus 1. Plainly the 70 years' Captivity, foretold
by Jeremiah, were determined by that law. These years
are a series of 10 Sevens, 7 multiplied by 10 equals 70,
each year, in the series, answering to a septennial
period, or period of 7 years in Israel's history under the
monarchy ; *i. e.* each year of the Captivity representing a Sabbatic Year (or every 7th year), which Israel
had violated in past time, refusing to give the " Land"
its covenanted "Rest" from cultivation. The "7 Weeks"
of prophecy, *i. e.* the first subdivision of the 70 Weeks
are, as Sir Isaac Newton quickly saw the "*compass of a
Jubilee*," *i.e.* 7 multiplied by 7 equals 49 years, ending
not only in a Sabbatic, but in a Jubilee year, year of
Israel's atonement, release and return, and full redemption ; and, in this case, as the history of fulfilment

shows, including the dedication of the Wall of rebuilt
Jerusalem. The "62 Weeks" next following the 7, are
"62 Sevens," or 434 years, these two subdivisions added together, making "69 Weeks," or "Sevens," *i. e.* 483
years, ending with the Advent of Messiah. So speaks
the Angel Gabriel, who revealed the prophecy to Daniel, and was called the Angel of the Advent, uttering
the oracle, and uttering its fulfilment also: "From
the Issuing of a word to restore and to build Jerusalem, unto Prince Messiah, shall be Sevens 7 and Sevens 62." Dan ix:25. The final "One Week," or one
7, stands removed from the 69 Weeks by the whole interval of time to elapse between itself and Messiah "cut
off." It is chronologically severed from immediate
sequence upon the 69th week, because of Israel's foreseen national rejection of their own Prince Messiah
without whose national acceptance the redemption
promised to Israel as a nation, could not come. Thus,
the Great Sabbatism, and Jubilee of Jubilees, due at
the close of the "70 Sevens," has been, by Israel's guilt
on the one hand, and God's suspension of His national
covenant with Israel, on the other, postponed "until
the time come" when Israel shall be in readiness to receive, as a nation, and hail with "*Hosanna!*" their long
rejected, yet returning, King. The "One Week," still
future, is a "Seven" of itself, and the entire 70 Sevens
run out into a Great Sabbatic Jubilee, when Israel,
nationally ransomed from their Gentile servitude, shall
return to their forfeited possessions, re-acquire their lost
inheritance under God's national covenant resumed,
and, forgiven their iniquity, their apostasy finished, and
their hearts renewed, enjoy their promised Rest, and
promised "Land," forever. Such is God's plan, a plan
of fixed, measured, and historic movement along the

ages, ruled by definite "seasons and times," and not by mere vague, timeless, and abstract ideas. The 70 Weeks of Years, announced by the Angel to Daniel, along with the Interval between the 69th and 70th Week, have as literal a fulfillment as had the 70 years of the Exile, or the Crucifixion of Christ, or the Destruction of Jerusalem by the Romans. Israel's dispersion to-day, is as truly a national punishment for the national rejection of Christ, as Israel's dispersion, and captivity for 70 years, were a national punishment for the violation of the Law of the Sabbath, and their national apostasy from God. Lev. xxvi:33-35 ; II Chron. xxxvi:21. The post-millennarian assumption, that Israel is *nationally cast away forever*, that God has *no national future for Israel restored*, and that Israel is now the " *Church*," is the one fundamental and false postulate that blinds so many to the true interpretation of the " 70 Weeks" of Daniel.

The final goal of prophecy is Israel's remote future. It lies on the distant horizon, or *Acharith Hayyamim*, *i. e.* at the end of our present age, or dispensation. By means of the Angel's Revelation, Daniel is made see, not only the End, but the Way thereto. He knows the Messianic Kingdom cannot come to Israel, except through Israel's national acceptance of Messiah. The Angel tells him that, even after the return from Exile, Israel will deepen in apostasy, rejecting their Messiah when He comes; that the rebuilt City and Temple will be destroyed as a punishment for their sins, and they themselves dispersed again, nor be gathered, save in the distant End-Time, through great tribulation ; and that God, who knows all things and sees the End from the Beginning, and all the Way, has "measured off 70 Sevens" with the Interval "and unto," as the allotted pathway at whose close the " **Mystery of God**"

shall be finished, and Israel as a nation be redeemed.
The *time* is delimited, and the Sabbath law holds its
ground, and shapes the prophecy. It dominates the
number 70, and the subdivisions of it, 7 plus 62 plus 1.
It is the vital reason of it. As all Harvests point to the
one final Harvest when Christ comes, so all Sabbaths
point to the one final Sabbath at the end of Israel's
weary world-week of 7 times 70 years' Captivity, with
the Interval "and unto" included, the time of the suspension of the covenant, when Israel, as a nation, is a
blank before God actually, although, by that same covenant, reserved to a glorious destiny. God's chronology, prophecy, and history, all end in a Sabbatism of
redemption, jubilee, holiness and rest, in the land
of Canaan; type of an eternal day! God has respect
to the " *Seven*" and to the " *Sabbath,*" in all His dealings
with His people. It is the law of the Sabbath that
shapes the times and seasons, the ages and the ends,
the cycles and the epicycles, equal or proportionate,
and is ingrained in all the processes of Nature. As
the earth's circular motion in her orbit, and on her axis,
gives roundness, not squareness, to the bodies of the
trees, and to the stems of vegetation, so it is the Law
of the Sabbath that shapes the growth of the rounded
times and seasons, articulates them, and runs them out
into an endless Sabbatic Jubilee. To that all things
tend.

The sub-distribution of the 70 Weeks, and the prediction of the great events connected with them, prove
these weeks to be literal measures of time, and not
mere symbols of abstract ideas. The numbers " count."
He " counts" who fixes termini " *from*" one event "*to*"
another. He chronologizes and arithmetizes, who
writes " *unto*" and " *until*," and the events connected

therewith prove that the figures " count." The 70 is at least not 71, 7 is not 9, 62 are not 26, and 1 is not 4. And, that *time* is involved, the lapse expressed by "*unto*" and "*until*," and the question, "*how long*," and the words "*measured off*" or "*decreed*," sufficiently declare. And, that the " Sevens" or " Weeks," are literal *Year-Sevens*, each Seven being Seven *Years*, and not Seven "*days put for Years*," is proved by the reduction of the last Seven to twice 3½ *years* through its reduction to twice 1,260 *days*, and by the nature and number of events predicted. It is of the first importance however, to observe that the prophecy of the 70 Weeks relates to the fortunes of the literal Israel, and to Israel as a nation, and is an answer to prayer and anxious investigation of the prophets concerning Israel, and the salvation promised, through Israel, to the world. The prophets had spoken of a suffering, and of a glorious Messiah, and of Israel's relation nationally to both the Suffering and the Glory. To Daniel, "searching what, and what manner of time" the Holy Ghost signified, when thus testifying, and inquiring the relation of the " what," and the "time," and the " manner" of it, to Israel's 70 years' Captivity, Dan. ix:2 ; I Pet. i:11 ;—to Daniel studying " in the Sacred Books (*Bassepharim*), and adding prayer to study ; the Angel Gabriel makes the revelation of the future. This Apocalypse is an answer, full, and precise, and in direct response to the points made in the prayer itself. It covers the prayer in the most perfect manner. It speaks in the terms of the prayer. The subjects of the prayer are (1) the *People*, " All Israel," " we," "us," " our fathers," Israel as a nation in their collective unity, or solidarity, ever since they were a nation, ever since they came "out of Egypt," vs. 7, 11, 20; (2) the *City*, " Jerusalem," vs. 2, 7, 12, 16 ; (3)the *Temple*, the

"Sanctuary," in the "holy mountain," vs. 16, 17, 20. The matter of the confession is sixfold (1) Israel's national "transgression," the apostasy in departing from the Covenant, vs. 11, 20; (2) Israel's national "sins," vs. 16, 18; (3) Israel's national "iniquity." v. 16; (4) Israel's want of enduring "righteousness," v. 18; (5) Israel's punishment as that foretold, in what Moses foresaw and predicted, vs. 11, 12, 13; (6) Israel's desolated Sanctuary, vs. 17, 20. All these he weaves into an agony of deep-drawn, plaintive supplication, imploring, beseeching, twisting, and undertwisting, his petitions and confessions, pleading, plying, and pressing his suit, bemoaning himself and "All Israel," and with the most solemn repetition of the dreadful name of "Jehovah, the covenant-keeping God," appealing to Him as God, and as his God, for immediate forgiveness and deliverance. The appeal is most touching, intense, and solemn,—"*O Lord, hearken; O Lord, hear; O Lord, forgive; and do; Defer not, for thine own sake, O my God; for thy people are called by thy name.*"* v. 21.

It is in answer to this paroxysm of devotion, surpassed only by the prayer in Gethsemane, that Gabriel, darting like a beam of light across the sky, "flies swiftly" and touching Daniel on his knees, gives him this prediction of the 70 Weeks. He tells him that the

---

* *Pesha*, means to rebel against a sovereign and break covenant allegiance, to go into open treason and apostasy by departure from God. *Hhattaoth*, means failures first, then gross sins, as intemperance, adultery, idolatry, refusing to hearken to God's prophets. *Avon*, means crookedness, perversity of will and disposition, a heart not right, unrighteousness, or want of straightness according to a rule, and always includes guilt and punishment. These were Israel's national character and condition. Daniel confesses all for his nation, just as David did for himself. "Seventy Sevens" are decreed in order to stop "the transgression," end "sins," and cover "iniquity." A grand *Apotelesma* is here, in this complex prediction, spanning both Advents, reaching not only to Messiah, but to Israel's ultimate and national redemption.

full redemption of his People, City, and Temple, will *not* come at the close of the Captivity, but only at the end of " Seventy Sevens," the last " Seven" following a long Interval which itself must follow the Sixty-Ninth Seven, at whose close Messiah comes. These " Sevens" are decided upon as the time for accomplishing the points in the prayer. What the Angel says is:

Verse 24. *" Sevens Seventy"—Shabuim Shibim*, are decreed upon thy people and upon thy holy city.

(1) *Lecalleh Happesha*,' to finish, or put a stop to *the* transgression.

(2) *Ulhathem Hhattaoth*, and to make an end of, or put away, sins.

(3) *Ulcapper Avon*, and to cover over iniquity, or condone it by reconciliation.

(4) *Ulhabi' Tsedek Olamim*, and to cause everlasting righteousness to come.

(5) *Velahhtom Hazon ve-Nabi*, to seal, close up, or verify, vision and prophet.

(6) *Velimshoach Qodesh Qedashim*, to anoint, or consecrate, a holy of holies."

Such is the opening announcement of the *Davar*, the word, that " went forth " from God in the ears of holy angels above, while Daniel was praying, v. 23, and which Gabriel flew swiftly to tell him. In the vision of Nebuchadnezzar, he had learned how Babylon, Persia, Greece, and Rome must fall before Israel's final glory should come, with Messiah's appearing in the clouds of heaven. In the vision of the four beasts, he had learned how the Little Horn from the fourth empire must first appear and be destroyed. In the vision of the Ram and He Goat, he had learned how the sore distress of Maccabean times must first supervene. And now, he is informed that Messiah will come *prior* to the time of coming in His glory; come at the *beginning* of the fourth empire after 69 appointed Sevens have passed away, as well as at the *end* of the fourth empire after the 70th Seven is completed; and that then, when the 70 Sevens are exhausted, the *Hexad* of blessing in v. 24, will be realized in Israel as a nation, and in their City and Temple, even as at the close of the 69th Seven, the meritorious ground of the whole redemption should be laid in the work of Messiah at His first appearing. Thus the *whole* future is grasped in one conception, and covered by this one prophecy. And now, the Angel calls on Daniel to apply his mind to the revelation given, and to discriminate. " Let him that readeth understand!"

Verse 25. "Know therefore and discriminate; *from* the going forth of a word to restore and build Jerusalem, *unto Prince Messiah* (shall be) Sevens Seven ; and (shall be) Sevens Sixty and Two ; she shall be restored and built, (as to) broadplace and rampart, and in distress (shall be) the times."

Verse 26. " And, *after* those Sevens Sixty and Two, shall Messiah be violently rooted out, and (there shall be) nothing for Him ; and the city and the sanctuary shall the people of a prince, the one that is to come, destroy; and his end (shall be) in the overflowing ; and *unto that end* (shall be) war, a decreed (measure or limit) of desolations."*

---

* It may be objected that the *disjunctive* Hebrew accents, separating "decreed" from desolations" forbids this construction. I follow, however, Hengstenberg, Havernick, Lengerke, Maurer, Gesenius, Wieseler, Hitzig, Auberlen, rather than the R. V. which renders the words as subject and predicate; " desolations are decreed ;" The two clauses stand in apposition, "Unto that end shall be war; decreed (measure or limit) of desolations." So it may be objected that the *conjunctive* accents, binding "end" and 'war" together, require the rendering "Unto the end of the war shall be a decree of desolations," as Rosenmüller, and Ewald think. But the binding requires only the copula, "shall be;" "Unto that end shall be war." The article is wanting to the word "war" which, moreover, is not in the genitive.

Verse 27. " And he shall make strong (cause to prevail) a covenant, to the many, *One Seven ;* and he shall cause Sacrifice and Offering to cease, *Half of that Seven ;* and, upon wing of abominations (he shall come) a Desolator, even *until* the Consummation, and *until* that which is decreed is poured upon the one desolating."

Such is the literal rendering and force of this important prophecy.   And what we have here is

1. *Seventy Weeks*, or 490 years are delimited, or measured off from the course of time, for the purpose of accomplishing the six things enumerated in the *Hexad* of verse 24, viz., the termination of Israel's national apostasy, the hindering of the outburst again of Israel's sins, the covering over of Israel's iniquity, the introduction of abiding righteousness, the verification of what vision and prophet have foretold concerning Israel, and the consecration, in Israel, of a new

---

* Verse 24, Seventy Sevens=*Shabuim Shibim.*   The infinitives, with the preposition " to, " have a Gerundive force, i. e. *for the purpose of* stopping ; *for the purpose of* ending ; *for the purpose of* covering over.   The 70 Sevens all contribute to that End and Outcome in Israel's history.   Beautifully, Cocceius renders these infinitives, by " *ad coercendum, ad consummandum ad expiadum, ad adducendum, ad obsignandum, ad ungendum.*   Verse 25, Going forth of a Word=*Motse Davar.*   Seven Sevens=*Shabuim Shibim.* Sevens Sixty and Two=*Shabuim Shishshim Ushnayim.*   Prince Messiah =*Masiach Nagid.*   Verse 26, Nothing for Him=*Ain Lo.*   A Prince, the one that is to come=*Nagid Habba.*   Verse 27.   The Many=*Harabbim ;* the definite article is in the long pointing under the first Hebrew letter.   A Covenant=*Berith.*   Make strong=*Higbir.*   One Seven=*Shabua' Echad.* Sacrifice and Offering=*Zebach* and *Mincha.*   Half of that Seven *Hhatsi Hashshabua.'*   On Wing of Abominations=*Al Kenaph Shikkutsim.*   A Desolator=*Meshomem.*   Consummation=*Calah*, i. e. completion at the end of the Week.   The one desolating=*Shomem.*

The " Prince Messiah " v. 25 is not the " prince the one that is to come " v. 26.   The " prince the one that is to come " is not Titus, but the last Antichrist, " His end " —*Keits*—is Antichrist's end.   The subject of the verb "make strong," v. 27, is not Prince Messiah, but the Nagid or prince to come.   It is he who makes the covenant.   The "many " mean the masses of the Jewish people.   The "overflowing" alludes to the tide of judgment. The "poured upon" is pointed to by the vials in John's Apocalypse of which the verse, Dan. ix:27, is the outline and frame, from Rev. chapter iv-20.

Sanctuary, no Veil existing, the entire structure being a
" holy of holies. " To this end and outcome, the
" Seventy Weeks " are appointed or decreed. The
Hexad of blessing is the rich fruit, the ripe result, or
issue of the whole period. Israel, as a nation, and a
people, in their collective unity, will never more
become apostate, but, renewed by the Spirit, and
pardoned of their guilt, be a righteous nation, and mon-
ument of the truth of prophecy, and shall worship God
in their own land, and in a sanctuary where God will
dwell among them forever. This is the final goal or
ultimate *terminus ad quem* of the 70 Weeks, viz.,
Israel's final restoration and complete national redemption. This did not occur at the First Advent.

2. *Seven Weeks*, or 49 years, the close of which was a
Sabbatism, and in the history of the period of the Restoration, was made illustrious by the completed work
of Ezra and Nehemiah. The reader of the Revised
Version will see a colon placed after the words " Seven
Weeks " (:) representing the Masoretic punctuation of
the text, and used now in the interest of an interpretation which refers " *Prince Messiah* " not to Christ, but
to some other person, " an anointed one, " Onias III,
the high priest, or some other one, " cut off " in the
days of Antiochus Epiphanes, a century and a half before Christ. The Masorites, who pointed the text,
simply followed the Maccabean commentators and editors of the book of. Daniel, who misapplied the 70th
of the 70 Weeks of Daniel, to the times of the Maccabean persecution under the Greek, or *third* prophetic
empire,—whereas the prophecy refers to the closing
times of the final form, yet future, of the Roman, or
fourth prophetic empire,—and sought to teach that,
" from the going forth of a word to restore and build

Jerusalem unto an anointed one, shall be 7 Weeks;"
but not "7 Weeks and 62 Weeks."*   That the Angel
had a reason for dividing the 69 Weeks into 7 plus 62
there can be no doubt, and as little doubt is there that
the 7 Weeks cover the period of the Restoration not
from the first year of Darius the Mede, but from the
decree of Cyrus two years later, to the Completion
of the Restoration under Nehemiah.   While, therefore,
we note the memorable period of the Restoration and
mark its Sabbatic close, according to the "law of the

---

*The Masoretic accents (*of which the Angel was totally ignorant,
giving the sense of the passage with accents of his own voice, pausing where
he pleased*) are used not only as signs of interpunction, but often as a Rabbinic commentary on the text.   We are not bound by them in any case and
should scrutinize them carefully, especially in Messianic prophecies.   Of
great value, yet they are *no part of the sacred text.*   It is possible also that
we may not know fully the reasons of their location in important places,
and may impute wrong motives to the Jewish editors of the text.   That they
can be perverted is plain enough.   *We have a right to strip the text of all
accents, and accent for ourselves.*   Pusey says the Jews put the *Athnach*
where it is, "dishonestly."   Hitzig says no man, who knows anything
about Hebrew as a living language, could put it anywhere else than where
the Masorites have placed it.   Ewald, Bleek, Keil, Küper, Davidson,
Kuenen, Orelli, Riehm, all say it is in the right place, and Briggs remarks
that the vast body of scholars concur in this.   The question is, does Messiah
come at the end of 7 Weeks or at the end of 62, or 69 Weeks.   The truth is
that it is not in the power of the *Athnach* to settle that question, and it may
not only be perfectly harmless where it is,—notwithstanding, men pervert it,
—but really serve a good purpose.   Küper says it may be only a Rest-
Point, —*Ruhepunkt,*—and to draw attention to the fact that two independent
periods are named, but not to separate them in reckoning.   Auberlen says it
marks the fact that the two periods have distinct characteristics.   Kuenen,
Bleek, etc., say it means that the City was to be built during the whole 62
Weeks, and that Messiah was not Christ but some one 150 years before
Christ.   Canon Cook, in Speakers' Commentary, justifies the *Athnach.*
King James' Version, and others, reject it, as did Theodotion and the
Vulgate, and as have the majority of Bible translators.   The Septuagint
itself is neutral, an important fact.   Professor Green of Princeton, disputes
the right of the Revisers to retain it.   Prof. Briggs, *contra.*   He would be
a remarkable Messiah who should come at the end of 49 years, and then be
" cut off " at the end of 434 years more !   That would make him older than
Enoch, the 7th from Adam !   It is certain that, if the *Athnach* is to be used
for such purposes, neither Onias, nor Jesus, were the Messiah, and that he
has not yet appeared, and probably never will !   We have no objections to
the *Athnach.*   It serves an exegetical purpose, but not that of separating
the 62 from the 7 in reckoning.   The text might admit of one or two more !

Seven," we are not to negate the conjunction which connects the 7 Weeks and 62 Weeks, whether with or without interval, making 69 Weeks, or 483 selected years," from the going forth of the commandment to restore and build Jerusalem, unto Prince Messiah."

   3. *Sixty-Two Weeks.* These weeks added to the 7 Weeks are 49 years and 434 years, making 483 years of selected time " decreed upon the people and the City," for the purpose of accomplishing the building of the Temple and the City. "Know and *discriminate*" that there are measured times "Sevens Seven," and "Sevens Sixty and Two," *those* for the building of the Temple and the City, *these* for the building, fortifying, and completion of the City. " She shall be built, plaza and rampart, her broadstreet, her gates, her mural defenses. From the going forth of a word to restore, and to build Jerusalem," these 69 Sevens are delimited, and at the close of the 69th, expect Messiah. The Angel does not say that the last of these two periods is immediately sequent on the first, or that there are *only* 483 years from *Cyrus*' decree to *Christ*. There are times of arrest, distress, and inaction, intervening. Sacred Sevens are however, " *decreed upon the people and the city* " for accomplishment of God's Work. As history shows the characteristic of the " Seven Weeks " to be the building of the Temple and City, so it shows the characteristic of the " Sixty-Two Weeks " to be the building, fortifying and completion of the city, down to the time of Herod, who so grandly adorned both it and the Temple ; even "unto Prince Christ," born under his rule. This Advent of Messiah is the nearer *terminus ad quem*, or end, in the prophecy ; not the end of the 70 Weeks, but of the 69 Weeks taken together ; the end of the 62 Weeks. The end of the 70 Weeks, with

their included interval, is Israel's final redemption from apostasy, and their national conversion, recovery and glory in the kingdom.

The *ad quem* of the 69 Weeks is " Prince Messiah" soon to be cut off, or rooted out. The first *ad quem* gives us the First Advent when Messiah comes in humility, to suffer, die, and be thrust out. The second *ad quem* give us the Second Advent when Messiah comes in glory, to be accepted by " His own" who before rejected Him. The first is His Appearing ; the second is His *Re*-Appearing. Two Advents are here. The *Hexad* of blessing in v. 24, is the *ultimate ad quem*, Israel's glorious condition at the return of Messiah in the clouds of heaven, while 7 plus 62 Weeks give us the *nearer ad quem*, viz., the First Coming of Christ. Let our secular chronology be what it may, this is what the Angel says to Daniel, viz., that " 70 Sevens " are appointed for the purpose of bringing Israel's final redemption, and " 69 Sevens" are appointed for the purpose of bringing Messiah's first Appearing.

4. *The Crucifixion of Christ.* " After" the 69 Weeks —how soon after is not said,—shall Messiah be rooted out by violence, " cut off" by judicial execution ; "and there shall be nothing for Him !"* This is plainly the specification of a time for the death of the " Servant of Jehovah" of whom Isaiah says in chapter liii:8 : " He

---

* *Ve Ain Lo !* wrongly translated in King James' version " but not for Himself." The phrase denotes the absolute apostasy of the nation, and is best interpreted by, " He came to *His own, and His own received Him not!*" Even of His disciples it is said, " *All forsook Him and fled !*" and " As for His generation, who cared that He was cut off out of the land of the living, though He had done no violence, nor was deceit found in His mouth !" Matt. xxvi:56 ; John i 11 ; Isa. liii:8, 9 ; Zech. xiii:7 ; Psalms xxii:1. While the death of Christ was a substitutionary sacrifice for the whole world, this expression *Ve Ain Lo* has no reference to that fact, but marks the complete apostasy of the Jewish nation in the rejection of its King. " *We have no King but Cæsar !*" " *Not this man, but Barabbas !*"

was cut off out of the land of the living," and for the " Shepherd" whom Zechariah represents as saying, " They shall look unto Me, whom they have pierced," Zech. xii:10.   Neither " Palm Sunday" nor " Good Friday" lie within the 69 Weeks.

5. *The Second Destruction of rebuilt Jerusalem and the Second Temple.*   This is the result of Israel's consummated national apostasy.   Israel's great "transgression," the apostasy which led to the crucifixion of Christ, and caused the suspension of God's covenant with the nation ; the breaking of "Beauty and Bands," and the Destruction again, of the City and the Temple.   What the Angel informs Daniel is, that " Messiah" will come while the Second Temple is standing, and the Second Temple shall be destroyed because " Messiah" has been " cut off."   *After* He comes He is cut off.   *After* He is cut off, City and Temple are destroyed a second time.

6. *Interval, or the Continuance of the Judgment on both City and Temple, and on the Nation, down to a specified time.*   As the crime of Jerusalem transcended that of all other cities, so must the continuance of her judgment.   " Unto the End shall be War ; a decreed measure of desolations."   Though rebuilt and restored, with broad street and rampart, Jerusalem shall be besieged and destroyed, and judgment shall linger upon her, in the form of " War and Desolations," down to the End of the 70th Week.   Seventy Weeks are measured off ; Seven and Sixty-two pass away ; Messiah comes, and is cut off ; Jerusalem and Temple are destroyed ; and down to the End of the whole decreed time of judgment, war and desolations, involving a second Dispersion of the people, are the dark future for unbelieving Israel.   Yet not forever.   There is a " decreed measure" of national punishment.   It is the " times of the

Gentiles," and this *Interval* between the 69th and 70th Weeks, during which the national covenant is suspended, and Jerusalem lies prostrate under Gentile feet, and Israel is nationally cast away, is opened out by Messiah Himself, when interpreting this prophecy of the 70 Weeks, and resuming and enlarging it. " Jerusalem shall be trodden down by the Gentiles *until* the times of the Gentiles be fulfilled," *i. e.:* " *Unto* the End." Luke xxi:24 ; Dan. ix:26. Then it will be redeemed.

7. *A prince, the one that is to come.* This is not "Prince Messiah" of v. 25, already come, cut off, thrust out from the land, and nothing for Him. That one was the *Anointed Nagid.* But this one, yet to come, is the *Unanointed Nagid,* one spoken of as already known to Daniel, " *the* coming one," " *the* future one," in short, " *the Little Horn,*" Dan. vii:8-28, here called " *Nagid Habba,*" the prince that shall come, and " *Meshomem,*" the Desolator, and " *Shomem,*" one desolating, v. 27. It is here that the Anti-Messiah, the Antichrist, is found; one standing over against Messiah ; one who, like Messiah, has a " Coming ;" and who, like Messiah, is a " Prince," and like Messiah, makes a " Covenant," and with " Israel," too.

8. *The Seventieth Seven, or One Week.* This 70th Week closes the long *Interval* that follows the rejection of Messiah and destruction of Jerusalem by Titus, A. D. 70, and is divided into two equal periods of 3½ years or 1,260 days, and is the mother-seat and source of the same numbers found in John's Apocalypse ; this final week being John's twice 3½ years, or twice 1,260 days; the "One Seven" of Dan. ix:27, which reappears in John's Apocalypse, and is covered by the Seals, Trumpets, and Vials, opened, sounded and poured, during this " Day of the Lord ;" in short, an Epitome of the

Rise, Reign, and Ruin, of the last Gentile ruler, the
last Antichrist, who perishes beneath the outpoured
vials of divine wrath. This doom is administered by
Messiah Himself in person, who appears as the Amen,
the Faithful and True, to smite the Mock-Messiah of
the End-Time. It is of this " Nagid" Isaiah speaks,
calling him " that Wicked," Isa. xi:4, and again " the
Enemy coming in," or invading Palestine, " like a flood"
lix:19, and of whom Paul speaks in II Thess. ii:8, as
destroyed by the judicial breath of Christ's mouth,
when Israel's " Redeemer comes to Zion," and " All
Israel," for whom Daniel supplicated, and on whom
the 70 Weeks were determined, "is saved." Rom. xi:25.
At the opening of the " One Week" this Nagid enacts
a covenant with the Jewish masses, and, by his power,
makes it prevail during the whole week, yet only for
a week, *i. e.*, seven years. At the middle of the Week
he attains the summit of his power, abolishes the Jewish
worship and substitutes a worship of himself. During
the second half of the Week, or final 3½ years, or
1,260 days, he swoops like a vulture, desolating in his
rage mightier than an Alexander, Antiochus or Napoleon, and continues "even unto the consummation,"
which marks the exhaustion of the desolation decreed
on Israel and Jerusalem, and is the end of the measure
and the time appointed ; the end of the 70 Weeks. Then,
the Antichrist perishes in the flood-tide of divine indignation which breaks, like a stream of fire, upon him,
overwhelmed more fearfully than Pharaoh in the sea.

   9. *The Glorious Outcome for Israel.* This is the
Hexad of blessings already referred to in v. 24, due at
the close of the 70 Weeks ; the arrest of *the* transgression or apostasy ; the shutting of sins ; the pardon of iniquity ; the introduction of enduring righteousness ;

the confirmation of the prophet's word, and the consecration of a new sanctuary to God.   God and Israel as
a nation, are reconciled.   The apostates have perished.
New-born Israel serves God in newness of the spirit,
and not in oldness of the letter.   All is concrete, literal, exact, real; the 70 Weeks, the 7 Weeks, the Restoration, the 62 Weeks, the Advent, the Crucifixion,
the Destruction and Dispersion, the Interval, or Unto,
the 70th or One Week, the Antichrist, the Covenant,
the Half of the Week, the Great Tribulation, the
End of Antichrist, the Consummation, all is literal.
Two Advents are here in this wonderful " Word that
went forth," while Daniel was supplicating, and which
Gabriel fled swiftly to tell, and as Gabriel has stood up
at the one he shall stand up at the other!   Two Dispensations are here.   Two Ends are here.   Christ and
Antichrist are here.   The Times of the Gentiles are
here.   The Day of the Lord is here.   Two Judgments
are here.   Israel cast away, and Israel restored, are
here.   It is the acorn from which comes the whole tree,
the sketch in which is subsequently filled out the whole
picture.   It is the outlined programme of the far End-
Time and the pathway to it, for " All Israel," Dan. ix:7,
11, and End-Time bringing a Hexad of blessing, in a
Jubilee of Jubilees, a Sabbath Rest, and reversion of
the lost inheritance.   It is the time of Israel's national
resurrection.   Nor could the clock of destiny strike an
hour more opportune, or appropriate, than this, for
ransomed Israel's return from earbored servitude to
Gentile Nagids, the repossession of their land, forgiveness of their debts, and remission of their sins.
    Of this all-comprehensive, complex, and age-travel-
ing prophecy, much has been fulfilled already :   The
Return from Exile, the Restoration, the Distress of

Times, the Advent of Messiah, the Crucifixion, the
Destruction of Jerusalem, War and Desolations, and
nearly 1900 years of the Interval between the 69th and
70th Weeks.   Roman, Saracen, and Turk, have trodden
Jerusalem under foot, nor could the valor of Crusaders,
nor diplomacy, nor sword, redeem it to a *" Holy City "*
before the appointed time !   A consecrated *" Temple "*
made it so before.   A consecrated *" Temple"* shall make
it so again.   Much yet of this prophecy remains to be
fulfilled.   It is as certain that Israel never yet has realized the glorious outcome predicted by the Angel, as it
is that to Israel, nationally, the Sixfold Blessings of
verse 24th refer.   There is a deep genetic and organic
nexus between the work of Christ at His first Advent,
and the true relation of that work to Israel, as a nation,
at His second Advent, which accounts for the peculiar
atonement-term (Caphar) used in verse 24th, and be
cause of which interpreters have been wont to care-
lessly refer it to the first Advent, alone.   Certainly,
Messiah did atone for sin, and bring in everlasting
righteousness, in his own person, and prophecy was
verified, and the *" Church "* was consecrated as a *spiritual* temple, with an election out of Israel, as a New-
Born people, unto God.   But, as certainly, this mighty
work did not exhaust the prophecy.   Not once, in all
the New Testament, does either Christ, or do His
Apostles, quote or refer to this verse as fulfilled in His
Crucifixion, a point Kuenen and Graf, with many more,
have made the most of, but vainly against the Messianic
interpretation.   The Gerundive force of the Hebrew infinitives points to a continuance of events, both of judgment and of mercy, *during*, and *at* the close of, the 70
Sevens.   Not only the events of the Restoration from
Exile, Maccabean times, the first Advent, and the Cru-

cifixion, but also Pentecost, the establishment of the
Church, the rejection of Israel nationally, Missions to
the Gentiles, Apostasy in the bosom of Christendom
itself, and the whole development of the long Interval
into modern culture and civilization, both infidel and
Christian, *all* are covered by the "*Seventy Sevens*,"
decreed upon Daniel's down-trodden people and their
desolated city, *for the purpose of bringing in Israel's
final redemption, yet future, and not far away.* And not
less are the events of the 70th Week ordained to the
same End, and *must* transpire before Israel's Sabbatic
Jubilee can come. The entire "Times of the Gentiles,"
in which are the "*Seventy Sevens*," with the Interval,
must belong to the past, the Gospel have gone to all
Nations, the fulness of the Gentiles be come in, and
Judgment sit, before the Kingdom can be restored to
Israel. Then "*the* transgression" of Israel will be
stopped, and Israel's sins ended, and iniquity pardoned,
and a people, all righteous, be created, and the vision
and prophet be verified, and a new sanctuary exist in
which God will dwell forevermore. Jerusalem shall
once more, become the "*Holy City*," Israel a "*holy
people*," and both the center of a new and blessed age.
All the prophets declare it. Christ taught it in his
Olivet discourse concerning the End, looking through
Jerusalem's destruction and Israel's dispersion, forward
to Jerusalem's recovery and Israel's redemption, at His
Second Coming. The Apostles repeat it, in various
ways. John has portrayed it in glowing symbols.

What a study is the study of these 70 Weeks, the
study of Israel under four world empires, the study of
the civilized world's course, first of all, for six centuries
before the coming of Christ, if we add the years of
the Babylonian Exile. Of this earlier portion of the

" Times of the Gentiles, " *Israel* was 70 years under the Chaldean power, from Nebuchadnezzar to Cyrus B. C. 606 to 536, according to our conventional chronology, the Times of the Golden Head of the Great Colossus in its relations to the " holy people " the times of the Lion or Chaldean ascendancy, the center of civilization and culture at Babylon the center of the world's history.   Then under the Persians, 200 years more, from Cyrus to Alexander, B. C. 536 to 336, the times of the Silver Breast, the times of the Bear, the times of Zoroaster and the Fire-Worshipers, the center of the world's history and civilization at Shushan where Xerxes the Great, Mordecai, Esther, Vashti, and Haman, were ; the times of Marathon and Salamis.   Next 273 years more, from Alexander to Pompey, B. C. 336 to 63, the date of Pompey's conquest of Judea, the times of the Brass Thighs, the times of the Leopard, the times of Socrates and Plato, of the attempt to force Javanic culture upon the Jews, of the period of Macabean valor, of the wars of the Seleucids and Ptolemies, of the Syrian Antichrist, Antiochus, the times of Athens, " the eye of Greece " the center of the world's philosophy, science, and art, the times of Alexandria and the Septuagint Version, on down to the days of Caesar and Brutus, Scipio, Antony, and Cleopatra. Then, finally, 63 years more, from Pompey to Christ, the times of the dying gasp of the Roman Republic, when only the " dregs of Romulus " lived, presaging the coming Empire hard as iron and' wild as a ravening beast ; Imperial Rome, enriching the land and staining the sea with human gore ; the initial times of the Iron Legs and rise of the monster, exceeding dreadful, iron-toothed, brazen-clawed, devouring, breaking in pieces, stamping ; the later days of the Asmoneans and Herodians, the times of Augustus, Tiberius, and of Herod the Great when "*Prince Messiah*" was born ; Rome Pagan the center now of the World's civilization, and mistress of all the nations. Across this whole period of 69 Weeks of Years, with their attendant " Times of Distress, " all ruled in their course, by the " law of the Seven," for Israel's sake, the Angel's eye swept, and the prophet's glance was directed ; Israel still subject to Gentile supremacy, their necks under the Gentile yoke, their City trodden by Gentile feet ; a Simeon and Anna, a Zacharias and Elizabeth, a Joseph and Mary, sighing and waiting for Israel's Consolation.

But more. The vision of the 70 Weeks covers a wider and farther scope. The Angel's glance goes to the " End " of the painful road decreed to the tribes of the wandering foot, and weary breast. The gigantic empires of the Orient, robed in barbaric wealth, have folded their mantles and muffled their weird faces and flitted away. The classic ages of Greek and Roman story have faded from view. " Prince Messiah " has come and been " cut off " by His own. Gethsemane and Golgotha bring to Israel, crowned with guilt, no national deliverance from Gentile power. A suspended national covenant abandons the Jew to behold his City razed to the ground a second time, his " Temple " a second time consumed, and Judah a second time, with slaughter and chains, scattered, not only throughout the Roman world, but " among all nations." The " Arch of Titus " still stands, to tell the judgment.

The long Interval following that event,—the Roman " Times of the Gentiles," has already fulfilled more than 18 centuries of its appointment. Since Nebuchadnezzar saw in his dream, the " Great Image " of Gentile Power, and " a night vision revealed the secret to

Daniel," 2429 years have winged their flight, and Israel still abides, alone, and uncommingled, subject still to the foreign yoke, their land still trodden down by the Gentiles. These are days of the Iron Legs and Iron and Clay Feet and Toes ; the days of the Beast with Ten Horns; the days when, no longer, a single City is the center of the world's civilization, culture, and religion, but when each division of the parted Roman Earth has its own " Capitol " of light and power, and " Centers " of guilt and glory. These are the days of Israel under the hand of Rome pagan, Rome papal, Rome divided into Eastern and Western empires, Rome sundered again into a European States–System, Romano–Germanic forms of rule prevailing, and yet powerless to bring peace to the world; the days when the proud Colossus itself begins to dream of a Mountain Stone that may strike its toes, the days when Israel's Dry Bones in the Valley of Vision begin to move, the days when anxious nations forebode some crisis near, some great catastrophe, from which a new Center of World Unity shall lift its head, and Jerusalem the " Holy City," once more attract the eyes of mankind. Then will enter the final 70th Week, when, through " Great Tribulation," the " End " of Israel's long way will be reached, at last, and Gentile Power go down, and Israel's kingdom rise, the Hexad be fulfilled, and " Seventy Sevens " attain their full accomplishment.

And now, it might be deemed almost superflous to ask, do these prophetic numbers, in Daniel, the 70, the 7, the 62, the 1, the ½, import only abstract ideas, and not literal concrete measures of historic time? Because they are symbolic, and represent ideas, are they, therefore, merely schematic, and void of chronological value? They certainly " *count.* " They span the

"Times of the Gentiles." A word to restore and build Jerusalem certainly did go forth, and as certainly 69 of these Year-Weeks, and the Interval "*Unto*" in large proportion, have passed away. The Times of the Gentiles, *i. e.*, of the Colossus and the Four Beasts, are mathematically equal, being demonstrably commensurate. The Sabbatic law governs their whole course, and gives them their dimension and their limit.

The "*Seventy Sevens*" underlie the whole development of history and prophecy, since the Angel's word to Daniel, and determine not only the fortunes of Israel, but the fortunes of the Nations, and of the World. By these "*Seventy Sevens*" alone, the "Times of the Gentiles" are measured. Israel is the core of all history, as Christ is the center of All Israel, and the events of history are only those reverberating after-claps booming through the fields of space, of which God's purpose is the casual fore-stroke; or better, it is one vital organic process, or becoming, in which prophecy fulfils itself by stages, so that even in the sphere of human freedom, a divine causality pervades and shapes the mighty movement, from its first emergence to its final consummation. And measured time, and measured space, a true chronology, a true geography, the two eyes of history, are seen everywhere. The 70 Weeks of Years, not less than the four-empired Colossus, teach us this. All point to the End. Nebuchadnezzar and Cyrus; Alexander and Antiochus; Pompey and Caesar; Herod and Titus; Constantine, the Othos, and Charlemagne; Kaiser, Czar, Sultan and Shah; Cabinets, Parliaments, and Congresses, are but the servants of God, under His immediate control, ministers of his court commissioned to assert His counsel, though free from all intention of their own to execute His will, and fulfil the mystery of the "Seventy Sevens." Factors they were, as others are, unconscious of God's mind, yet none the less instrumental to promote it, a "Chancellor Rehum " and "Governor Tattenai" obstructing, a favoring Darius and Ahasuerus, an Alaric and Attila, an Omar and Saladin, a Charles Martel and a Napoleon, a Moltke and a Grand Duke Michael, all cooperating, with their Talleyrands and Chathams, their Bismarcks and D'Israelis, their Gortschakoffs and Cavours, to achieve the one great end to which all prohpecy is looking, and to which all history is tending, viz., the establishment of the Kingdom of Christ in glory on the earth. *They* mean it not so, but *God* means it so, and it shall be so, because " *Seventy Sevens* " are decreed on Daniel's people and his holy city. That is the reason of it, and of scimetars, javelins, the 10th Legion, Krupp guns, iron-clads and dynamite.

All Western politics stand in relation to that purpose of God,—Rome and all her daughters. The whole " Eastern Question " is a part of the mystery,— Constantinople, Syria, Palestine, Jerusalem, the Keys of the East, and Gates of the World. The course of history is no bewildering maze of shifting scenes and transient actors, all confused and unaccountable. It is governed by a rule, and marches to a destined end. Under that rule, Babylon succumbs to Persia, Persia to Greece, Greece to Rome, and Rome parted into ten Kingdoms, awaits the final Antichrist, her own destruction, and Israel's jubilee. Gothic devastations, Saxon invasions, Norman conquest, Feudal anarchy, Modern Independence, Reformation, Revolution, Discovery, Navigation, Commerce, Trade, Culture, Infidelity, Apostasy, Lawlessness, and Missions, the homeless Jew scattered everywhere, " known by the show of his countenance," "alone, " "abiding for Jehovah, " the whole course of history with its myriads of events, *all* is decreed, marked off, and measured, by the measurements of God in reference to Daniel's people, city, and temple. Under such a view, it is impossible to regard the prophetic numbers which shape the Times and the Seasons, the Ages and the Ends, themselves shaped by the ordered motions of the planets, God's great chronometers, as mere *ideal* symbols of abstract spiritual truths. No difficulties of chronology will justify a judgment so repugnant to the teachings of God's word. Least of all, will it avail in a prediction which is part of a plexus or connected whole, an organic scheme whose burden is the present and future fortunes of a special people, "elect forever," whose times are measured by a Sabbath law, and whose goal is crowned with a mighty Sabbath Jubilee. *Seven* times *Seven* are *Forty-Nine*, and *Ten* times *Seven* are *Seventy*, as truly as *Seven* and *Ten* are symbols of ideas in the development of the Kingdom of God.

E.   THE SIXTY-NINE WEEKS

But further still, and of vast importance in our warfare with the unbelieving Israelite, and the unbelieving believers of modern times, is the fact that our demonstration of the *Messiahship of Jesus of Nazareth* depends, chronologically, upon the literality of the 70 Weeks of Daniel. Otherwise Paul's argument as to "the fulness of *the* time" when God sent forth His Son, and Matthew's assertion that, " from the carrying away into Babylon, unto *the* Messiah, are fourteen generations," and other like passages of Scripture, must be surrendered. It is a serious matter to say that every attempt to calculate

the 70 Weeks has ended only in " ignominious failure."
Whatever ignominy attends the effort to bind the 70
Weeks together, in unbroken sequence, and so annihilate the Intervals between them, there has been *no*
failure in determining the distance from Daniel to the
First Advent, to such extent as to make the demonstration of the Messiahship of Jesus of Nazareth, a final
and invulnerable one.   Not less important is the literal
view for Israel's conversion in days to come.   The
great events that shape the world's destiny, at both Advents, are involved here.   The 70 Weeks relate to both
these Advents, and the Interval between them ; to Israel
and the Nations ; to Christ and Antichrist.   They have
a starting-point or *terminus a quo*, and a closing-point or
terminus ad quem, in history.   The starting-point is from
the " *Motse Davar*," or " going forth of a command," to
" restore and build Jerusalem," Dan. ix:25 ; let that command be a word from God, or a Persian edict.   In their
subdivisions, 7 of the 70 Weeks reach to some epoch
unnamed in the prophecy, while 62 more, added to
the 7, reach "*unto* Messiah the Prince," *i. e.* to the
First Advent, when Messiah is cut off, followed
by Israel's excision as a nation.   Over-glancing the
great Interval, we touch the 70th Week, which ends
with Israel's complete redemption, as specified in Dan.
ix:24.   Thus, the end of the 69th week brings us to
the First Advent and Israel's " *Fall*," while the end of
the 70th week brings us to the Second Advent and Israel's " *Rising again*," or " *Reception*," as " *Life from the
dead*."   So Paul understood it, Rom. xi:12, 15, 25, 26 ;
and Peter, Acts iii:19-21 ; and Christ, Luke xxi:24, 28 ;
and John, Rev. xii;10 ; xv:2-4.   In Daniel, the 70th
Week shows Antichrist's overthrow, Dan. ix:27.   In
Luke it shows Israel's Redemption, Luke xxi:28.   Both
concur.

While we hold to the literal character of the numbers in Daniel, we are not to be understood as meaning that, in the present state of chronological science, any one has yet appeared who has been able continuously to suit the prophetic numbers as to the distance between Daniel and Christ with our received Chronology; *i. e.* accepting B. C. 536 as the date of the Edict of Cyrus, or "going forth of a Word to restore and build Jerusalem," the starting point, or *a quo* of the 70 Weeks. No one has yet been found skillful enough to make 536 equal 490. This, however, is far from admitting that the numbers in Daniel are merely symbolic. All computations have proceeded on three assumptions, none of which have been proved ; the first that B. C. 536 is an infallible date, the second that no interval exists between any of the sevens, and the third that all the Weeks must be counted successively; to which a fourth may be added, viz.: That the *ad quem* like the *a quo*, may lawfully be made a sliding point, a varied date to suit a varied computation. God's chronology may be, and assuredly is, undoubtedly exact and literal, a perfection to which the calamity of ours is still a stranger. Nor are the events of ancient history, or regal lines of ancient succession, in a much better condition.. The conclusion of some that, because *our* own erroneous chronology fails, it must be the same with God's, is hardly according either to Whately or Hamilton. In spite of our failures the 70 Weeks of Daniel will remain literal to time's end, as the 70th will prove, and as the 69 have already proved, no matter what fate attends *our* conventional manipulations. It has been the custom to defend the literality of the 70 Weeks by allowing a large margin for the *a quo*, a margin extending even to 90 years, the *Motse Davar*, or issuing of the Edict to " restore Jeru-

salem," being distinguished from another edict, though
part of it, to " build the Temple." On this ground,
supported by the thought that the participle "*going*"
might mean a process of utterances, or continuous
series of different Edicts for different ends, one to
" restore the people and build the House of the Lord,"
another to " build the city," and another to complete
the fortifications, or defences, and finish the City, the
beginning of the 69 Weeks, or 70 Weeks,—which is the
same thing,—has been fixed, now at the Decree of Cyrus, now at that of Darius Hystaspes, now at the Order
of 7th Artaxerxes, and now at the Grant and Letters of
20th Artaxerxes, Longimanus. Similarly, the *ad quem* or
end of the 70 Weeks, or 69 Weeks, has been placed,
now at the Advent, now at the Baptism, now at the
Triumphal Entry, and now at the Death of Christ. In
the first series we have a margin of over 90 years ; in
the last, a margin of 33½ years, or 37. And yet the
two *termini* of the 69 Weeks are as fixed as the " hills
of Olam,"—one the Return of the Jews from Babylonian Exile, the other the appearance of Messiah. The
Edict of Cyrus cannot be evaded. By divine appointment, Koresh, Cyrus II, the son of Cambyses, "Cyrus
the Great," "Cyrus the Mule," was God's "Shepherd " to whose mouth the order was committed to restore Israel and build both the Temple and the City.
" Jerusalem shall be inhabited ; the Cities of Judah shall
be built. *Cyrus* is my Shepherd, and shall perform all
my pleasure, SAYING of Jerusalem, *She shall be built ;*
and, to Zion, *Thy foundation shall be laid !*" Isa. xlix:-
26-28. Nothing is plainer than that. The Edict of
Cyrus,—whenever it was—was the " *Motse Davar* to
restore and build Jerusalem," the immovable *a quo* of
the 70 Weeks. The distinction, therefore, which as-

serts that the Edict of Cyrus related alone to the building of the *Temple*, but not of the *City*, is untenable as it
is superficial, and fails to justify a slide of the *a quo*
from B. C. 536,—or whatever the true date may be,—
to any point historically nearer the Advent. Whatever
subsequent republication, or further enforcement, of
that Edict there may have been by any of the Persian
princes, the *starting point* of the 70 Weeks is, by God's
authority, fixed at the Order of Cyrus. That much, at
least, is literal.

And as to the *ad quem* of the 69 Weeks, or "*Unto
Prince Messiah*," it is no less so. It has been the habit
of uncounted critics and commentators to imagine
that the words "*Unto*" and "*Messiah*," are alike vague,
indefinite, and obscure,—if not " symbolical,"—the
one as a point, the other as a person ; and the slide has
been used correspondingly, different interpreters to-
bogganing from Cyrus himself to Onias, or Seleucus,
and thence to Christ at his First Coming, stopping not
short, however, of Christ at His Second Appearing, in
order to learn what "*Messiah*" means; and, as to the "*Unto*," sliding precisely the same distance, and with the
same result of agnostic dubiety; winding up their orien-
tation by rendering the words, in Daniel, "Many shall
run to and fro, and knowledge shall be increased," by
"Many shall rush up and down and be confused, and
not understand !"*

---

* The R. V. retains, without any marginal reading, the rendering in
King James' translation, "run to and fro." Long ago, Cocceius more correctly rendered the verse, *Multi scrutabuntur, et major fiet cognitio:* Many
shall closely investigate, and greater will become the knowledge, *i. e.* of this
book.   Dan. xii:4.   Badly Michaelis: " Many shall wander in error, but
yet knowledge shall increase."   Better Hitzig and Ebrard: "Many shall
zealously peruse," etc.   Hævernick: "Many shall strive after the knowledge
of this prophecy, and so shall it be increased."   Lengerke: " Many shall
wander in the darkness of this prophecy, and so shall knowledge come to

The divine word, however, fixes the *ad quem* or close of the 69 Weeks, as infallibly as it does the *a quo*, regardless of our protean-figured and many-faced chronology. "From the going forth of a word to restore and build Jerusalem unto Prince Messiah shall be Sevens Seven, and Sevens Sixty and Two," *i. e.* from the *Motse Davar* to *Mashiach Nagid* shall be 69 Weeks of Years. The reduction of the last Week, by the Angel, to twice 1260 *days*, and to twice 3½ *years*, demonstrates that the rest of the weeks are of the same chronological value. Dan. xii:7, 11, 12. As to the "word" to "go forth," it was not any backspoken word to Jeremiah, whose writings Daniel was reading, for that contained no order to restore either temple or city, Dan. ix:2, nor was it the word that went forth to the Angel-world, announcing the purpose of God, and because of which Gabriel, appointed, "flew swiftly" to tell it to Daniel, for this was the word of the Prophecy of the 70 Weeks itself, ix:21, 23, 24–27. It was the Decree of Cyrus, as the analogous expression in Esther, "*Yetse Davar Malcuth,*" "*Let there go forth a royal word,*" shows a Persian Edict; the word from God put in the

---

them." Better are Gesenius, Maurer, Fuerst, Winer: "Many shall thoroughly go through this prophecy (turning over its pages again and again), and so the knowledge of it shall be great." And Kliefoth, "Many shall set out upon an investigation of this prophecy," etc. There is a beautiful figure in the Hebrew verb, *yeshotetu.* The root (*shoot*) signifies to "rudder about," or sail on the ocean in search of land; to circumnavigate in order to make discoveries as do mariners on exploring expeditions; voyagers. Then, applied to the land, it denotes traveling here and there, up and down, spying out, prying into, and going through, inquiring, observing, examining, and so increasing knowledge. So shall it be, as to this deep, wide, and wonderful prophecy, in the End-Time. "Many," not a few.—"shall eagerly study," not read superficially, "this whole prophecy of Daniel, and so the knowledge," *i. e.* "the inward perception" (*haddaath*) of its contents, "will become great." Compare Amos viii:11, 12. How many earnest souls are "searching" the meaning of these blessed prophecies to-day, "eagerly," like men out on the ocean sailing in quest of land! It is a sign of the End. "The wise shall understand!" Dan. xii:10. That is the promise.

heart of Cyrus, sent forth by his own hand, and confirmed by his royal successors; the word to build and
finish the House of God, which involved the City as
well, "*Saying* of Jerusalem *She shall* be built, and to
Zion, Thy foundation *shall* be laid," a word performed
"according to the commandment of the God of Israel,
and according to the Decree of Cyrus, and Darius, and
Artaxerxes," Ezra i:19; Isa. xliv:28; Ezra vi:14; the
word that went forth " in the first year of Cyrus, king
of Persia," Ezra i:1, and, according to *our* Chronology,
B. C. 536. That is the *a quo* of the 70 Weeks. To
maintain, under such a commission as Cyrus, the
"Shepherd," received, that *his* edict intended only the
building of the Temple, but not of the City, because
"to restore and build Jerusalem" is not distinctly expressed in the decree, is not only to refine too far in a
critical way, but to contradict the fact that, in pursuance of that same Decree, the returned Exiles, not only
laid the Temple foundation, but built for themselves
even " ceiled houses," for whose extravagance the
prophet reproved them. It is the core of the accusation of Chancellor Rehum to the obstructing Artaxerxes that the people builded the City. Hagg. i:4; Ezra
iv:8. Nor was the Decree of Darius aught else than a
reproduction of the lost firman of Cyrus, Ezra vi:1–11,
enforced by his own, adding no new permission, vs. 11–
15. Nor were the Grant and Letters of Artaxerxes
Longimanus aught else than permission in terms to
build the "Walls and the Gates," and continue the
work already begun upon the " City," and for 90 years
carried on. B. C. 536—445=91. Neh. i:2; ii:1. Ezra
vii:7. Whatever building of the city was done during
90 years, was in pursuance of the order of Cyrus,
repeated and re-inforced. So much for the *Motse Da-*

var, the starting-point of the 69 or 70 Weeks.   It
was the Edict of Cyrus, the "Shepherd," of God's
people.*

And, now, as to the *ad quem* or closing date and
event of the 69 Weeks.   It is "Prince Messiah," "*Mashiach Nagid.*"   The nouns are in apposition.   The absence of the article "the" does not detract from a definite reference to Christ.   "Prince Messiah" in Dan ix:
25, and "Messiah" to be "cut off" in v. 26a, are one and
the same person, the future anointed King of Israel, of
whom David in suffering, and Solomon in glory, were
eminent types, the "Lord's Anointed," the Prince of
the House of David, whose expected appearing was
Israel's hope.   Contrary to many critics it must be held
that "Mashiach," in the above texts, is not a mere vague,
indefinite ideal, attributive, or appellative, a blind ad-
jective descriptive of some uncertain *"anointed one,"*
Cyrus for instance, Onias III, or Seleucus, or "some
other man," a "Great Unknown," but is a distinctive
designation, the personal name of Him of whom the
prophets have spoken, and whose genealogy Matthew
and Luke have recorded ; the Ruler out of Bethlehem,
and the Heir to David's throne.   The fundamental passages for this are Ps. ii:2, and Ps. xlv.   Post-Biblical
pre-Christian Judaism, resting on Old Testament
ground, continued to use the word as a proper name,
the name of the Coming One, *"Mashiach"* and *"Hamma-
shiach."*   In II Sam. xxiii:1, David is called "Messiah."
In Dan. ix:25, 26a, the term denotes the Priest-King of
Israel, for whom was reserved the true *mitre* and *crown*
of David's race, when that terrible word went forth

"It must be remembered that the Edict of Cyrus gave permission to
the Jews to rebuild their City as well as their Temple."   Prof. C. H. H.
WRIGHT, D.D.   *Zechariah*, etc., p. 23.

against the wicked Zedekiah, the word that forms the completed *a quo* of the 70 years' Captivity, the word sounding amid the flames of the burning Temple, ruined City, overthrown House of David, and Judah borne away captive in chains to Babylon : *"Away with the mitre !   Off with the crown !   This is not this !   Up with the low !   Down with the high !   Ruin !   Ruin ! Ruin !   Even this shall be no more, until That One come whose right it is, and I will give it Him !"*   Ezek. xxi;25. To "That One" the prophets gave witness, the Priest. King, *Mashiach Nagid*, to suffer for Israel, be rejected, despised, "cut off," rooted out, and "nothing for Him !" Ezekiel's " Until " is Daniel's " Unto," the Advent of Christ.   We delight in the utterance of Hengstenberg, here, that "the non-Messianic interpretation of Daniel's prediction will remain false as long as God's Word is true, and that is to all eternity !"

But, admitting all this, the question recurs, as to the force of the word *"Unto ;" "Unto* Prince Messiah." Six inspired New Testament Targums on the text settle the question, and fix the *ad quem*, or close of the 69 Weeks, at a definite point, all sliding excluded.   That point is not the Baptism of Christ, nor His Triumphal Entry when hailed, for a moment, as king, and then rejected, nor the Death of Christ, which occurs *"after"* the closing point, but is the Advent of Christ,—His *Birth.*

Our first inspired Targum on the text is that of Matthew, a Jew, who, writing in the Hebrew, and for the Jews, in order to show that fulfilment of Messianic prophecy, and recording the genealogy of Jesus, uses the same expression, *"Unto* Christ,"—yet with the definite article *"ad ha—Mashiach,"* found in the prophet, the article indicating a special reference to Him of whom the prophet spoke, " Unto *the* Messiah." He does so, moreover, in connection with the statement that certain Magi from Babylon where Daniel had received the prophecy, and over whom he presided as chief of their order, came to Jerusalem inquiring, " Where is he who is *born King* of the Jews?" Trisecting the whole period of Israel's history from Abraham to Christ, into equal periods of ." fourteen generations," he says, speaking of the last, that " from the carrying away into Babylon, unto the Messiah (the King of the Jews) are *fourteen generations*," Matt. i:17. He thus gives us the *a quo* of the 70 years' Captivity, and declares the *ad quem* of the last period, and of the whole period to be " the *Birth* of Jesus Christ." i:18. This is absolute. If we allow 40 years for a generation, in *round numbers*, then, from the Captivity to the *Birth* of Christ, the year when Cæsar enrolled the world, are 40×14=560 years. If we subtract the 70 years' Captivity, then 560—70=490 years, the precise measure of the period found in the 70 Weeks, the end of the Exile being the *a quo* of the 70 Weeks. The " 14 generations" of the evangelist are commensurate with the " 70 Sevens" of the prophet, less the 70 years' Captivity, which the prophet excludes.

Matthew ; 560 minus 70, equals 490.

Daniel ; 70 multiplied by 7, equals 490.

A double witness by two independent calculations, both which make it impossible that the *ad quem* of the Messiah to be " cut off " should ever reach either His Death, His Triumphal Entry, or His Baptism, but that it must and can only be A. D. 1. An apparent discrepancy, however, of 7 years, or One Week, an error, not of chronology, but of computation, meets us. From the Captivity to Christ, is, according to Daniel, 69 Weeks, or 483 years, while according to

Matthew it is 490 years, *i. e.* in round numbers. If, remembering how exact computation is by the " Seventy
Sevens," and how less precise that by " generations " is,
and allowing for the difference, regard a generation as
39½ years, this allowance brings the two into perfect
harmony, and we have, from the Captivity to Christ,
14 multiplied by 39½, equals 483 years. The two will
then stand :

Matthew : 14 multiplied by 39½, equals 483 years.
Daniel : 69 multiplied by 7, equals 483 years.

It seems that by two different modes of reckoning,
one by exact " Sevens," the other by less precise and
rounded " generations," yet both governed by the law of
the 7 (7 multiplied by 2 equals 14) a difference of " One
Week," or 7 years is made, this difference accounted
for in Matthew by the round numbers, but in Daniel by
the fact that the " One Week " is separated from the 69
and placed after the long interval following the 69, and
thus the harmony of the prophet and evangelist is perfect, the *ad quem* of the 69 Weeks being fixed immovably
at the *Birth* of Christ. Is this merely *"ideal"* or *"symbolic,"*
or due to " *the trickish nature of numbers ?*" Or is it the
wisdom of God, both revealing and concealing? The
whole question is solved, for the *ad quem* of the 70
Weeks is not the *First* Advent but the *Second*, the close
of the " One Week " still future, while the *ad quem* of
the 69 Weeks is not the *Second* Advent but the *First*.
The Great Interval between the 69th and 70th Weeks,
by reason of Israel's rejection of Christ, is opened out
by our Lord Himself, in Luke xxi:24, the Roman
" Times of the Gentiles." Daniel's *"Unto* the End shall
be War," ix:26, is our Lord's " *Until* the Times of the
Gentiles be fulfilled." There is a double " *Unto*" in
Daniel, " *Unto* Messiah," and " *Unto* the End," the one

the *First* Advent, the other the *Second*, the 70th Week still future in Daniel, Matthew calculating in round numbers, and this explains the whole problem. The *ad quem* therefore, of the 69 Weeks, was the "*Birth of Jesus Christ*," that memorable time when the Temple of Janus was shut, and the Roman world was at peace, men dwelling in good will toward each other, and "Glory to God in the highest," was sung, and the salute of "Peace on earth, to men of good will" was poured from on high. It was that notable time when Augustus Cæsar enrolled the world, and shepherds were tending their flocks by night, and "Glory" flamed in the sky, and Gabriel, who gave the prediction to Daniel 500 years before, brought out his heavenly orchestra, and choir, and made the welkin vibrate as he played the overture of *Mashiach Nagid, Gloria in Excelsis;* that to-be-long-remembered year when the Star of Bethlehem shone like a gem set in nocturnal blue, and the moon silvered her way with unwonted smiles, and Jupiter, Saturn, and Mars, paraded, glittering in splendor together along the Zodiac's path, and gift-bringing Magi came in barbaric gold, and Herod was troubled ; that melody-year when music was floating everywhere "in the hill country of Judea," and Elizabeth sang her song, and Mary warbled her sweet and thrilling *Magnificat*, and Zacharias intoned his *Benedictus*, and good old Simeon sank, overjoyed, to his rest, breathing his holy " *Domine ! Nunc Dimittis !*" *Mashiach Nagid* was "*born!*" Glorious Christmas *ad quem* it was! Ring the bells! This much,—thank God,—is literal and not symbolical, real, and not ideal !

Once more. Gabriel himself is a Targum on the text, to fix the *ad quem*. He gave the prophecy of the 70 Weeks to Daniel. He knew the 483 years were out.

He went to Mary to tell her that He, whom she soon would bear, was the *Nagid,* "the Son of the Highest," to whom the Lord God would give "the *throne* of His father David." He saluted the Shepherds, saying "Good tidings! There is born to you *this day,* in the City of David, a Saviour, *Christ the Lord!*" He employs the same words he employed 536 years before, when speaking to Daniel. "This day," is the *ad quem* and "*Christos Kyrios,*" *Christ the Lord,* is simply the Greek for the Hebrew "*Mashiach Nagid!*"

But there is another Targum still, the Targum of Peter on the same prophecy. He has an eye on both Advents. He is looking at Eschatology, and Soteriology too! Daniel says of himself, that, "in the year one, of Darius," he was "searching," (*Binthi*) in the old prophetic Scriptures (*Bassepharim*) the *a quo* and *ad quem* of the 70 years' Captivity, and all concerning Israel's promised salvation, and the Advent of Israel's promised Messiah, when Gabriel came and spoke of the 70 Weeks, and Messiah "cut off." Peter says that the old prophets "searched" the "what time," and "what manner of time" Messiah's Spirit that was in them made evident when "foretestifying the *Sufferings of Messiah* and the *Glories after these.*" I Pet. i:10. None deny that Peter's reference is to Daniel. Christ is Messiah, and we have Peter's inspired word for it that the "*Mashiach*" predicted by Daniel, to be "cut off," was neither Cyrus, nor Onias, nor Seleucus, nor "some other man," but Jesus Himself.

Yet another Targum runs to salute us. It is the Targum of Paul. He assures us that the One predicted to come in "the fulness of *the* time," did come and that it was *then* God sent forth from Himself, or *ex-apostolized* from heaven, His Son "becoming from a

woman," and " becoming under law " to buy out, as a
" ransom," them that were " under the law," that, from
Him they " might receive the sonship." Jubilee was
the design of Messiah's manifestation. Paul is a par-
aphrast on Daniel, telling us that " Mashiach Nagid "
was the " Son of God," and that the time of His Incarnation and Advent was " the *pleroma* of *the* time " appointed, in otherwords, the close of the 483 years. The
" Word made Flesh " was the answer too. Two other
Targums are enough to quote in confirmation of the *ad
quem.* One is from Prince Messiah Himself, interpreting this prophecy as He stood with the 69 Weeks behind Him, and His Crucifixion and Jerusalem's destruction before Him. He had already told His disciples
that He must be " cut off," and that Jerusalem and
Temple must be destroyed. He now expounds, still
further, the ancient prediction, and says that by the
words of the Angel to Daniel, " *And unto the End*,"
ix:26, are intended the Roman " *Times of the Gentiles*,"
at whose close Israel's glory comes. This is the *Second
Unto* or *Second Advent*, at the End of the 70th Week, just
as the *First Unto* or *First Advent* was at the close of the
69 Weeks. Standing within two days of the point
called " *After* " in the " *After* Sevens Sixty and Two
shall Messiah be cut off," or 33½ years " *After* " the Advent, He opens the Great Interval between the 69th
and 70th Weeks. Surely, the " *Unto*" and the " *After* "
are not the same point. The *ad quem*, and *after* the *ad
quem* are not one. The other Targum is that of John.
To him it was reserved, under the direct teaching of
Prince Messiah raised, in heaven, to one of the " Glories after His Sufferings," to expound the *un*anointed
" *Nagid*," or " prince that shall came," Dan. ix:26b, as
the " *Meshomem* " or " Desolator," and the " he " of v.

27, as the " *Beast* " slain by the sword-stroke, yet reviving, and ascending from the Abyss, and whose
monogram is "666," the last Antichrist, Israel's last oppressor, the Little Horn of the 4th Empire. That
" Nagid," bent on universal conquest appears at the
opening of the " One Week " following the Interval, as
the Mock-Messiah of the End-Time, the Rider on the
white horse of the first apocalyptic seal. It is then, as
in Daniel, he maĸes his " Covenant " with the Jewish
masses, and his times are the twice 3½ years, or twice
1260 days, of the final 70th Week, at whose close the
true Messiah comes for his destruction and Israel's final
redemption, the " *Unto* " of the whole 70 Weeks,
with their included Interval, the Second Advent. It is
the clearest demonstration possible, that the 70th Week
is *not* at the First Advent, and that the *ad quem* of the
69 Weeks is none other than the *Birth* of Christ.

Thus, these six New Testament Targums of Matthew, Gabriel, Peter, Paul, Prince Messiah Himself,
and John, combine, in harmony, to interpret for us the
Prophecy of the 70 Weeks and to assure us that, not
the Cross and the Cry, not the Jordan and the Dove, not
the Hosanna-march from the slopes of Olivet, is the *ad
quem* of the "Sevens Seven and Sevens Sixty and Two,"
but Gabriel himself and Glory above with Peace to
men of good will below, the Star and the Cradle, Angels and Magi, Shepherds and Songs ; in short, Beth-
lehem-Ephratah little among the thousands of Judah
but great by reason of the Advent of Prince-Messiah,
"the Ruler of my people Israel," the *Birth* of Him who
was " *born* King of the Jews." The 69 Weeks were not
unto " Messiah the *Priest* " atoning on the Cross, nor
unto " Messiah the *Prophet* " entering on His public
ministry, nor unto Messiah hailed momentarily, as a

" *King*," by the crowd, then crucified to-morrow, but
unto Messiah the " *Prince* " of the House of David, and
Heir to the throne of His father.   His Messianic Kingdom, as predicted by the prophets, did not come in
His day.   Expressly it is said He is " cut off " and *"there
is nothing for Him."*   The *Birth* of the *Prince*, and King
only by right but not yet by enthronement over the
"House of Jacob " was the *ad quem*.   Such was the close
of the 69 Weeks, or 483 years, in the year of the decree
of Cæsar Augustus to enroll the world, 30 years before
the 15th regnal year of Tiberius, and according to *our*
chronology A. U. C. 747, or 748, or 749; according to
the Bible, A. D. 1.

The "Seventy Sevens," therefore, are *not* mere *"ideal*
spaces void of chronological value," as the ultra sym-
bolists would have them.   They are proved, by Matthew's " generations," by the reduction of the last
"Seven" to *"days,"* and by confirming history, to be
exact measures of historic time.   Worthless, utterly, is
the objection that, according to *our* Chronology the distance from the Decree of Cyrus to the Birth of Christ
is 536 years (B. C. 536—A. D. 1), while, according to
Daniel,—rather the Angel,—it is " Sevens Seven, and
Sevens Sixty and Two" or 483 years.   A whole Synod
of chronologists must retire before the statement of
the Angel, and, adjusting their *own* chronology to that
of the Bible, grounded on a true text, either make away
with the difference of 57 years between their reckoning
and that of God's word, or submit that this difference
may be accounted for on some principle of sacred computation perfectly in harmony with their own conclusions.   On the basis of a true text, the verdict will
always be for the Word of God as against all the objections of Science.   The demonstration that *"Jesus of*

Nazareth is the Christ," is absolute and irrefutable from the statements of Gabriel, alone, who both gave the prediction of the prophecy of the 69 Weeks, concerning Messiah, and presided at its fulfilment, interpreting the same.   How much more so from the combined testimony of Prophets and Apostles, Christ, Angels and men!   Moreover, Christ was to come *not before* 483 years had passed away, and *certainly before* rebuilt Jerusalem was destroyed.   Nor was Jerusalem to be destroyed till some time after Messiah was cut off.   The Incarnate ' Glory" was to enter and tread the Second Temple, Hagg. ii:7.   All Israel knew that Christ was to be expected while yet the City and the Temple were still standing, and under the Roman power, and at a precisely defined time.   Manner, Place, Time, Circumstance, all were predicted with unerring literality. *Ideal* time is as great an outrage on the facts, as would be an *ideal* Bethlehem, an *ideal* Gabriel, an *ideal* Augustus, and that latest invention of idealists now so popular—an *Ideal Christ!*   It matters nothing, absolutely nothing, what *our* chronology may object. God has not suspended the faith of believers in His Only-Begotten Son, nor the demonstration of the Messiahship of Jesus, upon the Eponym Canon of Assyrians, Babylonian Tables, Egyptian Hieroglyphs, Cuneiform Inscriptions, or any of our Systems of Chronology.   Either Messiah has come, or the Jew is powerless to prove his own past national existence, exile, and return, the destruction and rebuilding and destruction again of his City and his Temple, or the truth of any one of his teachers from Moses to John the Baptist.

If the *Birth* of Christ is the *ad quem* of the 69 Weeks, then we must surrender, at once, the cherished dates at which so many of us place the *a quo* of the 70

Weeks, *i. e.* the 7th Artaxerxes Longimanus, B. C. 457, and the 20th Artaxerxes Longimanus, B. C. 445. These are the dates accepted by a vast body of evangelical scholars, such as Ussher, Prideaux, Tregelles, Pusey, Wright, Alexander, Newton, Hengstenberg, Hævernick, Hofmann, Auberlen, Stanley Leathes, Anderson, Pember, Sir Henry Rawlinson, Wilkinson, Dean Milman, etc., etc., on the ground that *only* by this means can the literality of the 70 Weeks of Daniel be maintained, and the Weeks be computed. "The work of the Restoration," says Professor Wright, "cannot be considered as really accomplished until after the date of Nehemiah's visit to Jerusalem, B. C. 445, and not even then. And so long as the desolations of Jerusalem were not repaired, the *70 years' Captivity* were not to be considered at an end!"* This is the agony of interpretation! The order to restore and build must not go forth till a special request was made to fortify the City! *i. e.*, the Decree *to* restore and build was to be first issued 91 years *after* the decree of Cyrus!—536—445=91, and 71 years after the Temple was finished! The 70 Weeks are to be dated nearly *a whole century* after Gabriel delivered the prophecy, and Cyrus released the Exiles!! So Sir Henry Rawlinson: "The 70 Weeks of Daniel can *only* count from the reign of Artaxerxes Longimanus by whom the command to restore and build Jerusalem,—street and wall,—was given."† "*Street* and *Wall!*" This is defect. "To restore and build Jerusalem" is not merely "Street and Wall." Hengstenberg labors manfully to prove the certainty of this mode of computation, but fails to justify it. Professor Drummond, of London, says it is

---

* Wright: Zechariah and his Prophecies, p. 23.
† Rawlinson's Herodotus IV, 217.

Hengstenberg's "one telling argument," not dreaming of its fatality. Auberlen sees the prodigious difficulty, and tries to reconcile it with the purposes of divine discipline in promoting *faith* and *expectation !* Kliefoth justly declares it is impossible to accept the *a quo* B. C. 445, or any *a quo*, other than the edict of Cyrus. Pro. fessor Briggs holds to the *a quo* from Cyrus, but remains entangled in the mode of our computation, as does Professor Milligan, these last betaking themselves to the ideal theory of numbers, while Dr. Rowland Williams admonishes us that it is time to "cheerfully throw overboard all Messianic interpretations of the prophecy," and rest in the " Maccabean exposition " alone; an exposition which makes " confusion worse confounded."

We must abandon the idea that the Decree of Cyrus did not involve the building of the City, or that, because it was arrested for a time in its execution, therefore it was not the decree, the *Motse Davar* referred to in the prophecy, and the true *a quo* of the 70 Weeks. Our chronology must take care of itself. The Word of God must stand, as it will. When chronologists and antiquarians have decided who *"Darius the Mede"* was, determined the true lines of Persian succession, and proved that B. C. 536 is an infallible date for the Decree of Cyrus, it will be time to think that Daniel's prophecy is the work of some Maccabean romancer, and that the law of the "Seven" does not control Israel's history, and the destiny of nations. The Assyrian monuments, while, like the Egyptian and Babylonian, confirming the Scriptures at many points of contact, collide with them in many more, and, in some places, undoubtedly, some errors of transcribers and editors of the Hebrew text have obscured and rendered difficult

of harmony the Historical Books, and parts of the prophetic page. This must be admitted. It comes to this
that Modern Criticism has discovered the problem of a
"Jewish Chronology" without being able to solve it.
The prophecy of the 70 Weeks, however, and the record
of Matthew, stand invulnerable. Criticism, even in the
hands of such men as Wellhausen and Robertson Smith,
is, nevertheless, beginning to see that the Bible contains
a "symmetrical system of numbers," and has its own
methods of computation. And what is more wonderful
still, the Bones of dead Israel are speaking, and the Sun,
Moon and Stars are fighting, in their courses, for the
Bible, pointing out where the text has been corrupted,
and where the emendation must be made. The Grave-
stones of the Caraite Jews-, the descendants of the Ten
Tribes, authoritative and genuine as any Assyrian Eponym Canon or monuments of Egypt or Babylon, and
three Eclipses, two of them foretold in Scripture, one
by Amos, one by Isaiah, the other the eclipse of Thales,
a standard among astronomers, all appear, with the
Books of Judith and Tobit, the last literature we have
of the tribes of Simeon and Naphtali, to fix the date of
the carrying away of the Ten Tribes, and the fall of
Samaria, at B. C. 696, and not 722, our conventional
date, and to demand, not only a redemption of the Hebrew text, from its past adjustment, in several places, to
erroneous heathen chronology, but to lower the whole
reckoning of the Hebrew monarchy to the extent of not
less than 25 years!* We can rely, with confidence, on
God, who gave us His holy word, that He will watch

---

* Melanges Asiatiques. V. 121. 1886. Chowlsen's Achtzen Hebr. Gra-
binschriften. 1865. Strack's Firkowitch u. s. Entdeckungen. 1876. Bosanquet's Messiah the Prince. 1869. Dr. S. Davison, in Jewish Chronicle
Oct. and Nov. 1868. Zockler's Handbuch d. Theol, Wissen. Art. Chron-
ologie. Yol I. 1883.

over it, and that no weapon of false criticism, or error of textual corruption, that has been formed against it, in the past, or is now, shall ever prosper. To deny the literality of the 70 Weeks of Daniel, in face of the confirmation of this by both Testaments, and by history itself, on the ground of "Chronology" is only to repeat in this respect, what, in other respects, has been done. and a thousand times refuted. It will be our mercy, if, adhering to God's Word, in spite of all scientific objections, we continue to affirm, notwithstanding the errors of many of its devoted defenders, and of its enemies, that God's measures of time are literal and not ideal, and that from the "going forth of a word to restore and build Jerusalem, unto Prince Messiah," not less than 483 literal years did elapse.

F.   THE SEVENTIETH WEEK

And now, for the 70th week itself. The effort to connect it immediately with the 69th has led to results in exegesis, both amazing and amusing. Never was the hopelessness of any task more thoroughly evinced than here. Chronology is made the scapegoat for exegetical offences. Centuries of the keenest criticism, the utmost ingenuity of men, invention racked upon the wheel, have all been subsidized to save, if possible, the prophecy, by a method that could only compromise it. Jeremiah's 70 years are said to mean 7 times 70, or 490 years, Daniel being the redactor of his predecessor's calculation! The 490 of Daniel include the 70 of Jeremiah! That is, 70 equal 490! Again the 7 and 62 are said not to be consecutive, but both to date from the same point. The 62 include the 7. That is, 434 equal 483! Look at the Babel of results! The different starting-points, or *termini a quo*, from which the 70 weeks are dated, are respectively, B. C. 655, 606, 604, 599, 588, 538, 536, 457, 455, 454, 445, 444, the extremes varying by *two centuries!* so placing the close of the 70th week when Israel's apostasy is finished, and the promised glory realized, and the Kingdom is come, at B. C. 165, 116, 114, 109, 98, 48, 46, and A. D. 33, 35, 36, 45, 46! Curious, indeed, the struggles of interpreters! Even Auberlen, binding the 69th and 70th weeks together, understands by the 70th week the whole time from the Death of Messiah to the Destruction of Jerusalem, that is, the final week is from A. D. 33 to A. D. 70, or 7 years equal 37 years! Less valiant than Professor Leathes, he is unable to explain why, if the 70th week is sundered by the Angel from the 69th, and placed *after* the Interval that follows the 69th, it should yet be construed as *preceding* that Interval. Also the close of verse 26, last clause, " has no sense," as Rinck remarks, if it is referred to the destruction of Jerusalem already mentioned in the middle of the verse. And he is right in this. What mean the words, added, after Jerusalem's destruction, "*And* unto the End, shall be war, a decree of desolations ;" if the End is already Jerusalem's *destruction?* What else *can* it mean than the *Interval* which our Lord Himself describes when interpreting this very verse, Luke xxi:24 ? an Interval whose End is the End of the 70th week? Ewald, starting from B. C. 588, brings the 7 weeks to B. C. 539, the 62 to B. C. 105, then, subtracting 70 years' captivity, bounds back to B. C. 175, then adding 7 years, the 1 week, shoots forward at last, to B. C. 168, the time of Antiochus Epiphanes, when Israel was finally redeemed! Graf, and Wellhausen start from B. C. 606, 604, which put Israel's redemption at B. C. 116, 114; Prideaux Pusey, and Leathes, date from B. C. 457, which makes the 70th week end A. D. 33, the middle of the week, when Messiah is supposed to be "cut off," being the end of the week itself! That is, 33 equal 29½! To condense much into little, Desprez makes 49 equal 54, 434 equal 429, and 429 equal 490! With Dr. Rowland Williams, 490 equal 434, 434 equal 364, 494 equal 427, and 7 equal 11! With Eichhorn, Hitzig, Wieseler, 490 equal 441, and 70 equal 49! With Bertholdt, Bleek, and Rosenmuller, 490 equal 424, and 424 equal 420! No wonder that there has been a recent Hegira to the "ideals!" As to the order of the subdivisions of the 70 weeks, with Hofmann, Delitzsch, Wieseler, Volck, as even Isaac Newton suggested, it is 62 plus 1 plus 7, the distance between Antiochus and Christ being made 49 years; that is, 49 equal 170! Some, like Hilgenfeld, and Hitzig, say the order is only 62 plus 1, the 7 being included in the 62. Others, like Bosanquet, say it is 1 plus 62 plus 7, the last week being put first!

Some, like Ewald, exclude, others like Orelli and Riehm, include, the 70 years' captivity. The vast body of interpreters hold, however, that the Angel's order is the right one, 7 plus 62 plus 1, although blind, in great part to any *Interval*.

Still more. Some hold that "Prince Messiah" is Cyrus or Seleucus; others that he is Isaiah, Judas Maccabæus, or the People; others that he is Onias, Christ, or the prince to come, *i. e.*, Antichrist. "*His* end" is "*its* end," the City's end; the "cutting off" at the *close* of the 69th week is said to be the same as the "causing oblation and sacrifice to cease" in the *middle* of the 70th week; the "covenant" made for one week, with the Jewish masses, by the "prince to come" is supposed to be the "New Covenant" in Christ's blood,

made with believers; in the words "cut off, and nothing
to Him," the expression and "nothing to Him," is
supposed to mean the vicarious "but not for Himself"
of King James' wrong translation; the "he" in "he
shall confirm," is taken for Christ, instead of Antichrist; "unto an anointed one" means unto the consecration of Onias, or the Baptism of Christ; the "Holy
of Holies" means a Person and not a Place; the death
of Christ occurring "*after*" the 69th week, and long
before the 70th, is said to occur at the close of the 70th
or in the middle of the 70th, the end of the 70th being
its own middle, and the end of the 69th besides!

What a mass of worse than Hibernian absurdities, of
which these are but a few specimens, in the reckoning
of the 70 weeks! What a dark labyrinth, compared with
which the Cretan one was a wide and sunlit boulevard!
No wonder that in despair, Hengstenberg, who insists
on "exact fulfilment," should yet say of the 70 weeks,
"Their terminal point is a *vanishing one, more or less*, and
does not admit of being chronologically determined
with *minute precision.*" * So Küper, his able disciple;
"We are not to look for strict chronological exactness.
The numbers, *though having a certain value for post-exile
time*, are yet *not specially historic*, but *specifically symbolic ! ! !*" † So Stanley Leathes in reply to Kuenen;
"Chronology *fails* us as to the last week." ‡ Even Auberlen says, "We are not to expect *exact* chronological data." ‖ And Pusey: "We have not the Chronological *data* to fix it!" § And Orelli: "The historic
fulfilment certainly does *not fit exactly* in a chronolo-

---

* Christol. III. 2, p. 185.   Riehm. Mess. Proph. 152.
† Das Prophetenthum. 375.
‡ O. T. Prophecy, 236.
‖ Der Prophet Daniel, 157.
§ Daniel, 240.

gical point of view." * And Kuenen, who puts the 70th week in B. C. 121—114, and calls it the time of *the* Antichrist (!) says "We readily grant our interpretation does *not fully* agree with chronology, but it is *tolerably exact ! ! !* "† So, also, Professor Drummond of London, who denies the Messianic interpretation of the 70 weeks, and holds the Maccabean, yet confesses "The Maccabean interpretation is opposed by *serious chronological difficulties.*" ‡ Is it any wonder that Professor Briggs should say in reference to this matter, that "the efforts of interpreters have ignominiously failed? ‖ Is it not a wonder that his own view binding the 69th and 70th weeks together, should still be given? § Surely, all men will agree with Bosanquet, saying, "Every fresh interpretation only adds to the force of our conviction that *some radical error lies at the foundation of all our Christian interpretations*, and, till it is discovered, the 70 weeks of Daniel will remain unexplained and inexplicable to the comprehension of every unprejudiced inquirer." ¶

---

* Die alttest, Weissag. 526.
† Prophets and Prophecy iu Israel. 272.
‡ Jewish Messiah. 260.
‖ Messianic Prophecy. I. 53.
§ Ibid. I. 424.
¶ Messiah the Prince. 48.

Part 2

THE 1,260 DAYS, OR 3 ½ YEARS

Like the 1000 years, these much abused prophetic numbers have been the subject of great and various discussion. Whence come they? Of what are they a part? To what are they related? How often are they taken? When mentioned, is it always the same period that is denoted, or do they represent two different, equal, and successive, periods? What do they import? Are they merely ideal and symbolic, or do they represent actual historic time, literal and exact? Are they Days put for Years as the Reformers held, on the Year-Day Theory, or are they simply Days of 24 hours? Do they stand for the 1000 years, and cover our present Dispensation from First to Second Advent, as Professor Milligan holds? Are they the half of a Great Week of 2520 years which covers the Times of the Gentiles as Mr. Guinness holds? Are they the period referred to by our Lord in Luke xxi:24, when predicting the down-treading that follows Jerusalem's Destruction? And is *this* period of down-treading, in Luke xxi:24, the same as *that* of the treading under foot the Holy City, 42 months, in Rev. xi:2? Or are they the last 3 ½ years of the profanation of the Sanc-

152

tuary under Antiochus Epiphanes, when the Abomination of Desolation stood in the holy place? Or do they refer to a Roman occupation of Jerusalem, in the time of Titus? These questions form a labyrinth of confusion sprung from various systems of interpretation, and meet the student, everywhere. At one time taken ideally, at another literally, and when taken literally then conceived of as years, and yet again as days, then, still further, applied now here and then there, all hope of attaining certainty seems to vanish away.

    1. To clear up this confusion, and dissipate these clouds, it is necessary to observe that, in Daniel and John, we find *one and the same measure of time represented by four different forms of expression,* viz., (1) " time, times, (dual number) and the dividing (or half) of a time, " Dan. vii:25; xii:7; Rev. xii:14; (2) "half week, " Dan. ix:27; (3) " 42 months, " Rev. xi:12; xiii:5; and (4) " 1260 days " Rev. xi:3; xii:6. These numbers are commensurate. The word "*time*" here denotes a *year* as in Dan. iv:16; where it is said, concerning Nebuchadnezzar, " Let 7 *times* pass over him," viz., the seven years of his mania, and, as in Dan. xi:13, where it is said of the King of the North that he shall return "at the end of *times*, even *years*." The " time, two times, and half a time, " are, therefore, 3 ½ *literal years*. This is the first point. The next point is that these 3 ½ years are precisely a ½ Week of Years, or ½ Seven of Years. The third point is that this ½ Week, or 3 ½ years, is exactly 42 months, reckoned according to the Jewish or prophetic calendar, at 30 days per month; that is, 30×42 equals 1260 days. The last point is that the 1260 days are by consequence, the same measure of time as the other numbers just men-

tioned ; that is, a ½ Week of Years equals 3 ½ years, or 42 months, or 1260 days.

Nothing, therefore, is more absolutely certain, than that the *ultimate source and seat of the* 1260 *days is the Half Week of Years, given us by the Angel, in Daniel,* ix:27. First, we have the 70 Weeks of Years, *Shabuim Shibim,* which are determined, or measured off, not from the 2300 evening-mornings, Dan. viii:14, but from the whole course of time, upon Daniel's people and the Holy City, and at whose close the events of verse 24 are to be realized, that is, the ending of Israel's apostasy, the shutting up of Israel's sins, the reconciliation of Israel to God, the introduction of abiding righteousness among them, the verification in history of what prophecy foretold concerning them; and the consecration of a new Sanctuary to God. Then we have this whole period subdivided, as already seen, into 7 Weeks of Years or 49 years, ending with some unmentioned event in the prophecy. Then 62 more weeks of years, added to the 7, that is 69 weeks of years, 483 years, to the " cutting off " of Messiah, or Crucifixion of Christ. Next in order, follows the Destruction of Jerusalem by Titus. After this the Long Interval occurs between this and the "End." Dan. ix:25, 26. Then comes the 70th Week of Years, or last *Seven,* divided into two equal parts, each a half Week, Dan. ix:27, this " One Week " being still future to us.

The correct translation of this whole section of prophecy, so condensed and full of meaning, has established the fact that the *Anointed Prince* in verse 25, " cut off, " v. 26, is *not* the *unanointed "prince that shall come,"* in v. 26, but wholly a different person. The former is Christ, the latter is Antichrist. The one enters history *before* the Great Interval begins, the other enters *after* it is gone. The one appears at the First Advent, in this prediction, the other at the Second Advent, or "End" of Israel's sad punishment. The 70th week, therefore, is the Week of the unanointed Nagid to come, the Desolator, upon whom the vials of wrath are poured, and opens with the *Parousia* of Antichrist, the Rider, or Mock-Christ, of the first Apocalyptic seal, the last Anti-Messiah, whom, coming in his own name, the unblieving Jews will receive ; a man changing times and laws, enacting and violating covenants, abolishing the Jewish cult, hating Christianity, setting up a New Heathenism, making of himself a God, and persecuting the people of the Saints of the Most High. Dan. ix:27 ; vii:25 ; xi:44, 45 ; xii:7. The beginning of this Week of Antichrist is not signalized by any event, named in the prophecy.

When it shall commence, is not stated, save at the close of the Interval, or Times of the Gentiles. The first half of the Week is not developed. The middle point of it is clearly marked by his causing the "Sacrifice and Meat-Offering,"—"*Zebach*" and "*Mincha,*" to cease, and setting up the Abomination of Desolation. Dan. ix:27 ; xi:36. The last half of the week is undeveloped also. The End, or Consummation of the Week, is declared expressly to be the accomplishment of what God has determined, and in which this unanointed Nagid, or Desolator finds his doom, under the outpoured wrath of Heaven. In short, what we find is this, viz., that Dan. ix:24-27 *is simply the Outline or Frame of the whole history of Israel from the close of the Captivity to the Second Advent*, and that Dan. ix:26, 27, *is the whole of John's Apocalypse, from chapter vi-xix, epitomized, the Old Testament Skeleton of which the Olivet Discourse by our Lord, and John's Apocalypse, are the*

New Testament outfilling. The 70th Week is Antichrist's Week, and this determines for us, absolutely, the 1260 *days.* They are the 3 ½ years, twice taken, of the *"One Week"* of Dan. ix:27. *That is their source and their seat.* They represent the *Great Tribulation* in the last days, and the fortunes of Israel at that time, Dan. vii:25 ; xii: 7 ; xii:1. They are literal days of 24 hours each ; the 42 months are literal months, and the 3 ½ times are literal years.

3. The expression, *" time, times, and half a time,"* or 3 ½ years, occurs thrice in Daniel and John, viz., (1) Dan. vii:25, the period of the domination of the Little Horn of the Roman Empire over the Saints of the Most High, *i. e.* the faithful Jewish people ; (2) Dan. xii:7 ; the period when the last Antichrist of whom Antiochus was the type, ceases to break the power of the Holy People, the Jewish People ; (3) Rev. xii:14 ; the period of the flight, and sojourn in the wilderness, of the Sun-clothed Woman, or Jewish Church of the End-Time. The expression, *"42 months,"* occurs twice, viz. (1) Rev. xi:2 ; the period of the treading under foot of the Holy City ; (2) Rev. xiii:5 ; the period of the persecuting power of the Beast, or 8th head of the revived Roman Empire. The expression, *" 1260 days,"* occurs twice also (1) Rev. xi:3, the period of the prophesying of the two Jewish Witnesses, after the manner of Moses and Elias ; (2) Rev. xii:6 ; the period of the Sun-clothed Woman's flight, and sojourn in the wilderness. Seven times in all. The Woman's sojourn in the wilderness is said to be " 1260 days, " and a " time, times and a half, " which proves that *these* two measures are *one and the same period.* The identity of the Little Horn of the fourth empire with the Beast in John, and the final Antichrist of Dan.

xi:45 ; xii:7 ; proves that the " time, times, and a half," and the "42 months, " of these, are *one and the same period*. The period is, demonstrably, the same length or measure, in all.

The only question is, Are these variously designated times all *contemporaneous?* That they are *equal*, is confessed. Are they *identical?* For example, Is the period of the prophesying of the two witnesses, identical, not merely in length, but in location, with that of the Beast's 3 ½ years, of persecuting power ? We are certainly safe if, with so many excellent interpreters, like Baumgarten, Hess, Hofmann, Delitzsch, Christiani, Koch, Volck, Rinck, Hebart, Luthardt, Godet, Alford, Ellicott, Seiss, etc., we take these numbers as actual, equal, and literal measures of historic time, yet future, and not as mere ideals of trouble. And we are safe, if with all these,—save Hofmann,— we *deny* that they are *all* contemporaneous and identical as to location, even as Kliefoth himself denies. Hofmann, however, holds that only *one-half* of the 70th Week is occupied by all these, viz, the *second* half or *last* 3 ½ years, the *last* 42 months, the *last* 1260 days, and that the first half of the week does not enter here at all. "All are contemporaneous !"* He compares those passages in Daniel where the Greek Antichrist, Antiochus, treads down the Holy People. Dan. viii:13, 14, 19 ; xi:12 ; to which he adds xi:31 ; and identifying the same with the *second half* of the week in Dan. ix:27 ; xii:7 ; and vii:25 ; sees *only* that *second half*, and to this refers *all* the numbers just mentioned, not merely in Daniel but in the Apocalypse also. It is only, in part, we can agree with Hofmann, here. Antiochus was simply a *type* of the last Antichrist, and the passages

---

* Schriftbeweis, II. 2., p. 686.

in Dan. viii:13, 14, concerning the taking away of the
" *Continual,*" and in xi:31, concerning the setting up
of the " *Abomination,* " give us only historic *types* of the
times of the last Antichrist. The 2,300 evening-mornings do not furnish us with "One Week" capable of division into two equal parts, although having direct
relation to, and foreshadowing, the One Week in Dan.
9:27, as, also, constitutively entering into it.

It is significant that while Antiochus was a type of
the final Antichrist, to a certain extent, there are features in the photograph of the Antichrist that we do
not find in the history of Antiochus. The *type,* Dan
xi:21-35, melts insensibly, according to the law of perspective and prophetic representation, and passes over
into the *antitype* seen in Dan. xi:36-45 ; xii:1-7, which
looks to the " End-Time," and not to Antiochus at all,
but far beyond, as even Hofmann himself most conclu-
sively shows. The close of *both* the great divisions of
the book of Daniel (i-vi), (vii-xii), is identical with the
Second Advent, a fact Auberlen unhappily overlooked,
limiting the second half of Daniel to Maccabean times.
It is not the times of Antiochus that are reproduced
when Antichrist comes, but his own times emerge.   It
is also significant that the "2,300 hundred evening-morn-
nings" are not named anywhere in John's Apocalypse,
and that the 1,290 and 1,335 days, lie beyond the last half
of the 70th Week. What is perfectly clear is that Daniel's
" One Week" for the revived Beast of the fourth empire, is resumed and filled out in *both* its halves, partly
in the Olivet discourse, then completely in John, the
first half covering 6 seals and 6 Trumpets, the second
half the 7th trumpet or 7 Vials.   And what is also clear
is that the prophesying of the two Witnesses occupies
the *first half* of the 70th Week, during which the

Christian Jewish Church of the End Time is formed in the Holy Land. It is no less clear that the down-treading of the Holy City and persecuting times of the Beast, lie in the *second half*, for the simple reason that it is only when the Witnesses have "*completed*," or "*finished*" their testimony, that the Beast which ascends out of the abyss, comes to the height of his power, makes war against them, and slays them, Rev. xi:7. Hofmann, therefore, errs, in referring Dan. ix:27 to Antiochus, as greatly as Auberlen and the Church, in general, in referring it to Christ. It belongs to neither, but only to the *Little Horn*, Dan. vii:25, the last Antichrist, Dan. xii:7 ; the Beast, Rev. xiii:5, whose *Parousia* is at the beginning, the point of whose supremacy is at the middle, and the close of whose mission is at the End, of the Week. In this, Fries, Karsten, Schultze, Kliefoth, Splittgerber, Mühe, Däschel, Grau, Rinck, Köhler, Koch, Christiani, Volck, etc., etc., all agree. The true title of this last week divided into 3½ and 3½ or twice 1,260, is simply the *Rise, Reign, and Ruin* of *the Antichrist*. Its opening is the *Parousia* of Antichrist. Its close is the *Parousia* of Christ. The *first* 3 ½ or 1,260 is the period of the Witnesses, forming the Jewish Church and a contemporary resistance to the Antichrist. The second 3 ½ or 1,260, is the period of the Great Tribulation, Dan. xii:1 ; Matt. xxiv:22, 29 ; Rev. vii:14 ; xiii:5 ; the time when the people are given into Antichrist's hand, the time of the woman's sojourn in the wilderness, the time of the down-treading of the Holy City, the time of the Beast's dominion, the time of the desolating abomination, the time when the power of the Holy People is broken, the time when the covenant, or treaty with the masses having been violated, the Sacrifice and Meat Offering have been caused to

cease, and new heathenism introduced, of which the
Antichrist is the head. Here we cannot be mistaken.
In both Daniel and John, the photographs point to the
same individualized Antichrist, a military Rider, Conqueror, and Persecutor. The subject of the prophecy
is the same, the Jews; the empire the same, the Roman ;
the place the same, even Palestine ; the time the same,
the End Time ; the 3 ½, or 1,260 the same, viz.: the half
of the " One Week ;" the Judgment the same, viz ; the
Destruction of the Antichrist ; the Judge the same, viz :
the Son of Man coming in the " Clouds of heaven ;"
from "Heaven Opened ;" the Kingdom the same, that
which is given to " the People of the Saints of the Most
High ;" the Deliverance the same, that of the survivors
who are " written in the Book ;" and the End of the
Week the same, viz.: Israel's full redemption, the resurrection of the faithful dead, and the millennial age.
And all these being the same, and events of the 70th
Week with their issues, it follows that the 3½ or time,
times, and a half ; or 1,260, or forty-two months, or ½
Week, twice taken, are the same. They, therefore,
represent neither merely ideal time, nor the 1,000 years,
nor the whole time from Jerusalem's destruction by
Titus to the Second Coming, nor the half of a Great
Week of 2,520 years, nor the last 3 ½ years of Antiochus, nor are they all contemporaneous and identical,
although they are equal measures of time, nor do they
represent the period of Mohammedan or Papal domination dated in their last half, either from A. D. 525,
566, 606, or 725, according to the continuous Historical Year-Day Theory ; but in their first half, or
1,260, are the period of the prophesying of the
two Jewish witnesses, and, in their second half, the
"shortened days," Matt. xxiv:22, the "short time" of

Satan cast out of heaven and coming down in great wrath, the period *between* Israel's Conversion and the Destruction of Antichrist at the Second Coming of Christ. Rev. xii:12, the period of the last "Great Tribulation," Dan. xii:1 ; Matt. xxiv:29 ; Rev. vii:14.*

4. The importance of the foregoing cannot be overestimated. The defence of the literality of the 3 ½ years, 42 months, or 1,260 days, stands or falls with the defence of the literality of the 1,000 years. It has been very logically objected, and with great force, that if the Year-Day Theory is exegetically correct, and the prophetic numbers are not literal, but only "miniature measures of time" standing for larger proportional cycles of time, "a day for a year," then " the 1,000 years *must* mean, at least, 360,000 years." Mr. Guinness has sought to meet the force of this objection, in his work on the " Approaching End of the Age," by the argument that as the 1,000 years are " not a time of waiting" or " expectation," but a joyous " fulfilment," they are not amenable to the objection made.† This is the view of Professor Birks, whom he takes as his guide. All the prophetic numbers are to be interpreted, he assures us, upon " the one uniform scale of a day for a year,"—save the 1,000 years. And this, it is urged, must be so, because (1) they are all typical; (2) they all represent astronomical cycles; (3) the revealing Angel ex-

---

* The eschatological equation is this, viz. : (1) Dan. ix:27 equals vii:25 equals Rev. xi:2, xi:7 equals xiii:5, the 3½ of the unanointed prince, the Horn of the 4th Empire, the last Antichrist, of whom Antiochus was the type, and the Woman's sojourn in the Wilderness, the *second half* of the Week, which is Rev. xii:6 and 14. (2) Rev. xi:3 equals Dan. ix:27, the 3½ of the two Witnesses, i. e. the *first* half of the Week. Both halves are in Dan. ix:27, therefore the text is twice used in these equations. M. Godet is right when he sees clearly that the Israel in John is the Israel in Daniel. The 144,000, are the " People of the Saints of the Most High," and the Jewish Christian Church of the End-Time.

† Approaching End of the Age. 306, 307.

pressly informed Daniel that the 70 Weeks—*Shabuim Shibim*—were weeks of *days* put for years, actually "announced as 490 *days*"; and (4) because the events of history have proved to us that these 70 Weeks are weeks of years, and are all fulfilled.* It is with no pleasure to ourselves we are constrained to differ from men so great, able, and good, and such noble defenders of the pre-millennial doctrine. It is to differ with the Reformers, with many excellent scholars, with men like Faber, Woodhouse, Cunninghame, Elliott, and Cumming. But the interests of truth, in this relation, leave us no other alternative. In answer to the foregoing, it must be said, first of all, that the 1,000 years are, by Mr. Guinness, declared to be an astronomical cycle as truly as the 1,260, and therefore the circumstance that these 1,000 are not a period of "waiting" will not exempt them from the law that would make them also a "miniature measure of time," 1,000 for 360,-000! They are certainly a "prophetic number," and "*all* the prophetic numbers must be interpreted on the one uniform scale of a day for a year!" And, moreover, "*all* are typical," according to Mr. Guinness. But further, it is contrary to fact (and here lies the fundamental and fatal mistake) that the Angel revealed to Daniel that the 70 Weeks were Weeks of "*Days* put for *Years.*" That is incorrect. The Hebrew term, "*Shebua*,"—"*seven*," does not always mean 7 *days*. It means no more than the term "*Septem*" in Latin. It may mean hours, days, weeks, months, years, bushels, acres, Pharaoh's lean kine, or the sons of Sceva:— *which* it is, can only be gathered from the "context, and from the nature of the case." True, indeed, the He-

---

* Ibid. 302, 303.

brew term is the common term for an ordinary week, but the proof that it is so used, in the texts where it occurs, is gathered from the " context and the nature of the case." It is incorrect to say that it "*always*" and "*necessarily*" denotes 7 days. And that, in the prediction of the Angel it cannot mean *days* is established beyond all doubt, by the *events foretold* and impossible to occur in 70 weeks of *days* or " 490 *days* " *i. e.* 1 year, 4 months, and 10 days, prophetic time; as also by the organic connection of the prediction with the previous 490 years during which the Sabbatic year law was violated 70 times, and, for which, 70 years' captivity were decreed. We are not dependent (as Mr. Guinness supposes) on the subsequent fulfilment of the Weeks to know whether they are days or years. Still further, it is incorrect to hold that the 70 Year-Weeks have "*all* been fulfilled." Only 69 of these weeks have passed into history, the 70th being still future. Neither the Angel nor Daniel knows anything of a Year-Day Theory. The " *Seventy Sevens,*" as Daniel understood them (and as the Angel gave them), were Sevens of Years, a *Year for a Year*, 70 times 7 *Sabbatic* Years, *i. e.*, 490 *years.* They included the rebuilding of the Temple and City after the return from exile, the Advent of Messiah, the second destruction of both Temple and City, a long interval of second dispersion, and the Rise, Reign, and Ruin of the last Antichrist, with Israel's final deliverance. A period of 490 *days* would not be chosen by the Angel, as a time in which to represent the occurrence of these stupendous events. And, once more ; the prediction is neither " figurative, " nor " typical," but plain, unfigured and literal prophecy. No symbols are here. Even were it symbolic, yet this does not deprive the numbers of their literal value.

And it is just for these unanswerable reasons, *the " 1,260 days" cannot be taken to mean 1,260 years.* What-ever "applications" on a larger scale, men may make of them, whatever theories of interpretation men may build on such applications, no matter how interesting or marvelous the astronomical discoveries of M. Ches-eaux may have been, one thing is eternally sure, viz. : That the 1,260 *days* in Daniel and John, cannot be dis-lodged from their vital organic relation to the 70th Week of Daniel. They are half of the "One Week," in Dan. ix:27. That is their only and ultimate seat and source. They spring from there alone, the *fons et origo* of their being. And because of this, they are days standing for days, a day for a day, and not a day for a year. The 70th Week is the last in a series of 70 Weeks of the same co-ordinate character and chronological value. To hold otherwise, and interpret otherwise, is to wreck the whole prophecy, and make it wild, absurd, and ridiculous to the last degree, contradicted by Scripture and History alike. A child must be able to see that, if the last half of the 70th week equals 1,260 *years*, the first half must equal 1,260 *years* also, and by parity of reasoning, the whole 70th Week must equal 2,520 *years*, and, by a necessary consequence, each one of the 69 co-ordinate weeks of the one series must equal 2,520 years. And, this being so, then the 70 Weeks must equal 70 times 2,520 *years*, or 176,000 years. That is, the Angel informed Daniel that, from -the *Motse Davar*, or Decree of Cyrus, B. C. 536, to the First Ad-vent and Death of Christ, no less than 176,400 years would elapse, or more than 17 times the distance from the Creation of Man until now, allowing man's time on earth to be 10,000 years ! By what right, on the Year-Day Theory, shall we interpret the last half of the 70th

Week to mean 1,260 *years*, and not the first half also?
And if so, then by what right interpret *one* of the 70
Weeks to mean 2,520 years, and not *all* the weeks in
the same way? It is because the 70 Weeks are Year-
Weeks and not Day-Weeks standing for Years, that the
" 1,260 *days*" expressly so called in Scripture, are *days
standing for days and not for years*, and belong not
to centuries on centuries past, but are the last 3½
years of the Antichrist to come.   And, if the 70th
Week belongs, as the Church supposes, to *Christ*, and
not to *Antichrist*,—if it follows in strict chronological
sequence upon the 69th week, as is generally assumed,
then with what face can we, as we do, interpret the
first half of it as that occupied by the ministry of our
Lord in Galilee and Judea, 3 ½ literal years, instead of
the 1,260 years, and the second half of it during which
it was said the covenant was further confirmed with
the many believing Jews up to the death of Stephen as
3 ½ years instead of 1,260 years also? By what right do
we say that the 70th Week is "*fulfilled*" in those 7 years
or " One Week" in the midst of which Christ was " cut
off," on the Day-Day Theory, taking the numbers literally, and then wheel about and say, it is " *not fulfilled*,"
and apply it, symbolically, to the Papal or Mohammedan Antichrist, dating its first half from somewhere
in the neighborhood of B. C. 606, and its last half somewhere in the neighborhood of A D. 1914? The times
of this ignorance God has undoubtedly winked at, but
now, as undoubtedly, since light so clear has been shed
on his Word, commands all interpreters, everywhere,
to repent!   How much longer will the Church, disre-
garding Israel, continue to "apply" the 70th Week of
Daniel, first, to A. D. 30–37, and next to the period from
B. C. 606 to A. D. 1914, treating with positive disdain

the labors of faithful men, who would redeem God's word from the "ignominious failures" of its professed expounders? Who cannot see that, in Eschatology, the Church is involved in an error as deep and broad as she was in Soteriology, before the Reformation, an error of which one day, she will be ashamed? The word of the Puritan Robinson, " I am verily persuaded, I am very confident, that the Lord has *more truth* yet to break from His holy word," is only what every patient student of prophecy has felt to be true.* It is only by a great inconsistency, that they who hold the Year-Day Theory, and apply the 70th Week of Daniel either to the Mohammedan or Papal Antichrist, and the Reformation, so spiritualizing the prophecies concerning Israel, can hold to the final conflict of Israel with the last Antichrist, and to Israel's national conversion.

5. What we reach then, as an incontrovertible fact is this, viz.: That *the precise measurement of the* 3 ½ *times, or years, the* 42 *months, the* 1,260 *days, is fixed*

---

* " Nor is it all incredible that a Book which has so long been in the possession of mankind, should contain many truths which are not yet discovered."—*Bishop Butler.*

" Even now, after eighteen centuries of Christianity we may be involved in some enormous error of which the Christianity of the future will make us ashamed."—*Prof. Alexander Vinet.*

" All our efforts to arrive at a more perfect knowledge of the Scriptures, imply that hitherto they have been understood but imperfectly."—*Dr. Woods of Andover.*

" The time is coming when all the dark places of the Scripture will be elucidated."—*Prof. Moses Stuart of Andover.*

" There are many passages of Scripture reserved to quell some heresy yet unborn, and confound some error that hath yet not a name."—*Robert Boyle.*

" The Truth is a hill not to be commanded, but commanding error that now is, and is yet to be."—*Lord Bacon.*

" Patefacta omnibus veritas, sed nondum est occupata. Multum ex illa etiam futuris relictum est. Qui ante nos ista moverunt, *non domini nostri, sed duces* sunt."—*Seneca.*

" Accessu temporum, multis noviter infunditur quæ forsitan priscis doctoribus cœlata monstratur."—*Cassiodorus.*

unalterably by a comparisou of Scripture with Script-ure. Never are 3 ½ "times" described in Scripture, as 3 ½ "*days*," but always as 3 ½ "*years*," or 1,260 "*days*." The word "time" never denotes a day of 24 hours, but in prophecy is substituted for the word "year." A comparison of Scripture with Scripture proves this. If, taking a "time" for a "year," we re-duce the 3 ½ times, or half week of Daniel to days, what we get is 360 days plus 720 days, plus the 180 days equal 1,260 *days*, and if to this, we add 30, we get the 1,290 *days*, Dan xii:11 ; and if to this we add 45 more, we get the 1,335 *days*, Dan. xii:12 ; and this is precisely the calculation of the Angel himself. And that these 1,260 days *are* the second half of the "One Week" of years in Dan. ix:27, is clear, (1) because the "*Keren*" or Horn of the 4th empire, Dan. vii:25, is the unanointed "*Nagid*," or prince to come, the Desolator, ix:27, who appears in the 70th Week at the close of Gentile times, the period of supreme power for the one, being 3 ½ years, and for the other, the last half week, identical peri-ods ; (2) because both these characters are the last Anti-Messiah and persecutor of the Jewish Saints in the End-Time, Dan. xii:7, xi:45, of whom Antiochus Epiphanes, the "*Melek*," or wilful King, Dan. xi:36-39, and the Horn of the 3d empire, Dan. viii:9-13, was the type ; (3) be-cause the Horn of the 4th empire, the unanointed prince to come, the last Anti-Messiah, and John's first Beast, Rev. xi:7, xiii:1-8, and 8th personal head of the Beast, Rev. xvii:8, 11, xix:19, 20, are *all one and the same animal*, a compound, diabolical, divine, human brute ; a Beast, a Man, a Devil, a God ; the self-exalting, self-degrad-ing, blaspheming *factotum* in heaven, earth, and hell !

That great scholar, Professor Heinrich Von Ewald, was, therefore, right, when, comparing Scripture with

Scripture, he says, " The 1,260 days, or 42 months, during which the Holy City is trodden down, Rev. xi:2,
are that short, predetermined period, that *last* 3 ½
years of the One Week, which in the second part of Daniel, and since Daniel, is the fast standing formula for the
extremest tribulation immediately preceding the Advent of Messiah ; a number which John in Rev. xi:
2, and xiii:5, designates in a *new way*, as 42 months, and
which Daniel designates in xii:7-10 *as literal days*."*
So, also, Professor Orelli, " That these weeks (in Daniel) are *spaces of 7 years* is seen by comparing Dan. ix :
27 with vii:25 and xii:7."† So Küper, in his classic work
on Prophecy, " That, by the *Shabuim* or *Sevens*, in Dan.
ix:24-27 ; we are to understand *Year-*Weeks, results
not alone from their relation to the 70 years' Captivity
Dan. ix:2 ; *but from the* 1290 *and* 1335 *days* in xii:11, 12 ;
which stand connected with the " time, times, and half-
time, " vii:25, xii:7 ; that rise out of the 70th Week divided into two equal parts, and to whose last half an
excess of 30 and 45 *days* are added, for further explanation."‡ Contrary to Mr. Guinness, Dr. Pusey affirms,
what all Hebrew scholars will recognize as correct,
that " In prophecy, ' Weeks ' are Weeks of *Years*, and
not of *Days*. There could be no ambiguity in the people's minds. The period could not be 70 Weeks
of *Days*, or a year and about 4 months. The events
are too full for it." ‖ In like manner, Professor Stanley
Leathes : " The principle of reckoning by *Sabbatic*
years is here implied."§ And Professor Drummond, of
London, in the same way, " From a comparison of Dan.

* Johan. Schriften II. 223.
† Die alttest. Weissagung. 525.
‡ Das Prophetenthum. 382.
‖ Approaching End of the Age. 303. Pusey on Daniel. 170.
§ Old Test. Proph. 196.

xii:7, with xi:11, we learn that 3 ½ *times* are equivalent with 1260 *days,* and therefore must be 3 ½ *years. This period is treated in Dan ix:27 as Half a Week,* and hence it is evident that the Weeks are Weeks of *Years.*"* These testimonies might be multiplied, but are already sufficient to show that the effort of Mr. Guinness *to break up this Stronghold and Citadel of Futurism,* Dan. ix:24-27, by importing into it the Year-Day Theory, is unsuccessful. The Scripture itself repels it, as it repels the assertion, wholly unjustified, that the Angel announced the period of 490 years "*as* 490 *days.*"† We must decidedly demur to that, and *that* gone, the Year-Day Theory is gone! The fact stands patent, from the organic connection of all prophecy that Dan. ix:26, 27, is the frame or skeleton of John's Apocalypse, chapters vi-xx; that the 3 ½ times in John, *are* the 3 ½ times in Daniel, the Beast being the Little Horn, and therefore the 1260 *days are not days put for years, but days put for days,* being 3 ½ literal years still *future* to us, at the End of the Times of the Gentiles.

6. Were the Reformers, therefore, involved in a false view when, believing the Pope to be an Antichrist, they adopted the Year-Day *Theory,* taking the 1260 as years, dating from about A. D. 606 or 725? Were the translators of King James' Version, who so materially affected their version by this theory, false in their Protestantism?‡ We answer *No,* intensely *No.* The alliance of the Year-Day Theory with Protestantism was unnecessary. Protestantism did not need to stake its great movement upon making the 70th

---

* Drummond. Jewish Messiah, 204.

† Guinness Appr. End of the Age, 302, 303.

‡ See a series of valuable articles in the " *Truth,*" April, May, June, July, 1888, by Benjamin Douglass, Esq., Chicago, published by James H. Brookes, D. D., St. Louis, Mo.

Week of Daniel cover the whole time from B. C. 600
to A. D. 1920, and then limit that week to the 7 years
in whose midst Christ was crucified! We must beware of the conclusion that, if the Year-Day Theory
has no exegetical foundation, then Protestantism was
unjustified. This is a mistake into which we have
often fallen when defending the Protestant *"application"*
of the symbols of Daniel and John to the Papacy, as
against an *exclusive* Præterism which sees in them *only*,
a reference to Maccabean and Neronian times, and an
exclusive Futurism which denies every and any reference
to the past or the present. No less amenable to just
criticism is that *exclusive* Presentism, or Continuous
Historic and Protestant interpretation, which denies to
these symbols *any* relation to the past or the future.
Protestantism is justified even without any calculation
of 1260 *years*, even as Præterism, within certain limits,
is justified wholly apart from any calculation of
1260 *days*. The events of the 6th decade of the first
century, or the Neronian times and Roman Jewish
war, even as the events of the 16th century, or Refor-
mation-time, do not stand or fall with the strict interpretation of the 70th Week in Daniel. Protestantism
existed before Joachim took the 1260 days for Years.
It is independent of any calculations as to Israel's future.
It became entangled, hopelessly, as to prophetic interpretation, when it made the Church of Rome, the Harlot, mean the *false Israel* on the one hand, and Protestantism the *true Israel* on the other. But it did not err
when, seeing the wonderful *analogy*, between the features and photographs of the last Antichrist, and those
of " *Deus Dominus Noster Papa* " at Rome, it declared
that the gleam of the Antichrist glimmered in the
countenance, and the acts of the Antichrist were re-

flected in the conduct, of his imperial Holiness. Yet all, *imperfectly;* even as imperfectly in Nero, and in Antiochus, other features were represented.

We must beware of *narrowness*, in our views of God's word, while yet we must adhere to strictness, in allowing Scripture to explain itself. Grammar, Lexicon, Usus and Organic Unity have their inalienable rights. The *Eschata* are *Eschata*, and *Israel* is *Israel*. And yet foreglancings of the End meet us all along the way to the End, and, for that End, all the previous steps are a signal and vast preparation. All history is in some sense, " *typical.* " That which *has* been, *is*, and that which *is*, *shall* be. The view that God operates all things by number, measure, weight, and proportion, and that, as Newton saw it, the universe is " a system of identical laws evolving analogous phenomena, " the material related to the moral and religious, as the shadow to the substance, and that a profound sympathy exists everywhere in all God's works, no matter in what sphere occurring, is a truth not less of Science and Philosophy than of Scripture and Theology. While "*application*" is not " *interpretation,* " yet God's word is as elastic as it is rigid. The law that moulds a tear upon the cheek forms a planet in its orb. The "*Septate Law*" already was mirrored in the Jewish Calendar in Sevens of various dimensions, even as it is mirrored in Nature in the same way, and also in History. And it is written in the heavens, if M. Cheseaux and others are correct, in astronomical cycles corresponding to prophetic numbers. We must admit this. Still, for all this, Astronomy is not exegesis, even as Geology is not, though both confirm the Scripture. Concede, here, all that the advocates of the Year-Day Theory, demand, yet, when it comes to a question of Biblical interpretation,

" 3 ½ years " are not, and cannot be made, " 1260 years " even as " *Daniel's people* " cannot be metamorphosed in- to the " *Gentile Church.* "   Concede all that is justly claimed for *types* and *typical applications,* yet the Roman Imperator, celebrating his triumph in the Capitol, was as little the subsequent Emperor Julius, or Augustus, as Antiochus, Nero, the Pope, Mohammed, or Napoleon, were, or are, the final Antichrist.   The " 1260 days " are dejected Satan's " short time " Rev. xii:12 ; and to afflict the Saints 1260 *years* under the last Antichrist's rule is more than God is willing to permit.   We may not con- found things which God has distinguished.

RECONCILIATION OF VIEWS

It is often asked, may not the Year-Day Theory, or Presentism, be *reconciled* with Futurism, or the Day- Day Theory, the one for Protestantism, the other for Israelism?   And we might also ask, may not the Day- Day Theory, have a double reference, first to the past, and next to the future?   In short, may it not include Præterism as well as Futurism, even though Præter- ism on *its* scale, like Presentism on *its* scale, is only an imperfect shadow of the final Futurism?   *Why not?* May that not be applicable to the different ecclesias- tical schemes of prophecy, which Leibnitz said of the different philosophical systems of men, viz., that they are " *true in what they affirm, but false in what they deny!* " How many devoted and eminent scholars are among the Præterists!   How many, not lest famed, are among the Presentists?   And what a streaming galaxy among the Futurists?   Præterists, like Ewald, say the proph- ecies can be " *shaped to suit* " the events of the Be- ginning, or Nero-Time.   *Presentists,* like Thiersch, say the prophecies can be " *shaped to suit* " the events of the

End-Time. Futurists, like Leyrer, say the prophecies can be " *shaped to suit* " the events of Middle Time, and of Historic Christianity. All use the same expression, " shaped to suit," though writing independently of each other. There is, certainly, a deep unconscious testimony, here, to some deep truth not yet fully developed from the word of God ; a truth of great importance in reference to the structure, relation, and design of prophecy, as well as to the law of its application. May it not be true that the *Exclusivism* of each of these three great systems of exposition is the *bane* of that clearer, broader, deeper, higher, rounder-sightedness which would bring into perfect fellowship and unity of utterance all students of prophecy, careful only not to confound things that are distinct, and not to deny the reference claimed by each ? This does not involve the vagaries of any, but does confess the truth that cannot be successfully gainsaid by any. The Apocalypse was a support to the early martyrs in the time of Decius and Domitian. None can deny it. The antecedent events of the Nero-Time were typical of still future things.* It did provide

---

* I hold strongly to the *Domitianic date* of the Apocalypse, A. D. 95, or 96, as against Canon Farrar's repetition of exclusive Prætei ism, and suppression of the evidence, both external and internal, on which the early church relied with unbroken uniformity for 500 years. Whoever desires to see the demolition of the præteristic date, A. D. 69, will find it in Lardner and Woodhouse, in Hengstenberg and Kliefoth, in Godet's " Studies on the New Testament, " in Milligan's Appendix to his " Revelation of St. John, " in Elliott's, " Horæ Apocalypticæ, " not to mention other works. I have reviewed Canon Farrar's representation in the " *Truth*, " October 188᠊, edited by Rev. James Brookes, D. D., St. Louis, Mo. Alford's Prolegomena to the Apocalypse is excellent in its refutation of the speculative criticism that makes the Apocalypse a Book written *before* the Destruction of Jerusalem by Titus. Thiersch, Ebrard, Schultze, Harnach, and Volck, vigorously oppose the earlier date, and it is᠊to be regretted that Dr. Schaff, in the later edition of his works has changed his former and better view, on this question. The reaction against this extreme Præterism is setting in strongly, to-day in Germany. The " Nero hypothesis " ought to be driven out of exegesis. In

consolation for the sufferers of the Middle Age and
Reformation times.   And, as surely, it will be Israel's
strength in that awful crisis which shall close the Gentile Dispensation. *It is meant for all time.* And
what else as the final book of the future glancing with
prophetic vision, from time to time, from John to the
Second Coming, should it be, and viewing all as one,
than the Revelation of Him who announces Himself as
Præterist, Presentist, and *Futurist,* all in one, Jesus
Christ, " who *is,* and *was,* and *is to come!*" Rev. i:4.

---

the well chosen words of Professor Thiersch, " John's Apocalypse had something greater for its object than the events of the time of Nero and his successors.   All those interpreters are fast chained in error who see only herein
the fall of Jerusalem, and a Roman Emperor as the object of the visions.
The events of that time served as a *means,* appointed by Providence for the
anticipation, representation, and *understanding of future things,* the
shadows of a yet more decisive drama to occur at the end of the Christian
age." *Die Apost. Zeitalter,* 226.   The fact that the antecedent events of
the 6th decade of the first century are, to a certain extent, mirrored in the
Apocalypse written A. D. 95, or 96, even as all earlier events are mirrored in
later prediction, does *not prove* that the Book was written in Nero's time.

Part 3

THE CAUSE OF ERROR IN DETERMINING THE 70 SEVENS

The whole effect of our discussion, thus far, is to produce the conviction that the stumbling-block in the way of reckoning the 70 Sevens is not in the prophecy itself, but in our own *ignorance*, "not knowing the Scriptures," or in a *false chronology*, or, if not that, then in a *false mode* of computing the Sevens, and the Genealogies, or in both together. Something is wrong. The Angel says, that Many, in the time of the end, shall be like adventurers at sea, turning their rudder this way, then that, on the wide ocean, in search of land, yet finding none, but at last, by means of their very *erring*, shall increase knowledge, and come to shore. So has it been with the writer of these discussions! If we *accept* the Cyrus Date B. C. 536—not as infallible, for we do not need this,—but only as approximately correct, and if it is proper to count the 69 Weeks *unbrokenly*—then the solution of the mystery of the 70 Weeks is absolutely impossible. Neither an Angel, nor an Œdipus, could achieve it. The substitution of the lower dates (B. C. 457 and 445) will afford us no relief. It is impossible that 536 should be 490 or 483. It is impossible to ignore the Cyrus decree as the *a quo* of the 70 Weeks. If we take 457, then 79 years, or if we take 445, then 91 years, *pass away between* the Return from Exile, under Cyrus' decree, and the Edict to restore and build Jerusalem! *Nearly a whole century expires after the Angel's word to Daniel before the oracle he delivers, even begins to be fulfilled!* Before the *Davar* goes forth, two generations of restored exiles go down to their tombs! This is intolerable, and only proves that it requires greater faith to believe an absurdity than it does to believe a miracle. It is undeniable that, after a temporary suspension of the work, from 2d Cyrus to 2d Darius, 16 years, Ezra iii:8, 11; iv:5, 24, the work was resumed 2d Darius, the decree of Cyrus having been found at Achmetha, and republished by an order of Darius, with another of his own annexed, and was "finished" in the 6th year of his reign; *i. e.* 21 years, exactly, after the decree of Cyrus was first made. It is undeniable, also, that the people "builded the *City*" as well as the "*House* of the Lord," under and in pursuance of Cyrus' decree, and during the first years following its first publication, and that this was the gravamen of the complaint in the letters missive of Chancellor Rehum, Governor Tattenai, Bishlam, Shimshai, to the Persian king, and the cause of the wrath in the renowned Osnapper's conglomerate swarm all ready to assail, like bees, the laboring captives. Ezra iv:12,16,21. Hagg. i:14. During the early part of the 7 Sevens the reconstruction of the dwellings was begun. And just because of these facts, they who insist on calculating the 70 Weeks, now from B. C. 457, or again from B. C. 445, are compelled to *first count* the 7 Weeks as immediately sequent upon the Decree of Cyrus B. C. 536,—(for the release from Exile, the Founding of the Second Temple, the Obstruction, and the Resumption, cannot be denied to have taken place when they did take place),—and then carry these same 7 Weeks *forward*, after they are left behind, and *count them a second time*, in order to form a new starting-point for the whole 70! By this means 49 years are *added* to the Angel's prediction, and actually *inclosed* in the Sacred Sevens, so that the Angel is made say that 490=490+49=539, or that 483=483+49 =532. That is, with the 7 Weeks *behind* the reckoner, they are yet *resumed, thrown forward*, and *recounted*, not only the 62, but even the final 1 week, being attached in order to secure an *ad quem* for the 70 Weeks, or 490 years, either the year of our Lord's Baptism, or the year of His Crucifixion! Such is the almost universally received computation. Schematized, this grotesque conception stands thus:

Cyrus, B. C., 536. / Temple finished, 515.	80 to 90 years. / 7 Sevens. / 60 to 70 years.	Edict to restore and build, 457, 445.	7 + 62 + 1 = 70 sevens. / 49 + 434 + 7 = 490 years.	Baptism or death of Messiah, A. D. 28, A. D. 30, or A. D. 33.

And this is the orthodox *quod erat demonstrandum*, in our apologetics and polemics, against all Jews and Pagans, in proof of the Messiahship of Jesus of Nazareth, from the 70 Weeks of Daniel! Jesus was the true Messiah, according to Daniel, who predicted His Advent to be 483 years after B. C. 536, *because* Messiah died just 490 years after B. C. 445!! Is it a wonder that Rabbi Isaac, in his *Chizzuk Emuneh (Rampart of Faith)* the arsenal of English and French infidelity in the 18th century, should say, "Those who will examine the books of the Nazarenes will find that there is nothing

clearly known amongst them concerning either the beginning or the ending of the 70 Weeks, one placing
them here and another there, so that there is no agree-
ment." *   It is worse than this. From 80 to 90 years
fly away *after* the Return from Captivity, and 60 to 70
years expire *after* the Temple is finished, *before* the
Edict to restore and build the City is issued !   If the
Angel said so, we should assent without a murmur, but
there is no reason why *we* should say so, then say the
Angel said it !

The temptation is plainly immense to amateurs in
chronography to *repeat* the 7 Sevens, seeing that, by
the extra 49 added to the 483 years, or 62 Sevens, we
get the sum of 532 years, $483+49=532$, to which add.
ing the 4 years' error in our Dionysian Era, we have
exactly the 536 years from Cyrus to Messiah, *i. e.*, just
76 Sevens, and then proceed by the tools of a higher
criticism to amend the lower Esdrine text, and defend
the reading of the Septuagint !   The bait is glittering !
The diagrammed conception would be this :

Cyrus.	7	+	7	+	62	=	76 Sevens.	Prince.
B. C. 536.	49	+	49	+	434	=	532 years.	Messiah.

the Dionysian 4 making the 536 !   The trouble, how-

---

* The *Sepher Chizzuk Emuneh*, or Book of the Fortress of Faith.—
Munimen Fidei, was written by Rabbi Isaac, son of Abraham, a cultivated
Polish Jew, and orthodox Caraite or descendant from one of the Ten Tribes,
and who died at Troki A. D. 1594.   It is the standard defence of Judaism
against Christianity.   Voltaire says of it, "The most confirmed infidels have
alleged nothing that is not already in Rabbi Isaac's Book."   (*Melanges III*,
344.)   It has been turned into Latin, French, Spanish, German, English,
and gone through Christendom.   It is one of the calmest and ablest polemics
against,—not the Bible,— but our special hermeneutics and handling of the
Bible, that ever was written.   The copy quoted from above (p. 342) is a
beautiful reprint of Rabbi Isaac's work, in parallel Hebrew and German
columns, edited by *David Deutsch, Sohrau in Ober Schlesien*, 1865. Pp. 395.
Baron Rothschild contributed 500 francs toward defraying the expense of its
publication.   It was replied to by Wagenseil, of Altorp, 1681. and again by
J. P. Storr, Tuebingen, 1703.   See *Etheridge, Hebrew Literature*, p. 444.

ever, is that the Septuagint says there are "77 Sevens," or 539 years, from Cyrus to Messiah. This, however, could be got rid of, just by reversing the *rôle* of the Dionysian 4, *i. e.*, *subtracting* the 4 from the 539 which gives us B. C. 535, only one year less than 536, and near enough for all practical demonstration. *Finis media justificat!* Why not add the extra 49 years? The answer is plain. It is dishonest. The sum of \$4.83 may be ledgered to mean \$5.36 in ordinary business, but by no. legerdemain in Biblical chronology can 7+7=7! It will hardly do to intimate that the Angel's purpose in mentioning 7 Weeks by themselves, was to pay a passing compliment to the 7 weeks next following the decree of Cyrus, then wink us to recount them in front of the 62, or start the whole 69 from one or other of the lower Artaxerxes dates! The Angel allows us no such liberty. He bids us "know and discriminate."

He tells us that, "from the *Motse Davar* to restore and build Jerusalem, unto *Mashiach Nagid*,"

1) *"there shall be 7 weeks;"*

2) *"and there shall be 62 Weeks;"*

No verb exists, and we are obliged to supply the copula *"shall be"* in the *first* clause, according to a universal law of grammar in all Semitic languages. Why should not our translation supply it also in the *second* clause? "There shall be 7 Weeks; and there shall be 62 Weeks." Doubtless, that was the reason why the colon, or Athnach, was placed after the 7 weeks, but which has been perverted to sustain a Maccabean interpretation. It separates the clauses into two independent statements, and Hitzig is perhaps correct when saying that no one acquainted with either writing or speaking the Hebrew language, could either point or translate the text otherwise. *Why did the*

Angel make two independent periods? Why not say "there shall be 69 weeks?" The conviction must certainly press itself, more and more, upon a thoughtful mind, that the *grouping* of the 70 Sevens into three periods implies a *separate* existence, *separate* characteristic, and *separate* interpretation, of each, and perhaps an interval, longer or shorter between each, and perhaps in the groups themselves.

The peculiarity of the sub-distribution into 7+62+1 is striking and of supreme importance. It is our duty to observe that nowhere does the Angel say that there are *not more* than 483 years between the going forth of a decree to restore, and Prince Messiah. What he does say is that there shall be *not less* than 483 years. The distinction is vital. Messiah will not come *before* 7 decreed weeks and 62 decreed Weeks have passed away. This much is absolutely certain. And if so, our mode of computation must be wrong if the received chronology is right. What we shall have to do, is to say that, from Cyrus onward,—yet perhaps not unbrokenly,—there shall be, *at least*, 7 Weeks or 49 years, and then determine, if we can, what the *ad quem* of these weeks is. Then, next, we shall have to say that, from the *a quo* of the 62 weeks onward,—yet perhaps not unbrokenly,—there shall be, *at least*, 62 weeks or 434 years, and then determine, if we can, what the *a quo* of these weeks is. In the 62 weeks the *ad quem* is distinctly stated, but not the *a quo*. In the 7 Weeks the *a quo* is distinctly stated, but not the *ad quem*. And the *ad quem* of the 62 is the *ad quem* of the whole 69. And these observations are vital. There is foresight and design in this concealment, and it is clearly meant to exercise our thought, by way of "knowing" and "discriminating." We are *sure* if we start

forward from Cyrus. We are *sure* if we count backward from Messiah. But we are *not* sure that we may
count unbrokenly either way. *Just there is the problem!* The Angel does not say that, after 483 years,
reckoned *unbrokenly* from the decree of Cyrus, Messiah
shall come, but only that after 69 decreed, or selected,
Weeks of years, will be His Advent.

If these remarks are correct, then it is possible, by
changing our mode of computation, to retain the date of
the Edict of Cyrus (B. C. 536), and explain the great
post-exile Prophecy of the 70 Weeks, without either
asserting that date to be infallible, or resorting to vain
ideals. Counting 7 Weeks or 49 years unbrokenly,
from B. C. 536, brings us to B. C. 487, but we are not
sure that this is the *ad quem* of these weeks. Counting
backward from the Birth of Messiah 62 Weeks, brings
us to B. C. 434, but we are not sure that this is the *a
quo* of these weeks. The sum of 49+434(=483) is not
536 years. Count as we may, we are ever confronted
with an excess of 53 years, 536—483=53, over and
above the 483, and if we allow for the 4 years in our
Dionysian era on which our reckoning is based, then
57 years face us, *outside* the 69 weeks, demanding explanation. We cannot discharge them. They will
not down at our bidding. Plainly, these 57 are *Gentile*
times, and no part of the *Jewish Sabbatic Sevens.* They
belong to an interval, or intervals, *somewhere* between
some of these decreed Sevens. This much is absolutely
certain. If the date 536 is right, and the decree of Cyrus
was the *Motse Davar* spoken of by the Angel, (and both
these we accept), it does seem clear that our whole
method of computation has been wrong for 18 centuries, and has plunged us into quagmires from which
there was no escape. It is plain as can be, that the

7 weeks and the 62 weeks do *not* contain the *sum of all
the years* between the Decree of Cyrus and the Advent
of Christ. The full number of the years between these
events is 483+57=540, less the Dionysian 4 which
gives us 536.

If we "know and discriminate" the Hebrew text
clearly, we shall find that the 7 weeks are assigned to,
and decreed upon Daniel's people and city, for the
actual work of restoring and building the Temple, City,
Walls, Gates, and Houses, and the religious, civil, and
political organization and reform of the returned Exiles. The books of Ezra and Nehemiah confirm this.
The *Characteristic* of the 7 Weeks is the *Restoration*,
This does not exclude the fact of further building and
adornment, or repair, during the 62 weeks following, as
was the case after the assault of Antiochus Epiphanes,
and under the splendor of Herod the Great. The whole
combined period was to be one in which there should
be the Times of Distress. "And in distress (or pressure, or straitness) there shall be the times." The
Characteristic of the 62 Weeks is Israel's deepening
Apostasy, notwithstanding all God's favor, a defection
so great as to lead even to the rooting out of Messiah
when He comes, a crime resulting in the wreck of the
whole Restoration, the re-destruction of the rebuilt
Temple and City, and re-dispersion of the guilty people during a long period succeeding. As to the *Characteristic* of the "One Week," or final 7, divided into
two equal parts, it is that of Israel's final *Redemption*,
the preservation of their Temple built a third time, the
possession of their land, and the destruction of "the
prince that shall come," with whom, in the madness of
their last Apostasy, Israel's masses have entered into
covenant, only to suffer tribulation, and who, as a Des-

olator Desolated, perishes under the outpoured vials of divine wrath. Such are the phases of the development.

The 70 Sevens, therefore, while covering, are yet *cut off* and *cut out* from the whole course of Gentile Times, and are limited to the accomplishment of a *special purpose*, named in the Hexad v. 24. Their sub-distribution opens the road to the goal. They are decreed with special reference to a special People, a special City, and a special End,—"*upon thy* people and *upon thy* city," and for the purpose of "putting a stop to *the* Apostasy, etc.," v. 24, *i. e.*, a stop to Israel's perpetual defection. They have nothing to do with *Gentile* development. They are not decreed upon Persians, Greeks, Romans, Saracens, Turks, Russians, English, French, Germans, or Americans, but only upon *Jews*. They have nothing to do with the affairs of Shushan, Athens, Rome, Mecca, Constantinople, St. Petersburg, London, Paris, Berlin, or New York, but only with the affairs of *Jerusalem*. They are *exclusive* Sevens, devoted to the special interests and fortunes of Israel and Palestine. They begin that way. They continue that way. They end that way. Their fulfilment is the execution of God's purpose with respect to the chosen people, chosen city, chosen land. They do not relate to the Church, or the Church-Period. The Advent of Messiah, His Baptism, Life, Death, Resurrection and Ascension, the Second Destruction of Jerusalem, A. D. 70, and the course of Christendom, all lie wholly *outside* their number, valleyed between the 62 and the final 7. They do not even condescend to notice Gentile "culture," "progress," and "civilization." Israel alone is their purpose, object, theme, and end.

And now, we are ready for our solution of their

mystery.   The assumption that the " Sevens Seven
and Sevens Sixty and Two," with the final " One
Week," are one compacted period cut out, without interval, from the body of Gentile Times, is contradicted
by the sub-distribution itself into 7+62+1, by their exclusion of all Gentile times, save the years that enter
into their own number, by the space between the Advent and the Crucifixion, seen in the word "After," by
the space between the Crucifixion and the Destruction
of Jerusalem, A. D. 70, and by an interval between the
Destruction of Jerusalem and the end, all these separately indicated spaces being but parts of the one
great space between the 62 and the final 1, so making
one interval out of all.   The Angel himself shows us
where *one* interval is, at least.   It lies between the 62
Weeks and the 1 Week, and its Characteristic is the
second long day of Israel's casting away and dispersion, and the down-treading of Jerusalem until Gentile
times are fulfilled.   And our Lord confirms, and interprets for us, the Angel's word.   Luke xxi:24.

Ezra the " *Shopher*," who lived to work under the
7 Sevens and help fulfil the Angel's oracle, tells us
where *another* interval is.   None better knew.   It lies
between the 6th Darius Hystaspes when the Second Temple was dedicated, and the 7th Artaxerxes
Longimanus when Ezra received his Commission under Edict from that King, the son of Xerxes and Vashti,
and repaired with a second colony from Babylon, to
re-inforce the first at Jerusalem, and organize and reform the people.   It is an interval of 57 years lying in
between the first 21 years next following the decree
of Cyrus, and the last 28 years of the first 49 years of
the prophecy.   In other words, as the 21 *years are* 3
Sevens, and the 28 *years are* 4 *Sevens*, it lies between the

first 3 and last 4 of the 7 Sevens. Ezra vi:15;vii:1-7. From 1st Cyrus, 536, to 6th Darius, 515, are Cyrus 9, Cambyses and Pseudosmerdis 7, and Darius Hystaspes 5 full years, 21 in all, or 3 Sevens.   How important an epoch for Israel was the 6th Darius, we may learn from the Behistûn inscription which, reared by himself and recording his overthrow of Babylon, a second time, in the 5th year of his reign,*—and from Zechariah's appeal to the lingering captives to escape the impending danger as Darius prepared to move on the revolted city," Ho!   Zion!   Deliver thyself!   O Dweller with the daughter of Babel!"   Zech. ii:11,— and from Zerubbabel's bringing home the Temple topstone, "with shoutings, Grace! Grace! unto it!" Zech. iv:7,—as also from the Great Dedication of the Temple, and the Great Passover attending.   Ezra vi:14-22.   It was at that eventful, epoch-making date, were sung the words of the 118th Psalm,

> " The stone which the builders rejected
> Is become the head of the corner !
>   This is Jehovah's doing ;
> It is marvelous in our eyes !
> This is the day Jehovah hath made,
> We will rejoice and be glad in it."

Great day for Israel!   Fit event to be the *ad quem* of the first 3 Sevens !

And now, a *blank* of 57 years occurs in the Sacred History between this great epoch 6th Darius, and 7th Artaxerxes which is the immediate date next recorded by Ezra.   True, indeed, the Book of Esther comes in between the 6th and 7th Chapters of Ezra, to tell us

---

* See Rawlinson's Herodotus IV. Appendix.   Records of the Past. Vols. I and III.   Bosanquet, Messiah the Prince, 201.   Wright's Zechariah, 291.

how a plot for the universal massacre of the Jewish people in 127 provinces of the Medo-Persian Empire, from India to Ethiopia, was devised by a vile Amalekite, and a decree from Xerxes secured for its accomplishment, and only frustrated by that heroic daughter of Israel, who, risking her own for the life of her people, said, in the courage of faith, " I will go in to the king though it be not according to the law, and if I perish, I perish !"   Esther iv:16.   But this belongs not to the Seventy Sevens decreed upon Jerusalem and her home-brought exiles.   It occurs in the early interval of the 57 years, and is part of the Times of the Gentiles.   Like all intervals, it is excluded from the count, even as the modern enfranchisement of the Jews in Europe belongs not to the Seventy Sevens, but the modern interval itself.

The 6th Darius is in Ezra vi:15.   The 7th Artaxerxes is in Ezra vii:1–7.   The interval following 6th Darius is found in the words, " Now *after* these things, in the reign of Artaxerxes, 7th year, Ezra came to Jerusalem."   The length of time over-leaped, includes the remaining 30 years of the reign of Darius Hystaspes, the full 21 of Xerxes the Great, and 7 years of Artaxerxes the Longhanded ; in all, 57 years.   No theocratic work appears to have been done after the great jubal epoch, for over half a century.   The mighty previous effort seems to have exhausted the people Love of ease, doubtless, and Gentilizing ways increased, until the Lord raised up Ezra to renew the Restoration a second time.   The prophets Haggai and Zechariah had passed to their tombs.   How important an epoch Ezra's mission under the Edict of Artaxerxes was, the whole world knows, constituting a Second Restoration, the reform of the people, the re-establishment

of the Nomocracy, and the complete organization of Israel into a body politic with its Temple cult revived, though not in its ancient splendor. The 57 years of interval, taken from B. C. 515, bring us down to B. C. 458, the 7th year of Artaxerxes. The next date given us, is by Nehemiah, Ezra's contemporary, who tells us that, in the 20th Artaxerxes (B. C. 444) under the fourth Persian Edict favoring Jerusalem and the Jews, he was commissioned as "*Tirshatha*," or Governor, of the City, to protect the sepulchres of his fathers, the tombs of the kings and the prophets being even then exposed, and complete the mural defences of Jerusalem, bulwark and tower. Neh. ii:1. Counting full years, again, the distance from 7th Artaxerxes to 20th Artaxerxes, or B. C. 458 to 444, is 14 years, or 2 Sevens more, in which Restoration work was done.*
The next date given us by Nehemiah, is 32d Artaxerxes, "12 years" of arduous labor having passed, the circumvallation finished, the Wall dedicated, houses erected, and further reforms effected. This brings us down to B. C. 432. Accused to the king, by the enemies of Israel, of a purpose to revolt from the Persian Crown, and declare the independence of Israel, now that Jerusalem was fortified, Nehemiah went to the Persian Court, reporting his labors, remained there some time with the king whose " cup-bearer " he had

---

* There is every reason to believe that Artaxerxes Longimanus, 3d son of Xerxes by Vashti, i. e., Amestris, and who was contemporary with Herodotus and Thucydides, was the King who sent Ezra and Nehemiah to Jerusalem and sanctioned the restoration of the fortifications. Ezra vii:1. Neh. ii:1–8. *Rawlinson's Herodotus*, IV. 217. According to Rawlinson, Wilkinson, Oppert, Heeren, Grotefend, Brugsch, Thirwall, Grote, Curtius, the 1st year of Artaxerxes Longimanus was B. C. 466–5. This would make the 7th Artaxerxes to be 459–8, the 20th to be 445–4, the 32d to be 433–2, and the 34th to be 431–0. "The Restoration of the City cannot be considered as really accomplished until after the date of Nehemiah's visit to Jerusalem, B. C. 444, *and not even then.*" WRIGHT's Zechariah, 23.

been, enjoyed the friendship of his old companions, doubtless wrote the book of Esther, then returned *"at the end of days,"* after *"all this time,"* and, finding old abuses revived during his absence, re-commenced and continued his reformation, ousting the Ammonite from the Temple, providing for the Levite ministry, purging the people, and closing the whole work of the Second Period of Restoration by the Sanctification of the Sabbath,—fit type of the coming *" Sabbatism,"* following Israel's final Restoration, and of the *"Rest* that remains for the people of God!" Neh. xiii:6, 7; v:14. How much time is included in the expression *"all this time,"* and *"at the end of days,"* and in the closing period of Nehemiah's labors *after* his Second Return from the Persian Court, is conjectural. No critic pretends to assign less than 2 years.* If we add these 2 years to the 12 already given, we have 14 years again, or 2 Sevens more, bringing us down to 34th Artaxerxes as the end of Nehemiah's labors, and conclusion of the whole double Restoration-Period, the *ad quem* of the

---

* Various writers hold that Nehemiah's return from the Persian Court was "probably" not before 11th Darius Nothus, i. e., 18 *years* after his departure from Jerusalem, Josephus saying that he lived to a high old age. Auberlen says this may be "probable." Kurtz says Nehemiah "appeared" under Darius Nothus. The text affords no support for any of these conjectures. Kliefoth rejects them. Even a "high old age" for Nehemiah would not, as Auberlen truly remarks, " require many years," and Kurtz's indefinite "appearing" argues nothing as to the end of the 7 Sevens, but only as to Nehemiah's longevity. Both Haggai and Zechariah survived, a short time, the 3 Sevens. Many scholars take the expression *"keits yamim,"* *"end of days,"* to mean *"end of a year,"* and, though the expression itself does not determine this, yet all the circumstances of the situation go to support it. Auberlen fails to find any *ad quem* for the work of Nehemiah. It is a *"vanishing point,"* as it is with most ! Sir H. Rawlinson gives B. C. 434, as *"about"* the date of the Book of Esther. Nägelsbach, Köhler, Schrader, Orelli, make Malachi contemporary with the period of Nehemiah's absence, the prophet thundering away at the Gentile abuses and increasing apostasy, while Nehemiah was at the Persian Court. See KLIEFOTH on Daniel, 319; KURTZ, Sac. Hist., 248; WINER, Realwort. II, 147, Orelli, in STRACK-ZÖCKLER's Kurtzgef. Komm., Malachi 494. Rawlinson's Herodotus III, Appendix.

7 Sevens, which we set out to find from God's word alone. If now, finally, we add to B. C. 430 the deficient Dionysian 4, we have, in these 434 years, the 62 Weeks, *without interval*, extending from their *a quo*, which also we set out to find, 34th Artaxerxes, down to the Advent of "Prince Messiah."

Clear as daylight is the fact that the Restoration Time was a Double Period, parted by an interval of 57 years ; a Double Period actually defined in Ezra by the dates 6th Darius and 7th Artaxerxes marking the boundaries of the interval between the two periods, the 1st Cyrus being the *a quo* of the first period, and 6th Darius its *ad quem*, a period of 21 years ; also taking 7th Artaxerxes as the *a quo* of the second period. Then comes Nehemiah giving us the *ad quem* of the second period, 34th Artaxerxes, a period bisected by his coming to Jerusalem in 20th Artaxerxes. Still more; he actually gives names to *both* these separate periods ; calling the first period " *the Days of Joiakim, son of Joshua, son of Jozadak*," Neh. xii:26, and again, "*the Days of Zerubbabel*," v. 49 ; and calling the second period "*the Days of Nehemiah the Governor, and of Ezra the Priest, the Scribe*," v. 26, and again "*the Days of Nehemiah*," v. 47. Ordinary readers might not detect these important distinctions, but they exist, defining two distinct periods, called "*Days*," by the activities of the holy men whose labors signalized the same. The *Times of Zerubbabel and Joshua* were one period. The *Times of Ezra and Nehemiah* were another ; just as we speak of the Times of William the Conqueror, and again of Cromwell. And these are precisely what we have in the first 3 *Sevens*, or "Days of Zerubbabel" on the one hand, and in the last 4 *Sevens*, or "Days of Ezra and Nehemiah," on the other. This, certainly, ought to be conclusive. Beyond all controversy, the men who lived in and labored during those *Seven Sevens* are the best witnesses of how they were distributed. And if we remember that Ezra himself was engaged in compiling the canon, and in the old Hebrew collection placed the books Ezra and Nehemiah *immediately after* the book of Daniel, to what other conclusion can we come than that he put them there in order to help us interpret the 7 *Sevens* of the 70 Weeks, and that the Book of Daniel with its sublime prophecy of the 70 Weeks is *not* a Maccabean production, but was known to Ezra? The divine interpretation of the 7 Sevens, as it stands in Ezra and Nehemiah, is this,

| Cyrus, B. C. 536. | 3 Sevens. 21 years. | 6th Darius H. | (57 years.) | 7th Artax. L. | 2 Sevens. 14 years. | 20th Artax. L. | 2 Sevens. 14 years. | 34th Artax. L. |

equals 3+2+2 i. e. 7 Sevens or 49 years, a double period divided by an interval of 57 years, the whole time from the *a quo* to the *ad quem* of the 7 weeks being 106 years, 49 of which were selected, or decreed, upon the City and People of Israel, for actual restoration and rebuilding work.

Thus we have inductively discovered *two* intervals between the 70 Sevens the one between the 3d and 4th of the 7 Sevens, the other between the 69th and 70th Sevens. *Both these intervals are put there by the sacred writers themselves, and are therefore the work of God.* The Angel, the Prophet, the Scribe, the Ruler, our Lord, all confirm them. This much is secure. We have learned, also, what is meant by the "*Seventy Sevens*" as distinct from "*The Times of the Gentiles.*" The one stand over in contrast against the other, even as Israel stands over in contrast against the Nations, and

Jerusalem against all other cities. The one belong to the Jews, the other portion to the Gentiles. If, still, a third interval may yet appear, by reason of the possibility of a revision of our secular Chronology, and also of our handling of the Biblical data, so harmonizing the regnal times of the kings of Israel and Judah, as also shortening the lines of Babylonian, Median, and Persian, succession, allowing for years of co-regent administrations, *it will be found, if at all, between the 7 and 62, and nowhere else*, with Malachi as the *a quo*. Nor would the discovery of such an interval disturb in the least, what we have seen, as already resting on the plain statements of the word of God.

We do not say that such an Interval exists, or that the Masoretic *Athnach*, the English *Colon*, found at the end of the 7 Weeks, indicates such an Interval, but only that, should Chronology require, hereafter, some gap between the end of Nehemiah's labors and the beginning of 434 years reckoned backward from the Birth of Messiah, *this would in no way affect the accuracy of the 7 Sevens as fixed and measured periods of historic time.* These Sevens did most certainly *begin*. They did most certainly *end*. Clearly, three of them run on from 1st Cyrus and end in 6th Darius. Prairie-like is the gap of 57 years. On its other side, are the other four of the Sevens, beginning *as Ezra declares they do, with 7th Artaxerxes Longimanus, Ezra 7:7, and which* MUST END *at a point* 28 *years distant, and so close the decreed period of the Restoration.* According to our received chronology, and the regnal years of Artaxerxes Longimanus, this closing point MUST BE 34th Artaxerxes, or B. C. 430. The 7 Sevens MUST HAVE a definite end, and this end is *required* to be 2 *years after* the 32d Artaxerxes, Neh. xiii:6.

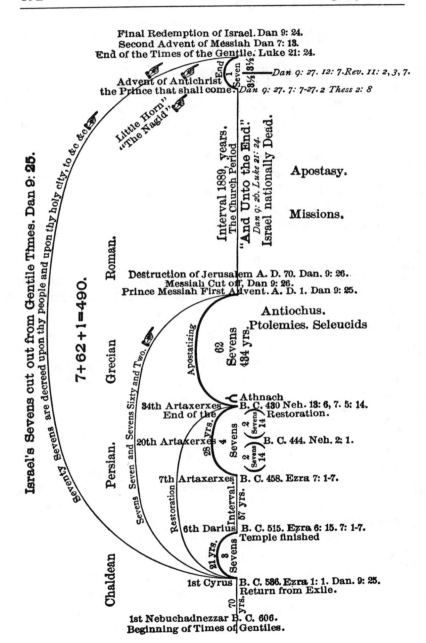

The Characteristic of the first 3 Sevens we know ; of the interval of the 57 years, the time of Darius, Xerxes, Esther, Haman; of Marathon, Thermopylæ, Salamis ; of Miltiades, Leonidas, Themistocles, the time of the shaking of the *Nations*, of the heaven, earth, sea, and dry land ! We know the Characteristic of the last 4 Sevens next following this interval, under the labors of Ezra and Nehemiah. The Characteristic of the 62 Sevens we also know,—Apostasy. From the death of Nehemiah and Cessation of Prophecy under Malachi, 250 years, or more, are an absolute *blank* in the History of the Jewish people, save what we learn from a fragment in Josephus.* Some intimation in the prophecies of Daniel and Zechariah, covering the Greek times especially, forecast the latter days of the third empire with great distinctness. But from 34th Artaxerxes to Antiochus the Great we have no history. Tradition preserved in Jewish books, reports some general facts, The 62 Sevens were the time of the Great Synagogue and the Sanhedrin, the final settlement of the Canon of Scripture, the rise of Rabbinism, of Pharisee, Sadducee and Essene ; the time of sore chastisement, when the Persian and Greek sceptres passed away, Israel's deepening apostasy visited by alternate strokes from the Ptolemies on the one side, and the Seleucids on the other, and again from Epiphanes, the Syrian Antichrist, who desolated the City, broke down the Walls, profaned the Temple, arrested the Worship, and set up Abomination in the Holy Place. The transient glory of Jewish independence won by the brave Maccabean heroes who fought the Antichrist of that time, soon glimmered away.†   The

---

* See Dean Milman's Hist. Jews. I. 443.

† The term "*Maccabee*," given to Judas, the eldest son of Mattathias, is the combined initial letters of the Hebrew words in the song of Moses.

Sibyl resumed her seat. The Hebrew Scriptures were turned into Greek. A vast body of apocryphal literature appeared. Asmonean and Idumean quarrels for crowns disgraced the temple splendor. When, at length, the 60th Seven saw the Gentile Eagle fly over the Holy Land, and Pompey make Palestine a province of Rome, the masses of the people, the Priests, Elders, and Scribes, Hillel, Shammai, and their schools, chafing under the Gentile yoke, longed for a Maccabean Messiah to come and save them, a Jewish Cæsar to wield an all-conquering scepter, annexing the world; while others more humble, and few, like Zacharias and Elizabeth, Joseph and Mary, Simeon and Anna, waited, and wondered, and watched for Him of whom all the prophets had spoken. The closed gates of the Temple of Janus, Israel looking to catch the first light from the "Star out of Jacob," is the End of the "Sevens Seven and Sevens Sixty and Two."

We know, also, the fact that, in the Prophecy of the 70 Weeks, only two specific events are foretold as occurring between A. D. 1 and the End, or 70th Week. One is the Death of Christ. The other is the Destruction of the Temple and City. Volumes are implied. More is said than is written. But only these are named. In 70 years after the Messiah has come, the whole work of the Restoration is wrecked! The Interval follows, 1800 and more years of which have

---

Mi Kamokah Baalim Iehovah?   Who is like unto thee, O Lord, among the gods?   Exod. xv:4.   *Makkab* is the equivalent of *Hammer*.   Judas *Maccabeus* was the Charles *Martel* of his day.   The word *Makkabi* was inscribed on the banner of the heroes who fought the Antichrist. and defied both Greeks and Romans, and bore in its face a charm like the "*In hoc Signo vinces*" on the Labarum of Constantine.   Every man, woman, and child, ought to read the Books of the Maccabees.   All earthly history has no valor superior to what the men of that time displayed.   The Apostle Paul has made their fame immortal.   Heb. xi:35-38.   They are the martyrs of the Law, battling Apostate Jews and Pagans, together.

already gone. Ever since "blood, fire and vapor of smoke" colored the sky over smoking Jerusalem, Israel has fulfilled the role in the legend of the "*Wandering Jew*." Awful, sad, weary, the way! But the End approaches. And surely, as God has already literally fulfilled 69 of the 70 Sevens or 483 years *decreed upon that people and that city*, so surely will He fulfil the 70th also, to *them*, in *their own land*, in their *own city*, and in 7 literal years of their *own Sabbatic time*.

In the light of these facts we discover what damage to the word of God, and to the Church of God, the existence of *one* time-embalmed error of exposition will bring, and indeed, has already brought! How, from century to century, exegetes and theologians, professors and pastors, transmit, as if by hereditary blindness, the thick eye scales of former generations, adding new laminæ of their own, and how, echoing the despair of others, and our own, we utter so boldly, precisely just what is not the fact, viz., that the numbers in Daniel are "*entirely symbolical*," and "*cannot be reduced to measures of historic time*." * Exactly the reverse of this is the truth. The one *assumption*, so absolutely false, that the Seventy Sevens flow on, like an unbroken river, and are to be computed in regular succession, has been the source of all this vital mistake. Israel divides both the sea and the Jordan. The spiritualizing, or idealizing of Old Testament prophecy, and the whole false conception of the character of John's Apocalypse have only made the evil almost incurable. Saturated with error is Commentary. From the days of Eusebius and Augustine, Jerome, Africanus and Syncellus. the Church has gone staggering like Elymas, groping for the door. Greek, Latin, Lutheran, Reformed, all are

* Briggs. Messianic Prophecy I, 426.

in the mire. The best men they have borne, have been
blinded, and thousands yet are. "Legion," "Myriad,"
is the brood of wild interpretations begotten of this
one prolific error, until commentaries have become
phantasmagorias and kaleidoscopes.   The India-Rub-
ber character of the Seventy Sevens allow 7 of them
to be pulled down to the Death of Christ, and the
next 62 of them to stretch to within 1 Seven of his
Second Coming!   And, because so accommodating to
our ignorance, we paste upon them the vague label
"*Sacred Times*," or profane them with the name "*World-*
Weeks!"   The restoring and building of Jerusalem is
the restoring and building of the "*Christian* Church,
the "*Spiritual* Israel," the "*Sacred* City!"   It is clear
that Chancellor Rehum, Governor Tattenai, the noble
lord Osnapper, and the Cis-fluvian Shethar-Boznai,
held no such views; nor did Joshua and Zerubbabel,
Haggai and Zechariah, Ezra and Nehemiah.   Ezra iv:
8–24; v:1–17. Neh. ii: 1–20. None of them ever made
the *a quo* of the 70 Weeks nearly a century later, or
nearly a century earlier than the Angel made it, and
their own living history, fulfilling the Angel's oracle.
declared it.   It was reseved for the Church, following
interpreters like Porphyry and Celsus, or some earlier
Alexandrite Maccabean, to say that the *ad quem* of the
70 Weeks abutted against Antiochus, or Christ, or Titus, or Onias, or the People, or all five at the same
time!   It took *Spiritual* Israel to do this!   It is time
that all this devout destruction of God's Word were
stopped, and that, at least, this part of " the transgression" were restrained. Perversion can go no farther.
Our "*modes*" and our "*ideals*" are not God's.   Our
ways and thoughts are not His. Six times six are
thirty-six, but Palmoni's wonderful numbering may

count Six at the opening, Ten in the middle, Four somewhere else, and Sixteen at the end, of a period 350 years long. It does not follow that, because Thirty-Six Times are decreed, or measured off, upon Babylon or Rome, London or Paris, Boston or New York, during three and a half centuries, that therefore 36=:350! The"*ergo*" is Hibernian! And yet the Church teachers, in great part, cling to this mummied delusion of near two millennia!   And the Jew looks on and smiles, and repeats to his friends our Christian Gentile demonstration of the Messiahship of Jesus of Nazareth, and *sotto voce;* tells them, and with truth, that evangelical Professors and Church Teachers are saying to-day, that the "Demonstration must be thrown overboard!"   If God does not one day smite the Gentile back with the Jewish rod, it will be because His truth has failed!

But God's word will stand!   The 70 Sevens are an Outline of the Philosophy of Universal History, and the Almanac of the Ages. They reveal to us an organic Unity and theologic End of History such as Herodotus and Thucydides never dreamed of, simply because they were unable to understand Israel's place in the "Times Foreappointed," Acts xvii:26, and Israel's relation to the Nations; a problem that baffled even the genius of a Hegel. It is to the credit of Bossuet, in part, and of Vico, both misled by the Church-idea of Israel, and yet more to the credit of those abler men, J. von Müller, Niebuhr, Brandt, Heinrich Leo, and the great school of which they are part, that the Jewish Captive, Daniel, is regarded as the "Father of Universal History,"—rather, God himself, who, by means of Gabriel, gave to Daniel, then to John, the true idea of the course of time, the place of Israel, and the destiny of Israel, as a People, and the Nations; unveiling their

times and their end.   We Gentiles put the whole into
our spiritual alembic, apply the heat of criticism, watch
it till it comes to double-bubble-bubble, then skim the
surface, and tasting the hot liquid, say: "Impossible that
the 70 Sevens can be historic time!"   The experiment
is vain!   The 70 Sevens cover the entire times of the
Gentiles from the fall of Babylon in the past, to the
fall of the greater Babylon in the present.   They begin with Cyrus.   They end with Christ at His Second
Coming.   They are *in* the Times of the Gentiles, but
not *of* them.   They are "decreed upon" the Jews and
Jerusalem, not upon the English and London, nor the
Irish and Dublin, nor the Scotch and Edinboro', nor
the Americans and Boston, or New York.   They belong to Palestine alone, and involve, in their outcome,
the solution of what politicians call the "*Eastern Question.*"   Rev. vii:2.   And, as the 69 Sevens have been
literally fulfilled upon the Jews and Jerusalem, in their
own land, so will the 70th Seven be fulfilled upon the
same people, in the same land, and according to the
law of their own Sabbatic Seven.   "The mouth of the
Lord hath spoken it!"   "It is the Utterance of Jehovah, Doer of these things!"   That is guarantee enough
against the Babeldom of unbelief.   The books of Ezra
and Nehemiah were written to instruct us how to interpret the 7 *Sevens* with the *Interval* between the 3
and the 4 Sevens.   Our Lord's Olivet-Prediction was
written to instruct us how to interpret the *Interval*, in
Daniel, between the 69th and 70th Sevens, and to point
us to the End and Israel's redemption at His Parousia
when Antichrist is destroyed.   John's Apocalypse was
written to foreshadow, in the 7 Epistles, the *Church-
side* of the Interval, then display the 70th Seven, the
Parousia, Israel's deliverance, and, unveiling the 1000

years, and the absolute End of the Ways of God, close
the Sacred Canon with a solemn warning that no man
add to, or take from, it.   Rev. xxii:18.   His magic lantern magnifies and intensifies with light all the great
events in that great "Day of the Lord!"   Marvelous,
to admiration, is the organic unity and progress of divine revelation from Moses to John, with Israel all the.
way! "It is the Lord's doing and wondrous in our
eyes."   The genius of a Plato, a Pascal, or a Newton,
the clairvoyance of all angels and all men, combined
and raised to the millionth power, would be powerless to construct such a book as the Bible!   Nor can
we better obey the voice of the Angel, bidding us
"know and *discriminate"* the 70 Sevens, than by passing
at once to the holy men and our Lord Himself, in
whose hands the true interpretation rests. And blessed
is the "wise" man, who, in the time of the end, *ruddering*
his way on the ocean of a stormy exegesis, and, long seeing no land, yet *"eagerly reads"* the prophecy of Daniel,
and through his very *" erring"* "increases knowledge,"
"understands," and, from the lookout on the top-mast,
hears, at last, the thrilling word, *Land ahead! ***

One further word, here. It will doubtless be asked,
how does the concession that the Cyrus date, 536, may
be admitted, and yet the word of the Angel to Daniel
be proved literally true, agree fully with the word

---

* INTERVALS in prophecy, and even in history, are frequent. A Gap
of more than 1800 *years* occurs between the first two clauses of Isa. lxi:2:
compare Luke iv:19.   A Gap of 57 *years*, spanned by the word *"after"* occurs in Ezra vii:1.   Compare vi:15 and vii:7.   This is the interval between
the first 3 and the last 4 of the 7 Sevens in Dan. ix:25, and not even hinted
there.   The interval between the 69th and 70th Weeks, expressed by "And
unto the End" is clear, in Dan. ix:26, and covers from A. D. 70 to beyond
the present time, i. e., *our whole Dispensation.*   The *same* Gap of 57 years,
seen in Ezra vii:1, is found also in Neh. xii:26, and xii:47.   The interval
between the First and Second Advents is overleaped in the Metallic Image,
Dan. ii:40–44, and in the 10-horned beast, vii:23-27.   A Gap of 60 years

of Matthew, who makes "14 Generations" from the carrying away into Babylon unto Messiah, or 560 years? Our answer, here, is the same as in reference to the "Sevens." The evangelist does *not* say that the *sum of the whole number of years* between the "Carrying away," under Nebuchadnezzar, and the Birth of Christ, is 560 years, but that the *"generations,"* counted according to a rule governing the construction of Jewish genealogies, and, in this case, unfolding the line of legal and royal succession, are " fourteen " in number. This must be so, for, if we consult the *three* periods described by Matthew as each consisting of "14 generations," we shall find that no two of them agree, and all three are different. Again, the computation varies from that in Luke's genealogy,—which has a different end in view. There is no conflict, therefore, between Daniel and Matthew, for the ˜simple reason that the *mode of computation* by " Generations," is just as peculiar as the mode of computation by " Sevens." There is an interval in the "Sevens." There are both intervals and overlappings in the "Generations." It is enough to have shown that the Bible is in perfect harmony with itself in this whole matter of the 70 Weeks, on which the Messianic demonstration depends, so far as the *time* of the Advent is concerned, and that the

---

lies in between verses 5 and 6 of Dan. chapter XI, from Ptolemy Lagi to Ptolemy Philadelphus. In I Cor. xv:23, 24 the *whole Millennial Age* is over-leaped between the verses; and the same overspringing and juxtaposition of events, in discourse, is found in John v:29. In the symbol of the sun-clothed Woman the entire distance from the First to the Second Advent is *annihilated*, yet *seen !* Rev. xii:1-10. In like manner, in our Lord's great Olivet prophecy of the End, the same wonderful feature of representation is displayed in ˙the strongest light. Matth. chapter XXIV. While a large amount of prophecy is *chronological*, a large amount also is *unconditioned by time*, events being seen in *space*, not in *time*, as stars are seen in the sky; seen, also, aˢ mountains are seen in the landscape. Hence the *Intervals*, revealed by further clearer revelation. So, all standard interpreters of every school agree.

"Sevens Seven, and Sevens Sixty and Two," precisely in the order in which the Angel has placed them, 7+62, are not to be dismissed as vague *"ideals,"* called "Sacred Times," or "World-Weeks," void of all chronological value, but are exact and literal measures of historic time.

B. LOCATION OF THE 70TH WEEK

If now we pass from the consideration of the erroneous method of reckoning the 62 weeks, to that of reckoning the 79th or final week, we shall not fail to discover another source of the perplexities in which, for centuries, interpreters have involved themselves. It is that of making the 70th week immediately sequent upon the 69th, and this in connection with the foregone purpose, *always to bring the 62 weeks, or 69 weeks, up to the Baptism or Death of Christ.* The delusion under which this effort is made, is that the 70th week belongs to the First Advent, and that the death of Christ occurred at its middle point. This denies to the 70th week its eschatological character, and attaches all the events in the Hexad of Dan. ix:24, and which relate to Israel's final Redemption, still future, to our Lord's First Advent. It identifies Christ with Antichrist. It interprets the words," And unto the End shall be war," v. 26, of the Destruction of Jerusalem by Titus, whereas Jerusalem is represented as *already destroyed,* and the words follow, in regular progressive order, the fact of that destruction, as clearly as the 62 follow the 7, and the cutting off follows the 62. *It contradicts our Lord's own exposition of the prophecy of the Interval following Jerusalem's Destruction, Luke xxi:24, and of Israel's final "redemption," Luke xxi:28,* and applies the prophecy, at this point, to the Christian Church, and the removal of the Old Covenant by the establishment of the New.   The false conception, schematized, stands thus :

First Advent.   Second Advent.
                          Times of the Gentiles
(3½ + 3½)———

instead of the true conception, thus :

First Advent.   Second Advent
                          Times of the Gentiles.
———(3½ + 3½)

Hengstenberg, dating the *Motse Davar*, or issuing of a word to restore and build Jerusalem, from B. C. 455, *his* 20th Artaxerxes, and allowing for the 4 years' error in the Dionysian Era, demonstrates victoriously the Messiahship of Jesus to those who fail to see how untenable that 455 date is.* Professor Drummond, of London, declares it is his "one telling argument."   He brings the end of the 69 Weeks up to A. D. 28, then interprets the 70th Week, divided into twice 3½, as immediately sequent on the 69th, the first 3½ being our Lord's ministry, the middle of the week His Crucifixion, the last 3½ *he knows not what!*   He is compelled to confess, with accustomed candor, that he takes the words " to anoint a holy of holies," to mean the unction of Christ by the Spirit, yet assuring us, as is well known, that nowhere in Scripture does a "holy of holies" mean a person, but only a place.   The last 3½ years perplex him, as they did Auberlen, and have done others, and he takes refuge in the invention that these last 3½, or 1260, in Dan. ix:27, as elsewhere, are *"a vanishing point, more or less,"* and *"minute precision is not to be expected"* (*!*)   Champion of "accurate chro-

---

* The alleged accuracy of Hengstenberg's date has been triumphantly disproved by Wieseler, Kleinert, Hofmann, Hitzig, Kliefoth, and many more, notwithstanding his great learning and labor to establish it.   Hengst. Christol. A. T, I. 541.   Wieseler, 70 Wochen, p. 79.   Kleinert, Dorpat. Beitrage II. 1–232.   Hofmann, 70 Jahre, p. 91.   Hitzig and Kliefoth on the texts in their Commentaries on Daniel.

nological precision" from B. C. 455 to A. D. 28, he abandons "precision" at last as a "vanishing point" that dwindles away! Auberlen and Leathes make the last half of the 70th Week equal 35 years, *"more or less,"* just as Professor Briggs, after making the 69 weeks reach to Messiah's Advent, says, "The final week is the *time* of His advent, in the middle of which He is cut off," i. e., cut off in the middle of the *time* of His advent!* Stanley Leathes says, "All after the middle point of the 70th week is foreshortened, and the *time* might be, so far as the language allows, *thirty-five years, or even more.*" (!)† That is, 3½ = 35 ! Drummond justly says of Hengstenberg's "vanishing point, more or less," that "It is a lame suggestion, for the prophet does determine the terminal point of the 70th week, and with precision." ‡ Pusey despairs of proving that the last 3½ years cover the preaching to the Jews, next following the Crucifixion, and adds, " We have not the chronological data to fix it." § The truth is that the last 3½ is "exactly" the size of the first 3½ of the same "One Week," and differs from it not so much as the thickness of a hair's breadth, neither more or less.

And yet, mindful of our own weakness, the power of educational prejudice, and the long struggle needed to *de*-educate ourselves out of an error sanctioned by great names, we may not be too harsh in our judgment on others. There is some palliation, some excuse, for men who are born in a fog. Until recently, the Church has been forced (1) to carry a bad translation of the

---

* Briggs.   Messianic Prophecy, I. 424.
† S. Leathes.   O. T. Prophecy, 286.
‡ Drummond.   Jewish Messiah, 266.
§ Pusey.   Daniel, 170.

Hebrew text in Daniel ix:24-27; (2) to support as bad
an interpretation; (3) to transmute the Israel of Prophecy into the Gentile Christian Church; (4) to expound
the prophecy regardless of the fact that it is the Sabbatic law that rules and shapes the 70 Weeks and its
subdivisions; (5) to delude itself with a false idea of
symbolism; (6) to lack a true view of the organic
structure, analogy, continuity, relation, and development, of all prophecy; (7) to sit blind to the inner connection of our Lord's Olivet Discourse and John's
Apocalypse, with the "Seventy Sevens" in Daniel; (8)
to remain a stranger to the true laws of prophetic representation, and the true development of the Ages and
the Ends.   Let this be the apology for honest but mis-
guided minds.

C.   New Testament Development of the 70th Week

What shall we then say of the 70th week, if it is not
immediately sequent upon the 69th?   Is it only *ideal?*
It is concrete, literal, and real, as are the 62 and the 7
that precede it, and the Interval also, in which we are
now living, and whose end is fast approaching.   The
development of Daniel's prophecy in the New Testament makes this all the more clear.   Just as the Olivet
prediction of the End, spoken by our Lord, *from His
advanced standpoint in history*, developed the Interval
in Dan. ix:26, so does the Apocalypse of John, *from his
own still farther advanced standpoint in history*, develop
the 70th Week.   We have the right, from what we
know of the law of prophecy, to expect this.   History
is the pre-condition of the further unfolding and new
outburst of prophecy, and the great crises in Israel's
history are the great epochs of prophetic evolution.
The importance of knowing this cannot be overrated.

1. When our Lord spake His Olivet word concerning the End, the 69 weeks were already *behind* Him, and He stood within two days of the expiration of the time involved in that word "*After*" in the expression, "*After* those threescore and two weeks shall Messiah be cut off." Dan. ix:26.

> "Two silent nights and days,
> In calmness for His far-seen hour He stays." *

The destruction of Jerusalem was not yet accomplished, but lay still *before* Him, at A. D. 70. He, therefore, *must needs*, when resuming Daniel's prediction which covered the whole time from the return from Exile down to the Second Coming, of which our Lord was about to speak, foretell Jerusalem's fall, as Daniel had told it, Dan. ix:26, and go on to *open out* the Interval following the same, precisely where the Angel speaking to Daniel, had placed it. Dan. ix:26; Luke xxi:24. It behoved Him, in few words, to also touch on the End, of which the Angel spoke, the final week. This is precisely what He did in Luke xxi:28, saying, "When ye see these things, Lift up your heads, for your *redemption* draweth nigh!" that very *redemption* foretold to come at the close of the 70th Week in Dan. ix:24. Perspectively viewing, *as one*, the Jewish-Christian Church, or Israel, of His own time, with the Jewish Christian Church to be formed under the testimony of the Two Witnesses in the End-Time, He declared that this "*Genea*" shall not pass away till all his words be fulfilled, and, by that promise, secured the indestructible and unamalgamated continuance of the "Jewish race" down to His own Second Coming. Hengstenberg himself, as Riehm rightly observes, admits that, in the

---

* Keble. Christian Year. Monday before Easter.

Olivet Prophecy, our Lord followed the law of prophetic representation found in the Old Testament prophets, and all the more so, since the disciples had asked a *double* question which needed a *double* answer, and in which the falling and rising again of Jerusalem and the Jewish nation were most intimately involved, as they were in the prophets themselves. He blended the near and the far horizons in one, in the same picture of the future. He looked, in a right line, through Jerusalem here, to Jerusalem there, and both were covered by His *Parousia*. "The Olivet prediction," says Riehm, "is like that in Daniel ix:24-27, in that *both group together and represent, as continuous, events in themselves, separated by wide spaces of time.*" * That is the very reason why the 7+62+1, though grouped closely, are yet *separated* in fulfilment by spaces of time between them. Ever since the days of Velthusen, this great law of prophetic perspective has been emphasized by the best interpreters, and Delitzsch has summed it up in a brief but clear expression : *"All prophecy is complex, i. e., it sees together what history outrolls as separate; and All prophecy is apotelesmatic, i. e., it sees close behind the nearest-coming, epoch-making turn in history, the summit of the End."* † So did Daniel in ix:24-27, the prophecy of the Seventy Weeks. So did Jesus, resuming and enlarging on Daniel, represent his Parousia and Jerusalem's destruction, as one, yet also Jerusalem's final deliverance. It is the wisdom of God—not to deceive,—but to preserve and quicken the expectation of the Second Coming of Jesus in every great event connected with Israel's history, and make Hope "spring eternal in the human breast." Prophecy moves on progressively, the later

---

* Riehm. Messianic Prophecy, 17.
† Delitzsch in Herzog. Real. Encyc. III, 286.

prophet resuming the former, and weaving into the web new matter at the point where the earlier had dropped his thread. Or, to change the figure, the 70 Weeks of Daniel are the original frame of our Lord's Olivet Discourse, onward from the end of the clause beginning with *"After"* in Dan. ix:26, i. e., from the close of the "Sevens Sixty and Two."   This is enough of itself to refute Dr. Kliefoth's aphorism that " *Symbolical numbers don't count.*" *

2.   Again, when John wrote the Apocalypse, A. D. 96, the Destruction of Jerusalem predicted by both Daniel and our Lord already lay *behind* him, by the distance of a full generation.   His historic standpoint was more advanced than that of our Lord, for history had made progress.   It was impossible that John's Apocalypse should predict the fall of Jerusalem, as the higher critics and some others, fond of the Nero Fable, say it does.   Far from his mind was the thought that Jerusalem should forever sink out of sight, and Rome arise a Christian City, the center of the world.   No! but Rome, New Babylon, *christianized,* should go down in the dust at the End of the Days, under Antichrist's blow, and Jerusalem, long down-trodden, shall rise from beneath the Gentile heel, shake off her chains, be redeemed with judgment, and shine as the central glory of the coming age.   De Wette saw that in 1852.   Not only were Messiah's death and Jerusalem's fall, and the "After" and 69 Weeks, *behind* the Seer of Patmos when, like prophets of old, he saw the visions of God, but well nigh 30 years of the Great Interval itself, named in Dan. ix:26, and Luke xxi:24, had passed away!

---

* He is compelled to refute it himself! "Moreover," says he, "the One Week *counts; it comes after* the 62 Sevens."   Uebrigens *zæhlt* das Echad: es kommt *nach* den 62 Siebenheiten."   *Das Buch Daniel's,* 376.

What remained of Daniel's prophecy, *unfulfilled at that time*, was to be resumed and further unfolded by the beloved disciple.   And what remained was (1) the remainder of the Interval itself described in Daniel in the expression "And *unto* the End," viz., the remainder of the "Times of the Gentiles," and (2) the *End* of those times, i. e., the 70th week.   And this is precisely what he did, the same "Spirit of Prophecy" who knows all things, and "moved" all holy men who wrote prophecy, guiding John, as he had guided our Lord and Daniel. It is for this reason we find in the Apocalypse (1) Our present dispensation, drawn in the 7 Epistles to the 7 Churches of Asia, chapters I–III, and (2) the End-Time itself, or 70th Week, divided, as in Daniel, into twice 3½ years, or twice 1260 days; the first 3½ covering the 6 Seals and 6 Trumpets, and the testimony of the Two Witnesses; the second 3½ covering the 7th Trumpet or 7 Vials, and the "Great Tribulation," the whole "One Week" of Daniel thus developed in John, and covering the contents of the Seven Sealed Scroll, closing with the Second Coming of Christ from "Heaven Opened," chapter IV–XIX.   It is the " Day of the Lord," or "Apocalypse of Jesus Christ" in judgment.   And, so far as regards Israel, it is precisely what Moses and the Prophets, and our Lord and His Apostles, did say should come to pass.   Compound myopic hypertropic stigmatism could hardly fail to see it, the light is so clear.   It is bright as the all-beholding circle of the Sun, unflecked by a spot, and undimmed, at noon, by a cloud.   The organic unity of the Three Great Predictions of Daniel, Christ, and John, is such as Science, proud of its doctrines of consanguinity, common descent, embryonic development, homology, and homogeneity, would be glad to hail, and to own!   In all these three great predictions concerning Israel, the Subject is the same (Israel), the Times the same (3½ 3½), the Enemy the same (Antichrist), the Place the same (Palestine), the Result and End the same (Israel's Redemption), and, therefore, the predictions the same, each enlarging on the other, the last the full picture of which the first was the general sketch. Can any one doubt what our Lord meant when He said, "This *Genea* shall not pass away till *all* these things be fulfilled?' He meant the "*Jewish Race !* *

D. The Great Prophecies Schematized

The great importance of this discussion justifies our lingering a moment longer on the organic relations of these mighty predictions. First of all a preliminary word.

The Prophecy of Daniel

The Colossus-Prediction, Dan. ii:33-35, 41-45, provides the first prophetic frame, or outline for the whole subsequent development of the World-Power and Israel's relation thereto, down to the Second Advent, and setting up of the Kingdom of Christ in outward glory on the earth. The vision reaches to the tenfold divided state of the Roman territory, the Ten Toes, and there it stops, ii:24. This is far beyond the time of Augustus.

The Beast-Prediction is the same truth under new forms, and from another point of view. Man's view of the Gentile Kingdom and Nations, is that they are the concentration of all material civilization, wealth and power. God's view is that they are predacious beasts,

---

* So Dorner, Hofmann, Delitzsch, Stier, Auberlen, Kliefoth, Küper, Volck, Schm dt, Schultze, Grau, Zockler, Rinck, Koch, Christiani, Luthardt, Hebart, etc., etc., "*Das Judische Volk als Solches; the Jewish People as such.*"

devouring one another. The Ten Horns answer to the Ten Toes, the Horns being, however, confederate under One Horn, an 11th, the last Gentile Ruler over Israel, and who perishes under a stroke from the Son of Man, coming in the Clouds of Heaven. vii:7-14; 19-27. Israel is triumphant.

The Prophecy of the Greek or Third Empire, and Israel's relation to it, gives us the Syrian Antichrist, Antiochus Epiphanes, the type of the last and Roman Antichrist, or Little Horn of the fourth Empire, Dan. viii:9-14; 19-27. Israel again, passing through the fires, comes out triumphant.

The Prophecy of the Seventy Sevens, again sweeps the vast future, giving us the relation of Israel to the Gentile power, from the Return from Exile, under Cyrus, down to the Second Coming of Christ. Three separate and independent periods of time, measured by the law of the "Seven," with fixed Intervals between the Sevens, subdivide the whole line of history, and include both Advents, as also Christ aud Antichrist. Again, Israel having been rejected, is recalled, and passing through the Great Tribulation under Antichrist in the last half of the last decreed "Sevens," comes out triumphant.

The Prophecy of the Second and Third Empires,—i. e., Persian and Grecian, runs over these rapidly, and displays the *Wars of the Ptolemies and Seleucids*, and times of *Antiochus Epiphanes*, until, at length, by a quick flight, overleaping all intervening time, the *type* Antiochus glides insensibly and melts into the *antitype* the last *Antichrist*, xi:41-45, who perishes " without hand," i. e., miraculously, while Israel's faithful living are spared, and faithful dead are raised, xii:1-3. Hovering over the Tigris, one saint tells another that the Tribulation shall continue only during the last half of the 70th Week, 1260 days, or 3½ times, and come to an end when Antichrist's power is broken. Then the Blessed time will come. Again Israel is triumphant.

And this is what Daniel gives us. Everything tends to, and concentrates itself in, the awful struggle, and the glorious issue, of the final Week. We have the Outline or Frame of that Week clearly before us, in its two equal parts, and we shall see how it is the *Basis* for our Lord's Olivet Discourse, and for John's Apocalypse. This prophetic frame of the 70th Week, in Daniel, is as follows :

I. THE ONE WEEK IN DANIEL.
(Dan. ix: 27).

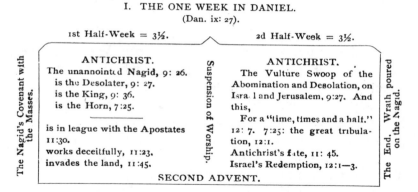

1st Half-Week = 3½.   2d Half-Week = 3½.

The Nagid's Covenant with the Masses.

ANTICHRIST.
The unannointed Nagid, 9: 26.
is the Desolater, 9: 27.
is the King, 9: 36.
is the Horn, 7:25.

is in league with the Apostates 11:30.
works deceitfully, 11:23.
invades the land, 11:45.

Suspension of Worship.

ANTICHRIST.
The Vulture Swoop of the Abomination and Desolation, on Israel and Jerusalem, 9:27. And this,
For a "time, times and a half." 12: 7. 7:25: the great tribulation, 12:1.
Antichrist's fate, 11: 45.
Israel's Redemption, 12:1—3.

The End., Wrath poured on the Nagid.

SECOND ADVENT.

Such is the *general frame*, or first brief outline of the 70th week, as given by the revealing Angel to Daniel. It is plain, clear, simple. The scene is in Jerusalem. And *"Israel"* does not mean the New Testament Church, but Daniel's people, and the "*City*" does not mean Christendom, but Jerusalem, first destroyed A. D. 70, then redeemed at last.

What a misinterpretation, big as all the geometrical dimensions, it is to refer this 70th Week to Christ and the First Advent, when it belongs to Antichrist and the

Second Advent! The grammatical and logical subject of the verb "shall make strong," **v. 27**, is not "Prince Messiah," but the "prince that shall come."

II.   THE PROPHECY OF OUR LORD.

(Matt. xxiv, and parallels.)

THE ONE WEEK.

| 1st Half Week = 3½. | | 2d Half Week = 3½. |

| Mock Messiahs coming. Matth. 24: 5. | "The Beginning of Sorrows." Matth. 24: 7, 8, and parallels. These events are figured in Apoc. chapter VI. Six Seals.

A time of tribulation. Matth. 24: 9—14. These in Apoc. VIII—XI. 14. The Six Trumpets.

False Messiahs and False Prophets. Wonders, Signs, Deceivings, Persecutions, &c. | The Abomination of Desolation. Matth. 24: 15. | "The Great Tribulation," Matth. 24: 15—28.

The Shortened Days for the elect's sake. Matt. 24: 22.

Tokens of the Advent. Matth. 24: 29.

Israel's gathering and Redemption. Matt. 24: 31. Luke 21: 28. | End of the Times of the Gentiles. Luke 21: 24. |

SECOND ADVENT.

Such the *frame* and *filling* of the 70th Week in the Olivet Prophecy, a *double* prophecy, which looks, perspectively, through Jerusalem of A. D. 70 to Jerusalem of the End-Time, and covers both the near and far horizons in its minute yet great and comprehensive expressions. As in the prophetic representation in Daniel, Antiochus insensibly glides into the last Antichrist, so here, Jerusalem and Israel of A. D. 70, glide into Jerusalem and Israel of the End-Time. The *Parousia* or *Advent* of the Lord, at the End of our own Age, is seen through the Judgment on Jerusalem at the End of the Jewish age, A. D. 70, which was itself only the Beginning of the War and Desolations decreed, Dan. ix:26, "unto the End." Remembering the double reference of the Olivet Discourse, the Tribulation for Israel, as a nation, *begins*, in its wide sense, with the Roman destruction of Jerusalem, and runs to the 70th Week, swelling to its fulness, in its last and strictest sense, during the last 3½ years. Then, "*immediately after those days*," are the tokens of the Advent. Matt. xxiv: 29. Then Israel is redeemed. Luke xxi:28. The Millennial Age dawns, for "*Summer is nigh*," and the "*Kingdom of God is nigh.*" Luke xxi:30, 31.

III. THE APOCALYPSE OF JOHN.
(Chapter VI—XX, 7.)
THE ONE WEEK.

	1st Half-Week = 3½.		2d Half-Week = 3½.	
Parousia of Antichrist. Rider in first Seal. Rev. vi:2.	1,260 days, 42 months. These are in Rev. xi:3, 7. Chapter VI—XI, 14. The Six Seals and Six Trumpets. The "Beginning of Sorrows," in Matt. xxiv:7, 8. The 144,000 sealed, vii:1-8. A time of tribulation, Matt. xxiv:9-14; Rev. vi:10; vii:14. False Messiah, and False Prophet, Wonders, Signs, Deceivings, Persecutions, War, Famine, Death, vi:1-17. Beast, Apollyon, Two Witnesses slain. Jewish Church formed. ix:11. xi:7. The Great Earthquake in Jerusalem, Rev. xi:13. The 1-10 of the City falls. 7,000 perish.	Abomination of Desolation. Beast at his height of power. Scenes in Jerusalem. xi:7-14. supreme.	1,260 days, 42 months. These are in Rev. xi:2. xii:6,14. xiii:5. Chapter XII—XX, 7. The Seventh Trumpet with the Seven Vials. The "Great Tribulation." Michael stands up. Conversion of Israel. Rev. xii:10, 11. The 144,000 safe on the earthly Mount Zion, with their Redeemer. Rev. xiv:1-5. Israel victorious. xv:2-4. Armageddon, The Slaughter, Antichrist destroyed, Jerusalem delivered. Rev. xvi:16. xiv:20. xix:11-21. All occurring at	The End. Parousia of Christ. Diademed Rider. Rev. xix:11.

THE SECOND ADVENT, WITH
THE FIRST RESURRECTION,
THE BINDING OF SATAN,
followed by
THE THOUSAND YEARS.

Such the *frame* and the *filling* of the 70th Week in John; the whole content of the Seven-Sealed Scroll. It is identical with that in Daniel and the Olivet discourse. The filling is complete, as becomes the last representation of "the mystery of God" foreshown to the prophets. The Olivet discourse was supplementary to Daniel's prediction of the 70 weeks. John's Apocalypse, in like manner, is supplementary to both. In the beautiful words of Professor Van Oosterzee, when speaking of the contributions of the successive prophets to the great picture of the future, "*Every prophet adds his own touch to it, until, after sufficient elaboration, the painters all withdraw, and the curtain falls."* * So is it here; Daniel first, Christ next, John last, all work, with more than a Raphael's power, on the *Great Scenes of the 70th Week*, each supplying his own touch, until it stands and glows complete, at last, as the Holy Spirit meant to leave it. One day, ere long, it will all be translated into actual history. What Daniel condenses in a *single verse*, Dan. ix:27, John enlarges, as by a magic lantern, to *sixteen chapters*, Rev. IV—XX. Paul embraces the same 70th Week in a single verse, also, in II Thess, ii: 8, its *two termini*, there, being (a) the *Parousia* of Antichrist, and (b) the *Parousia* of Christ, this same week bounded, in the Apocalypse, by the Mock-Messiah on the White Horse of the first seal, the last imperial head of Rome revived, Rev. vi:2, and the diademed True Messiah on the White Horse of the 7th Vial in Rev. xix:11;—the former the *un*anointed Nagid, in Dan. ix:26, invading the land, Isa. lix:19, the latter the *Anointed* Nagid in Dan. ix:25, spoiling the invader! And so we come to the *"End;"* the long-predicted, long-expected *"End."*

E.   THE END OF THE 70TH WEEK

And how magnificent an End it is, not merely ideal, but real! It is the End of the 70th Week, and crowded with marvels such as could only occur in a great bisecting epoch in history, as heralds of a new and glorious age. It is the End of the "Seven Times" of Moses, Levit. xxvi:28 ; the End of the Times of the Stonestruck Colossus, Dan. ii:35 ; the End of Israel's national Grave-Yard in which the Colossus still stands upon Israel's bones, Ezek. xxxvii:1–14, Rom. xi:15, Rev. xi:11;

---

* Person of the Redeemer. 104.

the End of the Great Interval or "Times of the Gentiles," Luke xxi:24; the End of Hosea's "Many Days"
of Israel's lone abiding, Hos. iii:3–5, and of Hosea's
"Two Days" of Israel's national death, Hos. vi:2; the
End of Israel's national apostasy, or finishing of Israel's
national transgression, Dan. ix:24; the End of the
Lord's indignation against the chosen people, Dan. viii:
19, 26; xii:7–13; the End of the desolation and the down-
treading of the Holy City by Gentile power, Dan. ix:
26, 27; Luke xxi:24. Isa. lx:1; the End of the *Diaspora*,
Isa. xi:11–16; xlix:22; lxvi:20; Zeph. iii:9, 10; Ezek.
xxxvii:21, 22; and Matt. xxiv;31, compared with Isa.
xxvii:12, 13; xix:23-25, and Rev. x:7; the End of the
Western Papal Antichrist, the Ghetto and the Vatican,
involved in Dan. vii:25; the End of the Eastern Islam Antichrist, and his Mosques Al Aska and Kubhat-as-Sakra,
resting on Zion, shrines of the adorers of "Allah Ma-
huzzim" shadowed in Dan. xi:36–45; the End of the Last
Antichrist, the *"Little Horn"* of the 4th Empire, in Dan.
vii:26, the *"Nagid Habba"* and *"Meshomem"* in Dan. ix:
26, 27, John's" *Beast*," "*8th Head*," the *Mock Messiah* in the
first Apocalyptic seal, Rev. vi:2, the "*Enemy*" invading
the land of Palestine and bent on universal conquest, Isa.
lix:19, 20, Paul's *"Man of sin,"* II Thess. ii:8; "*that
Wicked*" in Isa. xi:4; ruined at the Appearing of Christ,
Rev. xi:11–21; the End of the Great Tribulation, or
second half of the final Week, Dan. xii:1; vii:25; xii:7;
Rev. x:7; xiii:5; the End of the 1260, 1290, 1335 days;
the End of War, Isa. ii:4; Mic. iv:3; Ps. lxxii:7; the
End of Satan's constant accusation of God's people,
Rev. xii:10, and of his world-wide perambulation, Rev.
xii:7–11; xx:1; the End of the blinding veil on Israel's
heart, Rom. xi:25–31; II Cor. iii:13–16; the End of the
same veil now spread over all nations, Isa. xxv:7; Rev.

xv:4; the End of Christ's sojourn in heaven, Acts iii:19-21; Heb. ix:28; the End of Death's empire over the sleeping saints, Ps. xlix:14, 15; Hos. xiii:14; Isa. xxvi:19; Ezek. xxxvii:12 ; Dan. xii:1-3 ; Rom. viii:23; I Cor. xv: 23; I Thess. iv:12-18; Rev. xi:18; xx:4 ! In short, the End of the 70th Week is the End of our present Age, Matt. xxiv:14; a glorious End of Israel's woes, bringing the six great events in Dan. ix:24; the time when *"Lo Ammi"* and *"Lo Ruhamah"* will be said no more, and *"Ishi"* will be whispered, and not the ambiguous word *"Baali,"* Hos. i:8, 9; ii:14-23; the End when Zion shall no more be called *"Azubah,"* but *"Hephzibah;"* her land no more *"Shemamah,"* but *"Beulah;"* Jerusalem's names *"Derushah"* and *"Ir-Lo-Ne'ezabah,"* and her people,—"the ones expecting Jehovah,"—shall be dignified as *"Am Hakkodesh,"* the " Holy People," and *"Geulei Yehovah,"* the "Redeemed of the Lord !" Isa. lxii:4, 12; xl:31,—Glorious End it is for Israel!—the End of divorce, and widowhood, and death, when, as a young man marries a virgin, so Jerusalem's sons shall marry her again, and when, as a Bridegroom rejoices over his Bride, so the Lord will rejoice over her again; a double rapture, a double joy, Isa. lxii:5, the Lord himself "singing," and "silent in His love!" Zeph. iii:17. It is the End when the great Harlot is swathed in flame and sinks in the sea, and the greater Bride is arrayed in white and sits on a throne, Rev. xvii:16; ii:27; iii:21. It is the End when the Wedding has come, and the *"Hallel"* is sung ; the opening of the great Sabbatic Jubilee of Jubilees, along whose centuries the words go ringing *"Hallelu-Jah! for the Lord God Omnipotent reigneth!"* Rev. xix:6. The *"Kingdom"* has come, the Millennial Age, for *the End of the 70th Week is the Beginning of "the 1000 years!"*

F.   THE 2,300, 1,290 AND 1,335 DAYS

The 2300 evening-mornings of the Syrian Anti-christ's relation to the holy people, require but a brief discussion.   Daniel, in his vision at Shushan, while in the body at Babylon, beheld, under the figures of the *Ram* and *He-Goat*, the passing away of the scepters of Persia and Greece, and the rise of the Diadochian kingdoms into which the empire of Alexander was divided, Dan. viii:9–14.   Out of *one of these four* sprung from the 3d Empire, he saw a "Little Horn," *Antiochus Epiphanes*, waxing to greatness, southward, eastward, and into "the glorious land" of Palestine.   Self-exalting, it vaunted itself against the holy people and their rulers, "the host and the stars."   It overthrew and stamped upon them, and magnified itself even against God, the "Prince of princes," v. 25.   It abolished the Jewish worship, taking away the *Thamid*, or "*Established*," the "*Daily*," i. e., the morning and evening sacrifice and offering, and the whole Jewish cult as instituted by the law of Moses.   It "cast down the place of the Sanctuary," which God allowed to be trodden under foot because of Israel's apostasy.   One of the wonders was that "a host was given over" into its hands, along with the *Thamid*, by reason of apostasy, a large mass of Israel surrendered to the power of the Syrian Anti-Messiah who abolished everything that typified the true Messiah, and so, with the Jews themselves at his back, this *Miles Gloriosus* went on, like a revolutionary field-marshal, destroying the walls of the city, profaning the temple, placing in the sanctuary the statue of the Olympian Jove, and the Swine abomination, and, casting down the "*Truth*," burning the Sacred Books, as well as annulling the Sacred Worship, and, setting up old heathenism in its stead, practised and prospered, and did as he listed. The full account of all this we have in the books of the Maccabees. That this Horn into which the *four-parted* 3d empire runs out, is the *"Melek"* or *"King"* in Daniel, chapter XI, 29, 30, and *type* of the Horn into which the *ten-parted* 4th empire runs out, is undisputed. And that this *type*, Antiochus, glides insensibly, by a law of prophetic representation, into the *antitype*, the last Antichrist, the end of the 3d empire and the end of the 4th empire melting together in one, and seen in one, in Dan. xi:36–45; xii:1–7, is acknowledged by the best expositors. The description of Antiochus, in xi:21–35, is only the elaboration of the same Antiochus in viii:9–12; 23–25.

As Daniel went on gazing at the Horn's progress, he heard a holy one speaking, a certain saint saying to *Palmoni*, the *Wonderful Numberer*, *"How long shall be the vision* (as to) *the Thamid? How long* (as to) *the transgression desolating?"* (i. e., as to the taking away of the *Thamid* and setting up the Abomination), *and how long* (as to) *the giving both the people and the sanctuary a downtreading?"* viii:13, 14. The answer is, *" Unto evening-morning* 2300: *and the sanctuary shall be cleansed,"* v. 14. The *a quo* of the 2300 is some point anterior to the actual taking away of the *Thamid*, and plainly concerns its temporary continuance under the "craft and policy" of the Horn, in connection with the apostates, viii:25 ; xi:28, 30, 32. The *ad quem* is *not* "the cleansing of the sanctuary," as is generally supposed, but the end of the desolating transgression, or abomination, and of the downtreading of the people and the sanctuary, i e., of Jerusalem; in short, it is the end of the career of Antiochus. The word *"then"* in both King James' and the Revised English Version is an interpolation by the translators. It is not in the text. Palmoni does not say " Unto evening-morning 2300, *then* shall the sanctuary be cleansed," but " Unto evening-morning 2300: *and* the sanctuary shall be cleansed ; " and the Masorites have put an *Athnach* or *Colon* at the end of the 2300, just as they put the same at the end of the 7 Sevens, in ix:25. The end of the career of Antiochus in his relation to the Sanctuary and the people, was not the time of the Cleansing of the sanctuary, which was a month later, as we shall see.

Various have been the reckonings of the 2300 in this prediction, and none of the possibilities supplied by the history of the times of Antiochus and the Maccabees, have remained untried. The dispute is whether the expression *"evening morning," "Ereb-Boker,"* denotes a *whole* day of 24 hours, and the 2300 to be so counted, or whether it makes *two half days*, referring to the evening and morning sacrifice which Antiochus was to take away, so that the 2300 can only be counted as 1150 whole days. Scholars are divided here. Delitzsch, Wieseler, Hitzig, Kliefoth, decide in favor of 2300 *half* days, i. e., 1150 *whole* days. Hœvernick, Gesenius, Maurer, Auberlen, the older Christian, and the Jewish, Commentators, decide for 2300 *whole* days, or 6 years, 3 months, 20 days, prophetic time ; the phrase *"Ereb-Boker," " Evening-Morning,"* being the Jewish mode of designating a day of 24 hours, as when it is said, "And there was a *mingling (Ereb)*, and there was a *bursting forth (Boker),"*—i. e., a *twilight, followed* by night, and a *sunrise,* followed by day, extending to twilight again, —*"Day One."* Gen. i:5, 8, 19, 23, 31. In either case, however, 6 years, 4 months, 20 days, or 3 years, 2 months, 10 days, the 2300, and 1150, are less than *"One Seven"* of years, or *"Half of that Seven;"* in the one case

by 220, in the other by 110, days.   We decide for the
2300 *whole* days.

The *dates* of the vision of the Evening-Mornings, and
also of the Prophecy of the Seventy Weeks, are the
same, viz., 3d Belshazzar, i. e., 1st Darius the Mede as
King over Babylon, for this was the year, viz., B. C
538, when Cyrus took Babylon, delegating its government to Darius, and consequently was the year of Belshazzar's death, Dan. viii:1; ix:1; v:1, 31, i. e. the *second
year before* the Edict of Cyrus, releasing the captives
was issued.   In this year Daniel saw the vision of the
2300 evening-mornings, and was "astonished," not understanding it, "neither was there any one to cause him
to understand." viii:27. He fasted, and prayed, and
Gabriel came to bring him understanding of the vision,
by means of the Prophecy of the 70 Weeks. The 70
Weeks are an explanation, however, not only of the
2300 evening mornings, and Antiochus in his relation to
the End-Time, but a revelation, or vision also (*Mareh*)
of the whole future, of which the evening-morning
vision is an organic part; an unfolding of the *whole
mystery of God* concerning Israel and the Nations, down
to the sounding of the 7th trumpet. The vision of the
"Little Horn" of the 3d empire perplexed the prophet,
for other visions had told him of righteousness, peace,
salvation, a kingdom and glory for Israel, at the close
of the 4th empire, all earthly powers giving way. But
now, the almost total ruin of Israel restored, and of rebuilt Jerusalem and the Temple, under the 3d Empire,
in the times of Antiochus, confounded him. Must the
rebuilt City and Temple be assailed, and the Jewish
Worship suspended, and restored Israel again trans-
gress, *before Messiah comes to His people?*   The Angel
explains the *whole* matter now by unveiling the entire
future, in the prophecy of the 70 Weeks.

It was a part of the *ruddering*, foretold by the Angel to occur in the last days, that a sainted man, Mr. Miller, "erring about," and misled by crude pilots on the prophetic waters, maintained that, because, in the words of Gabriel, "I am now come to tell thee, therefore meditate *in the matter*, and understand *in the vision*," Dan. ix:23, the words *"the* vision" refer to the Evening-Morning vision which so greatly perplexed him, *therefore* the 70 Sevens, were 490 *years cut off, and cut out, from the* 2300 *Evening-Mornings*, which Mr. Miller's *"Year - Day - Theory"* taught him to regard *as* 2300 *years!* The fatal results of that misconception, and the prejudice excited' against prophetic study; are not forgotten, nor yet obviated, while still the same error is repeated and republished by a certain class of expositors, to the great injury of the truth. The year-day theory is, by the best and ablest scholars, repudiated as an invention unsupported by the word of God, nor is it needed to vindicate Protestantism nor the sublime doctrine of the constitution of all history and prophecy, under the law of proportionate cycles of time, larger and smaller. *The* 490 *years are not cut off from any* 2300 *years of any kind.* On the contrary, the 2300 evening-mornings, or 6 years, 4 months, 20 days, of the times of Antiochus, are a solid *part* of the 490 years, or 70 Sevens. They belong to the 3d, or Greek, empire in its four-parted condition, and are *included in the* 62 *Sevens* from 34th Artaxerxes to Christ, as any accurate interpreter must know. They lie between B. C. 176 and 164, the times of Antiochus, the Syrian Horn. They are not the times of Hildebrand or Leo. They fall in the 45th of the 70 Sevens, and are not cut off from the same.

While, however, the 2300 belong to the 45th Seven

in the past, they point *typically* to, and foreshadow, the 70th Seven in the future.   Their relation to the "*One Week*" in Dan. ix:25, is direct.   Seen from the prophet's standpoint, they lie in a right line, perspectively, with the times of the last Antichrist.   The prophet looks through them in vision, into their place in the 70 Weeks, first of all in the times of Antiochus, and next in the times of the last Antichrist.   In the words of Delitzsch, "Daniel perceives, in prophetic perspective, the *time of the End together with the time of Antiochus.*" The two visions are parts of one vast complex proph- ecy, which spans the ages, and looks to the Second Coming of Christ, and Israel's Redemption.   While it is of supreme importance not to identify the Little Horn of the 3d empire with the Little Horn of the 4th empire, lest the Messianic interpretation of the 70 Weeks be negated, it is no less important to recognize the organic relation of the one to the other, of Anti- ochus the "*Melek*," viii:36, to Antichrist the "*Nagid*," ix:27, and that the End of the 3d empire is a type of the End of the 4th empire, all ends being *one* end, and all ages *one* age, in prophecy, self-multiplying into a *series* of ends and ages, in regular advancing organism, and reaching to the final consummation, all persons and things preceding being types of all persons and things succeeding, and seen so, not less in Antichrist than in Christ.   That the last Antichrist makes a covenant with the Jewish masses in their own land, and chiefly in Jerusalem, in the last days, is plainly revealed, Dan, ix:27 ; xi:30, and underlies the whole representation in John's Apocalypse, Rev. chapter XI.*   It is then the

---

*It is not improper to add, here, a note in reference to Antichrist's "*Covenant*," or "*Treaty*," and which should have been inserted at p. 118.
    The common view held by Hengstenberg, Auberlen, Leathes, and all who regard the 70 Weeks as belonging to the time of the crucifixion, is that

"Two Witnesses" testify. That the Sacrifices are restored in pursuance of this covenant, and administered, for a time, under the "policy" of Antichrist, is as clear as that, in the middle of the Week, he "causes the Sacrifice and Offering to cease," and "changes times and laws," inaugurating a worship of his own, xi:31; vii:25; ix:27. The question that evoked Palmoni's answer, settles this. It is a threefold question in one: "How long (as to) the *Thamid?* How long (as to) *taking away* of the Thamid, and existence of the Abomination? How long (as to) the *Downtreading* of Jerusalem?" It is a question as to *Continuance* and *Discontinuance*, under the "craft and policy" of the Horn, and the permission of God. The Answer is "Unto evening-morning, 2300;" not Unto the Whole 7 years, or full "One Week," but "Unto 6 years, 4 months, 20 days," i. e., "Unto 2300 days."

It is not difficult to see the 2300 days here *set in* the frame of the 70th Week, the One Week, or 7 years, being 2520 days. We know tho duration of the downtreading. It is 1260 days, the last half of the One Week, or from the taking away of the *Thamid* in the

---

Christ confirms the New Covenant with many, one Week, and Isa. xxxiii:11 is quoted to support the view. It is also asserted that there cannot be a *"Berith,"*—*"Covenant,"*—without sacrifice, that *"Higbir Berith"* means to confirm the covenant in Christ's blood. and that the *"many"* are believers, Jews and Gentiles. Hofmann, Ewald, Wieseler, Bleek, Maurer, Gesenius, Hävernick, Füller, all translate *"make a firm, or strong, covenant,"* contrary to Fuerst and Hitzig who say *"make grievous or hard;"* and deny that *"Higbir"* means to *"confirm."* So the Revisers. Some, like Auberlen, make the *"One Week"* the subject of the verb. This is impossible, grammatically. The *Accusative of time how long,* can never be the *Nominative* to a Verb. Contrary to Auberlen and others, the subject of the verb "make strong" is not Antiochus, nor Christ, but the "prince that shall come." Contrary to Ewald, Wieseler and Ebrard. who hold that the "*Many*" are *Gentile* believers, after the Crucifixion, with whom Christ makes a firm Covenant, they are the *apostate Jewish masses* of the End-Time in alliance with Antichrist. See Matt. xxiv:12 ; Dan. xi:30, 32, 34, 45; II Thess. ii:8–10; Rev. xi:2. So Kliefoth Volck, Koch, Godet, Hofmann, Tregelles, and

middle of the week, unto the End of the Week, ix:27.
It is the time of the giving of the host and sanctuary to
be trodden down by the forces of Antichrist.   It is 3½
years or 1260 days, vii:25; Rev. xiii:5; the *half seven*, of
ix:27.   It is during this period he prevails to break the
power of the Holy People.   Dan. xii:7; vii:25.   This
disposes of the last 1260 days of the 2300, leaving 1040
still, the 1260 being the period of *Discontinuance* of the
Thamid, the 1040 being the period of its *Continuance*
under the sanction of Antichrist during a portion of
the first 1260, or from the time of the *first administration* of the restored Jewish worship to the time of its
cessation in the *middle* of the week.   And this disposes of the entire 2300 (1260+1040=2300.)   The One
Week is 2520 days.   The *difference* between 2520 and
2300 is 220 days, or 7 months and 10 days are needed
to complete the One Week.   This initial part (not
asked after in the vision, nor needed to be asked for
in the times of Antiochus, when the Jewish worship already was established, but required in the times of Antichrist and his covenant with the Jews when about to

---

all who refer to the 70th Week, the End-Time, save Christiani, etc., who
think it may mean confirming the covenant with the *Jewish-Christian
Church* then formed, Rev. xi:1, forgetting that Christ never confirms the
covenant merely for " *One Week.*" Auberlen, Hitzig, and others, affirm
that "*Berith*" can mean nothing else than the "Covenant of *God*," and not
of man with man, and that it never means a *treaty* in Daniel   On the contrary, Jonathan made a *Berith* with David. I Sam. xxiii:18, Ahab with Ben-
hadad, I Kings xx:34. Ephraim with Assyria, Hos. xii:1. Jehoida with the
Carites, II Kings xi:4, the Jews with Death, Isa. xxvii[i]:18.   And in Daniel
Antiochus makes a *Berith* with Ptolemy Philometer, xi:22, who is plainly the
"*Nagid Berith*," or "prince of the covenant,"—the formal league or tre ty
referred to in the following verse as "*hith-habberuth*," a "*treaty concluded*"
between Antiochus and Philometer.   So Gesenius, Ewald. Kliefoth, Ebrard,
Maurer, Volck, etc., etc.   In like manner, in Dan. ix:27, the "Covenant"
the Nagid enacts with the ' many," is an alliance between the last Antichrist and the Jewish masses by which their Worship is restored.   Doubtless they will worship the Nagid as "*Baal-Berith*," " lord of the covenant."
Judges viii:33, and call him "*El-Berith*," " God of the Covenant," Judges
ix:46, their covenant God !

re-institute their Worship,) can only be the period between the *enactment* of that covenant at the beginning
of the 70th Week, and the *first celebration* of the sacri-
ficial worship in pursuance of that covenant; i. e., 7
months and ten days are the period of the completing
of the rebuilt temple, and the preparation for its
formal dedication. It is not possible to think of the
Jews returning from their dispersion and long captivity, under the favor of some European, and perhaps of some Asiatic powers, and not rebuilding their
temple, nor re-instating Mosaism. Thus we have the
220+1040+1260=2520, the foreshadowing times of
Antiochus seen in the times of Antichrist; the 70th
Week of the 70 Weeks filled out, and so can see the
organism, harmony, perfection, and unity of all
prophecy.

The 2300, like the 1260, stand related to two other
measures of literal time, viz., the 1290 and 1335 days.
Dan. xii:11, 12.* How long *after* Antichrist's power

---

* *The destruction of Antichrist's power is the ad quem of the* 1260 *days.*
There is a difference as to the rendering of the answer to the question in xii:
6. Some render it, "When the *Dispersion* of a *part* of the holy people shall
have been *completed*." Others, "When the *Breaking in pieces* the *power*
of the holy people shall have been *finished*." The Revisors render it,
"When *they* have made an end of breaking in pieces the power of the holy
people." Hitzig, Lengerke, Gesenius, (last edition Lex.), in a Maccabean
interest, say, "*Dispersion*," "*part*," "*completed*." All others say, "*Breaking in pieces*," "*power*," "*consummated*." The spiritualizers and idealizers
say, that the "holy people" mean "*all Christians!*" or the "whole New
Testament Church!" The rationalists, as foolishly say, the "holy people"
mean Israel under the Maccabees! The oppressor of Israel, here, is not
Antiochus, but the last Antichrist, and the *time* the *last half of the 70th
Week, yet future.*
The question asked, v. 6, was, " How long,"—"*ad mathai keits happe-
la'oth,*"—to what extent,—*quousque temdem,*—"shall be the *End* of the wonders?" The answer is that *End* shall be "for a time, two times, and a
half," or 3½ years=1260 days. The culmination is *characterized* by an
event, the critics have translated variously. The verb rendered "to break in
pieces" means also to "scatter." The infinitive Piel (*nappets*) is here used
as a noun. The verb rendered "have an end" (*calah*) means also "to complete," or "consummate." The word rendered "power" means "hand"

is broken by the Coming of the Son of Man, Dan. vii: 8–27, that is, how long *after* the end of the last 1260 days, or close of the 70th Week, Dan. xii:7, shall be the *"Cleansing of the Sanctuary,"* is told in answer to the question, "O, my lord, and what shall be the *Afterness* of these things?" *Mah Acharith Elleh?* what more to follow? The linen-clothed, gold-cinctured *"Ani-Hu,"* hovering over the Tigris, answers the prophet, that, "from the time that the *Thamid* shall be *taken away* and the Abomination desolating put in its place, there shall be days 1290," xii:11, i. e., 30 days *beyond* the 1260; and this by a comparison of texts, is clearly the terminal point of the Cleansing of the Sanctuary, viii:14; xii:11. The linen-clothed man then adds a further period of 45 days more, saying, "Blessed is he that waiteth and cometh to the 1335 days," xii:12. And this point is, doubtless, the uprising of Israel's faithful dead to unite with Israel's faithful living in the Great Sabbatic Jubilee which begins the 1000 years.

The question of the prophet as to the *Afterness of these things*, xii, 8, was most natural. He would

---

(*yad*). The translations are "When the breaking in pieces the power of the holy people shall have reached its full measure."—Hoffmann, "When utterly shattered (*ganz und gar zerschmettert*) is the power of the holy people,"—Maurer. "When the breaking in pieces the power of the holy people shall have attained completion."—Füller. "When Israel shall be like a man *whose right hand is completely broken*, powerless in the grasp of his foe."—Kliefoth. "This is that complete breaking of the natural power of the holy people (*jene vollendete Zerbrechung der naturlicher Kraft des heiligen Volks*), which precedes their exaltation,"—Auberlen. That is, when Israel is driven to the last extremity, then the 1260 days will be finished, and the wonders of the End be completed. On the other hand, the literal rendering of the text is "*And when to end the breaking in pieces the hand of the holy people, then shall be ended all these*," that is, when *Antichrist's* power is broken, then the End of the 1260 days has come. Rabbi Leset translates, "And when there shall be an end to the crushing of the power of the holy people." So Dr. Philippson of Bonn. One would think, from reading the translation by the *Revisers*, that the Angel informed Daniel that when *"they,"* the armies of——"have made an end to *their own efforts* to break in pieces the power of the holy people!"—then the 1260 would close!

penetrate the far future of Israel's destiny ; a curiosity whose satisfaction is denied him, in a manner most tender and loving.   With affectionate address, the Angel, pronouncing his name, softly replies, " *Go thy way, Daniel, for the words are closed up and sealed till the time of the End*."   No more is now to be revealed. Enough has been told.   When the End comes the Seals will be opened by a voice from the throne calling the events to " *Come*."   Rev. vi: 2.   Many shall purify themselves, make themselves white, and be tried as gold is tried in the fire.   In the midst of increasing apostasy, the wicked shall do wickedly, while the righteous shall separate themselves to a holy fellowship, not following " the prince that shall come."   In the evening time it shall be light, and the wise, who eagerly peruse this book, shall understand.   Be perplexed no more.   For Israel redeemed, the glory shall soon follow the suffering. Dismiss all care.   The 1260 days shall be from the taking away of the *Thamid* and placing the Abomination to the destruction of Israel's oppressor.   *After*

The truth is, that the meaning of the text involves not only the complete breaking of the power of the *holy people*, but the complete breaking of *Antichrist's* power itself.   The end of Antichrist's power is the end of his breaking in pieces the power of Israel.   The interpretation is pregnant. Israel is delivered out of the Great Tribulation when He who is the "*Breaker*" breaks the breaker of His people.   Mic. ii:13, Hos i:11; Isa. xlix:24, 25; lix:19, 20, Rev. xix.11.   And this is in the last crisis when He who lifts his hand to heaven and swears, "*seeth that their power is gone !*" Deut. xxxii:36, 40; Rev. x:7; Dan. xii:7.   It was so foretold in the great Psalm that pictures the last conflict and Millennial glory.   "He shall break in pieces the Oppressor."   Ps. lxxii:4.   Then the "Standard is lifted against him," and the "*Goel* comes to Zion," Isa. lix·18, 19; Rom. xi:26.   Then the "*Blood*" of His saints is "precious in His sight," Ps lxxii:12-14; cxvi: 15; Isa. xxiv:21; Deut. xxxii:43; Rev. vi:10; xvi:6, for "*the Day of Vengeance is in His heart, and the Year of His redeemed is come*," Deut. xxx:41-43; Isa. lix:16; lxiii:1-6, the Day of the "glittering swo d," of " slaughter," and of the "wine press of the wrath of God Almighty."   Then. Antichrist's mission is ended, and Israel obtains the Kingdom.   The Eschatology of Daniel is simply the developed Eschatology of Moses.   Our exegetical foundation is a rock !

that, shall be 30 days more, reaching to 1290 days, the Cleansing of the Sanctuary, and Consecration of a holy of holies. *After* the 1290, shall be 45 days more, reaching to 1335 days, the Blessed Time when the just shall awake, and sing, and celebrate the Sabbath-Jubilee reserved for New-Born Israel, a ransomed race. *Go, Daniel!* Our communion is sweet, but be dismissed, now, for the vision is closed.   Israel's future is unveiled, their way and their end, their sin and their punishment, God's mercy and their glorious recovery. White-haired saint, a youth when carried from thy home, a captive threescore years and ten, talker with the Angels, and endeared to God, retire from the vision.   Remember that 70 Sevens have been decreed upon thy People and upon thy City, and that the End will speak.   The lions could not harm thee.   The satraps could not destroy thee.   *Go, blest prophet!* example to the Magi! fulfil the duties of thine office! In what remains of life to thee, be sustained amid the labors that await thee, by this assurance, heaven-sent to comfort thee, that thou shalt rest calmly in thy grave, and wake in the resurrection, to shine as the firmament's gleam.   To holy sleepers, the time is short. *Go! till the End shall be!*   Messiah will not only come, and suffer and die, and rise from the dead, but come again in His glory, and at His word the grave shall restore thy dust committed to its care.   Away with all doubts, anxieties, and vain interpretations.   Be of good cheer.   Believe and live.   Thou shalt stand in thy lot, in the end of the days, when Israel, for whom thou hast prayed, and toiled, and wept, and whose captivity thou hast shared, shall be "saved with an everlasting salvation, never to be ashamed or confounded, world without end."

Schematized, these great revelations of Christ to Daniel stand thus

SEVENTIETH WEEK.

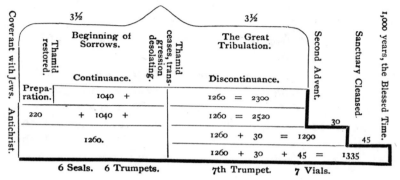

6 Seals.   6 Trumpets.   7th Trumpet.   7 Vials.

Thus ends the series of Old Testament prophetic numbers since the Exile and blotting out of God's visible kingdom on earth; 70 *years;* 70 *Sevens; 7 Sevens; 62 Sevens; 1 Seven; time, times and half a time;* 2300; 1260; 1290; 1335; all real, concrete, literal time. When we reflect that John's Apocalypse, from chapter VI to chapter XX, is a resumption of Daniel's 70th Week, and that John's personal head of the " Beast," " the 8th head," is the *Nagid* of Dan. ix:26, 27, typified in the *Melek* of Daniel xi:36, who is the Horn or *Qeren* of viii:9, and that John's numbers 1260, 1260, 3½, 3½, 3, 4, 7, 10, 12, 144, which he multiplies and combines, are all taken from Israel, and the 70th Week we shall not only see the organism and unity of prophecy, and Israel's place in prophecy and history alike, but the insanity of perverting these sacred measures of time into mere vague "*ideals* void of chronological value."

Before leaving the discussion of the 2300, it ought to be said, that, so far as the main interpretation of them goes, it is *indifferent* whether they are taken as *whole*, or *half*, days. In the one case they bear a certain relation to the *One* Week (2520 days) in the other to the *Half* Week (1260 days). What concerns us is to *beware* of the view of those who, by a forced identification of Antiochus, Dan. viii:9-14; xi:21-35, with the last Antichrist, the *Nagid* of Dan. ix,26, 27, and *Horn* of vii: 25, seek to identify the 2300 with 2520, or the 1150 with 1260, *and so limit to the horizon of Maccabean times all the visions in which we find the time-measures* 3½, 2300, *One Week, Half of that Week*, 2520, 1260, 1290, *and* 1335. By no possible manipulation of the numbers can the 2300 be identified with either half or the whole of the 70th Week. The times of Antiochus precede the First Advent; those of the Antichrist immediately precede the Second Advent. *The Græco-Macedonian Empire is not the ultimate horizon of the Book of Daniel.* By no artifice can we make Alexander's Empire the 4th prophetic Empire, or the 4th Beast, heavy, monstrous, and of iron-force, equal the leopard-footed Greek power, youthful and swift; nor can it be referred, as Zöckler, and others, would have it, to the reigns of the Diadochi, or successors of Alexander, or made correspondent with the 10 toes and the 10 horns. All this Orelli, with many others, properly reject as a violence to the text. The 4th Empire is the *Roman*, not the Greek. The End of the 3d Empire, in which the 2300 are found, is not the End of the 4th which is described as "One Week." *Antiochus* springs out of the *four*-parted 3d Empire. *The last Antichrist* springs out of the *ten*-parted 4th Empire. Nearly half of the 69 Weeks and the whole Interval between the 69th and the 70th Weeks, separate the two. By no right can we annex the additional 75 days to the 2300, but only to the last 1260 or 3½ times of the final Week which brings Israel's final Redemption.

Everything in the text, and context, compels us to see in Dan. ix:26, 27; xii:7; vii:25, an eschatological scene at the close of the 4th or Roman Empire divided into 10 contemporaneous kingdoms, confederate under the last Antichrist before whom 3 of them fall. Whatever *pre-illustration* the End of the 4th Empire receives from the End of the 3d, yet the two Ends, though standing in right line, *are not identical.* We can well agree with Hofmann, Delitzsch, and more, who hold that the vision of the 2300 Evening-Mornings, is "*both time-historical and eschatologieal,*" just as the Prophecy of our Lord on the Mount of Olives, relates to the destruction of Jerusalem A. D. 70, and the final siege and deliverance of Jerusalem, at the End of our present Age; i.e., it points to Antiochus, yet points to the Antichrist, as the "Terrible One," Isa. xiii:11, "That Wicked," Isa. xi:4, "The Enemy," Isa. lix:19, in short, to the *same* Antichrist, though represented by an Assyrian at one time, and a Chaldean at another. The generic and the individual, the time-historical and eschatological, are here interblended. But we must *avoid* the view that the unanointed "prince to come," Dan. ix:26, 27, relates to Antiochus, or that "*Prince Messiah,*" vs. 25, 26 admit both a Messianic and non-Messianic interpretation, i. e., refers to Onias, or any one else, and Christ, at the same time; a view no less objectionable than that of Auberlen and the Church in general, viz., that the *prophecy of the 70th Week relates to Christ alone and the time of His First Advent!* Grander scholars, or worthier defenders of the faith, never wrote upon prohecy. But in the points just specified, as objectionable, they have been in error; and the error is ever becoming more recognized along with the deeper scientific study of God's word. That the section Dan. xi:

36–45 describes the *last Antichrist*, and *not Antiochus*, (especially vs. 40–45), and is only the further development of Dan. xi:26, 27 has been established, in a masterly manner, by Tregelles, Rinck, Dæchsel, Kliefoth, Keil also, Burger, Beck, Kahle, and others, and that Dan. ix:21–35 is only the further development of Antiochus in Dan. viii:9–14 is made no less transparent. It is vital to remember these distinctions.   The blending of the End of the 3d Empire with the End of the 4th in one complex prophecy, Dan. xi:21–45, and the sudden and insensible transition from the one to the other (v. 36), overleaping the whole Interval between the Ends, is only what we find elsewhere in all prophetic study.

Part 4

The 144,000

We come now to the "144,000, a company *sealed out of every tribe of the children of Israel*," Rev. vii: 4, *prior* to the 6 Trumpet Judgments in the first half of the 70th Week, and found "standing on the Mount Sion" *after* these Trumpet Judgments are over, Rev. xiv:1. Is this number merely symbolic, ideal, abstract, representing "*the totality of believers in all ages, Jews and Gentiles,*" secure, at last, in heaven, or is it real and concrete, representing a definite number of the literal Israel in the End-Time, who have passed safely through the Great Tribulation, and survived to see the Advent? The idealistic and spiritualizing expositors affirm the first part of this question, and deny the second. We, on the contrary, affirm the second and deny the first. And we do so upon the ground of a strict exegesis based on the organic unity, analogy, identity, and teleology, of all prophecy, in both Testaments, concerning Israel. What we see here is the accomplishment of Israel's final redemption as foretold by Moses, the Psalms, the Prophets, Christ, and His Apostles.

The inner connection between Daniel's prediction, the Olivet discourse, and the Apocalypse, is alone suf-

233

ficient to establish this.   Supported by the consensus
of all other Scripture, it is redundantly confirmed.
When we remember that the entire Apocalypse, from
chapter IV onward, is eschatological, and brings the
"finishing of the mystery of God" with respect to
Israel, as foreshown to the prophets, Rev. x:7, and, therefore, as foreshown to Daniel in the 70 Weeks;—when,
also, we remember that, after the General Introduction
to the Book, chapter I–III, (which covers the Great
Interval in Dan. ix:26, and Luke xxi:24), the Special Introduction and matter of the Seven-Sealed-Scroll is divided into two equal parts, chapters IV–XI, and chapters XII–XIX, in order to correspond to the *two halves*
of Daniel's 70th Week,—6 Seals and 6 Trumpets in the
first half, the 7th Trumpet, with its 7 Vials, in the *second half*,—and that the Antichrist attains supreme
power in the *middle* of the week, commencing the Great
Tribulation, Rev. xi:7; xii:17; xiii:1, 5; and when, lastly,
we remember that the 144,000 sealed out of Israel in
the *first half* of the week, Rev. vii:1–8 (*before* the
Trumpet Judgments break, and the Great Tribulation
begins), are the same 144,000 who, *after* the Trumpet
Judgments are over, and the Great Tribulation has
ended, stand, at the *close of the second half*, triumphant
on the earthly Mount Sion with their Redeemer returned ; all doubt as to *who* the 144,000 are, ought to be
dismissed forever.   To spiritualize, or idealize, the
prophecy, is to negate it.   The scenes in Rev. xiv:1–5,
and in Rev. xi:1–14, are, both of them, earthly scenes
which occur during, and at, the close of Daniel's 70th
Week.   Already at the close of chapter III the Interval following Jerusalem's destruction, i. e., our Church-
Historical period, is ended, and the 70th Week, divided
into two halves, has come.   The vision in Rev. xiv:1–5,

is *proleptic*, and carries us by anticipation to the end of the second half of the week. The last trumpet has sounded; the last vial been emptied, and the Antichrist is overthrown. The Redeemer has already come to Sion, Joel iii:16; Isa. lix:21; Rom. xi:26; and Israel, chaste from the harlotry of the last times, and pure in holiness, Rev. xiv:5, stands before Him, and around Him, throned on Sion in His glory. Isa. xxiv:23; Micah iv:7. Already His feet have stood "upon the Mount of Olives which is before Jerusalem on the East," Zech. xiv:4. It is the End-Time we have here, and Israel's redemption.

Under another representation the 144,000 appear as the Sun-clothed woman of chapter XII; the Jewish Church, first, pre-Christian as the mother of *Messiah*, and, next, eschatological, as the mother of the Jewish *Nation;* in each case, of the "*Manly Child.*" Here, again, as in the older prophets, Israel is identified with Christ in His offices and work; Israel as "a Nation born in a day," and born to "rule the nations," Isa. lxvi:8; Rev. ii:27; xv:2–4. The pre-Christian and eschatological relations of the Sun-clothed Woman to Christ are both grouped in one Symbol for the sake of the organic unity. The woman represents the 144,000.* They are under the special care of Michael the guardian Angel-Prince of Israel as a nation, an Angel who has "stood firm" for Israel before, Dan. x:13, 21; Jude v. 9; and so stands again in Israel's last crisis. Dan. xii:1; Rev. xii:7. This settles the *time*, the *place*, the *people*, and the *event*, viz., the *time* of Antichrist's overthrow, Dan. xi:45; xii:1; the *place*, the Holy Land, Dan. xi:45; the *peo-*

---

* "The 144000, sealed out of Israel, are the Sun-clothed Woman who is miraculously preserved in the wilderness until the day of the Appearing of Christ." Koch. *Das Tausend. Reich.* 140.

ple, "the children of thy people," their posterity, Dan.
xii:1 ; the *event,* Israel's deliverance, Dan. xii:1.   The
Conversion is announced in Rev. xii:10, 11—at the middle
of the week, as the signal for the silencing of Satan's
age-long accusation against them (Compare Zech. iii:1-
5), and as the proof that the long-predicted kingdom is
at the door.   Sheltered from the Dragon, *this Jewish-
Christian Church of the End-Time is secluded in the wilderness for 3½ years, or 1260 days, the second half of
the 70th Week whose first half was the time of the
"Two Witnesses" under whose prophetic activity the Jewish
Church is formed.*   The final deliverance of Israel's
surviving election, and the resurrection of Israel's faithful dead, occur at the close of the week.   Dan. xii:1–3;
Isa. xxvi:19; Rev. xi:18; xx:4.

Again, these 144,000 are the same company figured
in true Hebrew style as Cithara-Players, triumphant
on the glassy sea mingled with fire,—a reminder of
the Red Sea lit with the Shekinah's blaze ; blending in memory and voice their first and and last redemption ; singing, more gloriously than Miriam, " the
song of Moses, the servant of God, and of the Lamb,"
Rev. xv:2–4; Deut. xxxii:39–43.   *Their Conversion and
victory bring the conversion of the Nations.*   All this is
in perfect harmony with the prophets, everywhere,
who make the entrance of the Nations, *as such,* into the
Kingdom of God, *follow* Israel's national conversion.
Deut. xxxii:43 ; Isa. lx:1–22; lxvi:5–20 ; Zech. xii:10–14;
xiv:9; even as the entrance of individual Gentiles increasing to a "fulness of the Gentiles," *followed* Israel's
individual conversion at the first, Acts xv:14–19.   After
the "fulness of the Gentiles," Israel, as a people, " all
Israel" is saved, Rom. xi:25, 26.   *After* Israel, as such,
is saved, the Nations *as Nations,* enter the Millennial

Kingdom. Rom. xi:12. So sing the 144,000 in the Apocalypse—the Cithara-Players on the glassy sea,— "Who shall not fear thee, O Lord, and glorify thy name? For thou only art holy; for *All Nations* shall come and worship before thee; *for thy Judgments are manifest.*" Rev. xvi:4. And these "Judgments" are the Trumpet-Judgments of the End-Time. Only a foregone conclusion, in bondage to an allegorizing, idealizing, or spiritualizing, exposition, can hinder any one from seeing this. Only such a prejudice can blind any one to the fact that the "*Benei Israel,*" or "*Sons of Israel,*" who are the 144,000, are not Gentiles, but Hebrews, the sons of Jacob and the seed of Abraham. They are an election out of the national 12-tribed Israel, called the "*Dodekaphulon*" in Acts xxvi:7, and the "*Diaspora*" in James i:1, that "*Genea,*" or race, which should not pass away till all our Lord had spoken should be fulfilled. Matt. xxiv:34. They are clearly defined, *as Israel,* by the use of Israel's covenant and national number combined and cubed with the number 10 raised to its third power; $10 \times 10 \times 10 = 1000$; $12 \times 12 = 144$; $144 \times 1000 = 144,000$, the whole election out of Israel ordained to survive the Great Tribulation and living to see the Advent. It means Israel of the End-Time, in their unity as one compact body. The totality represents a definite number of Israelites. The "*Benei Israel*" here are precisely the same as in Rev. ii:14, and everywhere else, in both Testaments, by unvarying usage; and by the term " tribes " is meant here, the same as in the expressions "Lion of the tribe of Judah," Rev. v:5; "names of the 12 tribes of the sons of Israel," Rev. xii:12; " sit on 12 thrones judging the 12 tribes of Israel," Matt. xix:28; "the tribes of the land shall mourn over Him," Rev. i:7; Matt. xxiv:30; Zech. xii:10; and

so connects this vision with that in Ezekiel, where "the
land is divided to the 12 tribes of Israel" in their final
restoration. Ezek. xlviii:13; xxi:22. What gives prime
importance to this vision is the fact that along with
the vision of the Countless Company in vii:9–17, it
forms the " Episode," as Alford and others call it, or
"Still-Standing Vision," as Ewald names it, or " Inter-
Act," as Reuss has it, *between* the 6th and 7th Seals, and
is not only an Interlude in the great Drama of the End,
but a Postlude, as well, following the opening of the
Day of the Lord in the 6th Seal, and also a Prelude, or
proleptic scene, anticipating the outcome of the Drama;
in every way a vision given for comfort and hope, in
the crisis where it stands. It points to the past and
tells how much of the Drama is accomplished. It explains the present, revealing the great tribulation, those
preserved from it, and those who fall therein. It looks
to the final future of the saved in victory, blessedness
and glory. To interpret this is to interpret most of the
Apocalypse.

That a *Contrast, Antithesis,* or *Distinction,* exists between the 144,000, Rev. vii:1–8, and the Countless Company, Rev. vii:9–17, is plain and undeniable. The chief
question is *What is that Contrast ?* It is not that the
144,000 are figurative and the Countless Company are
literal (Vitringa); nor that the latter company includes
the former (Düsterdieck); nor that both are martyrs,
the last including all the later martyrs (Paræus); nor
that John merely "hears" of the one but "sees" the other
(Grotius); nor that the 144,000 are a definite election in
contrast with others who are rejected, while the Countless Company is an indefinite number without an election
(Alcasar); nor that the two are the same company, viz.,
"the totality of believers in all ages," " the organic

whole of Old and New Testament Saints," "the whole Church," the "People of God," the "whole Spiritual Israel of God," seen under different circumstances, first before death, next after death (Augustine, De Wette, Ebrard, Hengstenberg, Keil, Riehm, Küper, etc.) ; nor "the *collective whole* of Jews and Gentiles in the 144,000, as distinguished from the *individuals* of that totality as seen in the Countless Company, the first on earth, and of the last in heaven" (Kliefoth, Milligan). None of these views are correct. Plainly, on the other hand, the Contrast is (1) That of an election "*out of the Sons of Israel*" standing over against an election "*out of every nation, and of all tribes, and peoples, and tongues ;*" and (2) That of a sealed and numbered company *on earth*, preserved to pass through the Great Tribulation, unharmed, and surviving to see the Advent, standing over against another countless company *in heaven*, who have fallen in the Tribulation and entered into the peace of God. The one are still living in their bodies, here on earth, not tasting death. The other are disembodied in heaven. The one are Jews. The other are both Jews and Gentiles, the martyrs of the 5th Seal with their "fellow-servants and their brethren," Rev. vi:11, over whom the holy benediction is pronounced, Rev. xiv:13, and who "live again" in the "First Resurrection," Rev. xx:4. The "tribulation" out of which they are seen "*coming*" as in long procession, is not that of the trials of the church from age to age, throughout her history, (though the vision may be *applied* thus), but is that of the definite 3½ years or 1260 days of the last Antichristian time, the second half of Daniel's 70th Week, the "Short time" during which the Devil's wrath is great, Rev. xii:12, and Antichrist's power supreme, Rev. xiii:5. So Delitzsch, Hofmann, Hebart, Lange, Volck,

Christiani, Karsten, Steffann, Rinck, Dæchsel, Starke, Weiss, Oehler, Schultz, Grau, Koch, Köhler, Kliefoth; the tribulation of the End-Time forecast in Deut. xxxii: 36–43; Isa. xxvi:20, 21 ; Jer. xxx:7 ; Dan. ix:27 ; xii:1, 7; Matt. xxiv:21, 22, and of which the tribulation that attended the Roman destruction of Jerusalem was but the type, Matt. xxiv:9–21, the near and far horizons seen in one.

Nothing in all the Apocalypse is more important than this, for, by a study of the parallels between this and our Lord's Olivet discourse, we find that "the beginning of sorrows," Matt. xxiv:7, 8, is what we have in the first 6 Seals, Rev. vi:1–17, the " End not yet;" and what we have in Matt. xxiv:9–14, is what occurs under the first 6 Trumpets, Rev. viii:1–13 ; ix:1–21 ; xi: 3 ; and what we have in Matt. xxiv:15–28, is the last Great Tribulation, under the 7th Trumpet, or the 7 Vials, Rev. xi:2; xii:6, 14; xiii:5, the near and far horizons blended by our Lord in one. It is the Jewish-Christian Church of his own time, and of the End-Time also, of which he speaks *there*. It is the Jewish-Christian Church of the End-Time only, of which he speaks to John, *here*. Under the "*Ye*" and the "*Your*" in Luke xxi:28, Matt. xxiv:33, He sees the 144000, described in Rev. vii:1–8 and xiv:1–5;—converted Israel; Luke xxiii: 39.

The passages of the Apocalypse that come under review in the determination of the 144,000, are

(1)   Rev. vii:1–8, the 144,000 sealed.
(2)   Rev. vii:9–17, the Countless Company.
(3)   Rev. xiv:1–5, the 144,000 on Mount Zion.
(4)   Rev. xxi:9–12, 24–27, the Bride, the Nations.

In reference to these it has been held, diversely, 1. That (1) and (3) are *Jews*, while (2) are *Gentiles*. 2. That

(1) are *Jews*, while (2) are *both Jews and Gentiles*, and (3) are part of (2).   3. That in all the four passages, (1), (2), (3), (4), as above, *all* are the totality of believers, the whole Church of Old and New Testament believers, in all ages, from the beginning to the end of the world, seen under variant circumstances.   This last is an *easy* way to dispose of a great problem! In accordance with these different views, it has been held (1) That John teaches *no* distinction between Jewish believers and Gentile believers, but that all are, without distinction, the " Israel of God ; "—Augustine, De Wette, Hengstcnberg, Keil, Riehm, Küper, Milligan, Fairbairn, David Brown, and the spiritualizing expositors in general.   (2) That John *does teach a distinction*, and a *Preference* of the Jew over the Gentile, in the Kingdom of God, i. e., an Ebionite Chiliasm.   So the whole Tübingen school of critics.

3.   That John *does teach a distinction*, but *no Preference;* Neander, Bleek, Düsterdieck, etc.

4.   That John *does teach a distinction*, but without any *spiritual* Preference of the Jew over the Gentile, yet *with an Economical Pre-eminence* or *Privilege, of Israel, as such*, in the outward constitution and form of the Kingdom in its visible and final glory. This is grounded in the fact that Israel, as a nation, is the "choice forever," and the seed from whom Messiah came ; a people indestructible and everlasting ; and that this distinction between Jewish and Gentile Believers is indicated everywhere in the New Testament, while yet both are spiritually one in Christ, the contrast being prominently marked in the promise to the Philadelphian Church, Rev. iii:9, in the difference between the Sun-Clothed Woman and the Remnant of her seed, Rev. xii:1, 17, between " the saints," and " them that

fear God," Rev. xi:18, and between the Holy City, New Jerusalem, the Bride, and the saved Nations, outside, who, in the New Heaven and Earth, are different from the Holy City, or the Bride, yet are enfranchised citizens and dwell around her, and bring their glory and their honor into her. So, Calvin in part, John, Owen, Ritschl, Köstlin, Volkmar, Hofmann, Auberlen, Baumgarten, Hess, Hahn, Roos, Rinck, Steffann, Da Costa, Roorda, Gebhardt, Luthardt, Koch, Köhler, Volck, Van Oosterzee, Saphir, etc., etc. According to this view, it follows that (1) the 144,000 in Rev. vi:1-8, and xiv:1-5 are identical. They are Jewish believers, and survivors of the Tribulation; (2) that the Countless Company, Rev. vii,9-17, are martyrs of the End-Time, both Jews and Gentiles; (3) that the tribulation in which they fall is the last 3½ years of Daniel's 70th Week, the time of the Sheltered Woman; (4) that the 144,000, are not all the believers existing on earth when the Lord comes, the Gentile Church, though reduced, being still extant and suffering; (5) that the 144,000 are not all, but only a part of the Bride in the New Heaven and Earth, the Bride being Israel and the adopted or engrafted Gentile believers; (6) that, outside the Bride, or Holy City, are the saved Kings and Nations, who are converted during the 1000 years, and have a right to enter into and frequent the New Jerusalem; (7) that the " *we* who are alive and remain, unto the coming of the Lord," Paul's " *Perileipomenoi,*" I Thess. iv:15, are not the 144,000, but the surviving portion of the Gentile Church, or portion of the Remnant of the Woman's seed, who, next after the resurrection of the holy dead, are " changed," and " raptured" with them " to meet the Lord in the air," I Thess. iv:17. In short, from first to last, Israel, as such, God's " choice forever," is the historic *Root* and *Basis*, not only of the " Church," but of the " Kingdom " in its outward glorious form forever. As Gebhardt says, " The distinction between Jewish and Gentile Believers, in the Apocalypse, is undeniable. The distinction between Israel and the converted Nations cannot be questioned," and again, " What we find in the Millennium, in a temporary, limited manner, will have place in the New World absolutely. As there, the " Beloved City " is the central point of the Kingdom of God, so is it here ; as there, the true Israel is a Nation of priestly kings dwelling at the center, serving God, and governing the world, so also in the final state ; as there the Nations bring their offerings, their princes, and their people, so also in the New Jerusalem. Only after Christ's second coming, are the Nations in the gross converted, and, in the final state, from the population of the New World around the City of God. Little as we are to think of an exclusion of the Gentiles from the dwelling-place of God and His priestly people, just as little are we to conceive an Identity of those living *in* and those living *round* Jerusalem. The distinction between Israel and the Nations remains forever."* This is certainly clear and true. As Israel is distinguished from the Church in the Millennial Age, though both are united, so is it in the final New Jerusalem State. The Bride is One ; the Holy City is One, composed of Jewish and Christian believers glorified. Yet, evermore Israel, as such, forms the basis of the Church, as also of the Kingdom, and is preserved as such. The 144,000 are distinct, although not separated from the Gentile heirs. And because of this, the "names of the 12 tribes of the *Benei*

---

*Doctrine of the Apocalypse. 184, 302, 303 and 304.

Israel" are graved on the gates of New Jerusalem, Rev.
xxi:12, and " the names of the 12 Apostles of the Lamb"
displayed on her foundations, Rev. xxi:14.   And this is
done, not to teach that only Jews are there, or none but
Jews are saved, but to hang the glowing signal out, and
let it glitter there to all eternity, that what was pledged
to Abraham in covenant has now been realized, viz.:
That in *him* and *his seed* all the nations of the earth
should be blessed.   That is the meaning of the 144,000!
That is the meaning of the names of " the 12 tribes of
Israel," and of " the 12 Apostles of the Lamb" upon
the groundstones and the gates of New Jerusalem!
Such is God's plan, and such " the End of the ways of
God."

What we have before us, therefore, as the result of
our investigation, is a series of great facts, viz., (1)
That Israel shall be converted when the fulness of the
Gentiles has come in, and the Times of the Gentiles
are fulfilled ; (2) That this shall be during Daniel's 70th
Week; (3) that the Apocalypse presupposes the truth
of all the Old Testament predictions, and the New
Testament ones, concerning Israel ; (4) that, as a people, Israel shall repossess their fatherland ; (5) that an
election, large indeed, shall be protected in the Great
Tribulation, and survive to see the Advent; (6) That a
Countless Company of Jews and Gentiles, both, shall
suffer death, and pass into the peace of God, and rise
again in the "First Resurrection;" (7) That Israel, as
such, shall stand victorious with the Lamb upon the
earthly Mount Zion, and dwell in the " Beloved City."
(8) That not only in Millennial days, but in the final
state, Israel shall be the Root and Basis, the Center,
and the Crown, of the glorious Kingdom of God.

These facts tell us, therefore, just what the *Contrast*

is between the 144,000 and the Countless Company in
Rev. vii:1–17.   They assure us also that the Christian
Church will not be removed from the earth, or become
extinct under persecution, but, reduced and suffering,
will also live to see the Advent.   They teach us also
that the "rapture" is the rapture of the Church, and
not of the 144,000, even as the prophets teach.   Isa. lxv:
17–22; Ezek. chapters XL–XLVIII, etc., etc.   Israel and
the saved of the nations abide on earth, the nucleus of
the Millennial Age.   As to the dwelling-place of the
risen saints this much we know, that, as Paul tells us,
the glorification of Nature *begins* with the resurrection
of the saints, and, as the Prophets tell us, Israel's land
becomes "like Eden."   The risen saints, moreover,
"reign on the earth."   Rev. v:11.   So far from this
view being wholly modern, it is ancient, and was the
faith of the early church for 300 years.   Even before
the Reformers began to see a part of the true interpretation, the Jesuit Cornelius à Lapide, in the middle
of the 16th century, "maintained that the 144,000 are
elect Israel, and the Holy City, Rev. xi:1, is Jerusalem
of the future." (De Wette.)   In the Lutheran Church
Spener held the same view (Bengel) as did Calixtus
(Luthardt) and in the Reformed Church, soon after, not
a few were of the same opinion (Steffan),   Even in A.
D. 1600, Pierre Launoy saw in Rev. chapters X–XII Israel's conversion. "the *Pas Israel*" of Paul, Rom. xi:26,
as, later on, the Moravian Brethren saw it in the promise
to the Philadelphian Church. (De Wette. Delitzsch.)
These facts, and the blazing light of modern exegesis,
only prove that God's truth *must* rise triumphant over
all false systems of interpretation.   Cocceius, the greatest Hebrew scholar of his day, is perfectly clear that
the "Pas Israel" of Paul, Rom. chap. XI, is the "Kol

Israel" of Daniel, chap. IX, although he is betrayed by
a spiritualizing method of interpretation to regard the
"Israel" of Daniel as the "whole Church!" Such is
the organic connection of all prophecy, such the continuity of God's plan, such the unchanging covenant of
God, such the unity of Scripture, and the utterances of
Christ and His Apostles that Israel, as such, *must* have
a large place in the closing book that sums and binds
the canon. Were Israel wanting here, the critic, versed
in Scripture, would allege the absence as a proof
that John's Apocalypse is not canonical; or, believing
it canonical, would ransack every library and mon-
astery, East and West, to find a genuine Manuscript, if
possible, with Israel's final fortunes in it. But this is
not needed. The great division of the Seven-Sealed
Scroll itself into *two halves*, corresponding to the two
half-weeks of the 70th Week in Dan. ix:27; the first 3½
years covered by the first 6 Seals and the first 6 Trumpets; the second 3½ years covered by the 7th Trumpet, or 7 Vials, the period of the Great Tribulation; in
short, the division of the Scroll, in its two great parts,
each a period of 1260 days, or 42 months, with Daniel's
"Little Horn," Dan. vii:2, 5, identified as John's Beast,
Rev. xiii:5, is enough to end the question whether
Israel is found here. As truly as the 144,000 are not
Gentiles, so truly the Jerusalem of chapter XI is not
that of Titus A. D. 70, but the Jerusalem of the End-
Time, whose deliverance is predicted, not less by John
than by our Lord, with the deliverance of Israel from
the grasp of the last Antichrist, at the end of the Gentile times.

The 144,000 are the *"Pas Israel"* of Paul in Rom. xi:
26; the *"Pleroma Israel"* in xi:15, whose conversion
brings such transcendent blessing to the nations, in the

last time. Zech. chapters XII–XIV. They are the *"Written in the Book,"* in Dan. xii:1 ; the *"Among the living and holy in Jerusalem,"* in Isa. iv:3 ; the *"Many"* of Daniel's people who have then been "turned to righteousness." Dan. xii:3. They are the *" Our Brethren"* of Rev. xii:10, identified also notably, in Matt. xxv:40, where the Son of Man decides the fate of nations according to their conduct toward Israel in the last tribulation. They are the "Offering" or *"Mincha"* brought by the Gentiles to the Holy Land, when the Lord appears in His glory to build up Zion, Isa. xi: 11–16; xlix: 22 ; lxvi:20; Zeph. iii:10 (*Revised Version*); in other words, the unspotted Israel of the last time, the holy *"Aparche,"* or *"First-Fruits"* of the Millenial Harvest of the Nations, Rev. xiv:4, 14–16; Matt. xiii:38–43; Rom. xi:16; Rev. xv:4. Still more, they are Daniel's "People of the Saints of the Most High," to whom the Kingdom is given, when the Colossus falls, and the Little Horn is judged, Dan. ii:44; vii:25 ; * Ezekiel's "exceeding great army," when the Dry Bones of the valley are quickened to life, Ezek. xxxvii:1–12, by the preaching of the word, and the blowing of the Spirit. They are *New-Born Israel*, at the Second Coming of Messiah, the nucleus of the Millennial Kingdom, redeemed under

---

*Even Keil, in Dan. xii:1-3, is compelled to say that "by the People of the Saints of the Most High is meant *das Volk Israel, das Volk Daniels.*" But then he spiritualizes it into *"all peoples ! Alle Volker; who belong to the New Covenant!"* on which Dr. Gröbler sharply remarks, " When Keil says this, he drags into the text what is wholly foreign to it. The prophet meant no such thing." (*Stud.* u. *Krit,* 1879, 4th Heft. 669.) So Bosanquet. "They are the *sons* of *Abraham,* the very same people as in Dan. xii:7:xii:1; Dan. ix:11,15,20,24;x:14; of this there can be no question." (Messiah the Prince. 13, 14.) So Auberlen. " They are the *People Israel* in contrast with the Gentile nations which were, for a time, to exercise rule over them, and we have no exegetical authority, or right, to think of any other. They are not the Christian Church." (*Der Prophet Daniel* 248.) So Volck. " They are the People who have been dispersed, outcast, and oppressed by the Nations, but to whom the Kingdom will be given at last, the people Israel." (*Chiliasmus.* 87.) It is useless to multiply authorities.

the echoes of the 7th Trumpet. Rev. xi:15 ; xii:10.
Otherwise, the advancing organism of prophecy is
broken. This, however, cannot be.

All the scenes in the Apocalypse of John from
chapters X to XX fall in that very epoch of time in
which the " Last Things " described in Ezekiel, chapter
XXXVII; Dan. chapter XII ; Hosea, chapter XIII,
and Isa. chapter XXVI, and in all the prophets concerning Israel, fall, viz.: after Gentile times are ended,
and the 70th Week has begun. Then God's covenant
relations with divorced dead Israel as a nation, are
once more resumed. We ought to have no difficulty
here. " The majority of expositors now," says Boehmer, agree that verses 2-8, of Rev. vii, mean an election
out of Israel, while verses 9-17 are an election of believers out of all Nations. This needs no proof, for the
words are so clear and express, that we rather need an
explanation how it is that any one could deny it."* So
Auberlen.   " The 144,000 are none other than converted Israel redeemed, through the storms of the last
time, into the Kingdom, to form there the nucleus of
the new and divinely organized life of humanity."†
Clear and right are the words of Professor Volck, who
says, " The 144,000 sealed from the 12 tribes of Israel, in
Chapter VII, are identical with the 144,000 standing on
Mount Zion, in Chapter XIV, and are not, as Keil and
others teach, the whole number of believers in all
ages. They are not, as Vitringa thinks, the sum of
evangelical confessors ; not as Ewald has it, all Christianity ; nor as De Wette and Hengstenberg hold, the
spiritual Church ; nor are they, as Düsterdieck views
them, included in the innumerable throng, v. 9.   All

---

*Offenbar Joham. 148.
*Der Prophet Daniel 385.

these views break the *fixed antithesis* between Israel and the Gentiles. Whoever, without prejudice, considers the vision, will be able to discover clearly the *express contrast* between a definite number out of the 12 tribed Israel who survive the Great Tribulation, and an innumerable throng, out of every nation, and of all tribes and tongues, who, during the tribulation, enter into the peace of God. He who is familiar with Old Testament prophecy, and what it says of Israel in the last time, will find nothing strange here."* In like manner, that able writer, Pastor Koch, defending Hofmann against Kliefoth, says, "The 144,000 are Israel of the End-Time who do not taste death, but survive to see the Advent of Christ, in contrast with another company who, through death, attain to heaven. They are, as Hofmann rightly conceives, the Israelitish Church of the Future, and upon the earthly Mount Zion where the Redeemer has come. It is not that Gentile believers have utterly perished in the apostasy, for Paul teaches the contrary. I Thess. iv:16, 17; nor that no Jewish believers become martyrs, for John teaches otherwise, Rev. vii:9. The countless company in heaven is "out of every nation, and of all tribes and tongues." But it is that, in the height of the apostasy, when the true Church is almost gone, *God will restore Israel, and preserve of Israel an election, undestroyed by the tribulation, who shall live to see the Advent.* Such is God's way."† " Wonderful," exclaims Luthardt, " are the ways of God! Israel ceased to be the territory of the Kingdom of God, that it might go to the Gentiles. But just *that* will, one day, '*provoke*' Israel. The first made last shall become the last made first. While, in the world of

---

*Volck. Chiliasmus 124.
†Koch. Uebersicht u. d. Heilsgesch. 56-64.

Nations the apostasy finds place, the Church of the End-
Time will be kept alive and preserved through Israel
restored—the 144,000 sealed and victorious in chapters
VII and XIV. When the tribulation waxes to its
height the Lord will come and show Himself on Mount
Zion." "The 144,000 are the Jewish Christian Church
of the Last Time, who have passed through the Great
Tribulation. They stand, not on the heavenly, but on
the earthly Mount Zion. It is the same thought that
we find in Rom. xi:26; the fulfilment of the promise
made to the Philadelphian Church."*

Is all this *only* abstract, ideal, schematic, merely
spiritual, and " of universal application to the Church,
in all ages?" Is it not concrete and real with an intensity under which even the symbol itself grows weak
and staggers? Who can doubt that Daniel's 70th
Week is the frame for John's Apocalypse and Israel the
key of its true interpretation? †

Spiritualizing expositors, like Hengstenberg, Keil,
R. W. Alexander, C. H. H. Wright, and idealizing
ones, like Bertheau, Riehm, Robertson Smith, and
others, may adhere still to the opposite view. but such
view is unsustained by a true exegesis. When that
eminent scholar, Dr. J. A. Alexander, still bound to the
Church-Historical theory of interpretation, said, "The
literal view rests upon the *false assumption* that the
apocalyptic prophecies are *exegetical* of those in the

---

*Luthardt, Lehre v. d. Letzten Dingen. 123 69.

† The 144,000 are *Jews*. So Andreas, Arethas, Ribera, á Lapide, Lam-
bert, Bullinger, Launoy, Grotius, Bossuet, Bengel, Hess, Hahn, Roos,
Baumgarten, Heinrichs Eichhorn, Neander, Züllig. Hofmann, Auberlen,
Luthardt. Karsten, Köhler, Koch, Rinck, Baur, Schultz, Steffans, Dachsel,
Starke, Lechler, Düsterdieck, Da Costa, Volck, Volkmar, etc., etc. "Most
expositors understand Mount Zion, Rev. xiv:1, on which John saw the
Lamb and the 144,000, in a literal sense." *Gebhardt. Doctrine of the
Apocalypse. 44.*

Old Testament, from which their images and terms are *borrowed*," * it was well replied by Henderson, Kitto, Davidson, Govett, and more, as now it is maintained by a hundred others, like Delitzsch, Hofmann, Volck, Luthardt and Auberlen, that there is *no assumption* in the case, nor *"borrowing,"* but that the *organic relation* of the prophecies, in both Testaments, to Israel's final future compels the interpretation, and that the later, more developed oracles upon the same subject *are* exegetical of the earlier ones. We can truly say of this chapter in the Apocalypse (VII) what the great Chalmers said of the 61st chapter of Isaiah, viz., "This chapter forms, altogether, a most regaling prophecy, and serves greatly to establish *the future Restoration of Israel as being the common subject of both the Apocalypse and the older prophets."* † We can say with Kliefoth, "The Apocalypse actually brings nothing more concerning the Last Things, than what is elsewhere found in the other Scriptures of the Prophets, our Lord's words, and the utterances of the Apostles." ‡ And, with Delitzsch, we can say, "The New Testament Apocalypse represents the Old Testament *Eschata* in their future temporal succession and order. It is, in this repect, the *Key* to the whole prophetic word. To spiritualize the prophecies concerning Israel, is to distort and negate the prophetic word itself." ‖ And we can say with Koch, " The Apocalypse of John not merely confirms the Old Testament Prophecy, but is the *Norm* for its understanding, for whatever the prophets have said of the kingdom of glory on this present earth, is

---

* Later Prophecies. 487. Scribner's Ed.
† Scripture Readings III. 335. Harper's Ed.
‡ Christliche Eschatologie. 16.
‖ Letter to the Writer, Oct. 9, 1886.

here repeated in the light of New Testament knowledge." *   And with Reuss, that veteran scholar, from
whom we dissent in so much else, we must yet say
that "the Apocalypse is no fancy of some exalted and
lazy dreamer, but responds to the felt need of the age
in which it was born.   Far from containing revelations
new and astonishing, as almost all past commentators
have imagined, it but gives to its readers what most of
them have already known and believed."† Nor, finally,
here, may we omit that word of Renan, so true and
impressive, even though bound up with a false interpretation, "The Apocalypse is the Seal of Prophecy,
the last word of Israel.   Let any one read in the ancient prophets,—Joel, for example,—the description of
the '*Day of the Lord*,' and herein he will find the germ
of the vision of Patmos.   Every revolution, every historic convulsion, became, for the Jewish mind, possessed with the idea of the establishment of a kingdom
of righteousness on earth, the prelude of a judgment
more solemn and definitive still.   At each event a
prophet lifted up his voice and cried '*Blow the trumpet
in Zion, for the Day of the Lord is near.*'   The Apocalypse is the last consequence and crown of all this remarkable literature which is the glory peculiar to
Israel.   Its author is the last great prophet, inferior to
none of his predecessors whose spirit and word he imi-
tates.   Almost his whole word is taken from the prophetic representations of the Old Testament, especially
from Isaiah, Ezekiel, Daniel and Zechariah.   The coming of the future reign of Christ is at hand.   It must
follow the destruction of Roman power.   The martyrs
are raised, the rest of the dead are not raised yet, and

---

* Das Tausend. Reich.   142.
† L'Apocalypse.   Introd.   10.

the kingdom of Christ is upon the earth, with its
central seat at Jerusalem, in the midst of the nations.
It will endure 1000 years, after which Satan will attempt a new reign, which God will disappoint by a
general and final judgment. *This is that Doctrine of
the Millennium spread so widely in the first three centuries,
which has reappeared constantly at different epochs, and is
supported by more ancient and formal texts than many other
doctrines now universally accepted."* With such a mass of
consentient opinion, rather of profound critical judgment, in every case built on the organic unity of all
prophecy, it must be impossible for any competent, im-
partial and intelligent mind, to evade the conclusion
that Israel is the key of this Book. It can only be
evaded by the adoption of a *spiritualizing* interpretation
which makes "Israel" mean the New Testament Gentile
"Church," and so confounding things different, negates
the prophetic word of both Testaments. The utterance of Luthardt, however, remains true, "Whoever is
at home in the prophets, and in the Apocalypse, will
soon find the right way which will conduct him through
all the apparent labyrinths of this wonderful book." †
This whole combined judgment of independent scholars
so eminent, of specialists so patient, and of writers of
theological views so different, multiplied as it might be
to volumes, only establishes the fact that the Apocalypse
is exegetical of the earlier prophets, and that as there,
so here, *Israel* is the cloud by day, and the fire by night!
It is a Jewish-Christian Book from the pen of the
apostle-prophet John. In the dark hour following
Jerusalem's second obliteration, Israel's second dispersion, and the persecution of both Israel and the Church

* Renan. L'Antichrist. 460-468.
† Lehre v. d. letzten Dingen. 174.

by the Roman power, it opens up a glorious future for all, "the Jew, the Gentile, and the Church of God;"— a future of blessedness and victory, introduced by the Second Coming ot the Son of Man, at the end of the Times of the Gentiles. In this respect John is the true successor of Isaiah, Ezekiel, Daniel, and Zechariah, yea, of all the prophets. In him Christ speaks as He speaks in them, the "*One Speaking*" in them all, the communication one and consistent all the way from Moses to John. " Israel,"—the literal Israel,—"shall be saved with an everlasting salvation, not to be ashamed nor confounded, world without end." Isa. xlv:17.

Part 5

THE 1,000 YEARS

A.   PROOFS OF THEIR HISTORICAL REALITY

These proofs are redundant.

(1) The *Identity* of these years with the " Third Day " in Hos. vi:2, the " Multitude of Days " in Isa. xxiv:22, the " Many Days " in Ezek. xxxviii:8, and the " His Days " in Psa. lxxii:7, is of itself conclusive of their historic reality, and definite chronological measure.   The *Eschata* that bound these " years " are identical with the *Eschata* that bound these " days," both at their opening and their close, while the differently named periods thus bounded, being commensurate, are identical.   If we schematize, or throw into linear form, this conception, the diagram will stand thus:

Opening Eschata.		The Third Day, Hos. vi:2.	Closing Eschata.
		Multitude of Days, Isa. xxiv:22.	
		Many Days, Ezek. xxxviii:8.	
		His Days, Psa. lxxii:7.	
	(A)	The Thousand Years, Rev. xx:1-7.	(B)

That is, the *Eschata* at the opening of the 1000 years (A) are identical with the *Eschata* at the opening of all

255

the other named periods; and the *Eschata* at the close
of the 1000 years (B) are identical with the *Eschata* at
the close of all the other named periods, which makes
the periods themselves not only commensurate but
identical; in other words, all are *one* period.

We have but to turn to the Apocalypse of John,
in order to see that the Old Testament *Eschata*, taken
together, in one combined picture, are the same events
that shine in the final New Testament revelation of the
future; these events grouped in the same way at the
opening, as also in the same way at the close, of the
Great Interval. These events at the opening (A) which
is the close of the 70th week, are the Parousia of Antichrist, the Gathering and Conversion of Israel, the
Great Tribulation, the Gathering and Judgment of the
Nations around Jerusalem, the Slaughter in the Holy
Land and final Conflict around the Holy City, the
the Parousia of Christ, Deliverance and Redemption
of Israel, the Destruction of Antichrist, the overthrow
of the Gentile Colossus or World-Power, the Binding
of the Dragon, the Resurrection of the Righteous
Dead, the Resurrection of Israel's Kingdom, and the
establishment of Messiah's Kingdom " over the whole
earth," and " under the whole heaven." These events,
accompanied by great cosmic changes and convulsions,
occur, in the Old Testament, at the opening of each of
the various periods, as above named; and in the New
Testament, at the opening of the 1000 years. The
events at the close of the 1000 years, are, in like manner,
the events at the close of the other periods, taken together, viz., the " Evil Spirit " that comes into Gog's
mind, the Release of Satan, the Redemption of the
Nations remote from Palestine, the Judgment on Gog,
the Resurrection of the rest of the dead, the Last Judg-

ment, the final New Heaven and Earth, and the final New Jerusalem. The Interval between these opening and closing events being literal in the Old Testament, it must be so in the New. Chronological there, it is chronological here. What was obscurely intimated there is eclaircised and unfolded brightly here.

This shows clearly the direct relation of each one of the Eschata to the 1000 years, and provides at once the answers to the several questions,—each a theme in itself—" What is the relation of the Church to the 1000 years?—of Israel to the 1000 years?—of the Nations to the 1000 years?—of Satan?—of the Second Coming?— of the rest of the dead?—of the land of Palestine?—of the Conflagrations?—of the Judgments?—of Antichrist?—of Gog?—of the New Heaven and Earth, and New Jerusalem? Where does each *Eschaton* stand in relation to the 1000 years, and to all the other *Eschata?* Which are on this, which on that side of the Millennial Age, and what the characteristics of the Age itself as foretold by all the prophets? The answers to these questions constitute no less than the clear *out*-rolling from one another, in temporal order and succession of the total Eschata, *in*-rolled and involute in one another in the earlier Old Testament revelation ; the Ends and Ages there confounded, but here unconfounded, and separately marked as successive, literal, and historic parts and bounds of time.

This argument, drawn from commensurate times, bounded by the same *Eschata*, is invincible. It is based upon the genetic unity, persistent continuity, and self-advancing organism, of all prophecy, from first to last forecasting the same future, opening the same Intervals, unveiling the same events, and struggling to reach the same end. What we see in each of the Old Testament germinal expressions for the 1000 years, is simply an embryonic pre-formation in its various growths and phases; an enigmatic mention of the *Millennium* to be announced at last, without enigma. It is with these *germs, or types, of the final Name* of the Interval, as it is with the early facts in Israel's history. Everything anticipates, and is prophetic. The judgment on Sodom seems marvelously like the Judgment yet to come upon the world. Every circumstance appears to be a type. The mission of Joseph to Egypt looks much like the mission of Israel to the nations. The 40 years' wandering in the wilderness foreshadowed a longer wandering among the Gentiles. The return from Babylon preluded a still more glorious return, in the latter days. Nay more, the actual pre-announcement of the future under terms indefinite, reserved to be defined by later light, is itself an anticipation of the final fact. All goes to show an organism and development in prophecy, the ground and guide for every true interpretation. If, as Hofmann beautifully says, " Every triumphal procession of the Roman General through the streets of Rome was a prophecy of the coming *Cæsar Augustus*,"* it is equally true that every detected Interval, in the Old Testament between the Advent of Messiah in His glory, and the final Judgment and Regenesis of all things, is a prophecy of the *Millennium*. It is the Millennium itself in prophetic embryo. Modern science shows designed connection in the different structure of the same organism, at different periods in its growth, and so builds its doctrine of homology and unity. "The most perfect being,—man,—presents himself, first, in imperfect pre-formation which imperfectly *prefigures*

---

* Weissagung u. Erfüllung. I. 15.

the perfect final form. So is it in prophecy and history."* The *Time-Designations* in Hosea, Isaiah, Ezekiel, the Psalms, and the implications in the Pentateuch, for the *Millennial Age*, are the archæology of eschatology. The End is contemplated from the Beginning. The identity of the Intervals represented by them, and of the *Eschata* that bound them, rest, not on any mere external accident, or similarity in prophecy, but upon the inner connection, and inter-connection, of the parts of prophecy, and the advancing organism of the whole along its fixed, original, and pre-determined lines. What looms in the End, lurks in the Beginning. For this reason, as Crusius says, Delitzsch agreeing, "The New Testament attributes to the Old Testament time a far deeper knowledge of the work of Christ than *we* could conclude from the Old Testament, *apart from* the New as its key." † And so is it with respect to the Millennium. Either the *whole* prophetic word is false, or the 1,000 years in John are literal historic time. Either the pre-formative expressions in Hosea, Isaiah, and Ezekiel, forecast the 1,000 years in John, *as chronological*, or the prophetic word in both Testaments is not a unit, nor an organism, but a mass of isolated sentences, a sheaf of incoherent oracles, ambiguous as the Sibyl's utterances. This cannot be. The proofs are "Legion" that the Bible is *One Word which "cannot be broken,"* *One Organic Whole*, to be studied as a whole, dealt with as a whole, expounded as a whole, each part an index to the whole, a complex, end-developing and one-aimed

---

* Orelli. Die alttest. Weissagung. 45. This statement must not be taken in the Darwinian sense of "Common Descent." Orelli does not mean it so. Man is the immediate work of God, yet all that goes before him is but the herald of his Advent on the Stage. This is God's wondrous work, and we may not deny it.

† Bibl-prophetisch-Theologie. 116.

whole, continually expanding and unfolding from narrower to wider, and obscurer to clearer, until. at last,
its hidden ages and ends, stand out in bold relief, displayed in all their brightness.   It is not that the New
Testament is "imported" back into the Old, in order
that there we may find ages and ends " borrowed from
the New," but it is that the discovery of the 1000 years
in the Old, is an inductive demonstration, scientific and
sure, that the writers of the New have said nothing
other than what Moses and the Prophets did say should
come to pass.   The denial of this involves the destructive statement that "in *every* form of prediction the laws
of prediction *preclude* exact and literal fulfilment." *
Such assertion assails as false the foremost argument
of the early Martyr-heroes who were called of God to
stand in the front line, "opening and alleging," in defence of the Messiahship of Jesus, against both Jew and
Gentile, that " the harmony between prophecy and fulfilment is the greatest and truest demonstration,—*me-
giste kai alethestate apodeixis,*—of Christianity." †   Nor
has Kuenen and his Dutch school damaged this position
in the least.   Nor is Idealism needed to help Apologetics.

B.   DEVELOPMENT OF THE 1,000 YEARS
IN THE NEW TESTAMENT

(2)   But another proof comes forward to salute us.
Nothing can be of greater interest to a student of God's
Word than to watch the development of the 1000 years
in the *New Testament*.   In the Old Testament, those
years are, first of all, implied, though not mentioned,
as introduced by Israel's deliverance and the resurrec-

---

* Briggs.   Messianic Prophecy.   I. 54.
† Orelli.   Die alttest. Weissagung.   75.

tion of the righteous, in Moses, Deut. xxxii:39–43, and David, Psa. xlix:14, 15, then gradually unveiled in Hosea's " Third Day," Hos. vi:2, more fully opened out in the " Many Days " of Isa. xxiv:22, and Ezek. xxxviii: 8, and finally, disclosed in Dan. xii:12, 13, as the blessed time following the resurrection of the just. So, in the New Testament, we have a like development of the Interval between the resurrections. First of all, since our Lord, in the Synoptists, has *nothing* to say of the resurrection of the wicked, He refers simply to the blessed age following the resurrection of the righteous, as a time when the just shall eat bread, and the righteous shine as the Sun, in the kingdom of their Father, Matt. xiii:43, Luke xiv:14, 15. That this kingdom is a kingdom of glory on earth, is the common teaching of both Testaments. But next, when our Lord has *something* to say of the resurrection of the wicked, in the Fourth Gospel, He employs a progressive method of discourse, advancing step by step, while grasping the total present and future in one conception, and, passing onward from one great thought to another, as plainly *wakes the suspicion* of an Interval between the resurrection of the righteous and the wicked, as He does of an Interval between the spiritual and bodily resurrections themselves. And it is the very Interval Hosea, Isaiah and Ezekiel saw. It lies, first of all, *wholly concealed*, then gradually unveiled, by our Lord, in John v:21–29, the classic passage constantly yet vainly quoted, by all Post-millennialists, to prove that no such interval exists. That very passage, however, proves the contrary! For, if we dismiss the wrong conceptions of it, taught by the Church, we shall discover, clearly, that in the exposition of His Life-Giving Power and Judicial Authority, as the Son of Man, our Lord, first of all, uses a most general expression covering *all kinds* of resurrection, the resurrection of the soul, and the body; and at different times, both now and hereafter, v. 21; next, as He proceeds from the general to the particular, He limits the expression to a purely *spiritual* resurrection, v. 24; next, He passes on to mention the *bodily* resurrection of those who are already spiritually raised, viz: the resurrection of the righteous, or of *some* that are in their graves, v. 25; then, finally, extends His thought to include the *bodily* resurrection of the *wicked* as well as of the righteous, *i. e.*, of " *all* that are in their graves," vs. 28, 29; the wondering crowd staring and listening, as His great discourse ascends to reach its climax. It is during the progress of His speech to this climax,— which sweeps His whole official work, as the Son of Man, at both Advents and all the way between, and beyond, yea, the *whole* future in one vast conception, both before and after His Second Coming, that the Interval after that Coming, viz.: *that* between the resurrection of the righteous and the wicked, begins to be detected and, at last, confirmed. It is manifest that different events, occurring at different times, are grouped together, regardless of any specification of the Intervals between. The whole time, present and future, is summed up in " the hour *that is coming* and *now is*," in v. 25, and the " coming hour " in v. 28, and which is of *larger extent* than the "coming hour" in v. 25; *that* referring only to the time of the righteous, *this* to the times of *both* righteous and wicked. Not a line exists to intimate the simultaneousness of the resurrection of these two classes, any more than the simultaneousness of the bodily and spiritual resurrections themselves. On the contrary, the " First Resurrection," foretold by Daniel xii:1–3, Isaiah xxvi:19, and

Rev. xx:6, is *here*, as plainly in v. 25, as the "Last Resurrection," taught by implication in Isa. xxiv:22, and
clearly in Rev. xx:12–15, is *there* in v. 29. *The juxtaposition of both, in general discourse, or in one mental conception, grasping the whole future, vs.* 28, 29, *does not
necessarily involve simultaneousness of occurrence.* The
Fourth Gospel has no other eschatology than is found
in the Apocalypse, and both none other than is found
in the Prophets, in Peter and Paul. It is the voice of
Christ that sounds in all. And this is of first importance in our age, and one of the best exegetically established and victorious replies,—after 60 years of hottest
conflict,—to the rationalists, and idealizers, who have
assailed the Fourth Gospel on the one hand, and the
Apocalypse on the other, as being uncanonical, and not
written by the same author, because of difference of
style, and chiefly of doctrine, and most of all in eschatology. The words of Gebhardt, familiar with the
whole controversy, are worthy to be quoted here, at
length. Commenting on John v:21–29, he says: "The
Evangelist and Seer hold essentially the same views
To an unprejudiced reader there can be no doubt that
the Evangelist, in most perfect harmony with the Seer,
expected that, after the completion of the earthly kingdom of Christ and the last judgment on Satan, and the
passing away of the present world, the final judgment
would take place; and that " *all the dead who, until then,
remain in the grave, would arise to be judged, in the general
resurrection.*" "As to John v:25, there has, unnecessarily,
been much controversy. *It can mean nothing else than
the " First Resurrection," in distinction from the general
resurrection to judgment.* If the two bodily resurrections do not come externally together, *in relation to
time* (as they do not) then the " *Last Day* " cannot pos-

sibly be anything else than the *Great Final Catastrophe* in its *Twofold Degree* of realization, viz; (a) The Advent and what it brings with it; and (b) The Final Judgment and what depends upon it; *both one and the same in nature, but in time and degree of realization, different.* When the Evangelist uses the name " *Last Day* " for this *Duality*, he intends nothing different from Christ's " *Day* " which " Abraham saw afar off, and was glad."* This is certainly correct.   Our Lord's discourse here, even as in the Olivet Prophecy, groups separate and distant events in one picture, after the manner of pre-exile prophecy.   The neglect to observe this law of prophetic representation, has turned prophetic theology into scholastic dogmatics and, blotting out the Interval between the resurrections and judgments, *has given to the Church, since Constantine's day, a series of Creeds and Confessions, aud Standards of Doctrine, wherein both the resurrections and judgments are made simultaneous, without interval, and placed as due at one and the same epoch of time!*   And this patent and palpable error of interpretation is one of the chief arguments, used by *post*-millennialists, against the *pre*-millennial coming of Christ!   The Church, however, has begun to see her error in eschatology, and in her creed-statement of the biblical doctrine, and to use her fresh light in defence of the truth.   "It is gratuitous," says Professor Stanley Leathes, in his reply to Kuenen, "and contrary to analysis, to *assume* that, *because events are mentioned in immediate juxtaposition, therefore they are to follow one auother in immediate chronological sequence!*" †   Plainly so !   That one clear observation overthrows, and con- signs to oblivion forever, the ordinary interpretation of

---

* Gebhardt. Doct. of Apoc., 4ˉ2–404.
† Old Testament Prophecy. 286.

John v:21-29, by post-millenialists. Allow that one false assumption for one moment, and prophecy stands self-convicted of irreconcilable contradictions, and Kuenen and his Dutch school wave their flag in triumph!

C. THE TWO PASSAGES, DANIEL 12:1-3 & JOHN 5:25-29

(3). Before we advance farther it is of the first importance to advert to the celebrated passage. Dan. xii: 1-3, in connection with John v:25-29. If we open the theological textbooks we have been accustomed to study, or the ordinary commentaries, we shall find that, upon the question of the resurrection, *these two passages are uniformly quoted, first of all, to prove a universal and simultaneous resurrection of the dead. They are the exegetical stronghold of post-millennialism, and are alleged to deny clearly the interval of* 1,000 *years between the resurrections, and to affirm the contemporaneous occurrence of both.* Nothing is more incorrect than this. The passages cannot be equated, nor does either teach, or even imply, a simultaneous resurrection of the righteous and wicked. The points wherein these supposed parallel passages agree are fewer than those in which they differ. They are only parallel in part, *i. e.*, in respect to the "*First* Resurrection." In Dan. xii:1-3, *only* the resurrection of the righteous is taught, *i. e.*, of Israel's faithful dead, contrasted with which is the non-risen condition of the wicked destroyed from the face of the earth. In John v:25-29 the resurrection of *both* righteous and wicked is taught, but not asserted as simultaneous. There are no proof-texts for any such doctrine in all the Bible. The Old Testament does not and cannot contradict the New, by abolishing the interval of the 1,000 years which separates the resurrection of the wicked from that of the righteous.

Were it true that *"at that time,"* Dan. xii:1, when
Antichrist comes to his end, Dan. xi:45, a simultaneous
resurrection takes place, or that Dan. xii:1-3, even implies such a thing, no exegetical talent possible to angel
or man, could reconcile this polar antagonism to other
Scriptures.   The true rendering of Dan. xii:1-3, in connection with the context, is " And (at that time) *Many*
(of thy people) shall awake (or be separated) *out from
among* the sleepers in the earth-dust.   *These* (who
awake) shall be unto life everlasting, but *Those* (who do
not awake at that time) shall be unto shame and contempt everlasting."   So, the most renowned Hebrew
Doctors render it, and the best Christian exegetes, and
it is one of the defects of the *Revised Version* that—for
reasons deemed prudent, doubtless, by the Old Testament Company—it has allowed the wrong impression
King James' Version gives, to remain.   A false doctrine is thereby, through defective rendering, given
color from the Word of God which repudiates it at
every step.

Not *all* awake "at that time," but only *many*.   The
"These" who awake, " at that time," are the righteous
of Daniel's people, the as many as are "written in the
Book," Dan. xii:1 ; they, of whom the " instructed
many," and they that "understand," xi:33, are the types,
the " Many " who are " turned to righteousness," with
those who have turned them, Dan. xii:3.   The " *Those*"
who do not awake, at that time, are the wicked dead,
Isa. xxvi:14, whom John calls the " rest of the dead,"
Rev. xx:7, and whom the pre-Christian Hebrew Teachers, the *"Maskilim,"* called *"Shear Hammethim," i. e.*, the
"Remainder of the Dead."   They include the "Slain of
the Lord," Isa. lxvi:16; the "carcasses" of the anti-
christian host rotting on the field of the last conflict

with the Beast; and described as *"an abhorrence"* to all
beholders, Isa. lxvi:24; Dan. vii:26; Rev. xix:17-21; xiv:
20. "Dead, *they* shall not live; Deceased, *they* shall not
rise." Isa. xxvi:14. The grammatical and logical subject of the verb "awake," Dan. xii:1-3, is " *Many out
from among the sleepers;"*—not *all.* The grammatical
and logical subject of the verb "come forth," John v:
25-29, is " *All that are in their graves,"*—not merely
many. In John, the "come forth" belongs to *both* the
clauses, "they that have done good," and "they that
have done evil," because *two classes* are *included* in the
"All that are in their graves." In Daniel, on the contrary, the "awake" belongs to only *one* of the classes,
viz., the " *These,"* because only *one class* is the total of
the "Many *out from among* the sleepers." It cannot
belong to the " *Those"* from whose company *"These"*
are separated by means of the resurrection.

In brief, *"Many out from among"* cannot mean *"All
that are in."* The angel who spoke to Daniel was a
better logician than to say that a part is the whole.
The common Church-Doctrine of a universal and simultaneous resurrection is not the Doctrine of the Word
of God. It rests on bad exegesis, misconception of the
text, and disregard of the law of development in prophecy with respect to the Ages and the Ends. Dan. xii:1-3,
teaches only the *"First Resurrection,"* as does Isa. xxvi:
19, its Old Testament "Companion-Piece," as Delitzsch
cal's it, and as does Rev. xx:4-6, its New Testament
"Companion-Piece." *And it is this first resurrection that
is taught in John v:25.* Daniel sees the Second Advent,
the Deliverance of Israel's surviving 144,000, the resur_
rection of Israel's faithful dead, and the Blessed Age
beyond; "the 1000 years," when he stands in his lot·

For a full discussion of the passages, see "*The Presby-terian Review. Notes.* Jan. 1884." *

D. 1 CORINTHIANS 15:23-28

But furthermore. This same Interval between the resurrections in John's Gospel, is still more clearly indicated, though not opened out fully, or named, in Paul's first letter to the Corinthian Church, when discussing the doctrine of the resurrection, 1 Cor. xv:23–28. He tells the Church that Christ comes (1) to *assume* the kingdom ; then, after this Messianic reign is closed, and His mediatorial work accomplished, (2) to *deliver* the Kingdom, "that God may be all in all," v. 28. Two horizons are here. Two Ends are here. And one Interval is here, as the best interpreters all maintain. The 1000 years, and the analogy between the quiet mode in which Paul assumes as well as asserts their presence, and the similar mode in which Isaiah xxiv:22 does the same, is very striking. They are the Age, to which Paul

---

*Professor Briggs (Mess. Proph. I. 42), "*Some* are to rise to receive their everlasting reward, and *Some* to shame and eve lasting abhorrence." Professor Birk's (pre millennialist), ' The words *These* and *Those*, in Hebrew, seem always to distribute something named before *i. e.*, *Of the Many* who awake, it is said *Some* will rise to glory, *Others* to shame and contempt." (Outlines Unfulfilled Prophecy 225). This is intolerable! for (1) *Many* does not mean *all.* (2) The preposition "*out from*" is not superfluous. (3) The "these" and "those" do not distribute the "*Many*," but the whole mass of the *sleepers*, of whom the "*Many*" are only *one* class. (4) Only "*Many*" awake, not *all* the sleepers. Excellently does Dr. Tregelles say, "The word rendered *Some* in our version is *never* repeated in any passage in the Hebrew Bible, *in the sense of taking up distributively any general* class *previously named*." Excellently does Petri also reply, ' So long as you construe the ' Sleepers' with the ' Many' your philological acquirement can only be absurdly applied; for the partition is manifest." (De usu Accent. S Cod. Hebr. Aphor. xiii: § 5.) Excellently Fuerst also. "In Daniel xii: 2, the *substantive verb*, frequently omitted, is to be supplied." So Cocceius, the best Hebraist of his day. "No universal resurrection is taught here. These who *are* unto eternal life are distinguished from those who *are* unto eternal shame and contempt. The *former* awake at the time specified xi:45, xii:1. To carry the verb 'awake' into the second member of the verse is to add to Scripture which I dare not do." (On Daniel xii:2.) So Saadias

tells us, the "Creature" is looking, Rom. viii:18–23, the millennial age following "the redemption of the body," the Sabbatic Age when Nature herself puts on her new dress, and wears a new smile. And, finally, this great Interval, suspected and implied in John v:21–29, unveiled in part in I Cor. xv:23–28, and opened still more in Rom. viii:18–23, blooms forth revealed in full, and stands disclosed, by name, as "*the* 1000 *years*," in Rev. xx:1–7. That is the crown of the whole development. Thus, the mode of progressive revelation is the same in both Testaments, viz., organic, the one and only true mode of all instruction, viz., from the general to the particular, and from the obscure to the clear. The harmony is perfect, and from Moses to John, God's word is without a contradiction. The 1000 years appear everywhere, as following the Second Coming of Christ.

E. FURTHER PROOF OF THE HISTORICAL REALITY

But still further reasons exist to show that the 1000

---

the prince of Hebrew scholars, the two Kimchis, Abarbanel, Bechai and Maimonides. So Dæchsel, "Some Jews and Socinians, interpreting right, yet argue that in the Old Testament, the resurrection of the wicked is not taught. This error lies in assuming that the time when Michael stands up, viz., the Advent, is the *Absolute End* which it is not, but only the *Relative* End. (Bib. Hebr. Accent. on Dan. xii:2.) Keil says he is "*surprised* to find the word *Many* here where the word *All* might have been *expected ! ! !*" (Keil on Daniel, p. 481.) Professor Briggs says, "Daniel has not learned that the *heathen* will rise from the dead also !" (p. 427), only Israel! *i. e.*, he did not know, Isa. xxiv:22.

"The Church idea of the resurrection is unbiblical. The resurrection is *not simultaneous but progressive, at different epochs.* A plurality of time-points is clearly distinguished: (a) the resurrection of individual believers out from the mass of their own number as a result of the *Descensus ad inferos.* Matt. xxvii:50-53: (b) the resurrection of all believers. John v:25; I Cor. xv:23; (c) the resurrection of the wicked, or rest of the dead, Isa. xxiv:22; Rev. xx:7; Acts xxvii:15; John v:28, 29. Church dogmatics have not reproduced accurately the Bible doctrine of the resurrections. In fact, in no other part of dogmatic study has so little been done as in Eschatology, because the subject matter is prophetic." *Rothe. Dogmatik III.* 73, 98.

years are not merely symbolic, but are a true measure of real and historic time still future.   And here, (a) first of all, the merest tyro at school, if asked to construe the sentences, "laid hold of the Dragon and bound him 1000 years;" "they lived and reigned with Christ 1000 years;" could only respond, if correctly, that the expression "1000 *years*" is the *Accusative of Time,*—standing absolute,—in answer to the question, *How Long?* It is not the Accusative of "Eternity," nor of "Spatial Ecumenicity,"—but of *Time, How Long.* That is its grammatical construction.   It tells the extent of time to which the Binding of Satan will go, te period of his non-deception of the nations, the duration of the priestly regency of Christ and His risen saints, the parallel blessedness of all who share in the " First Resurrection."   It is the Millennial Age ; *Time;* not *Eternity.* (b)   Again it is the same period of time that is called in Ps. lxxii:7, "*His Days,*" i. e., Messiah's Days of regal glory on earth,—the "*Yemot Meshicha,*"—"*Days of Messiah,*"—of the Hebrew Teachers, when "the righteous shall flourish, and abundance of peace shall be, so long as the moon endures."   It is that period on earth when patriarchal years return, and the centennarian sports as an "infant of days," and the days of God's people shall be "as the days of a tree," and they shall long enjoy, (literally "*make old,*") "the work of their hands." Isa. lxv:22.   It is not a poetic, symbolic, or merely ideal, prolongation of health, but actual longevity ; not "Christian ripeness," nor " beauty and germinations," but "length of days," which are "years," so that the "infant" will be more than " threescore and ten," and he who dies at the age of " a hundred years," shall be deemed as one signally smitten of God for his sins.   It is a literal period of time *before* which, *during* which

and *after* which, events take place, and *in* which agriculture, architecture, prayer, sin and death in measure,
all exist; therefore not eternity. It is the period which
in the Book Henoch represents human life as attaining
once more its pristine duration before the Flood, "the
Days of Messiah lasting 1000 years."* "We are compelled," as both Hengstenberg and De Wette say, " to
take these years seriously and literally, repeated, as
they are, six times, to impress them on our understanding." † Glasgow's interpretation of them as denoting
the "Gospel Age" is falsified by the actual history of
18 centuries of time since the birth of Christ. His application of the year-day theory to the Millennial Age
is without the slightest justification. The assertion
that "the Millennial *years*, like other prophetic years,
and the 42 months, *must* be taken as *days*, i. e.,=360,000
years, the standard prophetic measurement being *a day
for a year*," and, again, that "1000 are 360,000 *days*, like
the *days* of Daniel's weeks, each day denoting *a year*,"‡
is a series of assumptions and errors, clause after clause,
destitute of all exegetical foundation, and wholly speculative and imaginative. The Millennial Age is a
"Day," just as the Gospel Age is a " Day," and as the
Wandering in the Wilderness was a " Day," a Day
whose years, definite and known to God, are revealed
as "1000 *years*," and not as 360,000 *days* put for years. ‖

---

* Drummond. Jewish Messiah. 374.
† De Wette. Offenbar. Einleit. 5. Hengst. Offenbar. II. 402.
‡ Glasgow. Com. on Apoc. 477, 478.
‖ The Hebrew *Yom*, *Day*, is cognate with the Arabic *Ayam*, Sanscrit
Ayum, Greek *Aion*, Latin *Ævum*, and denotes either a longer or a shorter
period of time, *measured* by Hours, Years, Epochs, Ages, a Life-Time,
Events, or a Dispensation. Hence, "Day of Darkness," "Day of Wrath,"
"Day of Salvation," "Day of Vengeance," "Day of the Lord," " Day of
Temptation." The Day of Messiah's glory on earth is given us in *Years*,
1000 in number, just as the Day of Temptation is given us as 40 years. It
is an *Age*, an *Ævum*, an *Aion*, of measured time. Nowhere is a "Day for

But still again ; the Post-millennialists themselves, in their unwearied effort to fix the *terminus a quo,* or starting point, of these years, testify to the fact that they are historic, and not a mere ideal. Baffled in their calculations, they still renew them. Somehow or other, they are powerless to shake out from their conscience the indestructible conviction that " the 1000 years" *lie in between certain events in time,* one of which is the "Coming of the Lord," whatever that means, and another the " Resurrection of the dead," whatever that means, and, moreover, that, during these years, Satan is bound, and the Risen Saints reign with Christ, whatever these mean. These seem, clearly, to be actual time, and of definite and measured duration. They hold,

(a)   *That the* 1000 *years begin with the First Advent, and represent the whole Church Period down to the Second Advent.* This was the view of Augustine, Eusebius, Jerome, and the State-Church after the early martyr-period, the view of the Mediæval Church, the Lateran and Scholastic theory, still leavening Protestantism itself not yet wholly free from the traditions of Rome. According to this theory the 1000 years began with the Crucifixion, Satan being then bound by virtue of the Death of Christ. The " First Resurrection " is either regeneration, baptism, or the soul's ascent at death to glory, the reign of the risen martyrs being

a year" represented in Scripture as the "*standard* of prophetic measurement." Daniel's "Weeks" are not Weeks of *Days* put for *Years.* The "*Shibim*," or 70 " *Sevens*" are 70 *Sevens* of *Years.* The Year-Day theory has no place in Daniel, and none in John. The fatal error with Mr. Guinness, as with Professor Glasgow, and all who hold the Year-Day-Theory, is that they *assume* in their premises what they profess to find in their conclusions, viz., that the "*Shibim*" or "*Sevens*" in Daniel, are "*Days,*" which is contradicted by the whole prophecy. Similarly, there is not one iota to show that " the 1000 years" in John are 1000 times 360 *Days* put for *Years.* It is imagination.

that of their disembodied spirits in heaven, and the
promised rule of the 12 Apostles that of their spiritual
influence over the Church. Israel was forgotten.
Rather, the "Church" is "Israel." The absurdity of this
view is seen in this that it makes the Millennial reign
on earth, which begins with our Lord's Return, to be
that of His Sojourn in Heaven, a Millennium during
which the bodies of God's saints are still under the empire of death, and the "Times of the Gentiles" are still
running on; times of affliction and woe, and God-opposed world-power! Israel is still nationally cast
away, and in their national grave. The Colossus
of Gentile power still stands erect on Israel's prostrate form. The Apostasy is still deepening, the
Tares yet ripening among the Wheat. Antichrist
is still undestroyed, the Nations, as Nations, are still
raging, the whole tide of church-corruption, false
philosophy, false science, swelling to its height; a millennium of boundless ambition, avarice, and lust of military conquest in the name of religion and missions,
intemperance, oppression and crime of every sort, her-
esies and schisms of gigantic character, wars, dragon-
nades, and inquisitions, persecutions pagan and papal;
Satan's own; a millennium begun by devoting the
Apostles to the axe, Christians to the lions and the
flame, and sending John to Patmos, as a prisoner for
the truth and testimony of Jesus, to write his great
Apocalypse! This whole conception, false in every
way, rests upon an exegetical violence to God's word,
in sundering the strict temporal sequence of the 12th
upon the 11th, and the 20th upon the 19th chapters of
the Apocalypse, *so slipping backward the second half of the
Apocalypse and the* 1000 *years, also, across our whole dispensation, to attach their commencing date to the First Ad-*

vent ! This is the true magic of the post-millennial view improved, at last, by the dictum that " *Symbolical numbers don't count !* " It is associated with the allegorizing, spiritualizing, and idealizing, exposition of the prophecies concerning Israel and the Advent; a theory which taught the Church to say that, when Paul tells the Romans "All Israel shall be saved,"—i. e., the Israel to whom " blindness " had happened,—and who were nationally " cast away,"—it means '· the whole Christian Church ; " and that, when he repeats Israel's prediction that "the Redeemer shall come to Zion," for Israel's deliverance from the last Antichrist, and Israel's Redemption from Gentile power, it means "a great spiritual revival," but not the Second Coming of the Lord ! In short, we are in the *Millennium Now,* and have been so, *for nearly* 1900 *years !*

(b) *That the* 1000 *years date from Constantine, A. D.* 312. It is not necessary to dwell on the fact that post millennialism dates the 1000 years from Pentecost, from the Destruction of Jerusalem A. D. 70, and from the Death of each individual believer ! It is enough,—if passing by these literary curiosities, we confine ourselves to the more prominent commencing dates. Plainly, it was too much to be long believed, that 300 years of bloody persecution and pagan torture of God's saints should belong to the Millennial age of righteousness and peace, and "war no more." Accordingly, the commencing date, the *a quo,* of the 1000 years, was advanced 300 years along the line of history, so excluding the martyr-period. The blessed age begins with the accession of Constantine as the " First Christian Emperor," A. D. 312, the nominal establishment of Christianity, and the Union of Church and State. How Satan and the Church waltzed together around the tranquility of the so-called "Christian Empire," history has told us! Israel still is forgotten. The "Church" is "Israel." The Colossus has come down, i. e., Paganism! Antichrist has been destroyed, i. e., Nero, or Maxentius, or some one else! Such the theory of Grotius, Hammond, and even of a remnant in our own day; an "Idol of the Theater!" We are in the Millennium *now!* The Devil is bound *now!* The First Resurrection is *now!* It is essentially the Augustinian view, and amenable to the same objection.

(c) That the 1000 years date from Charlemagne, A. D. 800; another advance of 500 years, along the line of history, in fixing the *a quo!* Such the invention of that great and good man, Hengstenberg. The Beast, or Antichrist, is not the Pope, but God-opposed Heathenism and Barbarism, not to be destroyed under judgment, at the personal appearing of Christ, but gradually converted and peacefully overthrown by the preaching of the gospel. The Christianization of the German peoples, or European nations, by missionaries like Boniface, and the establishment of the so-called *"Christian State,"* as a result therefrom, is what is symbolized by the Rider on the White Horse in Rev. xix: 11–21! The 1000 years, therefore, *began* Christmas, A. D. 800, when Pope Leo III imposed the crown on the head of Charlemagne as the true successor of the Christian Cæsars, and revived the "Holy Roman Empire." That was considered a great piece of work in those days, although it required the lapse of the whole millennial age before Hengstenberg rose to let the world know how great it was! The Nations had never dreamed that Satan was chained! The Turk was not aware of it! It is morally certain that the German Emperor who stood three days barefoot, in a

hair-cloth shirt, in the winter time, at the castle gate of
Canossa, to do penance to an Italian priest, never suspected it! But nevertheless, the Devil was bound,
Christmas A. D. 800, and remained in Pit till A. D.
1789, when, loosed from his chain, he came forth and
began his old arts in the French Revolution, and the
Wars that followed. The 1000 years are gone forever!
The "First Resurrection" is the saints' passage to, and
appearance in, glory, at death, and the reign of the
risen saints "*on*" the earth is the reign of unraised
saints "*over*" the earth. Since A. D. 1800, or the
French Revolution, is Gog's "*little* season,"—not far
now from a *century*,—during which Gog and Magog
have beleaguered "the camp of the saints," i. e. the
"Church," the "spiritual Jerusalem," or "Beloved
City," called "Christendom," which is the "Holy
Land," by a revived Orientalism and Classic Paganism,
and by the general Heathenism of modern society.
This fiction is the grand-daughter of Augustine's fairy,
and incurs the censure that lies against the view of her
ancient sire. It belongs to the spiritualizing interpretation of the prophecies concerning Israel, and has
given occasion for the stirring Ode by Dr. Cox,

> "We are living, we are dwelling
>   In a grand and awful time ;
> In an age on ages telling—
>   To be living is sublime ; "

a hymn, which, as the line "Gog and Magog to the
fray," is reached by the praising audience,—has elec-
trified, with a nerve-thrilling enthusiasm, more crowds
of amazed and ignorant Christians, than almost any
other ecclesiastical war-ditty ever devised for public
worship. Modifying this view, Keil, the last great

representative of Hengstenberg, goes back to the Constantine date, and holds that "*so long as the State-Religion exists, the* 1000 *years exist,*" which, of course, rules out the United States, where Church and State are independent, from all share in the glories of the Millennial age! According to Keil the " First Resurrection " is literal, indeed, like the "*Parousia*" which, however, is no definite event, but a "continuous process from age to age, along the whole line of historic Christianity ; " a series of unseen individual risings from the dead, beginning with the Destruction of Jerusalem, A. D. 70 ! the attendant change of the living, however, not being mentioned, for obvious reasons !

(d)   *That the* 1000 *years date from somewhere, indefinitely,—in the future, i. e., from some unknown point* 1000 *years next preceding the Second Advent,* which may be either, 500, 1,000, 2,000, 5,000, 10,000, or 365,000, according to the uncertainties, or necessities, of the case. The other theories named, show us past pre-advent millennialism, and present pre-advent millennialism. This one shows us future pre-advent millennialism.   It is another advance along the line of history, the staking down of the commencing date of the 1000 years at *some* undiscernible point along the road, this side the Second Advent.   It is Whitby's "*New Hypothesis,*" as he named it, unknown to the Church for 1600 years, broached but once before Whitby was born, and instantly repudiated.   It is what is styled " *Chiliasmus subtilis,*" a " fine millennialism," a " spiritual " one, and by a French writer is humorously called a " *Chef d'œuvre de Sagacité !*" and is, to-day, the most popular of all the post-millennial speculations, bold, to the last extreme, in putting into God's word what God has left out, and leaving out what God has put in.

According to this " Optimist " theory, ever hissing
at what it calls " Pessimism," beguiled by a popular
catch ignorant of what either Optimism or Pessimism
means, the Church, by virtue of the Gospel, extension
of missions, revivals, operations of Boards, Clubs, and
Alliances, Moral Reforms, Societies, Contributions, Conventions, Assemblies, Circulation of the Bible, Church
Literature, and general Church agencies and activities,
will finally subdue Antichrist, convert the nations, bind
Satan figuratively, allegorically conquer the world, and
introduce the splendors of the Millennium.   It forgets
the words of the Saviour, that, the very time when the
gospel is sent as a " testimony to all nations," is the
time when " iniquity abounds, and the love of many
waxes cold," and " brother betrays brother ; " and the
words of the Apostle that, in the *Acharith Hayyamin*, or
last days "hard times" shall come.   Blind to the fact that
the inward corruption of the Church keeps pace with
her outward expansion, as Lange, Auberlen, Kliefoth,
Van Oosterzee, Alford, and how many godly men
have all so solemnly shown, and all history as well as
the reeking crime of Christendom to-day testifies, it
remains a stranger to the truth that the End-Time will
reveal these two contradictory facts as concurrent, viz.
the deepening of apostasy and the extension of the
gospel, enormous missionary activity, and enormous
departures from the truth.   Averse to confess what
every one sees, viz., the foregone tendency to change
the Church of Christ into an organization for the promotion of social and business relations, and mutual
temporal benefit, under the forms of religion ; the need
of regeneration, and the ignominy and scandal of the
cross ever disappearing before the formal profession,
outward success, and easy triumphs, of a Christianity

made pleasing to the world by all manner of indulgence, concession, and compromise; the pulpit rose-
coloring all things under the false lure of "Optimism,"
and the pew transferred to the theater, the club-house,
the euchre-room, the gay concert, and the temple of
mammon; the kingdom of God transformed into the
kingdom of this world, Satan disguised as an angel of
light joining the Church, the people delighted to have
it so, and supporting the gospel, and contributing to
missions, all the more while it is so; the inner spiritual
life of the Church decaying, the laws and government
of Christ in His own house set aside for the "wisdom,"
"prudence," and "policy" of Church rulers, lest
"financial interests" should suffer; it still assumes a
contract, under these conditions, to *convert the world to
Christ!* Enormous in pretension, as unfathomable in
the mystery of its way, it yet, while decking itself with
the garments of a world-harlotry, proposes to itself a
plan and a purpose which, already, the mouth of God
has declared to be false. All the social and moral
plague-spots, oppressions, and crimes, national, and
international, which 1800 years of advancing Christian
endeavor have been powerless to avert, and with all its
revivals powerless to extirpate, and which still bloom
in, fatten on, and disgrace, our "*Civilization;*" and all
the darkness and pollution of the degenerate human
heart, ever the same from generation to generation in
the birth of every individual, the millions multiplying
by an increase that outstrips even the progress of
Christianity; and all the vice embedded in our
"*Culture;*" and all the wickedness of Heathendom,
less wicked than Christendom; it proposes to remove by "*a continuous process*" of the same Christian
and Church development which for 1800 years has

shown itself utterly incompetent to achieve the task. And so the victory, foreseen by the prophet shall come to pass, the glory foretold arise and shine, the wolf and the lamb peacefully dwelling together, i. e. the wicked and the righteous, the leopard and the kid, the lion and the calf, allegorically cohabiting, and a little child, the Sunday school scholar, allegorically leading them. So long as *laissez-faire* is the law of Christian life, and Church permit to free indulgence, and the sun shines bright, and the grass is green, and the flowers are beautiful, and the canary sings in its cage, and money, and property, and amusements, and church contributions, and sociables, balls, orchestras, and dances, abound, the doctrine of an " apostasy " and a " judgment to come," and a " Day of the Lord," is incongruous with the situation, as Elijah at Ahab's table, or John the Baptist at Herod's banquet. Something grander than the Augustan " *nova ordo*," or the Jewish " *Yemot Meshicah*," or Sir Thomas More's " *Utopia*," or Plato's " *Republic*," will supervene, and Malthus' theory of population, which says that " men increase faster than their means of subsistence," and Darwin's theory of the " struggle to survive," will be proved by Christianity, Culture, Commerce, Trade, Mammon, Railroads, Telegraphs, Telephones, Graphophones, Chambers of Commerce, Syndicates, Companies, and Pools, to be vain dreams. Legislation and benches of justice, police courts and prisons, will be all right : governments all right ; newspapers, the present main-stay of crime, all right ; capital, labor, the social problem, corporations, bourses, and exchanges, all right ; total abstinence from all fermented drinks, material, moral, social, civil, and religious, all right ; seminaries, schools, universities, colleges, theology, homiletics, criticism, the pulpit and the platform, all right; alcohol, theaters, brothels, and breathing holes of hell, all right; the *Church* shining, the glory of the Lord risen on her; Buddha gone, Islam gone, Brahma gone, *Pessim* gone, armies and navies gone, the "Great Powers" at peace, the "Little Powers" also, the "Horns" no longer goring, and the knowledge of the glory of the Lord covering the earth as the waters do the sea. Arabian story will pale beside the wonders the "Woman," the "Church," will do, as she hides her leaven in the three measures of meal, "Shem, Ham, and Japhet," and swells the world's millions to the height of her own perfection! And all in historic time!

Alas! it is a deep falsehood;—a beguiling *"lie."* It is that *"finer form of Chiliasm"* which lauds the "Star-Spangled Banner, long may it wave!" and has taken possession, bodily, of what it calls our *"American Christianity,"* so much unlike the Apostolic sort!—It is the ordinary Millennialism of the spiritualizers, and of the pulpit, press, and platform, the millennialism ventilated in Church-Courts, Conventions, General Assemblies, Alliances, and Associations, and framed in special sermons, addresses, reports, and resolutions, published for the health of the soul. Discussion of it, there is hardly any, for "prudential reasons." It is that *"fine Chiliasm,"* false as fine, which, in common with the "coarse," or "Jewish," holds to a Millennium *before* the Advent and the Resurrection of the just;—Swedenborg's millennium, Robert Owen's, Fourier's, and St. Simon's, a socialistic and humanitarian Millennium, mixed with Christianity, and whose central idea, viz., that it comes *before* the Advent and the Resurrection, is, as Ebrard called it, the *"proton pseudos,"* or *"fundamental lie,"* through which all the Reformers, and the 17th Article

of the Augsburg Confession, clearly saw;—a millennium sprung from Origen, a Universalist, perpetuated by Rome all Arminian, fathered by Whitby, a
Socinian, and adopted by many godly and scholarly
Protestants, who, mistaking error for exegesis, spiritualize all the prophecies concerning Israel, or end
them in Maccabean, or early Roman times; a millennium without Christ to introduce it by judgment and
deliverance; a millennium of saints in the flesh, and of
the holy still in the grave; the precise Millennium of
the "heretic" Montanus, only wider than his Phrygian
Pepuza! *   Not a solitary text of Scripture is produced in its support, though challenged a hundred
times, except *"Lo, I am with you always, even unto the end
of the world !"*   It rests on a mistaken view of the purpose of God, and of the promise of the Spirit, violates
every principle of exegesis, depends for its success
upon the ignorance of its hearers, and the daring of its
preachers, and is one of the chief stimuli in mass-meet-
ings for prayer, where the leader, watch in one hand,
gavel in the other, times the action of God's Spirit,
calling for petitions "two minutes prompt," "short and
to the point," "next meeting this evening seven sharp!"
The Germans call it *"Phantasie !"*   Luther, whose
homiletic rules were three, "Step up freshly, Open
your mouth widely, and Get done quickly," and who
generally went straight to the center of his subject,
called it "a *Lie* forged by Satan to blind men to the
truth," and Delitzsch more urbanely styles it a "dis-
tortion and negation of the prophetic word," while
Lange calls its opposite "a pearl of true doctrine," Van
Oosterzee and Schaff assenting.   Refuted a thousand

---

* See Dr. S. R. Maitland's *"Eruvin,"* p. 197.

times since Bengel's day, it dies hard, the world loves it so! Absurd as it is, it remains, however, a witness to the truth that the 1000 years are not mere symbols of abstract ideas, but a measure of literal time, for whose coming the Church has waited 1800 years, and still waits in hope.

Thus, baffled at every step in its calculations, and contradicted alike by Scripture and the page of history, Post-millennialism has been compelled to creep slowly along the ages to find an *a quo* for the 1000 years, now here, now there, starting with the First Advent, and ending in some undiscoverable dream-date of the future *"somewhere,"* this side the Second Coming! In this protracted effort it has become responsible, by its impatience, for three "Great Panics" in Christendom, as to the "End of the World;"—the panics of the 6th, the 10th, and the 13th centuries. Had Hengstenberg lived sooner, to write earlier, we might have had another in the year 1800! Thus, discordant among themselves, the alternatives are either (1) to abandon what Professor Volck calls their *"Klopstockian Bloom-Time"* * altogether, and return to the early faith, or (2) wed the *"Ideal-Theory"* of prophetic numbers, repeating the dictum, *"Symbolical numbers don't count,"* dissolving the 1000 years into ideas of eternity, perfection, and ecumenicity, so teaching that when eternity is finished "Satan shall be loosed a little season," to play his old arts again, after which, "ecumenicity, eternity, and perfection" will begin again; the "little season" being "our whole Christian Dispensation;"—the words " when" and "expired" having "no reference to *time*," whatever! In presence of such an eschatology, the course for men,

---

* Prof. Christiani. Uebersichtliche Darstellung. 135.

not insane, is neither doubtful nor difficult to be decided.   By far the vast majority of standard interpreters,—and Alford and Delitzsch said it thirty years
ago,—have returned to the early faith of the Church,
and emancipated themselves from the allegorizing,
idealizing, and spiritualizing, perversion of the prophetic word.

And nothing is more just.   Let any one not en-
slaved to a theory, open the Apocalypse of John at
chapter xix:11–21, and xx:1–7, and say (1) that means
the *First* Advent and our present age, or (2) that means
Constantine and the overthrow of Paganism, or (3) that
means *Charlemagne* and the Holy Roman Empire, or
(4) that means a *Great Spiritual Revival* and the conversion of Antichrist 1000 years before Christ comes,
and he will see how repugnant such follies are to the
Theme of the Book, Rev. i:7, viz., the personal and visible Return of Christ from Heaven!   And, remembering the organic connection between the Seven-Sealed
Scroll and Daniel's 70th Week, (Dan. ix:27, Rev. chapters vi-xix,) where the Antichrist is the subject of discourse, he will quickly see how every false fixing of the
starting-point, for the 1000 years, makes 1260 days or
last 3½ years of the 70th Week itself, mean either the
whole, or a part of the entire Christian dispensation,
and the judicial overthrow of Antichrist at the Second
Coming, no less than his conversion 1000, or even 1800,
years before that event!   Such is the effect of following
Augustine's violent disruption of Rev. xx from Rev.
xixth chapter, and *sliding back* the commencing date of
the 1000 years to the First Advent; or, as others do,
to Constantine, or Charlemagne, or to "some point"
1000 years this side the Second Coming !

Let us dismiss, forever, this "Idol of the Theater,"

this human invention of a Church-Millennium, 1000 years before Christ comes! It is a false conception. In the words of Semisch, "There is not, in the entire Scripture, a single trace of such a millennium. The Second Coming of the Lord is none other than His coming to Judgment at the close of the present dispensation, and this close is far from being preceded by the peace and the delight represented by such a doctrine. The Apocalypse of John certainly furnishes the outlines of the Millennium. It is a *manifest misinterpretation* which, since the time of Augustine, has placed the beginning of the 1000 years, not at the Second Coming of the Lord, but in some point of time already past, or this side the Advent. *This cannot be.* The Millennium takes place *after* the destruction of Antichrist and his host, Rev. xix:11–21; xx:1–7. The "First Resurrection" Rev. xx:4, 5, expressly contrasted with that of "the rest of the dead who live not till the 1000 years are finished," v. 5, *cannot* have allegorical reference to the first stage of soul-bliss in heaven (Hengstenberg) nor to the mental process of the new birth (Augustine) nor to any spiritual resurrection in the Church (Whitby) in any sense. It can only be the "bodily resurrection of the bodily dead." *

---

* Chiliasmus in Herzog. Real-Encycl. I. 658.

Part 6

CHARACTERISTICS OF THE 1,000 YEARS

A. GENERAL VIEW

As to the Characteristics of the 1000 years, it is enough to name them briefly, as they are given us in the word of God. Like the New Testament, the Old is remarkably clear as to what shall occur at Messiah's Second Coming, and give complexion to the age following. A reference to the Scripture passages, herewith subjoined, will well repay the student.

1. Satan, the Cause of all the World's Woe, shall, together with his evil Angels, be imprisoned in the "abyss," chained, sealed, and locked up, beyond the possibility of getting out, during the whole Millennial reign. His power over man, and the nations, will be absolutely broken. Isa. xxiv:21,22; xxvii:1; Rev. xx:1, 2 A half week of years, previously to this, he has been dejected from heaven. Rev. xii:7–12.

2. Antichrist's kingdom, overthrown forever, and the kingdoms of this world with it, shall never be revived, nor Antichrist and his confederates ever reappear to dwell upon the earth. These, with the False Prophet, are cast alive into the "lake of fire." Isa. xxiv:21, 22; Rev. xix:20; xx:10.

3. There shall be but One Kingdom, in that day, the Kingdom of Christ, to which all the nations of earth shall be obedient, a kingdom "under the whole heaven," from sea to sea, and from the river to the ends of the earth. Ps. ii:1–12; lxxii:8; Dan. ii:44; vii:27; Numb. xxiv:17; Rev. xi:15; Zech. xiv:9; ix:10.

4. There shall be but One Religion, then, the Religion of Christ, alone. Christianity shall be co-extensive with the limits of the world. All false religious systems, and corrupt forms of Christianity, shall have disappeared, forever. Isa. xlv:23; lii. 1, 7–10; lxvi:17, 23; Zech. xiv:16; viii:23; ix:7; Rev. v:9–14; Zeph. iii:9; Mal. i:11.

5. All Idols shall be destroyed, of whatever kind. A presage of this, in primary fulfilment, was given at the First Advent, and is celebrated, not only in Plutarch's acount of the "Cessation of the Heathen Oracles," but also in the choral strains of Milton's "Ode on the Nativity of Christ." Isa. ii:8; xlii:17; Ps. xcvii:7; Zech. xiii:2.

6. "All Israel" shall be holy to the Lord; and this means, not the Christian Church, nor the Nations, but the Jewish people as such, the natural seed of Abraham. Their apostasy will be finished, their sin sealed, their iniquity atoned, and everlasting righteousness and holiness be brought in. Dan. ix:24; Isa. xxvi:2; Deut. xxx:6; Isa. lx:21; Jer. iii:17; l:20; Ezek. xxxvi:25–27; xxxvii:23,24; Zeph. iii:13; Rev. xiv:1–5; Zech. xiv:20; Isa. liv:13,14.

7. War shall exist no more.* This result of the

---

* The *Great Rebellion* of 1861-1865 in the United States, in defence of slavery, cost the Federal Government, the first year of its existence, $1,300.000 *per day*, the fourth year of its existence, $3,500,000 *per day*, or $27,500,000 *per week*, and left the nation encumbered with a Debt of about $3,000,000,000. The pecuniary cost of the War besides amounted to nearly

Binding of Satan, who is the instigator of all war, and
cause of all national and international collision, continues throughout the whole Millennial age. The
proof that Satan is *not* bound, *now*, is (a) the fact of
" *War*," in our present age, and (b) the fact that when
loosed for a " little season," at the end of this age, his
first effort is to excite the nations to " *War*," and (c) to
war against the kingdom of Christ. In the Millennial
age, however, all is peace, not only between man and
man, but also between the Nations. Isa. ii:4; ix:5;
Mic. iv:3, 4; Hos. ii:20; Zech, ix:10; Ezek. xxxix:9, 10;
Rev. xx:1–3.

8.   Harmony shall be restored in creation, between
man and man, and a covenant of peace be made
between man and the lower animal world. This also
is a result of the Binding of Satan, who first entered a
Serpent to practice his arts on mankind. Isa. xi:6–9;
lxv:25; Hos. ii:20; Ezek. xxxiv:25, 28; Mic. iv:3.

9.   The Land of Israel shall be transformed from
barrenness into beauty, and made fruitful, glorious, and
free from plague, and populated by a happy and
blessed people; the people to whom, by right, it
belongs. Isa. xxxv:1; xli:18, 19; Amos ix:13–15; Isa.
lxv:17–25; Zech. viii:3–8.

10. Patriarchal years will return, in which a man,

---

twice this sum. On the Federal side, not less than 300,000 men were slain,
or died of their wounds, or of disease contracted in the service. On the
Confederate side, as many more perished. To these 400,000 more of
crippled and ruined must be added, making a total of *ten hundred thousand
men* destroyed and disabled. At the close of the War the Federal Army
amounted to 1,000 000 of men, the Navy to 50,000. The *Standing Armies
of Europe*, to-day, amount to over 5,000,000 of men, with 10,000,000 of
reserves, the cost of the armies of Great Britain, France, Germany, Italy,
Russia, for the year 1888 being equal to $551,750,000. And these who fly
at each other's throats are " *Christendom*," said to be enjoying Millennial
Glory " *now*," while covered from head to foot with its own blood, and
steeped in its own crimes!

100 years old, shall be esteemed a child. Instead of saying, as we now do, that such an one has entered his "*teens*," it will be said that such an one has just entered his "*hundreds*." Isa. lxv : 20–22. The risen saints "neither marry, nor are given in marriage." Matt. xxii:30 ; but the unglorified are a "blessed seed, and their offspring with them." Isa. lxv:23.

11. Israel and Judah, or 12-tribed Israel, shall be re-united as One Nation, under One King, in their own land; and, enriched with spiritual gifts of wisdom, knowledge, and grace, be a blessing to all mankind. Thus, the promise to Abraham will be fulfilled. "In thy seed," etc., etc. Ezek. xxxvii:1–28; Mic. iv:8; Joel ii:27; iii:1; Zech. ii:14 ; Isa.x i:9 ; Jer. xxxi:34; Rom. xi:12–15.

12. Jerusalem and Mount Zion, by means of physical convulsion and geological changes suddenly effected through disruption, depression, fissure, and elevation, at the Lord's appearing, shall be "exalted" or "lifted high," above the surrounding hills, and the adjacent region be reduced "to a plain," like the Arabah, or Ghor, that runs from the slopes of Hermon to the Red Sea. "*All the land will change itself*," and the geographic center of the reconstruction will be determined by the boundaries of the ancient territory of Judah. All this the effect of the "Presence of the Lord," more awful than His "Presence" at Sinai. Isa. lxiv:1–4; Mic. i:3, 4; Judges v:4, 5; Ps. xcvii:4,5 ; Exod. xix:18, 24; Hab. iii:6, 10 ; Nah. i:5,6; Matt. xxvii:51, 52; Isa. xl:1–5 ; ii:2; Mic. iv:1 ; Zech. xiv:4, 5, 10, 11 ; Jer. xxxi:38–40.*

13. The City itself shall be built again, broadened, enlarged, and adorned with the wealth of the nations,

---

* See Physico-Prophetical Essays, by Rev. W. Lister. F. G. S. 111-160. London. Longman; Green, etc; 1861.

and the Temple made glorious by the "precious things" of mankind. Jerusalem shall not only be "lifted up," but made "fruitful as the Valley of the Jordan." Ps. lxxii:10; Isa. xxvi:15 (Revised Version). Zech. xiv: 10 (Revised Version). Isa. xxxiii:17. (Revised Version.) Jer. xxxi:38; Isa. lx:10–18; Hagg. ii:6–9; Jer. iii:17, and the last nine chapters of Ezekiel.

14. The "Outcast of Israel" and "Dispersed of Judah," gathered to enter the Kingdom, will return to their fatherland, from the East, the West, the North, and the South, to sit down with Abraham, Isaac aud Jacob, conducted thither by Gentile hands, and presented, as a holy *Mincha* or Offering, to the Lord Himself, revealed in His glory. Auxiliary to this great Ingathering of the Hebrew people, the River of Egypt, the Nile, shall be divided and dried up, and the River Euphrates also, to make way for the march of Israel returning under the protection of Eastern princes. A high road, moreover, out of Egypt to Assyria will accelerate the movement, and ships from Tarshish, and the Sea-Islands, will cover the Mediterranean, loaded with Israel's sons, their silver and gold, and the wealth of a world startled by the revelation of Christ in His glory. With ancient valor they shall press their way to the plain of Esdraelon where stands the Hill of Megiddo (Armageddon), and under "One Head," their Bozrah-Conqueror, move to possess the Holy City forever. "Great will be the Day of Jezreel!" Isa. xi:10–16; xxvi:13–16; xxvii:12, 13; xlix:12, 22, 23; Zech. x:10–12; Zeph. iii:9; Rev. xvi:12; Isa. lxv:19, 20; Matt. viii:11;— Isa. xxxv:8; xi;16; xix;23–25; lx:9; lxiii:1–6; lix:16–21; Rev. xvi:16; xix:11–21; Hosea i:11; Zech. xii:4-9.*

---

* The Valley of Jezreel or Valley of Megiddo, is the World-famed Plain of Esdraelon, where Barak defeated Sisera, and young Josiah and the Hebrew

15. Ten men, of all nations, that is, a large number, —in token of their recognition of what the Lord in His glory does for the Jew in the hour of his final deliverance, will "take hold of the skirt of a Jew," then honored beyond all others, and, detaining his step, beseech his favor, as he moves to the Holy City. The wiping away of the rebuke and reproach of Israel, brings the national conversion of the Gentiles, international concerts of prayer, and the concourse of men to the Throne of Jehovah, to worship before the Lord. Zech. viii:23; Jer. iii:17; Rev. xv:4; Isa. xxv:7, 8; ii:2, 3; Mic. iv:2 ; Isa. xlv:14–25. Apostolic Christianity was only a pledge of this.

16. A Perennial Stream of living water shall flow from the Temple-Rock toward the Mediterranean and Dead Seas, carrying life wherever it goes, and, with the renovation and transformation of the Holy City, monthly fruits shall grow upon trees on either side of the river. Ezekiel xlvii:1–12; Zech. xiv:8; Joel iii:18.

17. A Re-distribution and Division of the Holy Land shall be made according to the 12 tribes of Israel. Bounded, according to ancient covenant, North and South by the Euphrates and Nile, and East and West by the Sea of Oman and the Mediterranean, thirteen equal spaces of 50 miles each, the "Temple" and the "Holy Oblation" between seven on the North of the Tribes, each in their "lot," and five on the South, will cover the area where Israel dwells. The Glorification of the Land by means of the Temple-Waters, and the

---

Theocracy fell together before the might of Pharaoh-Necho. It stretches from Scythopolis to Mount Carmel, 30 miles long, and 20 miles broad. On account of the Hill of Megiddo, it is called in the Apocalypse "*Armageddon.*" It will be, in the final invasion of Palestine by the last Antichrist, the place of Encampment and Rendezvous, f r his Western confederates, the ten kings, even as Bozrah will be a scene of slaughter for his South-Eastern reserves and the Valley of Jehoshaphat the final and the fatal Winepress!

Redistribution of the Land go together. The name of the Holy City is *"Jehovah Shammah, The Lord is There!"* Ezek. xlvii:1–12; xlvii:13–23; xlviii:15, 35.*

18. There will be a Cessation of Sorrow, Tears, and Death, for God's people in that age. Although Sin and Death still exist, yet nowhere do we read that God's people are subject to the same. Elsewhere existing, though not reigning as now, yet among God's people these things never come. Isa. xxv:6–9; xxvi:1–4; xxxv:10. The universality of this exemption is reserved for the final New Heaven and Earth. Rev. xxi:1–4.

19. There will be a Sevenfold Fulness and Increase of Light, Solar and Lunar, in that day, when parted Israel are reunited in their fatherland. Isa. xxx:26; lx:19, 20; Zech. ii:5; Isa. iv:5.

20. There shall be a Restoration of Samaria, Sodom, and Gomorrah, less guilty than Jerusalem, in that day, and an alliance between them all, in covenant holiness, humility, and knowledge of the Lord ; as also between Israel, Egypt and Assyria. Ezek. xvi:46–63; Isa. xix: 23–5; xi:16.

21. A Yearly Concourse of people, from all nations, shall go to Jerusalem to worship. As already, in the Holy City, ages before, a Christian Passover was celebrated, and a Christian Pentecost was enjoyed, where " Parthians, Medes, and Elamites, and dwellers in Mesopotamia and in Judea and in Cappadocia, in Pontus and Asia, Phrygia, Pamphylia, in Egypt and the parts of Lybia about Cyrene, and sojourners from Rome, both Jews and Proselytes, Cretes and Arabians,'

---

* See Smend's Der Prophet Ezechiel. 338–393. Balmer-Rinck, Des Propheten Ezekiel Gesicht vom Tempel. 44–48. Tafel V. Das Gelobte Land. Major J. Scott Philip's "Address read to the British Association at Aberdeen." Chicago. 1879. Thos. Wilson, Publisher. Map.

all saw and heard "the wonderful works of God," so a Christian Feast of Tabernacles shall not only be celebrated for the glorious Millennial ingathering, and remembrance of Desert-Life and the tribulation gone forever, but shall become a stated service in the metropolis of the new kingdom. Zech. xiv:16; Acts i:9–12; John vii:2, 37–39; Rev. 22:17.

22. Israel shall be a Priestly Nation, as well as Royal, in presence of all Nations, offering perpetual spiritual sacrifice to God through Jesus Christ, an example of religious devotion to the whole world. Isa. lxvi:21; lxi:4–6.

23. The Jewish people and their Land, long divorced and desolate, shall be remarried with grand solemnities, as a New Bride to the Lord, over which He will joy with singing, and rest in His love. Isa. lxii:1–12.; Zeph. iii:15–17; Rev. xix:7–9; xx:9; Hos. ii:9.

24. The faithful dead of Israel will awake to share the joy of living Israel's Conversion to Messiah, and Restoration to the land of promise, and to celebrate the World's Sabbath, and Israel's Jubilee. Dan. xii:1–3; Isa. xxvi:19; Ezek. xxxvii:12; Hos. xiii:14; Rev. xx:4–6.

25. Not only shall the 12 Apostles sit on their thrones judging the 12 tribes of Israel, and the martyrs of Jesus bear eminent rule, but the vast multitude of those who have fallen asleep in Christ, in all ages, shall wake to share the joy, and, with those who are "changed," enter the glorious kingdom of God, and live and reign with Christ, 1000 years. The Church above and below shall be one. The Heavenly and Earthly Bride shall be one. Matt. xix:28, 29; Rev. xx:4–6; Rev. xi:18; I Cor. xv:23; I Thess. iv:13–18; Luke xii:35–37.

26. Around the Land of Israel thus glorious, and the Holy City, now the light of the world, because of the

glory of Christ, within it and on it, the Nations of
earth shall dwell in obedient and willing submission,
and, blessed in Abraham's seed, and free from Satanic
dominion, enjoy the Millennial Age of righteousness,
peace and rest. Ps. lxxii:6–20 ; Isa. lxi:11 ; lxvi:8–12 ;
Zeph. iii:9 ; Isa. xix:18, 23–25 ; Ps. xcvi:7–10; xcvii:1 ;
xcviii: 1, 2 ; lxxxix:15–17 ; Deut. xxxii:43 ; Rev. xv:4;
Zech. xiv:16. Here apply a vast number of the
Messianic Psalms.

B.   THE 1,290 AND 1,335 DAYS

Such are the main features of the kingdom that comes
at the close of the last 1260 days of the 70th week of
Daniel, the same 1260 days that we find in the Apocalypse of John. It is the work of Him who is "the
Lion of the tribe of Judah," " the Root and Offspring of
David," who has " the key of David," and whose name
is "the Bright and Morning Star," the " Star out of
Jacob," " the Lamb," who alone has "prevailed to open
the Seals," and disclose the future of Israel, the Nations,
and the Church. In one particular, Daniel is more
specific than John. It is in reference to the exact
intervals between the Destruction of Antichrist and the
Home-Coming of Israel, and between this and the
Resurrection. The time-points, and spaces, are given
with precision. In answer to the question, "O my lord
and what shall be the *afterness* of these things?" the
linen-clothed man informs him that 30 days *more* are
required *after* the 1260 days, and 45 days *more* are
required *after* the 1290 days, and that he is a
blessed man who waits and comes to the 1335 days.
Doubtless, the 30 days, after Antichrist's destruction,
are occupied with the triumphal Home-Coming of the
Sun-clothed Woman from her desert shelter, the return

of the Daughter of Zion to keep house, once more, in the " Beloved City." Who shall describe the scenes of that joyous eventful month ? " The ransomed of the Lord shall return with singing." Isa. xxxv:12. " From the ends of the land I hear songs; Glory to the righteous!" Isa. xxiv:16. "Great will be the day of Jezreel!" Hos. i:11. *Lo-Ammi* no more! *Ammi* forever! "betrothed in righteousness, judgment, loving kindness, mercies, and faithfulness." Hos. ii:6, 9, 19, 20. And then, the 45 days more! What can this month and a half be but that " All Israel," now together in the land, a converted nation, on whom the Spirit is poured, are beholding Him they have pierced, and mourning with bitterer tears than ever fell in the vale of Megiddo! It is the day of Israel's national and penitential sorrow. Zech. xii:9–14. But the sorrow is quickly turned into joy again, greater than ever, by the resurrection of the holy dead. He, who knew how to weep at Lazarus' grave, and to comfort Thessalonian mourners with his word, not only " appears in His glory," when he " builds Jerusalem," but " gathers the outcasts, and binds up the wounds of the broken in heart." Isa. lxvi:5 ; Ps. cii:13–22 ; cxlvii:2, 3. " Them that sleep in Jesus will God bring with Him." I Thess. iv:16–20. There is an Interval, then, between the Destruction of Antichrist and the full Redemption of Israel, and between this Redemption and the Resurrection of the faithful dead; 30 days elapse for the one; 45 days suffice for the other. Then, the 1000 years! David Kimchi, on Isa. lxv:5, and Abarbanel on Isa. xviii:3, say " the Resurrection will occur *after* the outcasts are gathered."* Others say " the Resurrection

---

* Weber, Syst. alt. pal. Theol. 357.

will take place *at* or *during*, the times of Israel's Restitution*" It is the same thing. From the East,
the West, the North, and the South, and from the
empire of Death itself, "they shall come, and sing in
the height of Zion." There is compensation, here, for
Ramah's sore lament; and Rachel, to whom it was
said, "There is hope in thine end, thy children shall
come to their own border," "refrains her voice from
weeping, and her eyes from tears, for her work is
rewarded, and her children return from the enemy's
land." Jer. xxxi:12, 15-17.

C. THE RELATIONSHIP OF THE RISEN SAINTS
TO ISRAEL— DISCHILLIASM

A question enters, here, of great importance.
Among all interpreters,—save the spiritualizers who
have an easy way of solving every problem,—the *Relation of the Risen Glorified Church, to Israel, converted
and restored, yet still in the flesh*, presents matter for
careful study and consideration. The struggle to the
light is full of interest. This problem troubled the
great Bengel. Rejecting the definite article *"the"* in
Rev. xx:4, before the words "thousand years,"—and
upon what seemed to him sufficient critical grounds,
Bengel developed a curious *Dischiliasm*, or doctrine of
two successive Millennia. Because, on critical grounds,
the definite article was excluded from verse 4, the 1000
years in verses 4–6 appeared to be distinct from the
1000 years in verses 1–3. According to this view the
First Millennium reached from the Epiphany of Christ,
the Destruction of Antichrist, and Binding of Satan, to
Gog's destruction and the First Resurrection, Gog being

---

*E senmenger, Eut. Jud. II. 895.

put at the end of the first 1000 years.   During this first
millennium the Nations, no longer deceived by Satan,
and taught by divine judgments, attain to the knowledge and worship of the true God.   The first 1000
years are the period of *Satan's Captivity.*   The *Second
Millennium* reaches from Gog's destruction and the
First Resurrection to the *Parousia* and Judgment of the
Great White Throne, and is the period of the *Reign of
the Risen Martyrs;* not, however, *on* earth, but *over* the
earth, with Christ in heaven;—the period of Israel's
blessedness in their own land.   In short, from the
Epiphany to the *Parousia* are 2000 years, bisected by
the *First Resurrection.*   Though militant, even to the
Last Judgment, still the Church enjoys a glorious
" Flowering Time " (*Flor der Kirche*) under the outpoured Spirit, not indeed before the Resurrection of
the Martyrs and Israel's return, but before the Last
Judgment or Parousia.   And this Church of the last 1000
years is Ezekiel's *Jerusalem below*, while the Risen martyrs and the saints in glory form the *Jerusalem above*
where Christ and those with Him, rule the world.
And these *two* Churches, the "Upper" and the "Lower,"
abide separate during the second 1000 years, yet to
blend in one, in the final New Heaven and Earth.
Such the first brave struggle in the line of exegesis, out
of that mediæval darkness on this subject in which
both Lutheran and Reformed were still held ; yet not
without previous beams of light from Spener, Vitringa
and Joachim.   Though "mixed and confused," the view
of Bengel was accepted, by many, as a relief and step
out from that spiritualizing and allegorizing mode of
exposition which robbed Israel of their future, negated
the prophetic word, and still afflicted Protestantism
itself.   It is a view that, *in part*, is still held to-day, by

some, among whom are Delitzsch and Auberlen, but
only so far as this, viz., that the Risen Saints, the Glorified Bride, "are *retired* into heaven, *from there* to rule
over the earth during the 1000 years.'

D.   DISCHILLIASM REFUTED— THE HABITAT
OF THE RISEN SAINTS

Deeper study, however, has produced more light.
No one, now, adopts Dischiliasm, and the large pre-
ponderance of the best judgment among specialists in
eschatology is adverse to the retirement of the Risen
Saints into heaven, from there to rule "over" the world.
Hofmann resists the conception and proves the inad-
missibility of rendering the preposition *"on"* by *"over."* *
A comparison of Rev. v:10 and xx:4 forbids it.   The
opinion rests, moreover, upon "the assumption that
the Holy Land is not transfigured during the 1000
years." †   As to the exclusion of the article, although
Bengel has been followed herein by Lachman, Tischendorf, Tregelles, and others, yet De Wette regards the
Manuscript authority for this as inadequate, the omission being not only "utterly improbable," but "contrary
to the context," viz., that the Binding of Satan is the
pre-condition of the Reign of Christ with His Risen
Saints.   The initial point, or *terminus a quo*, of the
1,000 years, in verses 1-3, is the same as in verses
4-6, therefore there are not *two* Millennia, but only
one Millennium, dating from the Advent and the
First Resurrection.‡   Delitzsch agrees that Bengel's
Dischiliasm is not proved by Scripture." ‖   Kliefoth,

---

* The Greek ἐπὶ with the Genitive never means *"over,"* but *"on "*
"upon."   Rev. v:10, ἐπὶ τῆς γῆς.
† Hofmann.   Weisssag. u. Erfüll.   II.   372.
‡ De Wette.   Exeget.   Handb.   Off.   Einleit.   173.
‖ Delitzsch.   Bibl-Proph-Theol.   137.

clearer than all, on this point, concedes the omission
of the article, v. 41, and says that, even did the manu-
scripts justify the omission, " yet such omission is easily
accounted for upon internal grounds ; for verses 1-3
are one vision, while verses 4-6 are another and distinct
vision. As in the first vision, the 1,000 years are first
named *without* the article, v. 2, and then *with* the article,
v. 3, so in the second vision, the 1,000 years are first
named *without* the article, v. 4, and then *with* the article,
v. 5." Then confirming De Wette's second reason, viz.:
That the initial point of the 1,000 years is the same in
both visions, he adds, " Since, however, both visions
1-3 and 4-6, *run parallel,* the 1,000 years are the same
period, in both."* They are, as Delitzsch says, " the
period when Israel enjoy the possession of their land,
and Jerusalem, the Seat of the First Christian Church
whence the gospel went forth, becomes glorious again
as the Mother-Church and the Mother-City of the
Kingdom of God."†

There is no exegetical ground, therefore, whatever,
for the doctrine of *two* millennia, and it is plain that the
doctrine that the Risen Saints are *retired* into heaven
to rule, *from there* " *over* " the world, and the Church
below, is critically unjustified. Such a view rests entirely on dogmatic grounds, arbitrary pre-suppositions,
apart from exegesis, and alleged " inconceivability"
and " incongruity " of the opposite view, and is therefore worthless. The assumption, moreover, that there
is no transfiguration of the Holy Land anterior to the
final Regenesis of all things, is at variance with the express letter of God's word, in many most notable pas-

---

* Kliefoth. Offenb. Joh. III. 268.
† Bibl.-Proph.-Theol. 136.

sages, and avoided only by regarding such passages as mere " poetry " or " artistic ornamentation." In opposition to this, it is our duty to say, with Küper, " The prophets of the Old Testament, like St. John in Patmos, are no mere Poets, nor Phantasts, but holy men of God who have spoken as they were impelled by the Holy Ghost."* " To interpret Israel's hope in the Kingdom, described by Ezekiel in chapters xl-xlviii, phantastically, we have no right," says Smend, " still less to interpret those visions spiritually, as is now almost generally the case."* Nor is there any authority for Düsterdieck and Kliefoth, Bertheau and Riehm, to interpret them *"ideally."* Even Kuenen has convincingly demonstrated that, and Orelli as well.

The Church of Christ, in the glorious Kingdom of Christ during the 1000 years, will be *One, not Two.* The " right of judging " given to the Saints at the coming of Christ, is to be explained from the word " they lived and reigned with Christ." The two expressions are of commensurate force. The power of judging belongs to the kingly office of Christ, and the power of life belongs to the priestly office of Christ, "a priest forever, not after the law of a carnal commandment, but after the power of an endless life.'" Heb. vii:16. And because of this, the co-regency and co-ministry of those who are one with Christ, at His Appearing and Kingdom, is not that of one part of the Church over another part of the Church, but that of the whole Church as One, " *on* the earth," and having " power *over* the nations." As Luthardt has admirably said, " There shall not be *one part* of the Church, the Gentile part, glorified in heaven, and *another part*, the Jewish part,

---

*Küper. Das Prophetenthum. 539.
† Smend. Der Prophet Ezekiel, 385.

glorified on earth. The Church shall be *one* with the Lord returned to earth in her midst, like the sun in the temple in New Jerusalem. The distinction still obtains, however, between the glorified church gathered around her Lord, in her glorified place on earth, and the outer unglorified humanity still liable to sin and death, yet freed from Satanic dominion, and subject to the dominion of Christ and his Church. The Earth, not heaven, is the place of the glorified Church. When the Bridegroom comes, He descends *from* heaven. For that reason, the Church goes out to meet him," even "to a meeting of the Lord, in the air," as Paul declares. I Thess. iv:17. By the wonderful ministry of angels the whole body of believers is gathered to Him from all places. The Bridegroom, however, is *on his way* to the Bride-chamber, therefore *turns not back,* but continues to move in the same direction He first took. The Church does not *remain* in the air, nor is she *retired* into heaven, but after her ascension, accompanies the Bridegroom hitherward to the Holy Place where He will celebrate the marriage Supper of the Lamb. Of a journey *backward* with the Bride to heaven, the Scripture knows nothing. The Bride glorified, her *Place* is also glorified.*

And thus the Bride above and the Bride below, the Risen Glorified Saints, and Israel in the flesh, redeemed, restored and holy, shall be One Bride, One Glorious Church in the Millennial Age, and share a Mutual Jubilee and Holy Sabbath. And what Luthardt has said concerning Israel and the Gentile Church shall be likewise true concerning Israel themselves. There shall not be one part of Israel in heaven, the glo-

---

*Luthardt. Lehre. v. d. letzten Dingen. 34, 52, 56

rified part, and another part of Israel on earth, the unglorified part. Israel's faithful *dead* will share with
Israel's faithful *living,* the joy of the Kingdom on earth.
As Weber has said, " The Jewish Christian Church
shall again revive. From the *Dispersion* shall the
living, and from their *graves* shall the dead be brought
back to enjoy, *together,* in the Holy Land, the promised
glory of the Messianic Age."* So Füller. " Not
merely those who survive to see the Advent, shall be
delivered from the Tribulation, but also many from the
sleepers in the dust shall be awaked, in order to enjoy
the Redemption."† " The confessors of Jehovah," says
Delitzsch, " shall be waked from their graves and form
with the faithful living, a glorious Church. Here is
the First Resurrection."‡ " It is at the coming of the
Lord Jesus that Israel is delivered. It is then also that
the First Resurrection takes place," adds Tregelles. ∥
" The prophets predict," writes Koch, " that Israel,
when Messiah comes, shall be delivered and their faithful dead shall rise. The whole great company of those
who have fallen asleep in Christ shall be waked to share
the glory of His Kingdom on earth. To Israel of the
End-Time, of whom the prophets have spoken, the
Church of all believers, gathered out from all the nations shall be added, and *together* all shall reign with
Christ, the 1000 years." § So also Kiesselbach: " The
prophet Isaiah in xxvi:19 says more than that the
faithful Israelites raised from the dust, shall be gathered, like the living, to their fatherland. He tells us
that these dwellers in the dust shall *sing.* They shall

---

* Delitzsch. Isa. xxv:19.
† Weber. Syst. alt. pal. Theol. 354.
‡ Füler. Daniel der Prophet, 321.
∥ Tregelles. Dan. xii:1-3.
§ Koch. Das tausendjahr. Reich. 144.

share the rapture of the Home-Coming ones from distant lands, and for this very purpose the pious dead of Israel shall be waked from their graves."* " Not merely," says Clöter, " the first converts from Israel together with a definite number gathered out from the Gentiles, but also the last converted Israel and all the holy dead shall share, *together*, the salvation in the Kingdom of Christ."†

So Hofmann: " Precisely that People whom the Tyrant, already pictured, would have destroyed, shall be delivered out of the unheard of Tribulation coming on the world in the last time, and shall enjoy the changeless and imperishable salvation. The two propositions, ' Thy people shall be delivered,' and ' many from among thy people shall awake out from among the sleepers in the dust,' are contemporaneous events. The Angel's purpose was not to teach the universality of the resurrection, but to *add* to the limited number of those who, in the flesh, survive to see the Outcome of things, the *many* from the dead who, also, should none the less have part therein."‡ And Baur to the same effect. " In the Millennial Kingdom the Patriarchs and Prophets, and all the righteous shall be waked to enjoy, with the living, the peace of this Kingdom which, like the heavenly Jerusalem, is painted in colors the most glowing." And this he assures us was " the faith of the primitive Church." ‖

E.   Further Confirmation

If more were needed to confirm the view that the Risen Saints are *not retired* into heaven to rule the

---

* Kiesselbach. Isa. xxvi:19.
† Das ewige Evangel. 191,192.
‡ Schriftbeweis. III, 399.
‖ Dogmengeschichte I. 320.

Church below, and the world, *from there*, the Scriptures
will supply it.   In Isa. xxvi:19, the dead are not
awaked to be retired to heaven, but to rejoice on earth,
and " sing " as they wake, and swell the jubilee.   In
Dan. xii:1-3, they rise to " *stand* " with Daniel in their
" *lot*," v. 13, and take the kingdom, *here*, vii:27.   And
yet, they " shine as the brightness of the firmament,
and as the stars forever."   They possess a true, real,
yet spiritual body, not like that of Lazarus after his
resurrection, but like that of the Lord Himself, who
tarried therewith 40 days on the earth ; a glorious body
even then, pervaded by the Spirit, and free from all
earthly limitations incident to His state of humiliation.
So, in the parable, when the Son of Man has come with
all His holy angels, and Wheat and Chaff are parted,
the " righteous shall shine in the kingdom of their
Father."   Matt. xiii:43,—the kingdom to come where
God's will is done " *on earth*."   Nor does Paul contradict this when speaking of the glory of the heavenly
lights, he adds, " So also is the resurrection."   I Cor.
xv:42.   " The manifestation of the sons of God " is due
to the manifestation, or Apocalypse, of the "Son of God,"
and is glorious as was the transfiguration on the Mount.
Matt. xvii:1-4.   To be raised and changed, and " *so* " to
be caught up and " *so* " to be with the Lord forever, *as
risen and changed*, does not require *a remaining forever
in the air, nor a disappearing, backward, forever in the
Heavens*.   That is not the language of Paul.   I Thess.
iv:16.

Even the Jewish teachers who saw in that far-reaching chapter,—the 40th of Isaiah,—the " Rapture of the
Saints " in connection with the revelation of the "Glory
of the Lord " which " all flesh " shall see " *together*,"
never dreamed of a detention in the air of the risen

ones, or of those changed and who are described as
" *The ones expecting Jehovah*." Isaiah xl:31, was to the
pious in Israel, what I Thess. iv:16 is to us, but nowhere in all their literature, biblical or post-biblical, do
we find either the view of aerial detention, or retirement to heaven, but always and everywhere, that of an
open, free intercourse among all, "in the land of the
living," where the righteous no more are entombed,
" nor die any more." The *Gemara Sanhedrin* preserves
the tradition of the house of Elias, saying, " The righteous, whom God will raise up in the first resurrection,
shall not return to the dust again, but *in them*,—during
the 1000 years in which He restores the world,—the
Blessed One will fulfil that word in Isaiah xl:31. They
shall renew their strength ; they shall *mount up* as with
wings of eagles; they shall *run* and not be weary; they
shall *walk* and not faint."* The song of the 4 living
creatures, and of the 24 Elders, is that the Kingdom of
the Lion of Judah's tribe, when He comes to reign, is
"*on* the earth," not "*over*" it. Rev. v:10. It is "in
This Mountain (even the literal " *Mount Zion* " where
" He reigns gloriously before His ancients," Isa. xxiv:-
23) that " the Lord of Hosts will make unto all peoples
a feast of fat things," and *here* " destroy the face of the
covering cast over all peoples, and the veil that is
spread over all nations," and " swallow up death in
victory." Isa. xxv:6,7. As Orelli beautifully says, "He
will bring to the nations a true and divine surprise,
when He takes away the covering that long enough
has veiled their eyes. They shall *behold Him*, then, as
the Dispenser of all Life and Grace, and taste how good
He is to those who bow before His majesty. By a

---

* Eisenmenger Entdeckt. Juden. II, 290. Mede's Works. 776.

second marvel, He will show His omnipotent Love,
abolishing Death with the Woe that has wrung from
man uncounted tears, and extinguish the curse which,
from the very beginning, has blasted the whole human
race!"* Such will be the character of the Millennial
Age, unchanged, till in mystery again its light shall fade
a moment, only to reappear in brighter glory and shine
eternally with the full splendor of an undimmed and
unsetting sun.

F. EXTENT OF THE TRANSFORMATION

To what extent the Glorification of our planet shall
go, at the Second Coming of the Son of Man, is a point
left undetermined in the Scriptures. How far, outside
the boundaries of the holy land the glorifying energy of
the Spirit will pass when once the resurrection has come,
what other cosmic convulsions and re-formations, besides
those foretold, will occur, it is impossible to decide.
Here, as in other respects, we "see through a glass
darkly." If, with Lange, Christlieb, Van Oosterzee,
and others, we regard the' *"Palingennesia"* or *"Anakai-
nosis,"* as a mighty Cosmical *"Process"* begun by catastrophe and convulsions in heaven and earth, at the Appearing of Christ, and completed at the close of the
1000 years, by similar changes, while yet the evolution
continues between, according to the law of geologic
ages, then of this much we are certain, that Palestine
is not the limit of the transformation. Scientific reasons come in here to confirm this conclusion. Geology
itself teaches us that our Planet was once a vast mass
of water, to the eye, that, only after some time, the dry
land appeared, that what is now land, was once submerged, and what is now sea was once land, and that

---

†Orelli. Isa. xxvi:19. Kurtzgef. Komm. 92.

all the mountains and valleys, and rivers and plains, are not of the same age.   And Scripture teaches the same lesson.   The earth and the world are expressly said to have been *"formed,"* and the mountains to have been *"brought forth,"* and the seas to have been *"gathered."* Scripture, in advance of Geology, foretold these phenomena before Science explained them, and the experience of the past should advise us what to expect in the future.   God's word will prove true, and that in the most literal manner, precisely where reason is blind, and a spiritualizing interpretation seeks to bridge over what men choose to call a "difficulty."   We know, from Paul, that, at the "redemption of the body," " the creature itself also, shall be delivered from the bondage of corruption into the liberty of the glory of the children of God."   Rom. viii:21.   It, too, shall share in the "power of the resurrection."   We may not attempt to be wise above what is written.   This much, however, is sure to faith, that He who establishes His Kingdom of glory on earth, and rewards the righteous with rule over the "cities " and " nations" of men, will find a fit place of abode for His saints who, like Him, are conquerors over the grave.   Holding this, we are, at the same time, also permitted to hold that the power of locomotion given to a "spiritual body,"—i. e., a body under the perfect dominion of the spirit, a body with motion "equal to the angels," and such as our Saviour had at His ascension and wore during 40 days, appearing and vanishing by turns, will enable the righteous, raised from the dead, to transcend the limits of earth, "mount up" toward heaven as on eagle's wings, "run" without sense of fatigue, "walk, and not faint."   Even now, clogged and infirm as we are, the power of our will lifts us at once from our seats and bears us with

ease along our way. How much more obedient.to the
volition of the saint will his resurrection vesture be!
As there is nothing to compel us to restrain the visible,
glorious personal Presence of Christ, to an uninterrupted stay upon earth during the 1000 years, so there
is nothing to forbid the motion of His risen saints. A
free and open intercourse between heaven and earth is
as believable a view,—an appearing and disappearing,
like that of the Saviour and like that of the bodies of
many saints who arose and went into the Holy City,
and there vanished away,—as is the scene of the Transfiguration, or the story of the post-resurrection life of
Christ on the earth. Angelic ministry, moreover,
waits on both Him and the Saints, and it may be that,
in the Millennial Age, that word of Israel's King to
Nathaniel will come to its full realization: *"Hereafter
ye shall see Heaven Open, and the Angels of God ascending
and descending on the Son of Man !"* John i:52.

G.   THREE PARTIES IN THE MILLENNIUM— THEIR RELATIONS, OBJECTIONS, AND ISRAEL TO BE A BLESSING

In a subject so vast as that of the 1000 years, some
further words are needed, in a general way. The
Kingdom is not composed of *Risen Saints* alone, nor
limited, as Professor Milligan, following Kliefoth,
would have it, to the "prompt victory" of Christ over
Antichrist, the World-Power, and Satan, in the coming
crisis.* " *Basileia* " means more than that one definite
action, and reaches even beyond the 1000 years. It
is Eternal as well as Millennial. In the Millennium,
however, Israel in the flesh is there, even as we Gentiles in the flesh are yet already " translated into

---

* Milligan, Revelation of St. John, 205.

the kingdom of God's dear Son." Col. i:13. It is to " New-Born Israel," the " Holy People," the " People of the Saints of the Most High," the Kingdom is given, at the close of the 70th week of Daniel. Dan. vii:27. Again, Israel and the Risen Saints, are not all. The *Nations* are summoned to rejoice with Israel in that hour of Israel's redemption. Deut. xxxii:43 ; xxxiii: 29. They all worship Israel's king in the moment of Israel's victory. Rev. xv:4. As many of them as have shown kindness to his *"brethren,"*—*"these My Brethren,"* —in the crisis of the Great Tribulation are welcomed to the kingdom, and inherit life eternal. Matt. xxv:31– 40; while the wicked are destroyed, II Thess. i:4–10, and go into everlasting punishment, Matt, xxv:41–46, and eternal shame and contempt. Dan. xii:2. The Lord's advent is not to annihilate the existence of the *Nations*, as such, but to overthrow their politics and rule, and scatter both like chaff, and then transfer the sovereignty to Israel. Dan. ii:44 ; vii:27; Rev. xi:15, 18; xii:10. The *Three Great Parties* of the 1000 years, are therefore, (1) The *Risen Saints*, (2) *New-Born Israel in the flesh*, (3) The *favored Nations in the flesh*. Such is the clear representation of the whole Word of God. Earth is beginning to realize the " Pattern shown in the Mount," and prepare for the full accomplishment in the final " New Heaven and Earth," at the close of the 1000 years. The Nations are the Fore-Court of the Temple; Israel and their Holy Land, are the Holy Place ; the Holy City and the Risen Bride are the Holiest of All; no Veil existing. To the perfect realization of this, all things are tending. The Invisible is the source of all Realities, and what *has* been in history is the Beginning and Type of what *will* be, only in greater perfection. David's kingdom shall be restored, and among the

" *sure mercies* " to David is the gathering of Israel, and the resurrection of the faithful to enjoy that kingdom together; and therein all Christians shall share, at Messiah's Second Coming. So Paul taught the troubled Thessalonians. A new Age heaves into view, *with Israel, the Risen Saints, and the Nations, in a new relation*, Jerusalem the central seat and throne of the earthly glory of the kingdom. Jer. iii:16–18 ; Isa. xxiv: 21–23. Dispute, and spiritualize as men may, yet this is the clear announcement of God's' word. Ewald is therefore correct when saying, " Of a glorified earthly Jerusalem, the prophets of the Old Testament frequently speak. Pre-eminently is Ezekiel's vision of the Resurrection the type of this, Ezek. xxxvii:1–14. As, there, *Israel* rises anew, so, here, in the Apocalypse, by means of the Messianic Judgment, and Glorification, shall *all true Christians, living and dead, and only such*, be gathered, and glorified, in order to reign with Christ, and fulfil this part of the Old Testament hope.* As to the alleged " incongruity of the glorified among the unglorified," and " how they will live," and " what they will do," and " what their condition," and " daily occupation,"—questions revived by Kliefoth, and repeated by others, though raised and answered ages ago; and, further, " will there be flies, and bees, and mosquitoes, in the Millennial age," as still others have sportingly asked; and, yet others again, as to " the habit of nature "—they all belong to that same unbelieving spirit, and cast of mind, that made a Socinus, some Schoolmen, and later profane wits, inquire " whether our Lord rose from the grave with His digestive organs?" " whether," as Cleopatra wanted

---

* Ewald, Joh. Schrift. II. 327.

to know, "the Saints will rise with raiment"? and "whence came the raiment our Lord wore when He rose?" and so, conclude, from all, to a *denial* of the literal resurrection of the body. Such inquisition, it becomes us to repel, with force, and rebuke into silence, holding, in spite of a thousand questions all men can ask and none can answer, in reference to every doctrine of Scripture, that it is far more Christian to believe what God has spoken, and give him the glory, as "Doer of wondrous things," than it is to idealize the prophecy, to suit our vain thoughts, and land ourselves at last into open rejection of the Word of God.

The Lord knoweth the thoughts of the wise that they are vain. Painful to the last degree is the ever-recurring style of objection we meet with in certain writers, as "*Is it reasonable?*" "*How remote from reasonable probability!*" It is "*inconceivable,*" "*incredible,*" and "*far from probable,*" and everything the mere natural man can object to the supernatural. We dismiss it all with the divine words, "O man, who art thou that repliest against God?" "Should it be a marvelous thing in *my eyes*, saith the Lord?" "The zeal of the Lord of Hosts will perform this." "The mouth of the Lord hath spoken it!" "It is the utterance of Jehovah, Doer of these things!" It must be so, as God has said. As to the Risen Saints, we know what their perfection is, and how near they are to Christ. It is the righteous man raised from the dead, who is the perfect man, ordained to dominion, in the Age to come. So Paul taught the Hebrews. Next to the Risen Saints, stands Israel, a New-Born Overcomer, with the right to rule the nations. The Kingdom of God *must* have its objective local center, on the earth, when Gentile supremacy is gone, and Israel's times have come. And that center will be Jerusalem; Jerusalem, that former "spiritual Sodom and Egypt, where our Lord was crucified;" where He finished His atoning work, over which He thundered His woes and showered His holy tears; outside whose gate His cross was erected; where He proved Himself the Prince of Life by rising from the dead; where He poured His Spirit and commissioned the Apostles to proclaim His gospel to the Nations; even Jerusalem, the seat of all grace for mankind, shall be the seat of all glory, too, *the sustaining center of the kingdom of the* 1000 *years.* Nor is there a "*carnal Chiliasm*" here. "Israel shall be among the nations as the *Dew* from Jehovah and as dropping *Rain* on the grass that waits for no one, nor tarries for the sons of men." Mic. iv:8. Of super-earthly origin, like "*Dew*" and "*Rain*," shall Israel's influence be, dispensing spiritual blessing everywhere. When Jehovah is "as the Dew to Israel," Hos. xiv:5, then Israel is as the Dew to the Nations. When Israel "takes root," again, and "buds and blossoms," it is then he "fills the world with fruit." Isa. xxvii:6. And, when he "blossoms like the lily, casts forth his roots as Lebanon, and his branches spread, and his beauty is like the olive-tree, and his smell as Lebanon," then it is that "*they* who dwell under his shadow shall return," and "*they* shall revive as the corn, and blossom as the vine." Hos. xiv:5–7. And that is Israel's resurrection hour, at the coming of Messiah, in His kingdom. Hos. xiii:14. Everywhere it is foretold that the "Spirit of Life from God" shall be given to living Israel in the flesh, as well as to dead Israel in the grave, when Messiah comes. The resurrection is the result of the "*Dew!*" "Life from the dead" is what God's "*Dew*" effects. A baptism of divine grace, an enduement from

on high, when " Jacob's Heavens drop *Dew*," and compared with which the First Christian Pentecost will
seem as nothing, yea, a " pouring out " upon the
Jewish nation of all heavenly blessing, in measure
mightier than ever, will be a " refreshing " and " anoint-
ing " that can never pass away.   When Messiah
" comes down like Rain on the mown grass, and as
Showers that water the earth," then Israel " comes up
like willows by the water courses."   Ps. lxxii:6 ; Isa.
xliv:3, 4.   When he lifts upon them the light of His
open face, then, sunlit, and wet with divine grace, they
sing together, as, with unveiled eyes they behold their
Redeemer, absent so long from their sight.   And their
Land shares in the blessing.   " *I will remember the
Land !* "   Levit. xxvi:42.   Where " thorns and briars "
have grown, and the populous city, deserted, has
become " a joy of wild asses," even there, " when the
Spirit is poured from on high," shall fruitfulness,
plenty, and peace, and safety, be found.   Isa. xxxii:13,
14.   The metamorphosis of the Holy Land moves
pari passu with that of the Holy People, the desert
becoming an orchard, and the waste a garden.   The
spiritual and physical shall be interblended.   The
entire physiognomy shall be that where the curse has
been lifted, and the blessing has descended.   " On
every high mountain, and on every high hill, shall be
brooks of gushing water," and " the moonlight shall
be as the light of the sun, and the light of the sun
sevenfold, in the day when Jehovah binds up the breach
of His people, and heals their scars."   Isa. xxx:18–26.
In the reunion of Israel and Judah, and the re-erection
of David's storm-struck Tent, and repairing of the
breach in David's kingdom, and restoring the same " as
in days of old," that is, as a visible dominion, with the

nations subject to the Lord's Anointed,—all these
blessings shall be fulfilled.

H.   THE EFFECT ON THE NATIONS

The *effect upon the Nations*, when Jacob walks in the
light of the Lord, and the Lord Himself reigns gloriously before His ancients, is impressively told by
Isaiah and Micah, in a picture, twenty-five centuries
long have failed to translate into practical life.   Jerusalem, the Christocratic center of the future, no longer
"Desolate" as now, becomes the object of attraction for
the world, the world-wide miracle, mystery, and magnet,
more potent than the Burning Bush which Moses saw.
One wonderful effect is produced.   The gazing Nations, influenced by the Messianic Judgment, the Sign,
the Glory, and what the Lord has wrought for His
people, combine to "go up" to the Mount where the
Temple stands, exalted above the hills and crowned
with the Glory-Flame.   Isa. ii:2; iv:6 ; Mic. iv:2.   No
idle curiosity directs their march.   The Judgment has
impressed them.   The deep *Desire to win Salvation*, the
resolve to bless themselves in Abraham's seed, inspires
their motion.   Clear rings their Watchword, *"Up ! to
the mountain of the Lord ! "*—the Design as clear, even
"to lea:n of His way ! "—and the Purpose as strong,
namely, *"to walk in His paths ! "*   Tired of their own
ways, and sick of their own paths, people and statesmen alike, yea "all nations" will seek to know the ways
of Christ, the King of the New Age.   The new code
that proceeds "out of Zion," so different from all other
codes,—the code Justinian, or the code Napoleon,—
viz., the code of Israel's King, and better than all codes,
national or international, is what arrests their mind.
Not " Culture," nor "Civilization," not the worn out

cry of the "Progress of Nations," is what they want, but the Zionite Law and the Zionite life ;—a divine knowledge and a holy obedience to Christ. Not Puffendorf and Grotius, nor Vattel, Burlamaqui, or Wheaton, but Christ, the "One Lawgiver," is what they long for,—Christ in His grace, Christ in His Power, Christ in His Kingdom, Christ in His glory. And, "like a flowing stream," Isa. lxvi:12, they "flow to the mountain of the Lord's House, set in the head of the mountains, and lifted above the hills, in the last days." Isa. ii:1. As from Babel the nations were *"scattered"* into all the world, so, reversely now, to Jerusalem all shall *"flow"* to be reunited. The "veil taken away" at Messiah's coming, they will adopt new Maxims, Policies and Customs, new Principles and Legislation. Not the Sermon on the Mount and the Ten Commandments will be incorporated in a Theodosian Code, but the whole Word of God, will be the "Law." The partial fulfilment of this great oracle at the First Coming of Christ, in an inward spiritual sense, to a portion of mankind, awaits, like Joel's oracle of the Outpoured Spirit, and Zechariah's oracle of the Pierced One, and the oracle of Amos concerning David's Tent, and all Messianic oracles of glory, a grander accomplishment. Not the wars of centuries and ages gone, and which have steeped the earth in human gore, not a new conflict with Antichrist ; no Armageddon scenes, nor winepress of God's wrath, with blood deep up to the horses' bridles, but *"war no more !"* the coulter for the sword, and for the spear the pruning-knife. Religion and Peace shall go together. What Kant declared a "possibility," and Charles Sumner lived to call "impossible," shall be a fact. In that day all the glory of man shall be brought low, his flags and forts, his iron-clads and

standing armies, his commerce and exchequer, his science, falsely so called, and vain philosophy, and "the
Lord alone shall be exalted." Isa. ii:11–22. Faithfully
does Orelli say, "*Certainly, the realization of this teaching
remains to-day far short of what the prophet predicts. The
'Christian Powers' still engage in strife, and the learning
of war exhausts the forces of civilized States. But a Divine Power, proclaimed from Zion to the world, will yet dic-
tate universal peace. And it can only heighten our reverence for the prophetic word when we find that, to-day,
after all our boasted advances in Culture and Humanity,
mankind has not yet risen to the height of the goal that
stood before the eyes of God's holy seers, more than two
and a half millennia ago!*"* We need no further
comment to assure us that the fulfilment of the oracle
of Isaiah and Micah concerning the Peace and Glory
of the Nations, can only come in the Millennial Age
that follows Israel's restoration at the Second Coming
of Messiah.

And the *Holiness* of the 1000-years' Kingdom will be
as remarkable as is the Sin of our present dispensation.
It is a blessed Chiliasm that is appointed for the Nations, a Sacred Sabbatism. Satan deceives the nations
no more, and the proof that Satan is bound, is that they
"*war no more*," nor stand in the way of the Kingdom of
Christ. Death holds empire no more over the sleeping saints of God. It is not, indeed, that Sin and
Death are unknown in the Millennial Age. Both exist
among the unglorified. Hengstenberg's thought that
"the continuance of sin is impossible because Satan is
bound," is not only adverse to the Scriptures, but to
the fact that the sinful quality in man must ever inhere

---

* Orelli.   Die Alttest. Weissag.   289, 290.

so long as man, in his whole person, has not passed through death, or been transformed while living. And this must be the case even under the highest culture and highest grace known to mortals this side the grave. Biblical Anthropology never treats the " Body, Soul and Spirit" as three separate and independent entities, but as integrated and mutually affecting parts of one organism. *"From Death to Life"* is the royal road, for the *whole* man, to perfection. He who, though innocent, was charged with human sin, has shown us this. And, therefore, though sinful in our best estate, we may not despair. The unregenerate body must pass through the grave, or be changed, before man's entire perfection is achieved, and he who sighs not for his resurrection, knows little of himself or of Christ. And here Hofmann's word is excellent, viz., that "the sinfulness of man would still remain in man, *even though Satan himself were dead!*"

On the other hand, however, not only will Satan be bound, but the *power* of Sin in men, and over men, not glorified as yet, will be broken, the fellowship of Sin will be gone, and, as a rule, the temptation to Sin be over-mastered, even though the possibility of Sin will not be removed, nor the existence of Sin be prevented. "Nothing," says Hofmann, "shall occur to undo the victory Christ has won over Antichrist." "Associated Sin," says Luthardt, "will exist no more during the 1000 years." "Sin has no more a universal might," (Delitzsch). "The first distinguishing feature of these times of requickening and restitution by the Holy Spirit, is freedom from all Satanic influence, the next is decadence of the power of sin." (Christiani). And though Sin and Death exist among the unglorified, yet Death will be rare because Sin is restrained and Satan's temptations destroyed.   It will be a " *Deutero-Adamite Life*," as Ebrard calls it, if not absolutely so, yet proximately so.   The enhanced energy of the new life of humanity will be such that, sharing in Israel's blessing, no mother among the Nations shall mourn the untimely loss of her babe a few days old, nor shall the old man fail to fill out his days, though they be " as the days of a tree," while he who, a hundred years old, is a " sinner " still, under such floods of light and of grace, will be counted as specially cursed of God, Isa. lxv:20. There can hardly be a doubt that the " blessed offspring " promised to Israel, in that day, and the " blessed seed " in whom " all Nations shall be blessed," implies a blessed offspring also among the Nations themselves.   Christianity will then celebrate its greatest triumph this side eternity.   The State will be the Church, and the Church the State, in a holy union, now that the Dragon is bound.   All places will be sacred, all hours canonical, the distinction between " sacred and secular," gone forever.   No strifes will exist, nor divisions, nor jarring religious sects.   Art, Science and Philosophy will then be consecrate, and mottoes graved on the doors and walls of institutions, —" *Christo et Ecclesiæ*,"—will not be mocked by creeds that crucify both.   No violence of climate will induce disease, nor recklessness of man drive to an unexpected grave.   In Israel's land, " the inhabitant shall not say I am sick, for the people that dwell therein shall be forgiven their iniquity."   Isa. xxxiii:21.   With Sin's destruction in the glorified, disease will be destroyed, and with Nature's smile the world will bloom again, and halcyon days return.

I. MODE OF LIFE AMONG THE RISEN

As to the mode of intercourse between the glorified and unglorified, there are many vain speculations. We only " know in part," and time will bring the answer to our various askings. The whole discussion binds itself to our conceptions of the Resurrection-Body,— what its needs, and what its functions, are. From the very first, the Jewish teachers were embarrassed here, and much divided in their views. The later Jews are not more clear. Saadias and Maimonides maintained that " they who rise in the resurrection, *eat, drink* and *marry,* and their bodily members serve them, for these are not in vain and they *die again.*"* It was an ancient view, and founded on the cases of the resurrection of the son of the Shunamite, and the son of the widow of Zarepta, " both whom," says Saadias, " ate and drank and doubtless took wives." On the other hand, Bechai and Abarbanel maintained that " they who rise in the resurrection *neither eat, nor drink, nor marry,* for there is no further need of these, after the resurrection, *nor do the risen righteous ones return to dust again.* They have their bodies, in which the fleshly functions have ceased, as in the case of Moses, when in the Mount with God."† Our Lord corrects both these views when, confuting the Sadducees, He replies that " they who shall be accounted worthy to obtain that world (*Olam Habba*) and the resurrection out from among the dead, *neither marry nor are given in marriage, neither can they die any more;* for they are *equal to the angels,* and are sons of God, being sons of the Resurrection." Luke xx:35,36. Saadias and Ben Mai-

---

* Eisenmenger. Eut. Jud. II. 943.
† Ibid 495.

mon said that the Risen "*eat, drink, marry, die.*"
Bechai, Abarbanel, Talmud and Cabbala, aver they
"*neither eat, drink, marry, nor die.*" Our Lord declares
they "*neither marry nor are given in marriage, neither can
they die any more,*" but says nothing as to the "eating"
or "drinking." What he teaches is that the children
of the resurrection are as the sexless angels. Beyond
the fact that Lazarus ate after his resurrection, John
xii:1,2, remains the fact that our Lord Himself, after
His resurrection, had a tangible and visible material
body, already free from the limitations of His former
humiliation, and possessed of resurrection-life, and yet
"*ate*" food in Jerusalem and at the shore of Galilee,
Luke xxiv:30, 41, 42, John xxi:12, and not only promised to the Twelve to "*drink* of the fruit of the vine,
new in the Kingdom of God," Matt. xxvi:29, but "appointed" them "a Kingdom," in which, said He, "ye
may eat and drink at my table in my Kingdom, and sit
on 12 thrones judging the 12 tribes of Israel." Luke
xxii:29,30. We can grossly carnalize this, on the one
hand, and as ethereally spiritualize it on the other.
The fact remains that the Resurrection Kingdom is "*on
the earth,*" and that the "children of the resurrection"
have material bodies, adapted to spiritual uses, and free
from certain physical functions. While we must shun
an Ebionite Chiliasm on the one hand, we must
equally avoid a Gnostic Chiliasm on the other, and not
rob corporeity of its rights in the resurrection, or dis-
solve, under the idea of "glory," the resurrection body
into a gauzy texture ballooning in the sky. Such a
conception is foreign to the whole word of God. The
risen ones shall have a human body, like their Lord's,
know each other, and be known, and live in relation to
the saints upon the earth, and to the Nations. Their

mode of immortality and intercourse are not revealed. It is enough for us to know that not more difficult is the faith of Christ's companionship with His disciples dnring the 40 days next following His resurrection. It is enough to know that Death is robbed of his empire, and that, as Professor Milligan himself admits in his able work on the Resurrection, our Lord's body was a true spiritual, glorified body, immediately upon His rising, and not first after his ascension, and that our bodies are to take the form and quality of His. Equal to the "*angels*" we shall be, in one respect. Like "*Him,*" we shall be, in another. As *both*, in all. "*Flesh and blood*" cannot inherit God's Kingdom, because "corruption" cannot "inherit incorruption." 1 Cor. xv:50. And yet "*flesh and bones,*" pervaded by the Spirit, and made incorruptible, is what our Lord's body was in *His* resurrection, Luke xxiv:26, a "glorious body," and "*like*" which—not "*equal*" to which—ours shall be at His coming. Phil. iii:21. In such bodies, the Risen Saints shall have fellowship with the unrisen in the Millennial Age. For the rest, our curiosity must be restrained, and will be, if we listen to the Angel's voice to Daniel, *Go thy way, Daniel, till the End shall be!*" Inquire no more. Be content with what is already spoken. Leave the unrevealed future to God. Sure we are of one thing. "We shall behold God's face in righteousness," and "be satisfied when we awake with His likeness!" Ps. xvii:15. Even so, *Lord Jesus!*

J. MILLENNIAL, NOT ETERNAL

That the Millennial Age is not the *Final* Age is made clear in both Testaments. The Kingdom of the 1000 years stands in relation to an Age beyond its

own limits, the *Endless Age.* It is a false construction
of the word *"Until"* in the expression *"Until* the 1000
years are *finished,"* Rev. xx:3, 5, 7, to say that the *end of
these years* is the end of the *Kingdom of Christ,* or of the
blessedness of Israel, or of the Risen Saints' reign with
Christ, or of the distinction between Israel and the
Nations, or between the Holy City and the outside dwellers. Even after the Judgment of the " Great White
Throne," and the surrender of the Messianic Kingdom
to the Father, the priestly co-regency of Christ and
His saints still exists. There is still a dominion of
Christ and His *Bride,* " *the Holy City,"* over the outside
"Nations" and the *"Kings"* in the New Earth, who are
distinguished from her, and " bring their glory and
their honor into her." And there is a condition of
things transcending that which we see in Millennial
times. In the New Jerusalem there is "no temple,"
and "no night." "They need no light of lamp, neither
light of sun, for the Lord God gives them light, and
the *Lamp* is the *Lamb."* Rev. xxii:23. It is plainly
said, "They shall reign forever and ever," v. 5. *This is
the last word on the whole subject. No more is spoken.*
"FOREVER!" And it confirms Paul's word, "FOREVER,"
in 1 Thess. iv:17. Their Kingdom is an *"everlasting
kingdom,"* Dan. vii:25. Christ's dominion has *"no end,"*
Isa. ix:5. "To the Son He saith, Thy throne, O God,
is FOREVER," Ps. xlv:6; Heb. i:8. The Golden Age
will disappear, Satan, let loose for a season, will cause
to fade away the beauty of the vision from the eyes of
all the nations girdling Israel's home and subdued so
long to Israel's sway. Unmindful of the centuries
when Israel was trodden down by Gentile pride, they
will become restless and averse to all divine dominion.
Then, after a brief final test, come the closing Judg-

ment and the farthest " End ;"—the door that brings the Endless Age. The last high point of the Apocalypse is gained, the *Absolute End of the Ways of God* to men ;—a vision of *Eternal Glory* toward whose unveiling all previous Revelation and all History have been the path, and on which the eyes of all prophets have been strained since the world began.

Part 7

IDEAL THEORY OF NUMBERS

A. THE LAST RESORT OF POST-MILLENNIALISM.

We have alluded to this already. Its present importance, however, demands a special notice. A favorite view with certain German writers and their English-speaking copyists, it seeks to evade the induction of a post-Advent Millennium by depriving the 1000 years of all chronological value, regarding them as only a symbol of " the *ideas* of *ecumenicity, perfection,* and *eternity.*" Three great antichiliasts have appeared in our generation, Hengstenberg, Keil, and Kliefoth, men of eminent ability, who,—had the task been possible for any to perform,—might have been expected to have overthrown the chiliastic faith of the primitive Church, and closed the appeal of modern times to this ancient historic witness. But, how unsuccessful the undertaking! What a splendor of scholarship, matchless in so much that is good, and what a persistence of misdirected aim in so much that is baffled at every step! Hengstenberg's theory,—though regarding the 1000 years as real time,—was repudiated as soon as born, finding but few defenders. The view of Keil,— now standing alone among exegetes,—was also rejected.

Few care to receive it. The idealistic symbolism of Dr. Kliefoth, supported by allegorizers, spiritualizers and idealizers of Old Testament Israel, changing the subject and contents of prophecy to suit their pre-conceived notions, now asks a suffrage everywhere, and wins it from such as, conscious that Post-millennialism is a failure in exegesis, seek for some ground on which to stand opposed to the Pre-millennial view. First of all Dr. Kliefoth *rejects Post-millennialism* in the strongest terms. He says, " *So much is certain, viz., that the* 1000 *years of our prophecy begin with the visible Appearing of Christ and His victory over Antichrist. Herein we agree with Bengel, Ewald, De Wette, Düsterdieck, Hofmann and his school, Ebrard, Auberlen, etc. All expositions which put the* 1000 *years in this our present time-course, whether dated from the Death of Christ,* (Augustine), *or from Constantine* (Keil), *or from Charlemagne* (Hengstenberg), *we must hold as a violation of the text.*" * *Pre-millennialism* he also rejects. "*How,*" continues Dr. Kliefoth, "are we to conceive of the 1000 *years* which fall *between* the Second Advent and the Resurrection and Final Judgment? Two conceptions are possible. *The first is that we take the* 1000 *years properly as a measure of longer or shorter duration.* So do, not only the expositors who put the 1000 years in our present period, but also the Chiliasts. *The second is that a symbolical number never counts, but only expresses an idea.* The idea expressed by the '1000' is that of *potentiated ecumenicity,*—because 1000 is the potentiated 10 number of *spatial* completeness,—and, since *time, in years,* cannot be applied to this *spatial* idea, all that is meant by what those years embrace, is '*Victory*,' the

---

* Offenbar. Joh. III. 287.

Basileia of the Lord over Antichrist, the World-Power
and the Devil. It is ecumenical. If we thus conceive
the 1000 years all difficulties fall away, and the Apocalypse stands in harmony with the rest of Scripture." *
He repeats the same in his later work, the *"Christian
Eschatology."* Without one solitary proof that the 1000
years of Satan's Captivity and of the Saints' reign with
Christ are merely ideal, and with singular boldness
of unsupported assertion that no place is found for
them as a historic period, he says, "The 1000 years
are *not* to be taken literally *because* the connection between Rev. xix:11–21 and xx:11–15 does not permit a
real period of 1000 years, but are to be taken symbolically, as are all numbers of the Apocalypse, that is, *as
not counting, but only expressing an idea.* The number
1000=10×10×10, that is, 10 raised to its third power,
expressing *the idea of absolute all-embracing Ecumenicity*,
and, reminding us of the ' One day with the Lord as
1000 years, and 1000 years as one day,' Ps. xc:4 ; II
Pet. iii:8, so represents *the idea of Eternity.* All that
is meant is that, after the Antichrist is destroyed, the
reign of Christ and His Saints shall be ecumenical and
eternal, and that Satan's power over men is universally
and eternally taken away." † And this " second conception" is the one Dr. Kliefoth adopts, a happy expe-
dient whereby the 1000 years are *abolished*, and the millennial problem solved. The 1000 number embodies
the two stupendous ideas of an all-embracing *Ecumenicity* and an inconceivable *Eternity !* It is the highest,
broadest, longest and roundest *"potentiation*," the symbolic *ne plus ultra* of inspired perfection, victory and
totality. Like Aaron's rod, it swallows all the rest.

---

* Kliefoth. Offenbar. Joh. III. 285.
† Ibid. Christliche Eschatologie. 246.

Thus *Pre*-millennialism and *Post*-millennialism both swept away at one stroke, by the same ideal broom, the doctrine of a *Millenninm* on this present earth, and in history, *disappears from the Scriptures altogether !* By this means,—the millennium gone,—*no Interval existing,* —Antichrist, Gog, the opening and closing Judgments, the Two Resurrections, the Transformation of the Holy Land and the final Regenesis of the whole Planet, *are brought externally together at the Second Advent,* and Eternity, the final New Heaven and Earth and New Jerusalem, are made immediately to follow Israel's conversion and the Resurrection of the faithful dead. Thus,—*an entire age blotted out of existence,* and Two Ends considered as One, the doctrine of the *simultaneous resurrection of all the dead,* righteous and wicked, is *in*serted in the Apocalypse through the *ex*sertion of the 1000 years. The exegesis is that of the annihilation of the millennial age. In this way the Old Testament Prophets, Christ and His Apostles and "all the rest of Scripture," are said to be *"brought into harmony"* as though they were not already in that relation, the "Third Day" in Hosea, the "Multitude of Days" in Isaiah, and the "Many Days" in Ezekiel, answering each other as face answers to face in water! The gifted author simply puts *out* of God's word what God has put *in*, and puts *in* what God has put *out*, inventing a contradiction between John and the Prophets, then, dissolving the same on one side, viz., in John, leaving it *un*dissolved in the Prophets, thinks that the word of God has been *"brought into harmony !"* The magic is clear, and the method is easy. *"Symbolische Zahlen nicht zæhlen ; Symbolical numbers don't count !"* a convenient way of denying that the " 1000 *years*" in John are the *"Many Days"* in Ezekiel, and of asserting that the *relative End* of this age is the *absolute end* of the next; no other Millennium seen than that of the Eternal State!

According to Dr. Kl. the 1000 years have nothing to do with *time*, but only with *space*. They represent " the *spatial* idea." What we have, here, is a species of exegetical transubstantiation. The figures 1000 mean "*space*," and the word *years* means "*victory!* " He soberly tells us "*Duration* is meant, *but not by the number*," and " *Time* is meannt, but whether long or short is *not told us by the number!* "* By what, then, may we ask, is it told? for, according to Dr. Kl. himself, " the 1000 years *begin* with the visible Appearing of Christ." They also *end*, and are said to " *expire*." If the " *number*," does not express " *Duration*," where shall we find the term that does? By what right shall we speak of " *Duration*" at all? Surely not because of the word " *Years*" for that means " *Victory* ; " and not because of the figures " 1000," for these mean " *Space !*" How, if Time is out of the question, determine the *unde* and *usque ad*, both which are admitted yet both denied, and denied while yet admitted? Events as well as dates limit duration. If all that Dr. Kl. is contending for is that we cannot say that the 1000 years are "*exactly* 10 centuries," we shall not be seriously grieved. We might shelter ourselves behind Hengstenberg's favorite " vanishing point," and reply that " Chronological exactness is not to be expected," and against which he could enter no demurrer! But, on such grounds, to enthrone the idol " Symbolical numbers don't count," and " all prophetic numbers are symbolical," and then " potentiate " the argument to a denial of

---

* Offenbar. Joh. III. 285.

these numbers altogether, as measures of time, is both curious and sad. All the more so, since the ideas of " Time," " Duration," " Beginning," are admitted, while still denied ! It might puzzle Palmoni himself to tell whence comes the idea of " Duration " if the " 1000 " only means " Space " and " years " only mean " Victory ! " What wonder if the " *Woe to Ariel*" should overtake teachers and people alike,—hungry but not fed, thirsty but not refreshed by such devices, while yet they dream the very reverse; that deep judgment of intoxication under which the head grows dizzy, " but not with wine," while looking at God's truth ;—that " deep sleep " and non-discernment of the Book of God, when the bright prophetic word itself becomes dark ! What wonder, if, under an exegesis, like this, the intellectual eyes of both ministers and people fail, and " the Book " becomes as a book that is sealed which men deliver to one that is *learned*, saying "Read this, I pray thee," and the Pulpit replies, " I cannot, for it is *sealed !* " and again it is delivered to one that is *not learned*, with the same request, " Read this, I pray thee," and the Pew answers " I cannot for I am *not learned !* " and, so, from Pulpit to Pew, and Pew to Pulpit, the " sure word," the " shining light," goes begging for recognition ! The Professor says, " It is " *Oriental !* " The Hearer says " I am not a graduate!" What wonder if God proceeds to do a marvellous thing in our day, even to smite *Japhetic* wisdom, and bring to naught *Japhetic* understanding ! It would, in no wise, be strange, if at last, the despised " Jew " might yet speak,—as Dean Payne Smith assures us he will,—and the Apocalypse beam brighter than ever before ! That day of illumination and restitution will bring a different interpretation from what, so many now hold. We have only, to wait a short time! *Then,*—when Lebanon is turned to a fruitful field,—" *the deaf shall hear the words of the Book, and the eyes of the blind shall see out of obscurity and out of darkness, and the meek will increase their joy, and Jacob shall not be ashamed, neither shall his face wax pale, but He shall sanctify the Holy One of Israel!*" Then *Japhetic* wisdom freed from its folly, will know the prophetic word, when Israel, converted to Christ, once more shall become our guide, and "*they that err in spirit shall come to understanding, and they that murmur shall learn doctrine!*" Isa. xxix:18–24.

The apostolic faith will suffer as little at the hands of Dr. Kliefoth, as it did at the hands of Hengstenberg, great and good as he was, or at the hands of Keil, great and good as he is, or at the hands of others, no less esteemed, yet to whom prophecy,—explained never so clearly by the Lord Himself,—appears an Egyptian Sphinx, or Isis, whose veil no mortal has drawn. "The truth is," as Rinck observes, that "*what these great and good men needed, was more light,*"—the need, of us all! What illicit assumptions! What tortuous explanations! What Bible-negating conclusions! Plainly, nothing is gained, either for *Post*-millenniasm, or *No*-millenniasm, by hoisting the flag "Symbolical numbers don't count!" To regard a number as symbolic does not require us to deny its chronological value. To affirm its chronological value is not to deny its symbolic character. The 70 weeks are both. So are the 1000 years. Irenæus and Lactantius, De Wette and Ebrard, Auberlen and Volck, Koch and Luthardt, and post-millennialists themselves, regard the 10×10×10=1000 as representing victory and peace, as truly as 12×12×1000=144,000 represents a perfect election out of Israel. But the Victory is not yet *absolute*, nor yet *eternal*, as Dr.

Kliefoth would have it. It is relative only, once more to be perilled, and put to the test, at the end of the 1000 years. To argue that the 1000 years are not literal because " not exactly 10 centuries," is a favorite logic with many who first assume in the premise what they propose to find in the conclusion; then, deducing the same, assert their finding as proved! It is the precise argument that the 70 weeks of Daniel, are not a literal measure of time, because *"not exactly 490 years,"* which they exactly are! This is worse than trifling. The proved identity of the 1000 years with Hosea's " Third Day," Hos. vi:2 ; Isaiah's " Multitude of Days," Isa.xxiv:22 ; Ezekiel's " Many Days," Ezek. xxxviii:8 ; and " His Days " in Psal. lxxii:7, evinces their value as a real' measure of time ; *nor does the exegete live who can show that they are not exactly ten centuries !* Düsterdieck, like some others, as Bertheau, Riehm, and Robertson Smith, has given away, just here, his great exegetical tact by accepting the snare of the Ideal Theory of Prophetic Numbers.

B. Professor Milligan's Work

The work of Professor Milligan, of Aberdeen, on the *" Revelation of St. John "* solicits a notice in this connection. Students of prophecy are aware that the great battle of interpretation is generally fought on the question of the 3½ years or 1260 days. Following the lead of Augustine, Hengstenberg, and Kliefoth, the Aberdeen Professor replies to the " strong argument " which holds to the literality of the 3½ years or 1260 days, by saying that " these numbers are merely symbolic ' and represent "not literal years," or " days," but only " the *idea* of trouble and distress." That is, a large.sized round number represents *unbroken* victory,

glory and eternity, but a number, whose countenance
is of less dimension, and distorted by a fraction, represents the *brokenness* of sorrow and woe. And that is
the reason why Daniel and John used the 3½. We are
not informed, however, why 1,000,000 was not chosen
by John as a sign in the one case, and 5⅜ as a sign in
the other. For all we can see to the contrary, 1,000,000
looks as cheerful and happy as 1,000, and 5⅜ as hag-
gard and sad as 3½! Besides, according to Dr. Kliefoth himself, the cubing of 10 to 1,000, is not the
highest "potentiation" of "ecumenicity," let alone the
idea of "eternity." When speaking of the Euphratean
horseman under the 6th seal, Rev. ix:16, whose numbers are given as *"twice ten thousand times ten thousand,"*
10,000×10,000=100,000,000×2 = 200,000,000, he tells us
that "the number stated at 200,000,000, represents the
10 number *potentiated to* 100,000,000 *then doubled in order
to show that the whole world is in war."** If 200,000,000
are the figures for an ecumenical *War*, it would be
hard to discover why an ecumenical and eternal *Peace*
should be potentiated only up to 1,000! A *whole world*
in peace, and forever, seems, if the numbers are not
literal, to require " *myriads of myriads* " as a symbol to
represent it, and not merely the minor cube of 10! But
if there is a *backlying reason* for 1,000 and 3½, as solid
as for the 70 year-weeks of Daniel ; if *the ideas expressed
by these numbers grow out of the relations of the same to a
Sabbatic Law, and a System of Cycles, Ages, and Ends,
inaugurated at creation, and engraved in God's whole pro-
cedure with His people;* if it is true that it has pleased
God to forecast the destinies of Israel, the Nations, and
the Church, and distribute the same according to fixed

---

*Kliefoth. Offenbar. Joh. II, 153.

measures of time, and that the close of the whole historic development is the World's Sabbatism, a " Day " of Joy and Victory which with God, " *is* 1000 *years*," then it is clear that while these numbers are indeed symbolic and express geat ideas, *yet they could never be other than exactly what they are, and are just what they are only because of their relation to the Law of the Seven, the Ages and Ends, Seasons and Times,* which God has ordained in the march of His Kingdom on earth. These numbers express *Time* as well as *Ideas.* It is a fact that 10 Jubilee periods are exactly 500 years, and these *doubled* are exactly 1000 years !

The absurdities that result from denying a chronological value to them, are both great and grotesque. We are instructed (1) that " the 3½ does not mean time ; " (2) It means " our whole dispensation ; " (3) It means the " little season " of Gog at the end of the 1000 years ; (4) It is " the period of the reigning of the saints ; " (5) Satan, during this 3½ period is " bound with respect to the saints," but " loosed, with respect to the nations," (6) the words " till," " after," " finished," " expired," " short season," have no reference whatever to time ; (7) the millennial age and First Resurrection are " now ; " and (8) all equal 3½, equal 1000, equal our dispensation, equal no time at all, but only an *idea.** The Professor frankly admits his " solution is not wholly free from difficulty," but claims it is yet " a fair interpretation," and is " in harmony with all other Scripture !"† We catch the echoes, here, of Kliefoth, as we do, elsewhere, in reference to the meaning of the " *Basileia*," viz., that it is not Christ's reign *during* the 1000 years, but only His

---

* Revelation of St. John, Lect. VI. *passim.*
† Ibid, 223.

complete victory over Antichrist, the World-Power, and the Devil.

The answer to all this is not hard to find. The 3½, not less than the 1000, does mean literal time. It is the last 3½ years of Daniel's 70th year-week, 69 of the 70 weeks being "*exact and literal*" time, as history itself has proved, viz., 483 decreed or selected years from the Edict of Cyrus, B. C. 536, unto Messiah the Prince, or Birth of Christ. Though sundered from the 69 weeks, by the long Interval, Dan. ix:26, the 70th week still *belongs to the same category of historic time* as do the *whole* 70 of which it is *part,* and the 3½ are the last half of *that* week, preceding the date when Daniel, waked from his sleep, stands in his lot. Dan. xii:13. In short, the 70 Weeks of Daniel are not merely and only symbolical, but are as literal as the 2300 Evening-Mornings. Either this, or *no* demonstration of the Messiahship of Jesus of Nazareth from Dan. ix:25, 26, on which, so far as the time of the Advent is concerned, the whole church has rested the demonstration, from the very beginning! To this length the Aberdeen Professor must go, if the Weeks of Daniel, from which the 3½ spring, do not express *time.* And, because the Interval of our Dispensation lies *between* the 69th and 70th weeks, as our Lord Himself, when expounding this prediction, shows, Luke xxi:24; Dan. ix:26, therefore the 3½ are *not* "our present Dispensation," as Professor Milligan would have it, but are the last half of the 70th week, and proper Signature of the literal End-Time.

And this settled, the whole argument of the Professor falls to the ground. That argument is that *since*

---

* Revelation of St. John, 202.

the 3½ *are not literal, the* 1000 *are not.* But the reverse of this assumption, as to the 3½, being proved true, it follows, according to the Professor's own method of reasoning, that since the 3½ *are* literal, *the* 1000 *are literal also.* Manifestly wrong is the statement, that, if we take the 1000 years literally, "it will be the *solitary* example of a literal use of numbers in the Apocalypse, and this alone is fatal."* We might as well say that John's 3½ is not the last half of Daniel's "One Week" divided into twice 3½ years, or twice 1260 days; or that John's "*Beast*" is not the "*Little Horn*" of Daniel † or that the 69 weeks were not 483 years. And, were it not that we know otherwise, we might suspect that Hume, revived, had written the following sentence, to wit, "The whole conception, in short, of the chiliastic view of the 1000 years' reign is compassed about with so many *difficulties* and *improbabilities*, with so many *notions* of which we can form *no clear conception*, or which, when we think we understand them, are *so incredible* in themselves, that, unless it be forced upon us by fairness of interpretation, there is no alternative except to abandon it."‡ So *Hume*,—save what follows the word "*unless*" (!)—would have said! "*Difficult*," "*improbable*," "*no clear conception*," cannot "*understand*," "*so incredible;*" it is Hume's vocabulary; the echo of Spinoza's voice to Oldenberg! So the Trinity, Incarnation, Inspiration, Revelation, Regeneration, Future Life, Resurrection, Second Coming, every supernatural work and truth of God, is amenable to precisely the same objections.

---

* Revelation of St. John, 202.
† The "Beast," the last revived Empire *is* the "Little Horn," the "8th Head" of the Beast. Both are one. "*Ubi imperator ibi Roma.*" "*L' Empire, c'est Moi!*"
‡ Ibid, 202.

Wherein, if once we adopt such mode of reasoning about God's word, are Hume and we of different schools? Why should it be thought a thing *"incredible"* that Christ should live on earth, the Glorified among the unglorified, 40 days after His resurrection? Why " incredible," improbable," even if " inconceivable," that God should ordain a Time-Course *after* the Second Advent and the Resurrection of the saints? Already, at His First Coming, " *many bodies of the saints that slept arose, and went into the Holy City, and appeared to many,*" and History still kept on its way! Why " incredible " that God should gather His saints, restore Israel, renew their lost inheritance, and give to Israel and His Risen Ones, co-regent power in the coming Age? Or is it only what is " *probable,*" that " comes to pass in the last days "? Was Noah's *Tub* " probable?" Was the birth of Isaac " probable?" Was the passage of the Red Sea, or the birth of Jesus, or were the three who ate with Abraham, then saved Lot out of Sodom, " probable?" Does the Church, to-day, really believe it is " probable " that multitudes of the Old Testament Saints literally rose from their graves, and visibly marched into the Holy City, and showed themselves to the Sadducees of that time? Do ministers really believe this? *Improbable! Incredible! Inconceivable! Absurd!* Surely this too is " *Ideal!* " if not " mythical! " It was Augustine himself who said, " I do not seek to understand in order that I may believe, but I believe in order that I may understand." It was Tertullian who spoke that deep word, so paradoxical and yet so true, *"Credo, quia impossibile!* " " I believe, *because* it is impossible! " Where Reason fails, Faith conquers. It was " Abraham's faith whereat Sarah laughed,"—as Lord Bacon finely says,—" and who, therein, was an image of natural reason ! " Splendid faith is this, a faith that is beyond philosophy, and throws some sand on the slippery slide-board of a spiritualizing exegesis which lands so many of our hearers into infidelity, and denial of the Resurrection itself ! Man's impossibilities are God's actualities. And such faith, in face of all improbability and impossibility, is just what the prophetic word requires. Nothing less will answer. Just where every one says *No*, God says *Yes*. " *Neum Yehovah !* " *it is the utterance of Jehovah, Doer of these things !* " Amos ix:12, a solemn asseveration, guaranteeing fact, and supporting faith in what natural reason rejects as improbable, incredible, impossible. That is the sole force of the expression, " *Neum Yehovah !* " And so Augustine grandly said, " It matters not what *I* say, what *you* say, what *he* says, but *what saith the Lord !* " " *Neum Yehovah !* it is the *Utterance* of Jehovah ! " And that's what's the matter in this case, as in so many others. A " fair interpretation " is demanded, and what Professor Milligan deems a " fair interpretation " we have already seen ; a compound of contradictions impossible to be defended, and resting on conjectures and imaginations so palpable that the Professor's candor is obliged to allude to them in anticipation of their criticism.* Are not Bengel, Hofmann, Delitzsch, Ebrard, Auberlen, Olshausen, Riggenbach, Rothe, Schmid, Van Oosterzee, Nägelsbach, Weber, Orelli, Volck, Luthardt, Oehler, Köhler, Christiani, Burger, Rinck, Stier, Godet, Alford, Ellicott, and a hundred more like them, "*fair interpreters ?* "

All persons will cordially agree that symbolical

---

* Revelation of St. John, pp. 223–226.

numbers are not to be "tossed about at our pleasure, or shuffled like a pack of cards, and that the 1000 years are not to be made 2,000, 10,000, 20,000, or 365,000 ; as the necessities of the case may require."* But it is not we for whom such necessities exist. The " necessities " belong to others who have made an indelible record *varying* the length of the 1000 years according to the " necessities " of their own nomadic starting-point, restless, wandering, and weary ; dating from (a) the Death of Christ, (b) Pentecost, (c) the Death of the Believer, (d) the Destruction of Jerusalem, (e) Constantine, (f) Charlemagne, (g) the Reformation, (h) the *Great Unknown Point* 1000 years this side of the Advent, the whole period being 1,000, 10,000, 100,000; or 365,000 ; " as the necessities of the case may require,"— even as the 3½ may be either the half, or the whole, of our present dispensation, Gog's little season !

Most persons will, moreover, question the genius which for the sake of symbolism robs the prophetic time-words of their temporal significance. This is what that able and devout man, Professor Fairbairn, attempted, decades ago, when toiling to prove that the " *First* Resurrection " means only the "*greatest in moral importance,*" but " *not the first in temporal order !* " The " necessities of the case " required that ! As well plead that the " last " must mean the " *least.*" The Angel's answers to the various questions, " *When ?* " " *How Long ?* " cannot be divested of their literality. The time-words " *Until,*" " *Unto,*" "*From,*" " *To,*" " *After,*" " *For a time, two times, and the dividing of a time,*" have temporal importance. " *From* the going forth of a word to restore and build Jerusalem, *Unto*

* Ibid, 203.

Prince Messiah," the selected 69 Sevens mean "*exactly*" 483 literal years. The answer to the question "*How long* shall be the Vision?" viz, *Unto* 2300 evening-mornings, means a fixed term of years, from one given point to another. The reply of a linen-clothed man, hovering over the Tigris, to the man this side the river, inquiring "To what extent shall be the End of these wonders?" viz, "*For* a time, two times, and a half," and then "an End will be put to Antichrist's power," means that, at the close of 3½ years, dated from the middle of the 70th week, Israel's faithful remnant will be delivered and Israel's faithful dead be raised. And so of all the other numbers, the 1000 years not excepted.

C. Organic Relation of Prophetic Numbers

But still further. It is not enough to content ourselves with saying that no exegete can show that the 1000 years are not exactly 10 centuries. We assert their literality upon the ground of their organic relation to, and connection with, the whole system of Biblical Chronology, both Historic and Prophetic, and from first to last. We have spoken of the "Ages" and the "Ends" as ordained of God, and the same is true of the "Times and the Seasons." All are established, firm as the ordinances of the heavens, and the dominion of the Sun and Moon, by whose motions they are measured, and whose offspring they are. Science, the boast of modern times, has nothing more fixed, nor more exact. Commissioned to "*divide*" the day from the night, and to be for "*Signs*, for *Seasons*, and for *Days* and *Years*," Gen. i:14, and "to *rule*," v. 17, these regent luminaries measure off, in silent revolution, the various stadia in the progress of God's Kingdom. The hierarchy of the Sun, Moon and Stars, in their rising and

setting, and in their stately movement, mute yet eloquent, perform imperial offices. They have their
Signiorities and Principalities, no mortals, nor angels,
may invade. They *"rule."* The motions of the Heavens are an administration. The Planet Earth also belongs to their order. They are *"Lights"* that reveal.
They *measure Time,* being given for Seasons, and for
Days, and for Months, and for Years. They *indicate
Events,* also, being ordained for *"Signs"* as well as "Seasons." It is from these alone we get the *"Times"* and
the *"Signs,"* the *"Signs of the Times,"* and the *"Times of
the Signs;"* solar, lunar, sidereal, telluric. Their march
is historic, their motion is measured, their meaning
prophetic. They are hermeneutical. They move and
shine, rise and fall, and put on their various phenomena
subservient to the will of God, rulers, significators,
measurers, and interpreters of His holy word. They
stand in organized connection with the whole structure
of prophecy, and are themselves a page of prophecy
and of history, declaring the glory of God, and the
wonders of His Way. In the combination of their
offices as measurers of time and indicators of events in
connection with the word of God predicting the Times
and the Signs of the Times, they are a species of Holy
Writ in bodily form, a living symbolism read, known,
and deciphered, by God's servants, in all ages, from the
beginning of the world. Evermore their study has
been connected with the knowledge of futurity, and the
approach of impending catastrophe. They have an
interest in Judgment and Salvation. What knowledge
the wise men of ancient times possessed concerning the
prognostication of events, Babylonian or Egyptian, was
derived from holy men who, taught from the first, as
Enoch, Noah, Abraham, Joseph and Daniel, were

taught by divine instruction, transmitted the same to coming generations. It was in the Symbolism of Sun, Moon and Stars, Joseph learned his destiny. It was by a "Star" rising out of Jacob Balaam visioned Israel's distant ascendancy. The Sun standing still on Gibeon, and the Moon in the Valley of Ajalon, were for "Signs" of Victory to Joshua, even as the retrogression of the Shadow on the Dial of Ahaz was to Hezekiah a "Sign" of his recovery. It was by a "Sign" in the Heavens, the Eastern Magi discovered the Birth of Christ, and so brought the News to Jerusalem. The Sign in the Heavens and the knowledge of the Times the Chaldean Astrologers had gained from Daniel's 70 Weeks, and from Balaam's prophecy, was a revelation that did not disappoint their expectation. The horoscope of the Nativity was sure. Caspar, Melchior and Balthazzar never dreamed of *"Ideals,"* nor an *a quo* of the 70 Weeks dated from 20th Artaxerxes! The "Sign" of the flaming sword in the sky over doomed Jerusalem, told only too plainly that the "Day of Vengeance" had come for that Christ-rejecting City. Our Lord Himself and His Apostles, like the Prophets of old, ever referred to the "Times" foretold as measured "Times," having a literal fulfilment, and to the "Signs of the Times," as signs in the Sun, and Moon, and Stars, in the Earth also, and in the Sea, and declared that, as then and before, so would it be in the *"End of this age,"* adding other " Signs " *

* If we are to credit Josephus, Origen and Diodorus Siculus, the Greeks learned all their Science of Arithmetic, the Mysteries of Numbers, Geometry, Astronomy and Astrology, from the Egyptians who were taught these and the art of foretelling events, by the Patriarchs, as the Babylonians and Persians were taught the same by the Hebrews. Moses learned in the Wisdom of Egypt, and Daniel, Master of the Magi, both reckoned the *Times and the Signs of the Times.* Nebuchadnezzar learned that "*the Heavens do rule.*" See *Origen Tom. in Gen. Caps 37–50. Whiston's Josephus. Antiq. Book I. Cap. VIII, p. 50. Booth's Diodorus Siculus, Lib. I. Cap. IV, pp. 24, 25; Cap. VII, p. 51. Lib. II.* Cap. III, p. 69. Dan. i:4, 5, 11, 17, 18–20; ii:13; v:11.

also, such as the days of Noah and of Lot. *"As it was"* before, *"So shall it be again!"* Sun and Moon, ruling and measuring the " times fore-appointed," and giving "Signs" of their approach, or presence, strange phenomena in all, Eclipses, Discolorations, Convulsions in the Earth, the Sea and the Waves roaring, high-tidal attraction, "the treasures of the Snow and Hail hid against the day of battle and of War," as Napoleon learned to his sorrow, even as Sisera found the "Stars" against him ; the storm-lashed sea roused at the "blast of Jehovah's breath" to whelm an Armada, or Lisbon shuddered into disappearance by a shock violent as in the days of Uzzah ; *all things* in the Cosmic System, above, around and below, with all the forces of Nature, are woven into prophecy to remind us that the face of Nature, not less than the page of Scripture, is designed to teach us the literality and reality of divine prediction in reference to the *Numbers* and *Times*, as well as in reference to the *Seasons* and *Signs*. The combination is perfect. The "Days," the ' Months" and the " Years," the "Times" and the " Seasons," the "Ages " and the "Ends," all are measured to the moment, and the "Signs" appointed to their places by that unerring One whose Works are "known to Him from the beginning," who "sits on the circle of the Earth," is "curtained by the Heavens," and to whose eyes past, present and to come, are as one. His Immensity and Knowledge, His Holiness and Majesty, should impress us ! He smiles at our *"Ideals,"* and mocks at our *"potentiations* ! " He tells us that a mutual sympathy exists between the moral and material in His plan of Working, an inter. dependence of all phenomena in the evolution of His Kingdom, that "there is a *time* for every purpose under heaven," that the End-Time itself is fixed, and that, *"in that day*," when Israel's crisis is come, and all things seem to fail, even then "God will answer the Heavens, and they shall answer the Earth, and the Earth shall answer the Corn, and the Wine, and the Oil, and they shall answer Jezreel!" Hos. ii:21, 22. And so, in the Age following, the 1000 years of Israel's glory in the Kingdom,—not too long a period of earthly compensation for their sore Captivities and wide Dispersions,— Heaven, Earth, Sea, and Dry Land, all Nations and all Things, will answer the Power that makes for Righteousness, and Resurrection, for Judgment and Millennial Glory ;—that high-point toward which all things have been tending, that *Sabbatism* toward which all previous Sabbaths, and all Times, and all Seasons, ruled by the "*Law of the Seven*," have, for centuries, been marching ; Sun, Moon and Stars, flaming in the van. To what other conclusion can we come than that Sun and Moon, the regent lights in the heavens, are God's complex Chronometer, the believers' Time-Piece, swung on the sky, to tell us what o'clock it is, in the march of the ages on to the 1000 years ?

It is by the study of this fact we attain the clear conception that the Periodology of Bible-Chronology is a measured system of Cycles, of smaller or larger dimension, yet always symmetrical, proportionate, and true ; all organized in one complex movement for the preparation, progress, and completion of Redemption. The " Law of the Seven" and of "periodicity ruled by the Seven," is as much a literal law of God in Chronology governed by Sun, Moon and Stars, as are the laws of motion and gravitation, in Astronomy, which Kepler and Newton discovered, or the law of division and integration in intellectual and material processes which gave to the systems of Hegel and Spencer all their

vitality. Ideler, Wieseler, Coleman, and Browne, have
demonstrated this. The literality of the 1000 years,
hereby, becomes an irresistible conclusion. What we
see in the Scriptures, as well as in Nature, is a law of
Seven everywhere in the ascendant, and grounded in
God's creative Week, even as that week was grounded
in Himself. What we have is (1) a Seven of Days, and
in the Ritual; (2) a Passover Week; (3) a Seven of Weeks
from Passover to Pentecost; (4) a Seven of Months the
Sacred Year of the Jews; (5) a Seven of Years, in the
last of which the "Land" must keep Sabbath, even as
"Creation" was meant to keep Sabbath on the 7th, the
hallowed, Day; (6) a Seven of Sevens of Years or
Jubilee-Period, bringing the trumpet of ransom, release
from bondage, freedom from debt, and return to lost
possessions; (7) a Seven of Decades of Years or the 70
years of Judah's Captivity; (8) a Seven of Septuagint-
Years, or 490 years decreed upon Daniel's people and
city; a Seven of Centurial Years, thrice taken, with
added decades of 6; or 7 times 360 years, the Great
Seven of the Times of the Gentiles, foreseen in the 7
times of Moses; and (9) a Seven of Millennaries, or 7
times 1000 years, the Great World-Week, or, better,
the Week of God, whose 7th thousand is the Sabbatism
of mankind, the Day that precedes the Last Judgment
after which is the Eternal State, or Seventy times seven
thousand, and seven hundred thousands of thousands,
the law of the 7 ruling without cessation, on to, and
into, and unto, and over, in ever-recurring and ever-
increasing cycles of time, eternal, rolling forever and
ever, world without end, never to end forevermore!
And to show how exact and literal God's time is, as
well as symbolical, each of these Sevens ends in a
"*Rest*" appropriate to each, a Day of measured duration.

The first brings the Weekly Sabbath, the second brings Passover, the third brings Pentecost, the fourth brings the Feast of Tabernacles, the fifth brings the Land-Rest, the sixth brings Jubilee, the seventh brings Judah's rest from Exile, the eighth brings Israel's rest from the final Antichrist and Gentile power, and the ninth brings, not only Israel's, but the World's, rest from the wars, calamities, plagues and wiles, of Satan, and unrestrained dominion of sin, and sore temptation, by which God's saints are tried and tormented in the present age, and in place of which they then enjoy the undisturbed communion, light, and life, and love, of God in Jesus Christ. *Literal,* from first to last, is every measure of time, every Season, Epoch and Age; literal as the Clock's tick, the Sun's brightness, or the Moon's motion, the days multiplying to a Week, the Week to a Month, the Month to a Year, the Year to a Period, a Time, a Season, Epoch, Age, the different measures all expanding, enlarging, and marching, all keeping step with the law of the Seven, revolving and swelling to reach the last great Octave of praise through ages of ages, giving glory to God and the Lamb. This genetic and organic relation of all Chronology to the development of the kingdom of God *betrays design.* There is a teleology in it. And the nexus between the 1000 years and these different measures of time, all alike ruled by the same law, and part of the one scheme so literal everywhere, makes it impossible to maintain that the "1000 years" mean "Space," "Victory," "Ecumenicity," and "Eternity," or deny to them a literality as intense as belongs to any of the rest of the prophetic numbers, ruled as they are by the same persistent law of the Seven.

Immersed deep in the truth were those Scripture-loving souls who not only saw in the 1000 years a measure of time, but in the 7 days of Creation, the *Form and Type* for the distribution of all the Times and Ages succeeding. And well instructed were they who saw in the Sun "a light to rule by day," and in "the Moon a faithful Witness in the heavens" to God's great pur pose of Redemption, both unfailing servants, measuring off in axial and orbital rotation those very "Times and Seasons" of which all prophecy had spoken, and bearing a commission to make *"Signs"* of their ex- haustion or approach. To *"search what time* and *what manner of time"* could not be a matter of indifference to such. *Palmoni* taught them better. The *Magi* knew it. And well were they indoctrinated who saw in heav- en's ordinances an unfailing testimony to God's faith- fulness, and understood the value of that soul-uplifting, cheering, word, sent to assure their faltering faith, and thrill new courage to their fainting heart;—"Thus saith Jehovah which giveth the *Sun* for a light by day, and the Ordinances of the *Moon and Stars* for a light by night, which divideth the *Sea* when the Waters thereof roar,—*Jehovah Zebaoth* is His name!—If those ordi- nances depart from before me, saith Jehovah, *then the seed of Israel shall cease from being a nation before Me, for- ever!* If Heaven above can be measured, and the foundations of the Earth beneath be explored, *then will I cast off all the seed of Israel, for all that they have done!"* Jer. xxxi:35–37. No! No! it cannot be! The Sun will sooner lose his splendor, and the Moon and Stars abate their shining, Arcturus and Orion pale away, and Mazzaroth and Pleiades be lost forever, the Himalayas reel, and Alps go plunging headlong to strike the Apennines, than God forget His covenant with Israel, or cease to watch the motions of the Spheres, or fail to count the number of their revolutions appointed to bring that 70th Week when Israel will be saved, and Israel's land redeemed; and that *7th thousand Day*, whose Sun and Moon with sevenfold light, still circling the Sky, will measure again the Kingdom's years, till Sun and Moon exist no more! Solar, Lunar, Astral, are God's Times, so long as Sun, and Moon and Stars abide, and governed by them are the 1000 years not less than were the 70 years' Captivity, or were the Sevens Seven and Sevens Sixty and Two that brought the Birth of Christ.

D. SUMMARY

What we have to say, then, upon the whole question is this. When Isaiah said that 65 years should elapse till the end of the kingdom of 10-tribed Israel, by means of Assyrian invasion, Isa. vii:8, he meant literal years. That was his "*idea.*" When Jeremiah foretold the 70 years' Captivity of 2-tribed Israel, by means of Chaldean conquest, he meant literal years. That was his "*idea.*" And when Daniel speaks of the 70 years' Captivity, Dan. ix:2; of the 70 Sevens decreed upon "All Israel" *and their City,* ix:24; and again, of the 7 and the 62 weeks, unto Prince Messiah; and again, of the 1 week, for the prince to come, the Antichrist, a week divided into twice $3\frac{1}{2}$ years, or twice 1260 days; and again, of the $\frac{1}{2}$ Week, ix:27; when he speaks of 2300 evening-mornings, viii:14; of a time, times, and dividing of a time; or $3\frac{1}{2}$ or 1260, again, vii:25; xii:7; then of 1290 and 1335 "*days*" or 75 *days* added to the 1260, so bringing the blessed time of promised glory in the land; his "*idea,*" or rather, the Angel's "*idea,*" is, that the literal Sabbatic Seven *dominates Israel's whole history,* ends in a Sabbath Jubilee,—the righteous dead and living sharing in the joy. And when John speaks of the Smyrna-perse-

cution, 10 days, Rev. ii:10; of the "little season" for the
altar-martyrs, vi:11; of the ½ hour preparation of the
Trumpet-Angels, viii:1; of the Scorpion-torment of 5
months, ix:5; of the attitude of the Euphratean horse-
men punctual to the very "hour, and day, and month,
and year," ix:15; of the "Days of the Voice" of the 7th
Angel, x:7; of the 42 months' down-treading of Jerusalem, and the domination of the Beast, xi:2; xiii:5; of
the 1260 days of the Sackloth-Witnesses, and next, of
the Sun-clothed Woman in the wilderness, xi:3; xii:6; of
the 3½ Days of the Witnesses unburied, xi:9, 11; of the
"time, times, and half a time," xii:14; and, last of
all, of "*the* 1000 *years*" of Satan's Captivity, the Saints'
reign with Christ, and non-deception of the Nations,
xx:1–7; when, furthermore, he says that, "*till*" the 1000
years are *fulfilled*, "Satan shall be sealed;" that, "*after
that* he shall be loosed a little season," xx:3, "*when* the
1000 years are *expired*," xx:7; and that, "*until* the 1000
years are *finished*, the rest of the dead live not again," xx:
5; his "*idea*," or, rather the Angel's "*idea*," is, that, *over
against all other literal and inferior time distinctions,* in
this prophecy, stand "*the* 1000 *years*" *as the one, unique,
distinguishing, and characteristic number of the Apocalypse,*
six times *intentionally repeated in the conclusion of the
Canon;* and that it is *the definite interpretation of those
other indefinite* yet, *equivalent expressions in the prophets,*
viz., "*Multitude of Days," and "Many Days," the special
measure of the Great Sabbatic Age that next ensues the
Advent of the Lord!* One law governs the construction of all these numbers, and the same rule of interpretation applies to all. They are alike literal and
symbolical.

Part 8

THE TESTIMONY OF THE SYNAGOGUE

A.   That the 1000 years are merely " ideal," is contradicted by the testimony of the Hebrew Doctors both before and since the Birth of Christ.   The voice of the Synagogue is against it, from first to last.   Targum, Talmud and Midrash, alike, upon the basis of Ps. lxxii: 7, have denominated the "*Yemot Meshicah*" or "*Days of Messiah,*" as the period following His Advent in glory.

As to the *Duration* of the Kingdom the Psalm declares it to be "*forever,*" v. 17, even while the sun endures, and "long as the moon, throughout all generations," v. 5.   So Daniel ii:44, and vii:14.   It is an "everlasting kingdom," a kingdom having "no end." Isa. ix:7.   It is the Biblical doctrine everywhere.   In the genuine Hebrew Sibyl (the Alexandrian) the same continuity and universality are ascribed to the kingdom, in the words, "Then shall He establish a kingdom over all men, *forever.*" *   In like manner the Book Enoch, yet not without limitation on the other hand, teaches the same "*eternal*" or "*olamic*" duration, extend-

---

* *Oracula Sibyllina ad fidem*, etc., etc.   III. 771, 776, 777, ed. Friedlieb.   Leipsic.   1852.   This portion of the Oracles, Book III. was written about B, C, 160, or in Maccabean times, the second century before Christ.

ing Messiah's reign to the "beasts of the field and fowls of heaven." *   The Psalms of Solomon, so full of spirituality and true devotion, written either in the times of the Maccabees, or subsequently in the times of Pompey and Cæsar, pray imploringly for the "gathering of elect Israel," the establishment of the kingdom in mercy and kindness," Messiah's "smiting the earth with the word of His mouth *forever*," and "the coming of a King to subdue the scepters of all the earth, *unto all ages*." † The Book of Jubilees, written before the Roman destruction of Jerusalem, emphasizes the same view, predicting a "king who shall reign on Mount Zion, *from eternity to eternity*," and Israel's "dominion over the whole earth, inheriting the same *forever and ever*." ‡   In like manner, yet not without qualification, the Apocalypse of Baruch, written while the Apostle John was still living, proclaims the Messianic Kingdom as "*forever*." ‖   This pre-Christian Jewish doctrine of the Eternal Duration of Messiah's Kingdom, was also the doctrine of the Jews in the time of Christ.   It was during the last passover of His life, when "certain Greeks came to see Jesus," He spoke of the "corn of wheat" that falls into the earth and dies in order to bring forth much fruit, and predicted the glorious harvest to follow His own crucifixion.   "And I, if I be *lifted* up, will draw all men unto me!   This He spake, signifying what death He should die."   John xii:20–33. The announcement astounded the people, taught, as they were, to believe that Messiah's person and throne

---

* Das Buch Henoch.   Dillmann's ed.   XC, 30–37.   XCI,17.
  † Der Psalter Salomo, in Hilgenfeld's "Messias Judæorum."   VIII, 33-35.   XVII, 39.
  ‡ Das Buch der Jubilaen.   (Dillman's ed. in Ewald's Jahrbücher, etc., 1850, 1851.)   I, 12.   XXXII, 42.
  ‖ Baruch. LXXIII.

are eternal, and shook their faith, to no small degree, in the Messianic claims of Jesus of Nazareth. They replied, promptly, to his words, "We have heard out of the law that *Messiah abides forever !* And how sayest thou, the Son of Man must be *lifted up ?* Who is this Son of Man?" John xii:34. They appealed to the *Torah,* by which they meant the whole revelation of God found in Moses, the Psalms and the Prophets, in support of their Jewish faith. Moses, David, Isaiah, Daniel, Ezekiel, Zechariah, all declare that Messiah *"abides!"* When He comes, He comes to stay. When He reigns, He reigns "forever." His throne is eternal. His Days are *"Yamim Yamim,"* *"Olammim Olammim,"* His Kingdom is *"Ain–Keitz,"* "without end," and He, Himself, is *"Abi-'Ad,"* the "Father of Unto," a " *Tsur Olammim,"* a "Rock of Ages !" Who is this Son of Man, to be lifted up ? Surely this Son of Man is not "Messiah !" So thought the people. Messiah cannot be mortal and die like other monarchs, for (Blessed be He !) " He asked life of Thee, Jehovah, and Thou gavest it Him, even length of days forever and ever." Ps. xxi:4. There is something in this most serious and earnest paschal debate that not only engages the head, but touches the heart.* What intense anxiety ! Messiah *"abides."* How then can He *"die ? "* And so spake the Rabbis of later times, represented by the judgment of Abarbanel, saying, "As respects the future kingdom of Messiah our Righteousness, and of which

---

* This is a clear illustration of the confusion that arises from not discriminating the Ages and Ends in prophecy, and the work of Messiah in each. The Jews quoted the Scriptures rightly, but interpreted wrongly, not seeing two Comings of Christ, and expecting at His First Advent what is due only at His Second. The like confusion exists, to-day, in the Gentile Church, many expecting at the Second Advent what is due only at the close of the 1000 years. Our eschatology is built on this error.

the prophet Daniel informs us, in chapter vii, he says, not that Messiah shall ascend from the Sea, but that He comes in the clouds of Heaven ; that is, His dominion comes not from the princes of earth, or spirits beneath the heavens, who rule this world, but comes by the special providence of God, and on that account shall stand *forever !* " It was the view of Rabbi Akiva whom Rabbi Meir quotes and then adds, "Of the *Cup of Life* the Holy Blessed God will give the Righteous Messiah to drink in the future Age. In the World to come the Holy Blessed God has said, I will cause *My Glory* to shine over all Israel, and they shall behold *Me* and live forever. Then shall they visibly see it when the Lord shall bring again Zion. Our Rabbis, of blessed memory, have taught us, that Messiah the Son of David, already exists in Paradise, and have a tradition that, in the Coming Age, there is no death for the righteous." "Peace be to Him!" exclaimed Rabbi Isaac, "for Psalm xlv speaks of King Messiah of whose government there shall be no end, as Isaiah says, but He shall reign eternally."

All these expressions of the Hebrew faith, as to the *duration* of Messiah's kingdom, are unlimited, and in perfect accord with the uniform teaching of the Scriptures.

But, if Messiah's kingdom is " Eternal," it is also " *Temporal*." If it is of unmeasured duration, not merely indefinite but absolute, transcending all temporal limits, it is no less a kingdom of measured duration, restricted to temporal limits, and bounded by great historic events. *One* in essence, it is *many* in forms. Its organic growth, from a seed to a tree, necessitates this. And this was the Hebrew faith, no less than the previous view. It is the biblical view also.

The word " *Olam*," " Ever," does not, of itself, and by fixed necessity, always denote the annihilation of time, but as frequently, in Hebrew usage, denotes simply unbroken continuance up to a special epoch in history, or to a certain natural termination. It has a relative as well as an absolute sense, a finite as well as an infinite length. It means " Here " as well as " Beyond," and applies to a kingdom that comes to " an End," as well as to one that has " no End." For this reason, a great World-Period, or Age, is called an " *Olam*," and World-Periods, or Ages, are called " *Olammim*," and in order to express infinite time, the reduplication is used, " *Ages of Ages*," " *Olammim Olammim*." It is therefore a false conclusion to say that because the term " *Le Olam*," " *Forever*," is applied to the Messianic kingdom, therefore the Hebrews contradicted themselves, when they assigned to it limits at the same time. Messiah's kingdom is Temporal and also Eternal, and *in both senses, Olamic*. The bondsman's free covenant to serve his master lasted " forever," but that only meant " till Jubilee." The Levitical economy was established to be " forever," but that only meant till " the time of re-formation." The Christian Church is " forever," in its present form, but that only means " till He comes." True to this view, the Jewish Teachers ever held to a *Temporal Kingdom of glory on earth*, in the " World to Come," *this side* the Eternal State in the final New Heaven and Earth. Therefore, we read in Fourth Ezra (Second Esdras in the English Apocrypha) that Messiah's kingdom is restrained " to 400 years,"* while in the Apocalypse of Baruch—both these productions written in the time of the Apostle John,—it is said to

---

* 4th Ezra, VII. 48.

'stand forever," yet only " until the corruptible world
is ended.''*   All this instructs us in the flexible, as well
as fixed, character of the term " forever."

As to the *Precise Duration* of this limited kingdom
of Messiah, various computations exist, based upon a
literal interpretation of various passages of Scripture,
and nearly all of them on the principle of *exact compensation* for Israel's various time of previous distress and
misery.   The one uppermost thought is that the
kingdom will bring a reward of happiness proportioned
to that of their past sorrow.   If one Rabbi teaches
differently from another, it is not that the one is to be
deemed false and the other true, but all are entitled
to the same religious respect.

According to Rabbi Eliezar, the time of Messiah's
kingdom on earth is limited to 40 years, that is, it
equals the period of Israel's wandering in the Wilderness.   This computation was based upon Ps. xcv:10,
" Forty Years long was I grieved with this generation,"
and upon the prayer in Ps. xc:15, " Make us glad
according to the days wherein thou hast afflicted us,
and the years wherein we have seen evil."   We may
smile, perhaps, at the computation as a puerile conceit,
but we may not smile at the deep devotion of the pious
Hebrew, and his deep regard for the Word of God,
apart from which he cared for no computation.   We
may think that, if the temporal measure of man's
reward is that of his transgression, then, not merely 40
years but immensely more must be Messiah's Days.
The Rabbis knew that as well as we.   Therefore, R.
Azaryah held that Messiah's Days are 70 years.   And
this was based upon the time of Israel's Captivity.

---

* Baruch, XL, XLVIII.

Jer. xxv:12 ; xxix:10–14. The term of Israel's enjoyment will, at least, equal that of their Exile.

But R. Dosa said, Messiah's Days are 400 years ; and so says 4th Esdras,—a computation based upon Gen. xv:13, which defines the times of Israel's Bondage to the Pharaohs. Messiah's Kingdom must, at least, equal the days of Israel's servitude in Egypt. R. Chiyya said, however, that Messiah's Days are 600 years, for it is written, "As the days of a tree shall be the days of my people," Isa. lxv:22. Surely not less than the life of the Olive, the Sedan and the Sycamine shall be the years of God's redeemed. Gentile scorn may curl the lip at these attempts, but could Gentile genius do better ? Yet R. Eleasar said, Messiah's Days shall be 1000 years, for it is written, that when Messiah comes to save Israel the "Day of Vengeance is in His heart," and (Blessed be He !) "the Year of His redeemed has come ! " Isa. lxiii:4, "a year of Remission and Return ; " and it is written, "a day in God's sight is 1000 years." Ps. xc:4. Therefore Messiah's Days will be a *Millennial Time*. And Elias, a Doctor of the Second Temple, and the School of Elias, both say Messiah's Kingdom is 1000 years for "the world's Ages are distributed upon the type of the creative week at whose close is the Sabbatic Rest." "The world shall last 6000 years from its creation, or 85 Jubilees from the time of Elias, then the Son of David will come and begin the World's Sabbatism." And R. Qatina and R. Jose say the same, adding that "Messiah's Days are the Days of Restitution for Israel, and are 1000 years." Israel's enemies shall be destroyed, for it is written, "The haughtiness of man shall be bowed down, and the Lord alone exalted in that day." Isa. ii:11. And in that day, it is said, " the

Lord's House will be exalted above the hills, and all
nations stream to it, and Jacob will walk in the light of
the Lord." Isa. ii:2–5.   And R. Moses Maimonides,
than whom "from Moses to Moses no greater than
Moses has lived," said, "Messiah's Days will be a long
time, and it must not be thought strange if the Kingdom endures some 1000 years."   And R. Bechai, great
rival of Maimonides, said, "When Messiah comes the
6000 years will have been completed.   Then the 7th day
shall go on, a genuine Sabbath and Eternal Life."   The
great Rabbi Jehoshua agreed but thought nevertheless
that Messiah's Days must be 2000 years, for it is written, "Make us glad according to the *Days* (plural),
therefore at least 2000 years or *two* days, for 1000 years
are *one* day."   Abimi, however, went higher still, saying, "Messiah's Days will be 7000 years, for it is written
of Jerusalem, As a young man marrieth a virgin so
shall thy sons marry thee, and as a Bridegroom re-
joiceth over the Bride, so shall thy God rejoice over
thee," Isa. lxii:5, and the marriage festivity lasts 7 days,
and with God a day is 1000 years."   Higher than all in
calculation mounts Rabbi Nachman who says, " Messiah's days are from Noah's time till now, for it is
written, 'This is as the Waters of Noah unto Me, for as
I have sworn that the waters of Noah should no more
go over the earth, so have I sworn I would not be
wroth with thee, nor rebuke thee.' " Isa. lv:9.   The
principle upon which these different computations were
made is manifest.   It is evermore that God's compassion
is, *at least*, equal to his justice.   One more remains.   The
highest estimate of limited time is that of Rabbi Je-
huda, who says, "Messiah's days are as long as from
the Creation till now, for it is written, ' Bind these
words for a sign on your hand that your days may be

multiplied in the land as long as the days of Heaven upon Earth.'" Deut. xi:21.*

Such is a specimen of the views of the Great Synagogue,—views perpetuated by the *Maskilim*, or teachers of the people, and afterward incorporated in the Targums, Talmuds, and later Jewish Books, and found in the Jewish Apocalypses, and pseudepigraphical writings. Hamburger tells us that the smaller computations appeared among the earlier, and soon gave way to the larger. Wünsche remarks that a 1000 years came, at last, to be regarded as the measure of the Messianic time. So Gebhardt, saying, " Eminent Rabbis fixed the duration of the Messianic Kingdom for 1000 years according to a combination of Isa. lxiii: 4; Ps. xc:4; (compare II Peter iii:8) in union with the reason that, as God created the world in six days, and rested on the seventh, so in 6000 years, as in six world-days, all will be finished, and the 7th thousand the great World-Sabbath will be celebrated." † It is plain that abstract idealism had nothing to do with these calculations. Along with this, also, was developed the strange idea of *two* Messiahs, grounded in the concession that Messiah, indeed, must be *mortal* like other kings, and *die*, if the Scriptures are true ; nevertheless His Kingdom is "forever;" it is "eternal." So Rabbi Moses ben Maimon (Maimonides) said:

---

* To spare wearisome repetition of reference, I refer here, once for all, to the sources whence the foregoing quotations are taken, viz., Eisenmenger, Entdecktes Judenthum. II. 912-920. Hamburger, Real Encycl. II. 775. Weber, System alttest. palæst. Theologie, 373. Wünsche, Neue Beitrage, etc. 280. Castelli, Il Messia Secondo gli Ebræi, Appendice, 297–335. Bertholdt, Christologia Judæorum, s. v. Messias. Drummond, Jewish Messiah, 315–318. Rabbi Isaac's Chizzuk Emuneh, or Munimen Fidei. 473. A vast amount of like literature is also found in Lightfoot, Schœttgen, his continuator, and Hilgenfeld's Messias Judæorum.

† Gebhardt. Doctr. Apoc. 277.

"Know this that Messiah must necessarily be *mortal* and *die*, but in His stead his son, or uncle, shall reign." And Rabbi Isaac, and others, speak in a like way. There is a "Messiah the son of Joseph," and a "Messiah the son of David." The apparent conflict of Scripture was not understood. The Mystery, the Incarnation and the Scandal of the Cross were, alike, a "stone of Stumbling and rock of offence." Messiah "*lifted up*" on the tree, yet "living forever," they could not understand. Yet as to the Doctrine of the Messianic Kingdom, it was to be *first of all* of limited time and extent. All the numbers used, and calculations given, are of the most *literal* character. They speak in realistic terms. The idea of "potentiated ecumenicity" never entered their thought. As little did Moses dream of "potentiated space and victory" when he wrote the xcth Psalm, and said, "A thousand years in Thy sight, are but as yesterday when it is past, and as a watch in the night," Ps. xc:4. And as little did Peter dream of it, when writing to the *Dispersed* of his people, who still waited for the fulfilment of Israel's hope and the coming of the Lord, "Beloved, *forget not this one thing*, that *one day* is with the Lord as *a thousand years*, and *a thousand years as one day*," II Pet. ii:8. The "one day" was in Peter's mind 24 hours. The "1000 years" were alike literal.

B.   THE *TERMINUS A QUO*

But the 1000 years are not only a definite measure of time, in Hebrew account; they have also a definite *terminus a quo*, marked by definite contemporary events. The Commencement of these years is

(*a*) *Dated from the close of the 70th Week of Daniel ix:*27; a week divided into two equal parts, or halves, 3½ and 3½ years, the first half being the "Beginning of

Sorrows," the second half being the " Great Tribulation," the close of the second the " End," the Middle-
Point of the Week marked by the "Abomination of
Desolation," and the whole denominated the " Dolors
of Messiah," or Birth-Pains of the Daughter of Zion
becoming the Mother of the Manly Child, and the Messianic Nation and Kingdom.   All this was founded on
the prophets, and how thoroughly it was verified by our
Lord in His great eschatological discourse, Wünsche
has shown in the clearest manner.   Blind to how
many things in reference to the First Advent and the
true Messianic Hope, which our Lord found it necessary to re-instate, in His conversation with Nicodemus,
yet both pre and post-Christian Judaism were open-eyed
as to many other things in reference to the Second Advent, but which they deemed due at the One and Only
Advent they admitted, an Advent for Judgment, Victory and Glory.   They saw clearly enough that the
Messianic Days, the Kingdom of the 1000 years, the
Millennium of their prophets, *followed* the Great Tribulation.   Attaching that 70th week, however, to the 69th
in immediate sequence, and history failing to bring the
fulfilment, they concluded that Jesus of Nazareth was
not the Messiah foretold by the prophets.   The relation
of the 70th week, however, to the Advent of Messiah
as a victorious and judging Prince, sent to restore the
Kingdom. of Israel, they understood.   The Jewish literature is crowded with evidences of this.   In the words
of Dr. August Wünsche, whose *"New Contributions from
Talmud and Midrash toward the explanation of the Gospels"* is of standard authority, to-day, " The Rabbis
divided the Year-Week preceding Messiah's Advent
into its several days, each day a year, and specified the
calamities that would mark this sevenfold period, viz.,

War, Famine, Pestilence, Betrayal, Oblivion of the
Law, Oppression, Persecution and Death, at whose
end the Son of David shall come. This they learned
from the prophetic books. One of the most celebrated
Baraithas * informs us that, *in the time when Messiah
comes, the House of God shall be a house of shame, the
teachers of the law shall go begging and none befriend
them, the Creed of the Sadducee shall prevail, the wisdom of the rulers shall stink, the godly shall be despised,
aud the faces of the people be like that of the dog, and truth
shall fail, and whoever avoids wickedness shall make himself
a prey.*" † With what emphasis the teachings of Jesus,
confirming to them their own interpretation, must have
fallen on the ears of His contemporaries! Was it possible that the best Jewish teachers of His day, disciples
of the school of Hillel, a lineal descendant of David and
grandfather of Gamaliel the teacher of Paul, should fail
to feel the force of His words? It proves to us Gentiles, at least, that *Jews* may *sometimes* be right in their
interpretation of their own prophets, while *Christian
Gentiles* may *sometimes* be wrong. The prophets, Hillel,
Gamaliel, Jesus and John, were all one as to the 70th
Week of Daniel. Not once did our Lord, not once did
His Apostles, ever refer to Daniel ix:27, as accomplished at His First Coming. Among the Rabbis, as
well as in Daniel, Christ and John, the 1000 years *follow*
the 70th Week.

(*b*) *Dated from the Overthrow of the fourth prophetic
empire,* Dan. ii:35, 44, 45. By way of eminence, the
"End" of that ten-toed political power was called "*The
End, Hakkets,*" in accordance with Dan. ix:26. It is

---

* The *Baraithas* are an independent collection of opinions, traditions
and interpretations, external to the Talmud.
† Neue Beiträge, etc. 302.

what the Apocalypse teaches. As for John, so for the Rabbis, Rome is the arsenal of Antichrist, the new Babylon that must be destroyed if ever Jerusalem shines again, and Messiah's Kingdom comes. As for John, so for the Rabbis, the thought of Rome's becoming a throne of Messiah, and Jerusalem a heap of eternal ruins, is the farthest possible from their minds. "*Roma*," "*Duma*," must be destroyed. The proud Colossus of Gentile supremacy over Israel must be broken. According to their twofold division of the Ages, based on the prophetic books, and according to the predictions concerning Israel and the Gentiles, were their constant proverbs, "The Most High did not make one age but *two;*" * and "Esau is the End of This Age (*Olam Hazzeh*), but Jacob is the Beginning of the Age to come (*Olam Habba*)." † The "Time of the End," the "Time to possess the Kingdom," the "End of the Days," the "End," they interpreted to mean the End of the Colossus in Dan. ii:44, the End in Dan. ix:26, the End of the ten-toed Roman Empire. And they were right, just where so many Christian interpreters are wrong. The Judgment described in Daniel chapter vii, they regarded not as the last Judgment closing the 1000 years or Days of Messiah, but as the Messianic Judgment, or part of the "Dolors" *preceding* those years; a Judgment connected with the "Gathering of the Nations" described by Isaiah, Zephaniah and Zechariah, and which Hamburger, Wünsche, Weber, and Gfrörer equate with the Judgment described in Matt. xxv:31-46. Eisenmenger quotes Abarbanel at length, as giving the view of the Hebrew Doctors, thus, "Rabbi Isaac Abarbanel in his book *Majene Jeshua*, folio 48, col. 3, writes,

---

* 4 Esdras VI, 25.   † 4 Esdras VII, 43.

When Daniel Cap. vii:10, says "the Judgment was set, and the Books were opened," he was not describing the Resurrection of the dead, for this was explained to him afterward in his fourth vision, xii:1–3. But the Judgment of which he here speaks, is that punishment with which the Holy Blessed God shall visit the *living Nations at the time of the Coming of our Messiah, when He shall annihilate their sovereignty and restore the Kingdom to the Jewish people;* for all this is conceived of under the figure of Judgment. Therefore, he says, 'Until the Ancient-One came and the Judgment was given to the Saints of the Most High.' The word *'Judgment,'* therefore, is here used in the sense of *dominion,* or *right of judging,* or *ruling,* the honor God will give to Israel, and is proof that it signifies the Reward of the Jewish people, and the Punishment of the Gentiles, their enemies, according to their works. For this reason it is said, 'The Judgment was set, and the Books were opened.' " * In like manner Rabbi Saadias Haggaon, chief prince and glory of all Hebrew scholars, wrote "Because Israel has rebelled against God, *their Kingdom* was taken from them and given to *those four monarchies* who shall possess the Kingdom in this present Age,—(*be-Olam-Hazzeh*)—and shall lead captive and subdue Israel to themselves, even until the Comng Age—(*ad-Olam-Habba*)—when Messiah shall appear and reign." † Nothing is clearer than that the *"End of the fourth Gentile Monarchy,"* after its development into its last ten-kingdomed divisons, is the Commencing Date of the 1000 years. And here again, the prophets, the Rabbis, Christ, Paul and John, all agree. Or, if Edom

---

* Eisenm. Entdeckt. Judenthum. II. 965.
† See Mede's Works. 536.

be taken, as some take it, to mean Ishmael, or Islam, then when Mohammedanism and Rome go down, and the central seats of both fall, Israel's times in the Kingdom of the 1000 years shall come.

(*c*) *Dated from the destruction of Armillus, the Last Leader and Last Antichrist.* All Jewish literature speaks of a combined assault upon, and siege of, Jerusalem under the leadership of one Great Enemy of Israel, the embodiment of the world's hatred to God and His people. In the pre-Christian Sibylline Oracles, Book III, lines 63–74, genuine lines of the old Hebrew or Erythrean Sibyl, B. C. 170 or 140, this Leader is called "*Beliar.*" In Baruch he is called the "Last Leader" in the "Time of Tribulation" which is divided into "two parts," or 3½ and 3½ in plain allusion to Dan. ix:27, and after which "Messiah shall be revealed," "the Resurrection take place," "the Kingdom come," and "men of all nations be subject to Israel's King." *
In the Targum of Ben Uzziel, on Isa. xi:4, which Paul interprets in II Thess. ii:8, the "Last Leader" is called "*Armilaus,*" plainly not derived from "Romulus," as Weber thinks, but from the Greek "*Eremolaos,*" the "Desolator of the People," which again is only another name for the "*Nagid Habba,*" the "*Meshomem*" or "*Desolator,*" in Dan. ix:27, a true "Apollyon." † In the pre-Christian Book Enoch the slaughter of Antichrist and his hosts will be appalling, Israel sharing in the vengeance, as Zechariah predicts.‡ It is a day when "sin is ready for a ceaseless bloodshed," and "when, from the blush of morning till sunset, they will kill one another, and the horse shall walk up to his breast in blood, and the chariot sink to its top." ‖ The point of

---

* See Drummond. Jewish Messiah. 121–129.   † Ibid.
‡ Book Enoch XC, 17–19.   ‖ Ibid. XCIX, 15. C. 3.

contact here with the fearful Armageddon and Bozrah
conflicts, and the last siege of Jerusalem and Valley of
Jehoshaphat, as pictured by John, are unmistakable.
Rev. xix:11–21 ; xiv:19, 20.   Compare Deut. xxxii:39-43;
Joel iii:13, 14; Zech. xii:1–9.   Here, again, the prophets,
the Rabbis, Christ and John are all one.   The Psalms
of Solomon, written a half century before Christ, speak
of "the Word of Messiah's mouth as the weapon in that
day." *   The 4th Esdras pictures the Jewish triumph
which it ascribes to Messiah as the "Lion of Judah,"
and "standing on the summit of Mount Sion," destroying with flame the "Eagle" that swoops with "wing of
abomination" upon His people. †   In Baruch the "Last
Leader" is slain by Messiah Himself on Mount Sion,
who thereupon in the End-Time erects "a dominion
that shall never be destroyed." ‡   He who delivered
Israel from Pharaoh, Sennacherib, and Antiochus, will
deliver also from Israel's last oppressor.   The "Last
Leader" of the Gentile force against Israel perishes
under a Messianic judgment, and then the Days of
Messiah, the 1000 years, begin.

(*d*) *Dated from the Resurrection of the Faithful dead.*
False, in every way, is the modern assertion, by many,
that the Pentateuch does not teach the resurrection of
the body, and the Prophets only a political and civil
resurrection of Israel, or that the notion of a literal resurrection of the body as held by the Prophets of the
Captivity, by the Rabbis, and by Christ and His
Apostles, was derived from the Persian eschatology.
In the admirable words of Hofmann, "There never was
a time when faith in a Redeemer to come existed apart

---

* Psal. Sal. XVII, 25–27, 37, 39.
† 4th Esdras. XII, 6–11.
‡ Baruch XXXV–XL.

from this Hope, nor has there been a time in history when this Hope *could* have made its appearance or *first entrance later than the First Promise in Eden.* Wherever the knowledge of *death by sin* went among the descendants of Adam, the knowledge of *redemption from death by sin* went by necessity also, involving the resurrection of the body." * These words are golden. False the assertion that the Rabbis herein followed Heathen ideas. Later Parsism, misapprehending the Hebrew doctrine, and borrowing from it, taught indeed a resurrection of the body, yet only at the time of the final re-creation of the Cosmos. Buddhism taught a resurrection, yet only as a soul-absorption, at death, into the absolute being whence it sprang. Mosaism, in opposition to both, taught the Resurrection of the righteous at the Coming of Messiah, the covenant Redeemer of "Abraham, Isaac and Jacob," and their believing seed, and taught it in connection with the gift of Canaan to the three great stem-fathers of the Hebrew race, *personally;* and Targum, Talmud and Midrash perpetually assert and emphasize the same. The Middle-Age Hebrew Doctors differed, indeed, as to the precise meaning of the expression *"at that time"* in Dan. xii:1-3. Maimonides on Isa. lxvi:5, Abarbanel on Isa. xviii:3, and others, like Saadias, Kimchi and Aben-Ezra, put the time of the resurrection of the righteous at the Advent of Messiah for victory and glory, as in Isa. xxv:1-9; xxvi:19. On the other hand, Bechai, Naphtali, the Book Enoch Hammelek, and others, put it at the "End of the Days," meaning thereby the close of the Messianic Days of glory on earth, the close of the 1000 years. Perplexity existed, and great debate

---

* Schriftbeweis. III. 490.

arose as to whether the "Heathen" should rise in the
resurrection, or only "Israel," and whether all or only
part of Israel should rise, and, if so, when? It was, in
fact, a *pre* and *post*-millennialist discussion, and embarrassed greatly by the fact that only *one* Advent of Messiah was admitted. The truth came to light, the Last
Resurrection, however, being assigned, not to Messiah,
but to God the Father. The great body of Jewish
scholars decided for the resurrection of the righteous
at the Advent of Messiah, to establish the 1000 years'
Kingdom And herein again, so far as this point goes,
they were right, and vastly superior to a thousand
modern Gentile commentators. They agreed with the
prophets, and by consequence their doctrine is that of
the New Testament, also, as Meyer, Olshausen, Stier,
Bertholdt, Weber, Wünsche, and others, have triumphantly shown. There is no better or clearer statement,
anywhere, of the Rabbinical Doctrine as to the resurrection than is found in Hamburger. Summing up the
results of his searching investigation, he says, "According to my judgment the Talmud Doctrine of the resurrection is that of a resurrection of the body occurring
at *two different times ;* first for the righteous at Messiah's Advent, and then, afterward, a long time, at a
General Judgment." Two Ends are asserted here, the
one a *relative* End at the Coming of Messiah to assume
and enter on His Kingdom at the close of this present
Age, the other, *after that*, the final, *absolute* End at the
close of the Messianic Days, or 1000 years, when the
Kingdom passes into Eternity. It looks immensely
like Paul's view and mode of expression in I Cor. xv:
23–28. To object to it as "*Jewish*," is an *ad captandum*
appeal to an ambiguous phrase, prejudice and ignorance, and ought to be repelled. The prophets, the

Rabbis, Paul and John are in perfect harmony here, on this point. Hamburger continues : " The Talmud speaks sometimes of the one, sometimes of the other, resurrection, and it is not to be wondered that this difference easily led to different conceptions. Even in the Gospels the resurrection to General Judgment is distinguished from that at the Advent of Messiah, this latter being only for the righteous, as in I Cor. xv:24, and Rev. xx:5. It is the Resurrection *out from* the dead and not the resurrection *of all* the dead. We give the sum of Jewish thought. Some teachers say that after a battle with Gog and Magog the dead shall arise. Others say, against these, that Gog and Magog, the Days of Messiah and the Resurrection-Time for the righteous are to be distinguished. The Gathering of the Outcasts will occur *before* the Resurrection. Again, the Gathering of the Outcasts will *precede* the Resurrection from the dead. So the Midrash on Psal. cxlvii:2, ' The Eternal builds Jerusalem, gathers the Outcasts, heals the broken in heart, and binds their wounds ; ' (1) the Building, (2) the Gathering, (3) the Refreshing, (4) the Resurrection. And with these views agree the Talmudic representation of the oftmentioned *"Olam Habba"* or *"World to Come,"* a period of time after the resurrection of the righteous, and for the Risen ones. So Maimonides, Alphasi, Tract Sanhedrin 92, Pirke of Rabbi Eliezar, 34, and the Palestinian doctrine, all make the resurrection *from* the dead, Dan. xii:2, ' *at that time,*' to be at Messiah's Coming prior to the Messianic Days and World to come. The doctrine of the Jewish Teachers is two resurrections at different times. So Rabbis, Saadias, Kimchi, Maimonides, Mannaseh ben Israel, Abarbanel, Nachmanides,

Chasdai, Albo, Abuhab, Chiyya, Eliezer, etc., etc." *
This is sufficiently clear.   In Rabbinic terms the Resurrection *out from* (*Min*) the dead, is called " *Techiyyath
Tsadikim*," "the Making alive of the Righteous," or
"*Techiyyath Hammethim*," the "*Making alive of the dead*,"
and differs from the "*Amdath Hammethim*" or mere
" *Standing up of the Dead*," which has no reference
whatever to "life" that is eternal.   The former expression, derived from the verb to "*live*," to "*make alive*,"
denotes a resurrection in which the sharers of it participate in the new life of the reunited body and soul, and
the continuous existence of the risen herein, to die no
more.   The latter expression, derived from the verb to
"*stand*," denotes simply, and in general, a resurrection
of the dead, without regard to eternal life, or specially
a resurrection to Judgment and the Second Death.
For him who *only* "stands" before God, there is no
"*making alive*," no rising to a new and eternal life.   The
body may live again, but not the soul.   It is dead.   The
"*Making alive from the dead*" is the " First Resurrection."   The *Standing up of* the dead is either specially
the "Second Resurrection," or a general expression indifferent in itself to the destiny of the two classes who
arise.   All goes to show how the Hebrew scholars,
studying their own prophets, regarded the Resurrections as *two*, and occurring at different times, the first
at Messiah's Coming, the second at the End of the
Messianic Days; in short, *two* Resurrections, and *two*
Judgments, with the 1000 years, the "Many Days" of
Isaiah and Ezekiel, and the "Third Day" of Hosea,
lying in between.   In the words of Hamburger, again,
"Among the Hebrew Doctors the propositions which

---

* Hamburger.   Real. Encyc. fur Bibel u. Talmud.   Theil I.   1052,
etc., etc.

assert the resurrection of *all* mankind, employ the expression '*stand*,' and refer to the last resurrection at the final Judgment of the World, while those which assert that the *righteous alone* share the resurrection, employ the different expression '*Make alive*.'" * This is important and reconciles the whole dispute among the Rabbis, as to *Who* rise in the resurrection. Those who do not rise in the " First Resurrection," Dan. xii:2, are called by the Rabbis, as by the earliest Hebrew teachers of the Synagogue, "*Shear Hammethim*," the "*Rest of the Dead*," which is, beyond all controversy, the source of John's expression "The *Rest of the Dead* lived not until the 1000 years were finished," Rev. xx:5, i. e., came not to *bodily* life ; a resurrection which he further qualifies by saying that he saw the dead "*stand*" before God and come into judgment ; a resurrection to the "Second Death." Rev. xx:12, 14. And this at the *close* of the 1000 years.

We know, thereiore, what the Rabbis mean when they say,—employing the word " *Techiyyath*,"—that " the Resurrection," i. e. the " *making alive*," " belongs alone to Israel," i. e. to the faithful dead, raised at Messiah's coming ; a resurrection extended to all proselytes who trust in Israel's Redeemer. And this was not, as Oehler inadvertently remarks, only " individual opinion,"† but was, and is, as Weber shows, in his System of the Old Palestinian theology, " *not an individual opinion, but general doctrine*."‡ And Professor Cástelli confirms the same, giving, as the result of his own study of the question, these words, " *The Gentiles*

---

* Ibid. 1055. Note.
† Oehler, Art. Messias in Herzog R. Encyc. IX 439.
‡ Weber, Syst. alt synag. palæst. Theol. 372.

are not, in general, excluded from this blessedness."*
Nothing is better established than that the Rabbis and
John alike, even as the Old Testament Prophets, and
Christ, and all His Apostles, make the resurrection *out
from* the dead a *terminus a quo* for the 1000 years.

Precisely as Paul gets his Greek preposition "*ek,*"
"*out from,*" from the Hebrew "*min,*" "*out from,*" in
Dan. xii:2, and from the Jewish belief of his time, so
John gets his "*loipoi ton nekron,*" "*the Rest of the Dead,*"
from the "*Shear Hammethim*" of the Synagogue,
founded on Dan. xii:2, and Isa. xxvi:14, 19, compared
with Isa. xxiv:22. The Millennial Age *follows* the
Second Advent and the Resurrection of the faithful
dead.

(*e*) *Dated from Israel's Repentance.* The 1000 years
cannot begin till Israel is ready to say "*Hosanna,*" and
hail their own Messiah. The doctrine of the Rabbis,
here, is that of all the prophets, of Christ Himself, of
Peter in Acts iii:19–21, of Paul in Rom. xi:26, and is one
of the two great burdens of John's Apocalypse. The
proverb of the Rabbis is universal, "*When Israel repents
Messiah comes !*" In Hosea, the beautiful picture of
the Days of Messiah and Israel's blessedness in the
kingdom, Hos. xiv:5–9 *follows* Israel's repentance, Hos.
xiv:1–4, and is accompanied by Israel's resurrection,
Hos. vi:2 ; xiii:14, which occurs at Messiah's Coming.
So, in Zechariah, the day of Israel's penitential sorrow
under the outpoured Spirit of Grace, Zech. xii:10–14,
precedes, most closely, the Coming of Messiah to the
Mount of Olives with His Holy Angels, Zech. xiv:4,
and the Days of Messiah's glorious kingdom on earth,
Zech. xiv:9. It is the common docrine of the prophets,

---

* Castelli, Il Messia, etc., Append. 297–355.

and the Rabbis well know it. The Targum of Jonathan ben Uzziel, on Micah iv:8, written before the destruction of Jerusalem, and based upon traditional interpretation, assigns Israel's sins toward Messiah as the reason of His absence and concealment from them, and the hindrance to the coming of the kingdom. " And Thou, Messiah of Israel, who art hidden on account of the sins of the congregation of Zion, to Thee the kingdom shall come." " The coming of Messiah," said David Kimchi, awaits Israel's " *Teshuvah*, Repentance. Messiah will not come while Israel is impenitent." Rabbi Levi said, in commenting on Solomon's Song, " If Israel shall *truly repent*, but for one day, then shall they be redeemed, and the Son of David shall suddenly come." So Rabbi Bechai in his commentary on the Five Books of Moses: " The future redemption of Israel is conditioned on Israel's *Teshuvah*. For so did our forefathers, in their deliverance from Egypt, repent and pray to God who heard their prayer in their time of trouble and then the deliverer, Moses, came." Impressive are the words of the Tract Sanhedrin folio 97, column 2: " All our calculations as to when Messiah shall come have failed, and the whole matter of His coming depends on nothing else than our *Teshuvah* and works meet for this." And the words of Rabbi Jehoshua, so full of truth, are not less striking, " Where there is no Repentance there is no Redemption. The Holy Blessed God will yet subject Israel to a prince whose decrees will be cruel like the counsel of Haman. *Then* Israel will repent, Messiah will come to them, and they will be godly."*

How firmly this doctrine was believed the opening

---

* Eisenmenger, Entdekt, Jud. II. 672, 673.

of the 16th century testifies.   How sincerely, blindly
and disastrously it was acted upon, not dreaming that
a *true* Repentance involved the believing recognition
of Jesus of Nazareth as the already Heaven-Sent Messiah, history has chronicled.   Messiah, once already
come, despised, rejected and crucified by His own
nation, will not appear to them so long as He is regarded as a Pretender to the throne, a Blasphemer and
Impostor.   In A. D. 1500, in the very throes of the Reformation, Rabbi Asher Lemle, a German Jew, sought
in Europe to call Israel to Repentance, proclaiming
that when Israel repents Messiah comes and restores
the Kingdom, proving, as well he might, his doctrine
from the Scriptures.   "He was," says Eisenmenger, "a
John the Baptist in the wilderness, but without the
Baptist's witness to the Son of Mary."   His mission
awoke the Jews of Austria and of Italy, then groaning
under Church-Persecution.   Like the Ninevites of old,
they fasted, they wept, they prayed.   Vain worship!
Messiah did *not* come !   Lemle died in despair, and A.
D. 1500 is known in Jewish history as the *"Vain Repentance Year."*   Disastrous was the moral effect.   Doubly
disastrous to the truth, for it sought to build *Chiliasm*
on the denial of the Messiahship of Jesus !   Israel's
pretended Repentance was nothing but a public act of
unbelief and repetition of their forefathers' crime !   The
"Blindness in part" had not been removed.   The teaching of the prophets, the doctrine of the Talmud, the
best tradition of the Jews, all was remanded to the lum-
ber-room of dead superstition, and the Hope of the
Coming of Messiah exchanged for sullen submission to
a hard and relentless fate for which no cure could be
found.   The apostasy deepened.   And yet, in spite of
all such vain and blind experiments, scarce better than

the work of Theudas, Judas, or Bar-Cochba, the doctrine still remains, and is insisted on among the orthodox, to this day. The one great postulate, the one thine needful for Messiah's Coming, is Israel's *"Teshuvah."* Not till then do the 1000 years begin. Impossible that the Millennial Age should lie this side the pre-condition of its possibility! And here, again, the Rabbis and Peter are at one, while they differ as to *"Jesus"* whom heaven has received till Israel repents, believing on His name. Acts iii:19–21.

(*f*) *Dated from the Advent of Messiah in the Clouds of Heaven, not to die, but live eternally.* Perplexing was the problem here, some saying Messiah must *die*, inventing two Messiahs; others holding that Messiah shall never die, but *live eternally.* But, in any case, the Kingdom comes only with the King from Heaven. Says Rabbi Bechai, "The Son of David, the Messiah, *shall never die, but live eternally, when He comes.* The 6000th year from the creation shall have passed away. Then the 7000th shall go on, a genuine Sabbath and Eternal Life. Of Messiah, King David (Peace be to Him!) has said, 'He asked *Life of Thee,* and Thou gavest to Him length of days, forever and ever!'" Ps. xxi:5. Perplexing! Insoluble! the problem of Messiah's coming *"to die,"* and coming *"not to die,"*—*one* Advent alone admitted! The solution of the perplexity we know. Messiah comes at His First Advent, *"to die,"*— but also to *rise again* and *live forever.* He comes at His Second Advent *"not to die,"*—but to *live and reign eternally.* The one point clear, amid all the confusion, is that the Advent of Messiah to set up His Kingdom of glory on earth and live and reign eternally, *His Advent in the Clouds, is the pre-condition of the* 1000 *years.*

And it is the faith of orthodox Israel, to-day, waiting
for Messiah's Coming, though still blind to Messiah
already come.   It is one of the *"Roots of Faith," "Sharshei Emunah,"* taught in all their schools, " We believe
in the Coming of Messiah," *"Biyath Mashiah,"* the Redeemer, at the time appointed, known to God alone,
and who will gather the dispersed of Israel, and restore
the government to the House of David.   We believe
in the Resurrection from the dead, *"Techiyyath Hammethim."*   We live in hope and expectation of the Coming of Messiah and our Return to our fatherland, the
land of Judah.   As long as our Goel is not come, we
are bound to *seek the peace,* and *obey the government of
the nation under which we live,* as directed by the prophet,
Jer. xxix:7, and *"abide,"* waiting for David our King.
Hos. iii:5, 6.*   " We believe that the real reward and
punishment will be distributed only at the period of the
Life Eternal in the World to come, *Olam Habba,* the
World of the Messiah.   For the wicked there is no
rest, no part in the World to Come.   Dead, they shall
not rise.   Their memory is consigned to darkness.
Isa. xxvi:14."†   How touching the Confession !   What
blindness !   What light !   The eyes see out of obscurity! " Blindness in part!"   But one thing shines
with noon-day effulgence : *No Millennial time for Israel,
no* 1000 *years of blessedness and glory, before the Second
Advent and the Resurrection from the dead.*

Such the doctrine of the Rabbis, such the faith of
the Synagogue, as to the *Terminus a quo,* or starting-
point of the 1000 years, or Days of Messiah in triumph

---

* It was this religious sentiment that made the Jews loyal to the National government during the "Great Rebellion" of the Southern States 1861-
1865.
　† Sharshei Emunah (Elements of Faith).   London.   A. M. 5575.   S.
I. Cohen, pp. 6, 10, 11, 37, 51, 53.

and glory on earth. The Millennial Age dates from (a) the Close of Daniel's 70th Week, (b) the Overthrow of the 4th prophetic empire, (c) the Destruction of Antichrist, (d) the Resurrection of the faithful dead, (e) Israel's Repentance, (f) the Coming of Messiah in victory and glory. These are the pre-conditions of it, and the prophets, the Rabbis, Christ and his Apostles, are one in reference to this one great fact, viz., *there is no Millennium until Christ comes in the clouds of Heaven.*

C. The *Terminus ad Quem*

But the doctrine of the Rabbis fixes also a *terminus ad quem*, or closing point, to the 1000 years. Here again, however, perplexity arises as to " Gog and Magog," even as among ourselves. From the reading of Ezekiel, chapters xxxviii and xxxix, it would *seem* that Gog is *pre*-millennial, and only *after* Gog's destruction, does God pour His Spirit on the House of Israel, bring again Jacob's captivity, and hide His face no more from them. Ezek. xxxix:29. On the other hand, from the reading of chapter xxxvii, and chapter xxxviii:8-12, 14, it is clearer still that Gog's invasion and destruction are " *many days after* " Israel has been re-born by the Spirit, gathered out from the nations, politically restored and established as a converted people, and dwelling safely in their land, unprotected by the means of warfare and defence, and trusting in God alone. Naturally enough, two views exist among the Rabbis, as among the Christians, in reference to the relation of Gog and Magog to the 1000 years, or Messianic Days of earthly glory. Weber gives them both.

(1). The war-march of Gog and Magog is *before* the beginning of the Days of Messiah on earth. The "*Many Days* " xxxviii:8, " *after* " which Gog invades, and is judged, are regarded by a few as the days intervening between the prophet Ezekiel and the Advent of Messiah. The " End of the Days " is interpreted to mean the End of this present Age, *Olam Hazzeh*, Israel having been regathered to their land, and having dwelt safely there a "long time." So the Jerusalem Targum says. " At the End of the days Gog and Magog shall march against Jerusalem, but perish by the hand of Messiah. They shall gather the Kings and Princes of the earth, and muster all nations for slaughter in the land of Israel, and in war against the Exiles returned to their home, but already, long time, the judgment has been prepared for them, and they shall be consumed by flame from the Throne of Divine Glory, and their dead bodies be given as a banquet to the birds of prey. Then the dead of Israel shall arise and receive the Reward of Works. All the nations are annihilated."* This conception of the relation of Gog and Magog to the 1000 years is a mixture of error and truth. That the Northern powers from beyond the Caucasus, aided by the extra-Palestinian nations hostile to Israel's re-possession of their land, will dispute that possession, *before* the 1000 years, or at the time of Israel's Home-Coming, is most likely, and apparently predicted. But that the nations will be annihilated and Israel alone survive, no people remaining for the Messianic sway, is in face of the whole Palestinian theology, and of the prophecy itself. Hence,

(2). The view that Gog's march and destruction *occur at the End of the Messianic Days of Israel's glory in the Kingdom restored to Israel,* that is, *at the End of the 1000 years*, the " Many Days " of xxxviii:8. And such

---

*Weber Syst. alt. pal. Theol. 370, 371.

is the force of the combined prophetic representation in Israel, Daniel, and Ezekiel. Such the special force of the strangely sudden, isolated, interposed, and entirely independent prediction of the post-millennial visitation of Gog. *"After Many Days thou shalt be visited."* Ezek. xxxviii:8. And this is the *terminus ad quem* of the 1000 years, the judgment on Gog which expands itself into the Last Judgment, when the Messianic kingdom is surrendered to " God," who appears on the scene for the final assize.

It is true that among the Rabbis there is much confusion, even as among Christians, confounding Gog with *the Antichrist*, and the End of the *present* Age with the End of the " *Many Days,*" or 1000 *years*, and ascribing to Messianic activity what the prophecy ascribes directly to the activity of God Himself. Hence the words of the Jerusalem Targum on Numb. xi:27, "In the End of the Days, Gog, Magog, and their armies, shall march against Jerusalem, and fall by the hand of Messiah Himself, and seven years of days shall the children of Israel make fuel of their weapons." Still it remains a fact that the Rabbis distinguished between Antichrist's destruction at the *Beginning* of the 1000 years, and Gog's destruction at the *End* of the same. " In *Wayyikra Rabba*, c. xxx," says Weber, " the time of Messiah and of Gog and Magog, are *so discriminated* that the latter *follows* the former, and *not the contrary*. The march, and judgment on Gog, are at the *End of the Messianic Age*. In *Tanchuma, Sophetim,* 19, it is clearly stated that the Nations of the earth shall first serve, as tributary States, the King Messiah. Then, *at last*, an *Evil Spirit* shall possess and impel them (Ezek. xxxviii:10) (Satan let loose), and they shall rebel against Messiah, and be destroyed by him. This is the last decisive conflict between Israel and the World of Nations."* The mixture here, of accuracy and inaccuracy is evident, and yet the doctrine remains that Gog's destruction is at the close of the Messianic Days or 1000 years, whose commencing date is the Advent of Messiah for Israel's final deliverance and redemption. Such the *terminus ad quem* of the Millennial Age. The Apocalypse of John has shed upon the whole subject, as Professor Volck remarks, "a clea and indubitable light."† Fixing his eyes upon the relation of Israel restored, to the strangely isolated prediction concerning Gog, in Ezek. xxxviii:8, John has cleared up the whole perplexity and asserted a *post-millennial* judgment on Gog as the transition step from the Messianic earthly kingdom of glory into the Eternal State. From first to last, all is literal.

---

* Weber.   Syst. alt. pal. Theol. 370.
† Volck.   Der Chiliasmus. 74.

Part 9

THE APOCALYPSE OF JOHN

It must be clear now, from the testimony borne by the Hebrew Doctors to the Designation of the 1000 years as the Messianic Days following the Advent of Messiah in His glory, that these years were not regarded as mere symbolism void of all chronological value, but were esteemed as a real measure of definite time. Gentile prejudice, construing Israel as the "Church" and negating the facts foretold concerning Israel, may indeed condemn, as "Jewish," the judgment of the Synagogue, among whose first lights were a Haggai, Zechariah, Joshua, Zerubbabel, Ezra, Nehemiah and Malachi, and repudiate, as "Judaizing," the literal exposition of both Old and New Testament prophecy in reference to the coming Kingdom and Israel's place therein. It is with some the customary criticism. The fact remains, however, that the best Biblical interpreters, of our time, do not share the prejudice that blinds to truth because a "Jewish" mouth has spoken it. As Gentiles are not always true, Jews are not always false, and a study of the manner of their labor on the Word of God, and their reverence for it, might, notwithstanding "Jewish fables," "Rabbinical conceits,"

379

and even their unbelief in Jesus, instruct some Gentiles
in an attitude toward that word with which they are
not now apparently familiar. "Blindness in part" has
happened to some of *us* in reference to the Second
Coming of Messiah, even as "Blindness in part" has
happened to many of *them* in reference to the First
Coming. And yet the day may not be distant when
*literal Israel will be for us a light as brilliant on the
Eleventh chapter of John's Apocalypse, as they are now
upon the Eleventh chapter of Paul's letter to the Romans !*
Even now, "Biblical Theology," "Old Testament Theology," "New Testament Theology," "Prophetic Theology," all cut loose from mediæval trammels, have vindicated for "*Israel*" a hundred texts in eschatology,
which the Church rejected a half century ago. It may
be but "a little while" and Jew and Gentile shall see
eye to eye, the Watchmen singing together when the
Lord "brings again Zion."

A. THE JEWISH BOOK

From what has been cited it must be plain to every
one, just what is the relation of that "*Jewish Book,*" the
Apocalypse of John, written A. D. 96, to the post-Bib.
lical and pre-Christian Apocalypses of the "Jews," and
what the relation of the "Jewish 1000 years" in John to
those Apocalypses and to the "Jewish" prophets on
which they were founded, as also the "Jewish-Christian
Church" of which John was no unimportant part. The
discovered "*Judaism*" of the book, and what it has in
common with the "Jewish " faith *before* the time of
Christ, and with Jewish writings *after* Christ, may lead
us to do what the Laodicean Council did in ancient
times;—extrude the Apocalypse altogether from the
Canon. Recent efforts in this direction are not want-

ing. The offense of the book is said to be that it is *"saturated with ideas born upon the soil of Palestine anterior to the publication of the gospel,"* * as though this were not the case also with Isaiah, Ezekiel, Daniel, Zechariah, almost every prophetic book of the Old Testament, and even the words of the Baptist!

In face of the *Title* of the Apocalypse which declares that its author is *"God,"* that He gave it by an *"Angel"* to John, and that John, as "His Servant," bore record of this *"Testimony of Jesus Christ,"* Rev. i:1, 2 ; and in face of the Curse on *"any man"* who shall "add to," or "take from," its content, alter, amend, or redact in any way, Rev. xxii:18, 19, certain critics, "blinking," as Lord Bacon would say, "in the noon-day, but clear-sighted in the night of their own notions," have discovered that it is either a patch-work by several, or at least, two, different uninspired authors, jointed and redacted, now by a Jew, and then by a Christian, either in different parts of the first, or of the first and second centuries, a non-Christian Jewish original vamped to a Judaizing-Christian copy, the whole fit only to be ranked with books like Henoch, Baruch, Esdras and the Sibylline Oracles. To such base uses have Völter, Vischer, Schürer, Dillman, like others before them, come! The conclusion that "the 1000 years" are a mere conceit because derived from a "Jewish, non-Christian source," and have been retained by a "Judaizing Christian redactor" of the carnal sort, is as discreditable to the reputation of the critics, as the methods by which they reached it, are offensive even to the Higher criticism itself. †

---

* "Il est tout saturé d'idees nees sur le sol de la Palestine anterieurement a la predication de l'Evangile." *Reuss. L'Apocalypse. Introd. p. 32.*

† One of the best things Prof. Briggs has done of late, is to repel this last assault upon the Apocalypse in a masterly way. His words will be

Not less strong is the case against the Idealists, whose favorite maxim is that " Symbolical numbers don't count," and that " the 1000 years " mean only "ecumenical potentiality," " potentiated ecumenicity," and " spatial victory ! " By such device, dissolving the 1000 years *out of time*, in order to make the Apocalypse canonical, the genius of the Greek Fathers is rivaled, who adopted the "*system of allegories in order to escape Chiliasm*," and so retain, as apostolic, a book which otherwise must be rejected, but which resulted in the expulsion of the book altogether !* Let the Idealism charm as it may, the historic evidence is com-

---

welcomed by all. "*It is a prematuie birth.* Nothing justifies the theory. The dependence of the Apocalypse upon the Gospels of Matthew and Luke, is clear. The eschatological discourse of Jesus is to our mind the Key to the Apocalypse. The Apocalypse of John and the discourse of Jesus agree in their pure and genuine development of *Old Testament Prophecy*, and contain none of those conceits and extravagances that is characteristic of the extra-canonical Apocalypses. We freely admit all that is common between the Jewish Apocalypses and the Apocalypse of John. There is so much of genuine prophecy in them, we are not surprised that the early Christians esteemed many of them as inspired;—apocalypses that followed the lines drawn by the Old Testament prophets—and thus reached many of the same conclusions that we find in the inspired prophecy of the New Testament. Grant all that can fairly be demanded in this regard, yet we find a simplicity, a power, a grandeur, in the Apocalypse of John, which exalts it above all the extra-canonical pseudepigraphs and *ranges it with the Old Testament Prophets, the discourses of Jesus, and the Epistles of Peter and Paul. It is the wouk of a Jew saturated with Old Testament Prophecy, under the guidance of the word of Jesus and the inspiration of God. It is the climax of the prophecy of the Old and New Testaments.*" Speaking of the *Title*, Rev. i:1, and the *Cuise*, xxii:18, 19, and the theory of two authors, one a Jew, the other a Christian, one writing A. D. 66, the other A. D. 95, he says impressively: "If these belonged to the *Jewish* original the *Chistian* editor would hardly have *retained* this curse upon *himself* for everything *he* had done ! If they belonged to the *Christian* author, what sort of a conscience must he have had *to pronounce a curse upon any one else* who should do with *his* work precisely what *he himself* had done with the work of another ? " This is a Damascus blade, and every lover of God's word will feel grateful to Dr. Briggs for this problem handed over to the Higher Critics to digest. *Presbyterian Review. Jan. 1888, pp.* 109-115.

* "Les Peres grecs à se jeter dans le systémedes allegories pour échapper au Chiliasme, et qui out fini par leur faire éliminer tout-à-fait l' Apocalypse du Canon de leurs E'glises." Reuss. Ibid. 36.

plete that no such view beguiled the mind of John, when the Patmos Visions passed before him. The 1000 years were but one of several time-designations, already current in the speech of *Jews and Gentiles*, both, not as symbols only, but as terms of literal time. They were the " *Yemot Meshicah*," the " *Days of Messiah*," in which "the righteous flourish," the one designation chosen, above all others, to represent that period. " They mean," says Keim, " the Golden Days of the terrestrial kingdom of Messiah between two Resurrections and two Judgments ; an introductory and transient kind of stage, in the sovereign reign and rule of God ; *a view which with noteworthy Christian alterations was followed even in the Apocalypse of John, and by St. Paul;* a period in any case to continue until the final New Heaven and Earth."* Professor Drummond's statement is loose and insufficient, when he says that " this particular view was adopted by the writer of the Revelation, and, which, no doubt, under his influence, became the prevailing opinion among those Christians who looked forward to a temporal reign of Christ."† For, first of all, it was not a "*particular*" view in. any sense, but the common faith of the flower of the whole pre-Christian Jewish and Jewish-Christian, as well as Gentile-Christian, Churches. Therefore, it was not " *adopted*" by John as a special theory, nor was the Christian Church indebted to John's " *influence*" for its prevalence, nor was it a mere " *opinion*," but a chief article of faith. Nor, once more, were " *those Christians*" who held it any others than whom Justin calls " right-minded," or " orthodox," people ; in short, the

---

* Keim. Jesu von Nazara. IV. 295–297.
† Jewish Messiah, 318.

apostolic and sub-apostolic Church, for 300 years. Nor did they believe that the reign of Christ was merely "*a temporal reign*," but like the great Hillel, ancestor of the great Gamaliel, Paul's teacher, held that Messiah's kingdom is "*not only for a time, but forever*." Far better are the words of Ewald, who says, " The hope of the 1000 years' kingdom *did not originate* with John. Plainly enough, it appears as an *already given, steadfast, and of itself a well-grounded, matter of expectation, familiar and needing only to be named, something peculiar and of the highest importance, and woven as closely as possible into the whole web of the Christian life.*"* That statement is just to the facts of history and the circumstances of the times. And, with this, Gebhardt agrees, saying, " The 1000 years with John, were *the grand interval between this present age, and the final one,* an interval in which Christ would reign in an earthly kingdom, *at least within the sphere of the Roman empire, and upon its ruins, the reformed earthly Jerusalem being its central point where the kingdom of the glorified would begin in a narrower compass, and as the prelude of the universal and eternal glory.*"† "The Seer," says Bleek, "*found this term, the* 1000 *years, already extant, and assumed that his readers were not unacquainted with it. He retained an expression already in common use.*"‡ And Dorner recognizes the facts of history, when he says, "*A point undoubtedly common to both Jewish and Christian apocalyptics, is the period of blessedness on earth, called the* 1000 *years.*" ‖

Not, therefore, from any such schematism as 10×10

* Ewald, Johan. Schriften, II. 324.
† Gebhardt, Doct. of Apoc. 284.
‡ Bleek, Einleit. N. T. 225.
‖ Dorner, Person of Christ, Div. I, vol. I. 409.

×10=1000 did the doctrine of the 1000 years spring in the Christian Church. Nor to such schematism was the pre-Christian Jewish faith indebted. Believing Jews and Gentiles found it in the Psalms and in the Prophets as they "searched *What* Time and what *Manner* of Time" Messiah's Kingdom should be, and to *that* period of time, when reaching it at the close of the 7-sealed scroll, or end of the 70th week, *he gave the name, already known, "the 1000 years."* No voice told him the number. Every Jew and Christian, every reader of both Testaments, knew full well that the 1000 years of Messianic glory in the Kingdom on earth, could not, and did not, lie in the Times of the Gentiles, or Times of the Beast, or Times of Israel's national rejection of Messiah, but *followed* the Beast's destruction, Antichrist's overthrow, Israel's conversion. It is one of the lights of the Apocalypse thrown back upon the Old Testament predictions. It *proves* that the period *following* the 70th week, when the six things named in Dan. ix:24, shall be realized to Israel and Jerusalem, and the Kingdom *following* the overthrow of the Colossus, Dan. ii:44, 45, and *following* the destruction of the Little Horn, Dan. vii:27, and the Blessed Time *following* the resurrection from the dead, Dan. xii:2, are *one and the same period*, "the 1000 years" of John ; and that this was the faith of the pre-Christian Jewish Church, and of the Christian Church itself, and was sealed, as true, by John, under the inspiration of the Holy Ghost. As De Wette observes, "*The faith of the Church was grounded in the Great Time-Reckoning of 7000 years for the World's course.*" What John did was, not to imitate the Babylonians, or the Persians, or build his Apocalypse upon the pre-Christian Jewish writings, or on any "fancies" of the Rabbis, or on the "Platonic

Cycle," but, guided by the Spirit, sketch our present Age, in the 7 Epistles to the Asiatic Churches, coming down to the proper End-Time in their Philadelphian and Laodicean states, then open out the *End-Time* itself in a series of gorgeous symbols, covering the whole time from John to the End, and unveiling the End itself with the utmost particularity.   That the Scarlet Woman, who rides the Beast, is not merely Rome Pagan, but Rome Ecclesiastical, and all her daughter hierarchies, and, last of all, apostate Christendom, "Babylon the Great," there is no doubt.   The symbols of " Beast" and "Woman" cover all, first by "application," last by "interpretation."   So also as to Israel. The Sun-Clothed Woman is the Jewish Church, first pre-Christian as the Mother of Christ, next Christian, then in her eschatological attire, the Mother of the "Manly Child," the Jewish-Christian " Nation" of the End-Time, born to rule the nations, the glory of God risen upon her, her light being come.   *The complex symbol embraces all, and looks to the End.*   What John does is to give an Apocalypse of Israel's future and glory in the Kingdom, and of the glory of the Nations *after* Messianic Judgment ; and, last of all, portray the final glory of Israel, the Church, the Nations in the New Heaven and Earth, following the Final Resurrection and Judgment at the end of the 1000 years. *What was true in the pre-Christian Jewish faith, he has preserved,* as matter of necessity, not because the Rabbis said it, but because the Prophets taught it, and our Lord foretold it, and the Spirit moved it.   *What was false, he rejected.*   In the words of Boehmer, "Whether in the 1000 years we find a reference to Ps. xc:4, or to the Jewish theology, or to the distribution of the world's course into 7 periods of a 1000 years each, as in the Book Enoch, is a matter of indifference.   In the latter case our Book would only prove *how well it appropriated the popular faith without adhering to its errors. It winnowed the chaff from the wheat.*   And, for this reason, we are compelled to regard the *two* Resurrections, between which lie the 1000 years, and the *two* phases of the Kingdom of God begun by them, as a doctrine which, like almost all others, finds its more definite expression now in the last time.   The eschatology of the Evangelist and Seer is one."*   So Wünsche, with the admirable word appended, *"The Apocalypse of John settled what the Jews disputed, as to the Duration of the Messianic earthly Kingdom."* †

Such is the *"Jewish"* origin of our Christian faith, the faith of the early Jewish-Christian Church, the faith of the pre-Christian Rabbis, the faith of God's people under the Old Covenant, the faith of the Prophets, a *Chiliastic* faith in a *Chiliastic* Kingdom of glory on earth, the Vestibule and Prelude to Eternal Blessedness.   It is from Jerome, chiefly, we get the sounding reproach that, to believe in a Pre-Millennial Coming of the Lord Jesus to restore Israel, raise His sleeping saints and establish on earth His Kingdom as predicted by the prophets, is to *"Judaize."*   And it goes sounding through Protestantism to-day, as it has gone sounding, since Jerome's time, through the mediæval Church, and is sounding in the modern Church, still.

No better answer has been made, none more deserved, to this assault upon the martyr-faith than is given in the earnest words of that eloquent and learned man, Dr. S. R. Maitland, published thirty years ago.

* Boehmer.   Offenb. Johann.   277.
† Wünsche.   Neue Beiträge.   204.

Speaking of this accusation of "*Judaizing*," he says,
"St. Jerome tells us repeatedly, and with mistaken
triumph, that to hold the Millennial doctrine was to
'*Judaize*.' This is certainly true, and one is glad to
have St. Jerome's testimony to the fact. It is important. Papias, Irenæus, Justin, Tertullian and others,
were only *maintaining that interpretation of the prophecies
which had been, as far as I can find, always held in the
Church of God before the incarnation of Christ*, and they
did this at a period when, I believe, nobody maintained,
or even had heard of any adverse opinion, or any other
interpretation of those passages of Scripture on which
they grounded their opinion. To be sure, this was
'*Judaizing*,' and so it was to adopt exclusively ' the
Jewish doctrine of a Messiah,' and the sacred books of
the ' Jewish Church.' *I am not frightened at words, and
do not see that I am to renounce a doctrine because it has
been held by the Jews !* And I must again say that I am
glad of such unexceptional testimony as Jerome's to
the fact that this was the judgment of the '*Jewish
Church*,' and that to hold the Millennarian doctrine was
to '*Judaize !*' It would not be difficult to show that
this ancient doctrine of the Church was maintained,
and unimpugned, *until the Christian Church began to*
HEATHENIZE."* Well said, and—a splendid ten-strike,
righteous as it is brilliant! true! And the conclusion
that the Apocalypse, in its doctrine of *two* Resurrections, and *two* Judgments, separated by "the 1000
years," *cannot be understood apart from a recognition
of the pre-Christian Jewish faith which holds the same
doctrine*, is, to-day the verdict of all scholars, not

---

*Eruvin, by Rev. S. R. Maitland, D. D. F. R. S. F. S. A. 173.

swayed by a false spiritualizing interpretation which negates and destroys the prophetic word itself. *

B. RELATIONSHIP OF THE 1,000 YEARS TO THE APOCALYPSE AND CHIEFLY TO ITS SECOND PART

To understand the relation of the 1000 years to the whole and chiefly to the Second Part of the Apocalypse is indispensable to a clear conception of the folly that would date these years from any point this side the End of the 70th Week, and the Second Coming of Christ. And here, we must take our time, and move cautiously. The *General Division* of the Apocalypse into *two* chief parts, analagous to the division of the Book of Isaiah, and the Book of Daniel, is already well understood, viz.: Chapters I—XI, and chapters XII—XXII. The relation of chapters I—III to the *Interval* between Jerusalem's destruction, A. D. 70, and the 70th Week in Daniel, Dan. ix:26, 27, viz.: that they cover this Interval, disclosed on its Christian side as the *Church-Period of development*, is also understood. This brings us at once to the *End-Time*, or 70th Week. Just as the 7 Trumpets preside over the 7 vials which issue from the 7th trumpet, and just as the 7 Seals preside over the 7 trumpets which issue from the 7th

---

*See Bertholdt. Christol. Judæorum, 35, 39, 176, 203. Eisenmenger, Eutdekt, Judenthum II, 901, 902. L:ghtfoot. Works XI. 296. Hamburger. R. Encyc. I. 1052. Weber. altsyag. pal. Theol. 354. Wünsche, Neue Beitrage, 204, 3ˑ1—3ˑ6. Meyer. Komm, Luke xiv:14 15. Joh. v:29. Acts xxiv:15. Olshausen, Matt. xxii:29, 30; xxiv:31. John v:24-29. Luke xiv:12-14. I Cor. xv:23 Acts xxiv:15. Stier, Reden J , Matt. xxii:19 Joh. v:26. Luke xiv:12-14. Matt. xxii:30. Rothe, Dogmatik II 73. foot. Tholuck. Joh. v:29. Heb. vi:2. Rom. viii:18-22. Van Oorsterzee, N. T. Theol. 53. Immer, Hermen. 294. John Owen; Epistle to Hebrews I. 541, Carter. Mede, Works 572, 776, 892, 893. Bleek, Lect, Apoc, 78, 79, 336. Stuart Apoc. I. 177. Elliott, Horæ Apoc. IV. 147, 150, 16ˑ, 183, 185. Note. Besides scores of others, as Delitzsch, Schmid, Volck, Grau, Godet, Luthardt, etc., etc.

seal, so the 7 Epistles to the Churches preside over the
7 Seals which issue from the 7th Epistle, Christ presid-
ing over all. Rev. i:12-16.

This is the organic connection. All the Epistles have
an eschatological reference. The Laodicean condition
of the Church, boasting of its wealth, culture and greatness, while yet Christ is exiled to the outside, and standing in its influence over against the Philadelphian
Church oppressed, yet faithful, small, yet looking for the
Coming of the Lord, *and to whom the promise of Israel's
conversion is made, and preservation in the Great Tribulation*, is the full picture of the state of things in Christendom *at the close of the* INTERVAL, Rev. iii:7-21. We come,
therefore, to the 70th Week, the End-Time following the
Interval, and, naturally enough, just what we should expect, we find, viz., that *John's Apocalypse is the resumption and development of what Daniel and the Prophets
have all spoken concerning this 70th week and its connection with Israel's Restoration at the Coming of the Lord.*
It is impossible to break this organic unity of Old and
New Testament prophecy. Therefore chapters iv and
v are General Introduction to the Opening of the Seals
and the solemn events of the End-Time. And, now,
we come to chapters vi–xi:14, which cover the first 3½,
or 1260 days, of the 70th Week, and include the 6 Seals
and the 6 Trumpets. In vi we have the 6 Seals, and
clear announcement in the 6th that "YOM YEHOVAH"
or "DAY OF THE LORD" has come.* The time is fear-

---

* " The *6th Seal* is the crucial point in Apocalyptic exegesis."—*Alford*.
"The *6th Seal* determines for us the whole question as to the entering of
the Day of -the Lord."—*Elliott*. " The 4 Seals are a common ground, the
5th rises out of them and is the special crisis, the 6th is the culmination, the
7th is the consummation."—*Lange*. "The first four Seals are the pre-signs
of the Advent as pictured by our Lord in His Prophecy on the Mount of
Olives, Matt. xxiv:6, etc., the 5th follows in strict connection with Matt.
xxiv:9; the 6th represents especially the Signs which mark the immediate

ful indeed! *"Who sha be able to stand ?"*   Mal. iii:2 ;
Rev. vi:17.   In answer to this question and for comfort to all believers whose hope is fixed on the victory
of God's Kingdom, we get the *Double Episode* in chapter vii, between the 6th and 7th Seals, viz., (1) the 144,-
000 sealed out of Israel, and (2) the Countless Company,
who, as martyrs of Jesus, have entered into the peace
of God ; the one a transaction on earth, the other a
scene in heaven.   What it teaches us is that, in that
awful day of tribulation to come upon the earth, blessed
are (1) the sealed out of Israel and all other servants of
God who shall survive to see the Advent, and blessed
are (2) the martyrs of Jesus, whether Jews or Gentiles,
who fall in that hour !   Their appearance in heaven is
the pledge of their rising again.   In that day some will
find a shelter under the Eagle-Wings of God, others
will pass through blood to glory.   Like their fellow-
martyrs, in all ages, they have been cruelly " judged
according to men in the flesh, but live according to
God, in the spirit." I Pet. iv:6.   Partakers of Christ's
sufferings, they are expectants of His glory, waiting
for the "First Resurrection." Rev. xx:4.   It is on their

---

entrance of the Day of Judgment."—*Düsterdieck.*   " The 4 Seals are the
ground of the 5th; the 5th *precipitates* the 6th which is the *crisis;* the 7th is
the nexus (*Knoten-ort*) of the preceding with the following series."—*Ewald.*
"The 4 Seals bring the ' Beginning of Sorrows,' the 5th brings the 'Great
Tribulation,' the 6th brings the sidereal and telluric signs of Judgment, or
beginning of the proper 'End.' "—*Klicfoth.*   " In these 6 visions of the
Seals we have just the same phenomena presented as in Matt. xxiv:6–9 "—
Gebhardt.   "The 6th Seal brings the telluric and sidereal commotions which
announce the last revolution and shaking of heaven, earth, sea, dry land and
the nations.   Heb. xii:26; Hagg. ii:6; Isa. xxxiv:4; Matt. xxiv:29.   It
points backward and forward; backward, being the answer to the martyr-cry
under the 5th Seal; forward driving affrighted men to cry *Who shall be able
to stand?*   It opens the Day of Judgment."—*Kübel.*   "As Rev. vi:4, 6–8,
'Sword, Famine, Pestilence,' answer to Matt, xxiv:6, 7; and Rev. vi:9, 19,
answers to Matt. xxiv:9,10, so Rev. vi:12–17, the *Sixth Seal,* answers to
Matt. xxiv:29,30, the *Portents* of the immediate presence of the Day of the
Lord : not the *Advent itself.* until the Judgments invoked by the martyrs,

graves the Holy Benediction falls, "Blessed are the dead who die in the Lord, from henceforth," Rev. xiv: 13. The Countless Company before the throne, are the souls of those whose altar moan, "How long, O Lord?" we hear in the 5th Seal.

And now, in chapters viii and ix we find ourselves under the 6 Trumpet-Judgments, let loose against apostatizing Christendom still impenitent notwithstanding the "Day of the Lord" has become a fact observable by all! This shows the power of sin! "Sudden destruction" seems to avail nothing! Signs in heaven and earth are mocked at by the wicked! As it was in the days of Noah, so now. Even under new judgments redoubling with intensity, judgments of "fire and blood," the world still perseveres to blaspheme! Such is the condition of the *"Christian State"* at the close of the first 3½ years, or 1260 days, of the 70th Week! Rev. ix:20, 21. *What is now left for God to do*, according to His plan for the development of His Kingdom on earth, when Europe, Asia, Africa and America are

---

descend on the earth, etc., etc. *After these* the Lord shall come. Matt. xxivth chapter forms a complete parallel to the 6 Seals, not only in events, but in order. The *Sixth Seal* brings us close to the Advent. Before the final blow is inflicted, the 'elect' must be gathered, chapter vii."—*Fausset.* "*All after the 6th Seal is but the expansion of that Seal, and development of the Day of the Lord.* The Trumpets and the Vials, and Characters described, from chapter vi–xix, only unfold the events that belong to the Day of the Lord."—*Volck.* " The 6th Seal gives the general view of the cosmic scenes of the Last Day."—*Luthardt.* "The Day of the Lord is here. The overthrow of Babylon. the Destruction of Antichrist, the Judgment of the Nations, all cosmic, civil, political and religious events, are involved here, only to be further unfolded under the Trumpets and the Vials."—*Hofmann.* "*Every allegorizing interpretation is excluded* from Lyra to Hengstenberg. The 6th Seal brings the literal 'End,' the 'Day of the Lord.' The *Parousia* is not described *here*, but is described further on. The view of Hofmann, Bengel, Düsterdieck, Ebrard, that this is the real '*End*' foretold in our Lord's prediction in Matthew xxiv:14, is the alone correct view. The *total End* is here, the *Dissolution* which, in the further development of the prophecy, parts itself into two great Acts, Rev. xix:11–21 and Rev. xx:11–15. *Between* these are the 1000 years."—*Christiani.*

in such condition—*what can He do* according to the sure word of prophecy ;—in this closing period of the Times of the Gentiles, this acme of apostatizing Christendom ;—*but call Israel into the field by His almighty grace, resume His covenant mercy to that people, let the apostasy ripen to its head, Satan do his best, then put in the sickle, tread the winepress, and reveal Himself from Heaven ?* It is all! *There is nothing else to be done ! The Crisis has come ! The middle of the 70th Week has been reached !*

And this is precisely what we have in the Second Part of the Apocalypse. At the close of the 6th Trumpet, and as if to prevent all misunderstanding, and to throw our minds back, once more, upon the page of Daniel, *Chapter XI hangs out the Programme, presents, in full view, the entire 70th week, in order to prepare the way for the scenes of the last 3½ years, or 1260 days of Antichrist's supreme power.* Nowhere is light more clear than just here, if only we had the eyes to see it. The darkest Chapter in all the Apocalypse, the place where more Apocalyptic systems have been wrecked than anywhere else, becomes the brightest, if only we dismiss our pre-conceptions of what it is, or ought to be, and, with finger on the text, follow its sun-clear, unclouded statements. *It interprets itself!* What we have is (1) *The first 3½ years* for the Two Witnesses, during which they exercise their reforming and prophetic activity, vs. 3, 7; (2) The *Middle of the Week* when the Antichrist, the Beast from the pit, Daniel's Nagid, ix:27, and Horn, vii:25, slays the witnesses v.7; (3). *The Second 3½ years,* or the Great Tribulation and down-treading of the holy city by the Beast and his armies, v. 2, also xiii:5 ; the period during which the sun clothed Woman, or Jewish-Christian

Church of the End-Time, formed under the preaching
of the Witnesses, is sheltered by the Eagle-Wings of
God, xii:6,14, and the "Dragon makes war with the
remnant of her seed," entering into the Antichrist himself, and giving him his "power, seat, and great
authority," xii:9, 17; xiii:1,2. (4) Then comes *the End
of the 70th Week*, in the sounding of the 7th Trumpet,
bringing the *Judgment on the raging Nations, the destruction of the Destroyer, the Resurrection of the dead,
the Reward of the righteous, and the revoking of
the Suspension of God's covenant relations with Israel,
symbolized in the opening of the Temple and the vision of
the "Ark of the Covenant,"* vs. 15–19. It is at the
middle-point of the week, that the scenes of the Resurrection and Ascension of the Witnesses in presence of
Israel who denied the Resurrection of Christ, because
unseen, are *openly displayed*, amid attending earthquake,
as both Ezekiel and Zechariah foretold should occur in
this Valley of Vision, at this time, and that one-tenth
part of the City falls, and 7,000 perish, and the rest, affrighted, "give glory to God," the sign of their conversion. *The entire Programme of the whole 70th Week is
here*, the whole Conflict between Christ and Antichrist,
presented in outline, first of all, in order to pass,
intelligently, to the last 3½ years, which embrace
the entire time coming after, from Chapter XII to XX.*

It is the merit of Kliefoth,—apart from his idealizing
interpretation,—that he has demonstrated the existence

---

* The period of 3½ years' downtreading of Jerusalem, xi:2, is *eschatological*, and different from the period of downtreading in Luke xxi:24, which
is *church-historical*. This, in Rev. xi:2, dates from the Slaughter of the
Witnesses, and is the *last half of the 70th Week*. That, in Luke xxi:24,
dates from the Destruction of Jerusalem by Titus A. D. 70, and is the *whole
Interval between the 69th and 70th Weeks*. Nothing can be more ridiculous
than to identify the 3½ here, with the Interval there, and *both*, with the
1000 *years*, as Professor Milligan and others, have done.

of the 70th Week here, and identified in the clearest manner, the "*Beast*," of John, with the "*Nagid*," or "prince that shall come," in Daniel ix:27, the "*Little Horn*," of Dan. vii:25, and by so many others, most clearly by Clöter, as the Mock-Messiah, the Rider in the first apocalyptic seal, at the opening of the Week. And it is the merit of Prof. Kübel, in the light, not only of older writers on Eschatology, but of more recent ones within the last decade, Burger, Ittamaier, Bisping and others, that he asserts, as incontrovertible, "the presence of the 70th Week, in two halves of 3½ years each, in which we see the downtreading of the holy city, and the Jewish-Christian Church as the proper Church of the End-Time; the end announced under the 7th Trumpet."* The whole tragedy of the day of the Lord is here, the Apostasy of Christendom, the Antichrist, the preaching of the Witnesses, their Death, Resurrection, and Ascension, the Conversion of Israel, the Anger of the Nations, the Revelation of the Wrath of God, the World-Judgment, the Resurrection from the Dead, the Reward of the righteous, and the Destruction of the Destroyer, all that is subsequent in the Apocalypse, down to Chapter XX, being but the exhibition of the *Dramatis Personæ*, the Beast, the Dragon, the Two Women, the 144,000, the Cithara-Players on the sea, Christ, and the development of these great events under the sounding of the 7th Trumpet, or pouring of the 7 Vials, during the last 3½ years, or 1260 days.

It is important to observe that this introductory scene of Chapter XI, while in part retrospective, is also proleptic. It *anticipates*. Just as between the 6th and

---

* Dr. Kübel, in Strack-Zöckler. Offenbar. 364. (1888).

7th Seals we had the Double Episode of Chapter VII, so here, between the 6th and 7th Trumpets, we have the Double Episode of Chapters X and XI, the one the *vision of the Rainbow-Crowned Angel*, the other the *vision of Jerusalem during the 70th Week.* As, in the Old Testament, the Lord Himself is personated by an Angel, called the " *Angel of the Covenant*," " *Malakh Habberith*," so is He personated here, in Chapter X, when coming to resume relations with lost Israel, and fulfil on Daniel's people and city, the *Hexad* of Blessing in Dan. ix:24. *Chapter XI is a vision of Jerusalem of the Future and the scenes there occurring, when the Jewish-Christian Church is formed, amid wonders mightier than at Sinai or at Pentecost.* Like Joshua and Zerubbabel, the Restorers of the Jewish Church and State, after the Return from Babylonian Exile, so do these Two Witnesses, the two " Sons of oil, standing before the Lord of the whole earth," labor for the Restoration of Israel returned from a longer captivity. Like Moses and Elias, one the founder of the Jewish nation, the other the reformer in the hour of its apostasy, so do these two Witnesses labor to the same end. Like John the Baptist preaching repentance and faith in the Messiah about to be revealed in His *First* Coming, so do these Witnesses preach repentance and faith, and prepare Israel for the *Second* Coming of Messiah. And, as opposition met all these men of God, in their work of reform and re-establishment, so do Antichrist and Satan exert their utmost endeavor to defeat, in this crisis, the purpose of God with respect to the chosen people, and, if possible, not only prevent the building of the Temple and the City, and the establishment o the Millennial kingdom, but show to the world that the Word of God is a lie. That is the object. It is the old trick and the old tactic, but with augmented malignity. What must ever be observed here for our interpretation, is that chapters X, XI, XII, are *all homogeneous*, and that the *action* or *movement* of the drama is not *cyclical*, curling back upon the past, *repeating* the same events over again, in new forms, so retrogressing to the opening of the Week, but is strictly *chronological*, no regress of time existing in the *progress* of the Drama.*

Chapters X, XI, XII, are chronologically sequent, unsunderable, and have to do with Israel under the 6th and 7th Trumpets. The crisis is present. The last call of the gospel has gone to the Gentiles. The fulness of the Gentiles has come in. Gentile Times are expiring. Apostasy has reached its height. The masses have rejected the gospel; Genuine Judaism longs for Restoration. Apostate Judaism seeks its

---

*The *"Cyclical,"* or *"Parallel"* theory is the *"Recapitulation and Repetition Theory"* of Augustine, holding that the Seals, Trumpets, and Vials are Parallel, each series starting from the First Advent and running on to the Second ; therefore a *"Returning to the beginning,"* at Chapters viii, the Trumpets, xii the Sun-Clothed Woman, xvi the Vials, and xx the 1000 years ; and a *"Repeating of the same things"* in different ways ; *"otherwise and otherwise ;"* *"now this way, then that way;"* no chronological succession of series possible. Of John, he says, *"Eadem multis modis repetit, ut alia atque alia dicere videatur;"* and again, *"aliter atque aliter."* So Bede, commenting at Apoc Cap viii, says of the Apostle, *"Nunc recapitulat ab origine,"* i. e. here at the Trumpets, he goes back to the beginning. In short, the Apostle is like a carpenter planing a board, or a musician drawing the musical staff, or a boy skating in a series of concentric circles, the motion is ever self-returning, repeating the same things (eadem). The result is that at Cap. xii also we are put back to the First Advent, merely because the *complex symbol* of the Woman shows the past and future of the Jewish Church, combined, for the sake of unity of representation, and genetic interpretation. *The inference was fatal.* In like manner at Cap xx, we are forced back to the First Advent. That is, *the 1000 years begin with the First Advent and run on all the way to the Second!* We have been in the *Millennium more than 18 centuries!!!* This stupendous error of Augustine, coupled with the *Figurative* interpretation ; in short, this *Pre-Advent Millennialism* dominated down to the Reformation. The *Symbolism* of the Apocalypse is indeed cyclical in several places, conspicuously so at Cap. xii, but the *action*, or Dramatic movement, not retrogressive but pro-opportunity to reject Moses and the Prophets and follow a new heathenism, under the last Antichrist. Lawlessness everywhere prevails. The Nations are raging in tumult of the last conflict, and the center of the struggle is Jerusalem. So all the prophets picture it. Antichrist is in the saddle. The world is now to change front, Israel in the lead as ever, sought to be destroyed, but yet redeemed. Judah's lion, Judah's banner, Judah's tribe, bear the brunt of the final action. They become " like David," and as " the Angel of the Lord." It is the one prophetic picture. To them God calls in the darkest hour Christendom ever saw,—the Gethsemane, the Calvary of God's true people, everywhere,—the time of the Cross in earnest, the time of martyrdom ! On an " election out of Israel," armed by his grace, and inspired with a valor all divine, God relies. *Against* them Satan rages. *For* them Michæl stands firm. *Through* them, come " the Kingdom, the

---

gressive, or chronological. The 6th Seal opens the Day of the Lord. All after that, is simply the development of events, partly contemporaneous, partly successive, but in chronological order up to Cap xx. There is *One Parousia*. There is *more* than One *Epiphany*. The *One Parousia* covers all the Epiphanies. For the sake of distinction, Critics have called the Scene in xix:11, etc., the *Parousia* or *Advent*. It is the *great "Epiphany of the Parousia."* The Cyclic, or Circle-forming Theory ("planetary motion;" Grau) is held by Hengstenberg, Ebrard, Hofmann, Luthardt, Thiersch, Burger, Steffann, etc., etc,, in connection with the *"Group Theory."* But this is not Augustine's *Repetition* Theory. On the other hand, the strict *Chronological* is held, yet not without some circling, by Bengel, De Wette, Ewald, Bleek, Reuss, Düsterdieck, Koch, Christiani, Volck. Füller, Rinck, Van Oosterzee, Nägelsbach, Weber, Züllig, etc., etc., in connection with the " *Group-Theory*;" also. Kübel says, properly, that a " *Dilemma* must be rejected." It is not " *either* one *or* the other ;" and Boehmer's remark is correct, " There is truth in both views." In fact, all recent expositors are substantially one. There is partial retrogression in the Symbols, but constant progress in the action. The truth is, the motion is that of Divine providence and History. It is that of Ezekiel's "Wheels." We are riding in the *Cherubim-Wagon*, or " *Merkaba*," of the prophet. Ezek. i:1-28. The μετὰ ταῦτα, in John, is always chronological, and is the *Acharith Elleh* of Daniel. Bengel's word is important: " Many separate the natural sequence of viii on vii ; xi on x; xii on xi; xx on xix, but each case vindicates itself."

Power, and the Glory." Our reckoning is clear. We
know just where we are; even in the Valley of Vision,
and in the 70th Week. We stand precisely where
Ezekiel stood when he saw the Dry Bones move;
where Zachariah stood when he foretold the last crisis
and the splitting of the Mount of Olives ; where Isaiah
stood when he saw the Enemy invading like a flood,
and Israel's Goel coming to Zion ; and where Jeremiah
and Daniel stood when they predicted Israel's "time
of trouble," and great deliverance. It is a violence to
God's word to spiritualize all this away, and refer it to
the Gentile Church. *That the Jews are already in their
land and city, in large numbers, and even with a Temple*
in process of erection, notwithstanding Lange's incon-
siderate word, that such a view is a " misapprehensive
literal conception,"* is " *the one grand presupposition of
the whole Apocalypse, and apart from which we cannot
understand the Book.*"† What we see here in Chapter
XI, is the beginning of the last conflict with Antichrist,
Israel's last oppressor, and hater of the Church of God,
and out of which Israel comes victorious, standing on
" Mount Zion " with their own Redeemer,—their
"*Goel*" come to them. Rev. xiv:1–5. Rom. xi:26. The
great Crusius, the greatest theologian of his day, saw
this in the last century, and decided upon the ground
of Chapter xi:1, 2 alone, against the perpetuation of
bloody sacrifices in the future Israelitish Church, as do
also Delitzsch, Luthardt, Orelli, Smend, Volck, Koch,
Christiani, and the vast majority on the same and other
grounds. The Israel of the End-Time is NEW-BORN-
ISRAEL, " serving God in newness of spirit, and not in
the oldness of the letter." The Altar of Burnt-Offering

* Lange. Rev. 223.
† Rinck. Zeichen 131.

is "cast out" with the outer-court where it stood.
The Vail of the Temple is now unknown to the
Sanctuary. The Holiest of all and the Holiest Place
are one. Only the Altar of Incense, the emblem of a
true spiritual worship, is seen. The true Israel are
" *worshipers* " in the " *Naos* " where only the priests
might go, and therefore a *priestly spiritual people unto
God.* It is also, after patient study, that Gebhardt
writes, saying, " Jerusalem, the Holy City, means,
here, the *local Jerusalem,* and is, *at the same time,* the
representative of the Jewish people." Matt. xxi:5; xxiii:37.
John has the future of Israel before him. The action
in xi:1 is symbolic, and imports exemption of the
measured worshipers, who are Jewish-Christians, from
destruction, and the exposure of the non-Christian
Jews, the not-measured, the outer-court, to the treading
down by the Gentiles. Once more, the Law and the
Prophecy, in their highest form of personality, *Moses
and Elias, will personally appear as two witnesses,* clothed
with sackloth, to prepare the Jewish people for the
coming of the Lord in glory, heralding His approach,
testifying of Him, and laboring for Him, in word and
deed. *They will publish the gospel to the Jewish Nation
for their repentance, prophesying* 3½ *years, or* 1260 *days,
at whose close Antichrist shall slay them.* In miraculous
attestation of His servants, God smites Jerusalem, and
thereby the City and the Jewish people, in the gross,
finally become converted. If Weiss thinks that " the
Seer no longer ventures to hope, with Paul, for the
final general conversion of Israel, but that *only a remnant shall be saved,*" I think much rather that ancient
prophecy about the remnant, Isa. i:9 ; x:22, 23 ; ix:27-29,
is fulfilled in the portion of the Jewish-Christian
Church intended in Rev. xi:1, while in xi:13 is meant

essentially what is predicted in Rom. xi:25–27."* This is manifest, and the best eschatologists admit it. *Chapters X–XII are undoubtedly connected with scenes in Jerusalem during the 3½ years' testimony of the two witnesses, and the formation of the Jewish-Christian Church.* In the words of Rinck, " *The land of Israel shall become once more, the theater of great events. Once more, Jerusalem shall be the middle-point of the history of the kingdom of God on earth, when Gentile times are ended. A Sanctuary shall be built, and preserved from Gentile profanation. There will be a mighty movement in the valley of dry bones, connected with the return of the Jews to their fatherland, in the time of the 6th Trumpet. And this we have in Chap. XI.*"† This is correct. It is the time of wide international wars and Christian apostasy, the time of the " grafting in again " of the natural branches into their " own olive tree," the time when " All Israel " is saved. Rom. xi:25,26 ; the end of the Times of the Gentiles. Cap. xii:10, is, beyond all question, the time of the Conversion of " All Israel," whose first instalment is announced, Cap. xi:13. The " Measured-Worshipers," the " Sun-clothed Woman," the " Our Brethren," the " 144,000," and the " Cithara-Players " on the glassy sea, all represent *Israel of the End-Time seen under different aspects, and in different relations, as the events of the 70th Week are developed.* The time of Caps. X–XII is the time when the Prophet speaks, then prays, and the Spirit blows, and dead Israel awakes ; the time when Michael stands firm, and Israel is delivered, bringing soon the resurrection of the faithful dead ; the time which also brings the fall

---

* Gebhardt, Doct. of Apoc. 258–262.
† Rinck. Zeichen v. d. Letzten Zeit, 133.

of the Colossus, the near destruction of the Antichrist, Israel's "taking root again, blossoming and bearing fruit;" the time that brings "the Kingdom, Power and Glory." It is announced in Cap. xii:10, as "now come" by a strong Prolepsis; the 3½ years or "short time" of Satan's rage, deemed as nothing.

The vast importance of Chapters x, xi fully excuse our protracted explanation, inasmuch as the understanding of these involves the understanding of all. To a well-disciplined mind, and skilled in God's word, nothing is more absolutely certain than that it is *the literal Israel* and the *geographical Jerusalem* we are here dealing with, and that the specific time before us, is the 70th Week of Daniel. The *Angel who lifts his hands to heaven and swears,*—one foot on the land and one on the sea,—in Rev. x:7,—is the *Same Person* who swears, in the same way, in Dan. xii:7, and Deut. xxxii: 40, the Creator of earth and sea, and now to assume rule over both; no other than "ANI-HU" (see page 73) the "Linen-clothed Man" on the banks of the Tigris, Dan. x:5, 6; and xii:7; the "One like a Son of Man," Rev. i:13-16, Jesus Christ Himself, who is personated by His Angel. Rev. xxii:8, 12, 13, 16. The *Object of the Oath is the same* in every one of these passages, and expressly declared to be (1) the *"finishing of the mystery of God foreshown to the prophets,"* and clearly to Daniel, even the finishing of the 70 Weeks decreed upon Israel, Rev. x:7; (2) the *"bringing to an end the time, times and half a time,"* i. e., the 3½ years, or last 1260 days, of the 70th Week, Dan. xii:7; (3) the *"making an end of breaking in pieces the power of the holy people,"* a victory to be accomplished at the close of these 3½ times; Dan. xii:7, and (4) the *"avenging the blood of His servants,"* the *"resurrection of the faithful dead, the over-*

throw of the Antichrist, Israel's deliverance, and the Joy of the Nations," Deut. xxxii:39–43; Dan. xii: 1–7. All these are the *one Object of the same Oath, repeated by the Same Person speaking in Moses, Daniel and John, concerning the same People, the Jews, and the same Time, the last* 1260 *days of Daniel's 70th Week.* And these *"Days"* are called the *"Days of the Voice of the 7th Angel,"* during which the *"Mystery of God shall be completed,"* Rev. x:7. What else can these "Days of the Voice of the 7th Angel," which are the 3½ years of the 7th Trumpet, be but "the 1260 Days" or last half of the "One Week" in Dan. ix:27 ? What else can *"God's Mystery"* be but the *Mystery of Israel's blindness* during the Times of the Gentiles, *and final conversion,* Rom. xi:25,—the *Mystery of Babylon the Great overthrown,* Rev. xvii:5, 16,—the *Mystery of long-working Iniquity at last destroyed as the Man of Sin is revealed,* II Thess. ii:7–10,—the *Mystery of the resurrection of the faithful dead,* Dan. xii:1–3; I Cor. xv:51,—the *Mystery of the Restoration of the Kingdom to Israel at the end of Gentile Times, with Christ revealed in His glory,—the Mystery of the regrafting of the Jew into his own olive-tree,* Rom. xi:24, and now, the Mystery of the conversion of the Nations, as such, and their engrafting into Israel in order to the formation of the visible *"Kingdom"* at Messiah's Second Coming ? Eph. iii:5, 6; Rev. xv:4 ; xii:10. It is nothing else, for these are the great events that occur *during,* and *at,* the close of the " Days of the Voice of the 7th Angel," which, beyond all successful denial, are hereby proved to be the last 1260 days of the 70th Week. The events of these 3½ years of the 7th Trumpet, are the Contents of the *"Biblaridion"* or *Open Booklet* in the protesting Angel's hand, sweet to know because of the glorious end they reveal, bitter to feel because of the painful

way thereto ;—a *Booklet*, like to Ezekiel's scroll, full of
"mourning, lamentation and woe," the prophet commissioned to preach concerning (not *"over"*) Israel, and
many nations beside.   Rev. x:8–11: Ezek. iii:1–11.
There is no other interpretation.   The *"What withholdeth"* is *"taken out of the way."*   The *Man of Sin is
revealed.   His last* 3½ *are come.   "There shall be no more
delay."*   Terrific will be the judgment of God, fearful
and rapid the strokes in the last Great Tribulation,
extreme the rage of Satan, and, sounding, the 7th
trumpet shall prolong its blast, the vials discharging their
wrath all over our *"modern culture and Christian civilization,"* until "the *Mystery of God is finished*," and the 70
Weeks decreed upon Daniel's people and city expire,
and the Hexad of Blessing be fulfilled as the Angel
foretold it.   Dan. ix:24.   Whatever else is involved,
this much is sure.

The position, then, of Cap. xi is clearly defined.   It
belongs to the Episode between the 6th and 7th Trumpets.   The events are in the time of the Antichrist, and
in Jerusalem.   It unveils the two halves of the 70th
Week, and what occurs therein.   The moment Israel's
Conversion begins, the 7th Angel begins to sound, Rev.
x:7, and *during that sounding the finishing of the Mystery
concerning Israel takes place.*   The chronological connection between Caps. x, xi, xii is as perfect as the
sequence of the 7th upon the 6th trumpet, and we must
not forget this.   It is Israel we have here.   *No new
subject* is introduced.   *No new time* different from that
of the 6th and 7th trumpets.   There is *no retrogression*
to the time of the First Advent.   The circumstance
that the plastic symbol of the Woman, or Jewish
Church, combines in the fulness of its representation,
the *Birth of Christ*, "the Manly Child," with the *Birth*

of National Israel, "the Manly Child," is in perfect harmony with Old Testament prophecy which *identifies
Christ and Israel in their work* on the Nations, and
gives to both the same names, offices, victory and
glory. The unity of the Jewish Church as the Mother
of "Messiah" and Mother of the "Manly Child," the
National Israel, is already asserted by the prophets,
whom John follows, in the clearest manner. (See Hos.
xiii:13; Isa. lxvi:7–9; Rev. ii:27.) This linking of past
and future horizons in Israel's history, this overleaping the interval between the two Advents in order to
present the total likeness of the Woman in one picture,
does not justify the *"Recapitulation theory"* of Augustine, which retracts the time of chapter xii to the First
Advent. Such Recapitulation has been the bane of all
Apocalyptic exposition since the day Augustine first
devised it. Chapters x, xi, xii are all *eschatological;*
under the 6th and 7th trumpets. The connection between the " Measured Worshipers " in xi:1, the "Rest"
who give God the glory, xi:13, the " Sun-Clothed
Woman," xii:1, the "Our Brethren," xii:10, is perfect.
And these together are no other than the " 144,000,"
and the "Cithara-Players" on the Glassy Sea ;—Israel
of the End-Time. All goes to show that *Israel's Conversion must precede the Kingdom of the* 1000 *years,* and
herewith, as Godet remarks, a world-wide revolution
changing the whole face of Christendom in the midst
of national convulsions and agonies, compared with
which all others have been as nothing." The combined exegesis of all the prophets, and the allusions in
the Apocalypse, not only to the plagues that attended
the deliverance of Israel out of Egypt, but also to the
times of the Restoration of Israel under Joshua and
Zerubbabel, and re–establishment of Israel in their own

land, drive us to this ; both these epochs being figures
of epochs greater to come ; the Exodus–epoch leaving
a whole generation dead in the wilderness, and found–
ing a Kingdom soon to be broken ; the Restoration-
epoch a paltry affair compared with what the sublime
predictions foretold ; the *Nations* still remaining in unbelief.   But this final epoch is crowned with grander
results.   It occurs in the midst of the last siege of Jerusalem, of the shaking of the Nations, Heaven, Earth,
Sea and Dry Land, the Redemption of Israel, and
the Advent of Christ.   A new order appears.   In the
impressive words of Orelli,   *"A mighty revolution is
soon to take place in the whole state of the world, the effect
of which will be to transfer the Center of the World's power
and glory to Jerusalem, a new evolution in the world's history, and new direction to the aspiration of the Nations."*
    We shall be able to go on, now, more rapidly.
Chapter xiii tells us what the Beast is doing during the
Second Half of the 70th Week.   He is working up the
" Great Tribulation," while the 144,000 are sheltered in
the wilderness, and Satan, bodied in the Antichrist,
expends his rage upon the " remnant of the Woman's
seed."   In Cap. xvi:1–5, we see Israel, redeemed from
the wilderness, and secure with their Redeemer come
to Sion.   The trumpet storms are over, including the
7th trumpet and 7 Vials.   *In the Vision of the 144,000,
here we have reached the close of the last 3½ years, or 1,260
days, for the vision itself is proleptic, like the other still-
standing visions of the Apocalypse.*   The connection of
the 144,000 with the preceding 13th Chapter is unmistakable.   It shows us elect Israel, now safe, *after* the
Antichrist's 1260 days are over, and the Trumpet-Judgments are gone.   Contrasted with another company in
Heaven, they stand on the earthly Mount Zion sing-

ing a " New Song." *They come to Zion with songs poured* OVER *their heads*, and learn the music they hear FROM ABOVE, and which only the redeemed of the Lord can sing. They are a holy people now. See Isa. xxxv:8–10. Rev. xiv:1–5—the *"All Israel saved*," of Rom. xi:25—the pleromatised last reserve, and new born bearers of grace and glory to the Nations, the "elder brother" brought into his father's house, amid music and dancing, such as the younger never has known. The rest of the Chapter is a brief *Programme* of the scenes under the Vials, a preparation for the resumption of the dramatic progress now moving swift to the End.

Chapter xv is the Introduction to the Vials, therefore proleptic also, forecasting the great result to the *Nations*. The Host on the Glassy Sea, with harps in their hands, sing *two* songs, the one decisive that the harp-bearing singers are they whose Mediator, in olden time was *Moses*, and who saw overwhelmed in the sea, flamed with the anger-blaze from the Pillar of Fire, their ancient foe, the other that now their Goel, or Kinsman-Redeemer is Christ, the *Lamb*, in whose blood they trust. The Moses-song recalls the deliverance from Egypt ; the Lamb-song the greater deliverance from sin and Satan's power.

And now come Chapters xvi–xix, giving us the Vials poured on the earth, intensely upon the seat or " throne " of the Antichrist, an account of the Harlot, the Armageddon scenes, the slaughter in the valley of Jehoshaphat, the great world-shaking earthquake, " the shock that splits the Mount of Olives," and shatters the " cities of the Nations," in that " day unique and only known to the Lord," Zech. xiv:4–7. *But not before Rome, head of the New Babylon, has already been destroyed by*

Antichrist himself and his confederates. A description of this and of the world's commercial wail because of it, we have in Chapters xvii and xviii. Already, the whole world is in arms, " 200 millions " of men moving in the East, apart from the Western forces in the field, Chapter ix:16. It is *after* Rome's fall, the Antichrist, inflated with his victory, returns to the East, under the 6th Vial, with all his forces, to annihilate the Jew, regain possession of the holy city, and exult in universal empire. It is his last march, his one supreme, self-confident effort, his fatal campaign! Meanwhile, *ecclesia pressa* presses through the tribulation to a martyr's crown! " *Here is the faith and patience of the saints!*" Rev. xiii:10. From the *rendezvous* at Armageddon, a united march is made upon the holy City. The moment of Israel's last crisis has come! The " *Beast* " stakes all upon the siege of Jerusalem, with Israel driven to the wall. Satanic madness rules the hour. History has never seen such a time! nor will again! Demonic rage is driving its last blow!

Then, after Heaven's arches have rung with the " *Hallel* " * over the Harlot's overthrow, and the

---

* At the great Jewish solemnities, the " *Hallel*," or cycle of Psalms, beginning or ending with " *Hallel-u-Jah*," " Praise-ye-Jehovah," was sung with thrilling effect. The Singers were a large company. Psalteries and Timbrels were used. The Cithara-Players, or " Harpers harping with their harps," were the *bass* accompaniment, the " loud-sounding cymbals " being struck by the priests to regulate the time. At the close of each section of Psalms, 200 trumpets blew together their exciting *tara-tan-tara*, the whole combination, vocal and instrumental, swelling to the octave and making, not only the temple-courts, but earth and heaven, ring with the " joyful noise." *Delitzsch, Der Psalter II.* 400. *Lightfoot I.* 958. *Binnie, Psalms,* 369. The *Hallel* was in memory of God's " *mighty acts*," " *the wonders he had done.*" It includes the "*mention of His mercies*," and " *of His power.*" It celebrates, (1) redeemed Israel's deliverance from Egypt, (2) the dividing of the Sea, (3) the giving of the Law, (4) the possession of the Land, (5) the Resurrection from the dead, (6) Messiah in His kingdom. It also includes (7) the triumph-song over fallen Babylon, (8) Israel's song in the land of Judah, at the End of the Days, (9) Israel's

Jewish Bride, below, is ready for the Wedding, xix: 1–10, comes a scene that beggars description, and mocks the loftiest genius of man to give it expression. It is the *Glorious Advent of the Warrior-Bridegroom* to fulfil his words to Israel, xix:11–21. John sees " *Heaven Opened*" and crowded with " white horses," indicative of victory, the King Himself in front of all, superbly mounted on his charger, white as the spotless snow. The " *armies of heaven*," the Hosts of Jehovah, follow Him, " *clothed in fine linen, clean and white*," the emblem of their sanctity. A vivid contrast now appears. As He who leads them,—the " *Faithful and True*," comes nearer, His eyes gleam like a flame of fire, the sign not only of discernment and omniscience, but of anger also, telling that " *in righteousness He doth make war*." Since, moreover, He comes as " *Prince of the Kings of the Earth*," to take to Himself His mighty power and reign, so " *on His head are many crowns*," emblems of the fulness of royalty that sat, usurpingly, upon the crowned horns of the Beast, and now to be wrested from him. As, once more, the Beast had a mystic name which wisdom alone could count, so the conqueror wears " *a name written that no man knows but He Himself*," a name divine. As He approaches closer to us, the sky now far behind Him, we detect Him as the *Bozrah-Hero*, descending over Edom, and moving toward Jerusalem, arrayed in crimson vesture " *dipped in blood*," in strik-

---

pardon in the Last Days, (10) Israel's song for their restored Jerusalem ; and, in the Apocalypse, ascends (11) from the 144,000 standing with their returned Redeemer, on Mount Zion. (12) is the song of the Cithara-Players on the sea of glass, and (13) is the *five-fold* rolling and thundering reverberation of the heavenly multitude, above, and Israel below, over the Harlot's ruin, the destruction of Antichrist, the marriage of the Bride, the Resurrection from the dead, and Millennial glory with Messiah in His Kingdom !

ing contrast with the *white uniform* in which His armies ride. It means that the *" day of vengeance" is in His heart, and the " year of His redeemed has come ! "* He comes *" to tread the winepress of the fierceness and wrath of Almighty God," " to sprinkle His garments with blood, and stain all His raiment ! "* It means that He comes to *" avenge "* the altar-moan of His martyred ones and confirm the solemn word of the Angel of the waters, *" Righteous art Thou, O Lord, which wast, and art, because thou hast thus judged ; for they have shed the blood of saints and prophets, and Thou hast given them blood to drink, for they are worthy."* Rev. xvi:5, 6. John tells us His mystic name. It is the *" Word of God." " Out of His mouth proceeds a two-edged sword,"* the symbol of judicial breath with which He *" smites that Wicked."* As He descends still lower, coming still nearer the earth, and passing the blue horizon line, close followed by His crowding and flanking hosts, we see a quivering, a glittering, of something bright as gold upon His crimson breast. What we see is a series of blazoned words upon His military baldric, diagonally drawn across His vesture, reaching from shoulder to thigh, and dazzling in characters bright and large that all His enemies may read them. It is His glorious title, " KING OF KINGS, AND LORD OF LORDS !" Moment of intense impression ! Moment of awful answer to Israel's prayer, *" O that thou wouldst rend the heavens, and come down ! "* Isa. lxiii:1 ; lxiv:1, In words of brevity, befitting a scene and crisis like these, the one so replete with majesty, the other so full of Woe,—the great result is stated." *And the* BEAST *was taken ! "* Rev. xix:20. Hallelujah ! He and the False Prophet, *" they twain,"* individualized, yet undivided in doom, go headlong and alive to the " Lake of Fire," while Israel, plucked as a brand from the burning, shines as a pillar in the temple of God ! The armies of the Beast perish beneath the sword of Israel's Great Deliverer, and their carcasses furnish a banquet for the eagles and the vultures invited to their supper by an Angel standing in the sun ! Rev. xix:20, 21.

And now, Babylon gone, Antichrist gone, the False Prophet gone, and Israel delivered, *Chapter xx:1-7 introduces us to the Arrest and Imprisonment of him who was the cause of all the mischief.* With visions, such as Oriental drugs produce, the Church has dreamt for centuries, that to *her* was decreed the power to *bind Satan* and bring in the days of Millennial glory on earth. The Object-Lesson here given, is to instruct her innocence that, to the Redeemer alone, in His proper person, belongs the prerogative to " *bind,*" at His Second Coming, the body of him whose head He "*bruised*" at His First. In other passages of Scripture the conflict with Satan is represented as being a personal hand to hand encounter, as when He speaks of Himself " entering the house of the strong man armed" " binding the man," and " spoiling his house," Matt. xii:28, 29; " through death destroying him that has the power of death, that is the Devil," Heb. ii:14 ; " making a show of principalities and powers openly triumphing over them in His own person," Col. i:15. In the same personal way, at the very outset of His career, He encountered this Evil One, in the time of His fleshly temptation, Matt. iv:1-11, and, after 40 days of protracted struggle, repelled him with victorious power, a prelude of greater victory yet to come. The Apocalypse reveals the Conqueror engaged in His last conflict, His last personal hand to hand grapple with His great antagonist. John watches the action in the vision, with intensest gaze, riveted, motionless, and with supremest, breathless, and almost panting, suspense, his pulse-beat quickening every instant. He seems to forget, for the moment, his usual calm contemplation, and snatches the opportunity,—as the coil of omnipotence circles and binds the limbs of that old ambulant monster who, 6,000 years long, had " walked up and down," promenaded, paraded, glittered, deceived, tempted, led captive, and roared, and did as he pleased, —to indulge the luxury of flinging at his head a string of academic epithets and pictorial titles the most unique and best befitting he could find. He confers all the degrees at once! He tells us that " *the Dragon* "— "*that Old Serpent*,"—"*the Devil*,"—and " *Satan*,"—four devils in one,—the " Dragon " with his crowns off, the " Serpent " with his head bruised, the " Devil " with his clamps on, and " Satan " with his mouth stopped,— was first " seized," next " chained," then " cast into the pit," after that " shut up," and finally " sealed.' The Seed of the Woman has given him a sore head, tight wrists, close ankles, a long plunge, a dismal hole, a sure lock-up, and reasonable time for reflection ;—the period of " 1000 years," not merely " three days," in which, as a " Stated Supply," in his own " Dark Dungeon," to gnaw his chain and study the question, as Dr. Kliefoth would call it, of " potentiated ecumenicity," and "spatial victory !" John seems perfectly delighted! It is an eternal satisfaction to him to watch not only the chaining, but the slinging, and hear the shutting of the iron bars, as they fall on the top of the Pit, and see the Seal superadded, massive, rocky, heavy, over-covering, and large as the Mount of Temptation! "*Amen!*" The world is now free from his wiles. Anarchy and Antichristianity are now perished from the earth. Bereft of his old companions, the Beast and the False Prophet in the lake of fire, Satan in the Pit, and alone, he sighs out his solitude, prostrate in a corner, wondering how long " 1000 years " may be, or if again the time will come when one more missionary privilege will be given him to overturn, if he can, the kingdom of Christ! Upon this great event, comes the announcement of a still greater and more solemn—the Resurrection of the righteous dead, the " *First Resurrection* " in which the Apostles, Martyrs and Confessors of Jesus made co-assessors and regents with Christ, live and reign with Him " the 1000 years."

Thus have we come to the close of the Second Half, or last 3½ years of the 70th Week of Daniel. The 7th trumpet has sounded, the last vial has been poured, the Advent is a fact, "*the mystery of God is finished*." A New Age is before us. *The high point of the whole development, after Chapter xi, is the Kingdom of the 1000 years, introduced by the Second Coming of Messiah.* Old Testament Prophecy is fulfilled. The Beast is given to tne flame. The Colossus is scattered like chaff. Gentile supremacy over Israel has ceased. The bones in the Valley of Vision have stood up, an exceeding great army. Leviathan is bound. The Kingdom is given to the " People of the Saints of the Most High." The "*Days of Messiah*," have come, in which the righteous flourish in a kingdom "under the whole heaven," and in which the "Beloved City " is the middle-point, and Israel, restored to nationality, is enthroned as the " Manly Child," ordained with Christ to rule the world.

In the light of this organic relation of the 1000 years to the previous dramatic action of the second part of the Apocalypse, we see the folly that would date these

years from any point this side the Second Coming of
the Lord.   Never was a violence, so monstrous to the
word of God, committed until the Church, as Maitland says, began to "*Heathenize*," and Origen and
Jerome, and Augustine, great, good and beguiled,
evaporated Israel's right to future recognition; and,
breaking as with hammer stroke the chronological connection, first between Chapters vii and viii, then between Chapters xi and xii, and next between Chapters
xix and xx, applied the symbols, concerning "Israel,"
to the "Church," *sliding backward the* 1000 *years, across
the whole dispensation covered by the 7 Epistles, and dating
these* 1000 *years from the death of Christ!*   That is the
way it was done!   That is the magic, mischief, and
monstrosity, of pre-advent Millennialism, which now,
abandoning its old arguments, raises the banner, "*Symbolical numbers don't count!*"

C.   Relative and Absolute Ends

But the *Relative End,* or End of "This Present Age"
is not the *Absolute End*, or End of Time and History.
The Millennial Age is not the Endless Age.   The 1000
years, therefore, sustain a relation to the Eternal State
in the final New Heaven and Earth, like that of a vestibule to the Grand Temple to which it is the Entrance.
Such is the scope and order of the Ages.   At the close
of the 1000 years, we encounter the Last Judgment—
and the Last Resurrection, followed by the final Regenesis of all things, the surrender of the Messianic Kingdom to God the Father, "the Son Himself subjected
to *Him* that did subject all things to Him, that *God*
may be all in all."   Rev. xx:11–15.   I Cor. xv:28.
Viewed in the light of a future scope, so great, Chapter
xx:1–7, seems itself an Episode, like Chapter vii, and

Chapters x, xi, in the vast evolution. Ever wider grows the view as we advance, expanding as we are carried along with the flow of time, till, like a minnow, borne by the stream and swept into the sunlit ocean, we are lost in depths and heights, and widths of space beyond our comprehension; expanses, bewildering, immeasurable, filled with glory ever shining; enlarging circles of the future ever opening out before us and vanishing as they recede to distances we cannot grasp; horizons swelling, breaking by distension, outreaching to the infinite, until imagination droops, and thought returns exhausted. Still, what we *can* learn, and *do* know, is this, that as the ultimate glory is not the result of human endeavor, so neither is the glory of the 1000 years. It, too, is the work of God, not by means of ordinary processes, nor by Church activities, nor by any merely natural laws of development, but the outcome of Judgment and Salvation which alone arrests the downward tendency of man, and alone defeats the arts and power of Satan. Not philosophy, Science or Education, nor Culture of any kind; not schools, colleges, universities or seminaries; not Christian civilization can restrain Israel's dark apostasy, convert Christendom (not to speak of Heathendom) destroy Antichrist, expel Satan, raise the dead, annihilate our Gentile politics, and establish the Kingdom of Christ in its glory. The Millennial blessedness is something *more* than Christian civilization, or Church and State Religion; something more than the progress of nations, or suppression by law of gigantic evils hurtful to human society; something more than glorified Judaism, or bettered Christendom. It is a new creation, as relatively great compared with Christendom, as Christendom is relatively great compared with

Jewdom ; a state where divisions and sects exist no
more ; where Mosque, Pagoda and proud Cathedral
find no place ; but where *"we all come in the unity of the
faith and of the knowledge of the Son of God, unto a perfect man, unto the measure of the stature of the fulness of
Christ,"* Eph. iv:13 ;—a state where we see no longer
"as in a mirror, darkly, but face to face, and know as
we are known," I Cor. xiii:12 ; a time when Jew and
Gentile, though distinguished in the plan of God, shall
yet be one in Christ, dwelling in communion of life and
love, and risen saints, all glorified, have constant fellowship with saints unglorified, who yet are nearer glory
than the saintliest of us now.   Heaven and Earth will
have come closer together in that 1000 years of peerless privilege and blessing.   That is one lesson we
learn from the study of John's Apocalypse, as also from
the prophets of the grey fore-time.   It is the doctrine
of God's entire word, and any *"view"* which makes it
impossible to preach that word as the apostles and the
prophets preached it, or leave on the minds of hearers
the impression they left, stands self-condemned at the
bar of eternal truth.   Not " codes," nor " confessions,"
nor "evangelical alliances," nor "large conventions of
our leading men," nor "Conferences," nor "Associations," nor "Assemblies," can accomplish this.   Not
" Boards," nor "Clubs," nor " Syndicates," nor " Sermons," nor " Review Articles," can give it birth.   It
comes by Judgment and Catastrophe, as well as by the
outpoured Spirit.   It comes by the Coming of the
"Lord Himself from Heaven."   Then, and then only, begin the World's Great Sabbath, Israel's Great Jubilee
and the Saints' Great Reign.

Part 10

THE 1,000 YEARS IN EZEKIEL

A. A preliminary word is needed as to Ezekiel Chapter xxxvii, before discussing chapter xl–xlviii, the favorite retreat of post-millennarians. The vast body of exegetes agree that the sublime symbol of the re-animated Bones in the Valley of Vision, prefigures the literal re-establishment of Israel as a nation, and organized body politic, in their own land, at the Second Coming of Christ. " The symbol," says Professor Briggs, "is a symbol of the resurrection of Israel as a nation, and their restoration to the holy land. It becomes associated in subsequent prophecy with the doctrine of a universal resurrection, because the restoration of Israel, that the prophet had in view, can be accomplished only in the resurrection of all mankind in the last great day, and their establishment in the New Jerusalem upon the New Earth."* It is perfectly correct that the civil, political, national and religious restoration of the "Whole House of Israel" in their fatherland, is here predicted. But it is contrary to the text and the whole word of God, to say that this

---

* Briggs. Messianic Prophecy. 277.

417

is "associated with the doctrine of a *universal resurrection*," either at the Second Coming of Christ, or at the Last Judgment, or that Israel's political rehabilitation "can be accomplished *only in the resurrection of all mankind in the last great day ;* or that this political re-establishment takes place " *in the New Jerusalem upon the New Earth;*" or that this view of the restoration (the view of Kliefoth followed by Professor Briggs) is " *what the prophet had in view!*" The eternal continuity of the Jewish Nation, existing politically as a separate entity, distinct from other nations *in the final New Earth*, with *New Jerusalem as the Metropolis of the Eternal State*, may be true, but it is not taught *here*, since Ezekiel clearly tells us that, " *many days after* " Israel's restoration, Gog's expedition shall march against the "Beloved City" and fire from heaven consume the invaders ;—a military promenade and divine judgment being scarcely appropriate in eternity, and on the New Earth, after the "first earth " has " passed away " and " no place is found " for either Satan, Gog, or their encircling swarms. Ezek. xxxviii:8–13. And the apostle John, who was somewhat skilled in the prophets, confirms this criticism, showing that Gog's march is against Israel restored, on the *old* earth, and *before* the old earth has vanished away. Rev. xx:7–10.

The view that this " *locus classicus* " is not a " *proof-text*," for the doctrine of a resurrection of the body, as Jerome and others taught, is incorrect. While the symbol prefigures Israel's political recovery in Palestine, it involves also a literal resurrection of Israel's faithful dead from their individual graves. A large number of the ablest scholars insist upon this. The epoch of occurrence is that of the literal resurrection of God's saints. Hos. xiii:14; Isa. xxv:8 ; xxvi:19 ; Dan.

xii:2, 3; compare Matt. xiii:43; I Cor. xv:24; Rev. xx: 4–6. The Hebrew term *"Mikkiverotheichem,"* rendered "out from your *graves*," Ezek. xxxvii:12, has, for its root, "*kever*" (*cover*) which never means death, nor the state of the dead, nor Hades or Sheol, but always an *individual grave*.* Employed as a symbol of the nations, or the field of slaughter, where dead Israel nationally sleeps, it yet imports the place of literal sepulture, and its use, in connection with the resurrection here predicted, involves the literal resurrection of Israel's faithful dead, and harmonizes with Paul's all-comprehending word when, referring to this very event, he says, "What shall the receiving of them be, but *Life out from the dead?*" Rom. xi:15; one of the frequent and strong antitheses in which he delights. It is great error to deprive God's word of its whole significance.

The *national* resurrection of Israel is accomplished in connection with the *literal* resurrection of Israel's faithful dead, at the time of the Second Coming of Christ. Then He will appear in His glory and build up Zion, gather the outcasts, heal the broken in heart, and bind up the wounds of His people. Ps. cxlvii:2–4; Isa. lxvi:5; Ps. cii:13–22. They shall come from the East, and the West, and the North, and the South, and sit down with risen Abraham, Isaac and Jacob, not in the "New Earth," after the 1000 years have expired, but *in Canaan made glorious on the old Earth.*

Time was, in Jerome's day, when the "Church" having swerved from her first faith, spiritualized this "*visio famossissima,*" as he justly calls it, and it became a constant "*lectio,*" or "*reading,*" in all the Churches.

---

* Kahle Bibl. Eschatol. 136–140. Craven, in Lange's Commentary, Revelation, Excurs. 366. I.

Israel was the "Church," Constantine was "Michael" standing up for Israel, the temporal supremacy of Christianity in the Roman Empire was the "First Resurrection." Even then the 12 Apostles sat on their promised thrones, and ruled the Kingdom by their various Epistles. With the cessation of the martyr-flame, and the erection of the State-Church, and her nurture by imperial patronage, the 1000 years, had dawned! *"Famous,"* indeed, was the vision of Ezekiel, a mirror in which the *"Church"* of the 4th century dreamed she saw her own face. Israel was snuffed out, as an offensive wick, by Origen, Augustine, Jerome, and Eusebius, a smoking flax quenched by Gentile hands, a light extinguished, impossible to be relumed. That time, through the mercy of God, and that notion too, have passed forever away, and Jerome's canon of interpretation, — "What things the Jews, and our people,—yea, *not* our people,—*Judaizing carnally*, maintain as events still *future*, let us (*orthodox*) teach, *spiritually, as already past*,"*—has been remanded to the age that gave it birth, save by some who still play the Alexandrian music, with the 4th century accompaniment, telling us that we are living in the millennium *"now,"* when the Devil is bound, and War is no more! So sang the Sibyl preluding the glory of the Augustan age, followed by the scenes under a Caligula, and Nero, a Vitellius and Caracalla!

Notwithstanding this, God's truth,—as a *Jew* once said, "is mighty and will prevail," and, as another *Jew* said, "God's word is not bound." Dead Israel shall rise again as truly as did dead Lazarus. The "House of

---

* "*Quæ Judæi, et nostri,—immo* NON *nostri, judaizantes carnaliter, futura contendunt, nos, spiritualiter,* jam transacta, doceamus." Jerome, in Ezek. xxxvii.

Israel," Dan. ix:7, 11 ; " All Israel," Dan. ix:7, 11 ; Rom.
xi:26; Israel as a "People," Rom. xi:1. Israel as a
"Nation," Jer. xxxi:36, shall yet reappear in history,
more glorious than ever. Their Dry Bones shall flourish
like the grass of the field, even in the Holy City, and
the dew-gemmed verdure of their resurrection will
adorn the now sad Valley of Vision. Isa. lxvi:14 ; xxvi:
19; Ps. lxxii:16 ; cx:3 ; Hos. xiv:5.

This is the place, by way of a moment's digression,
to speak of that great " *Change of interpretation*," which,
in the 4th century, came with the " *Change of the
Church's condition* " in the Roman Empire. It was a total
revolution, and signal departure of the whole Church,
from the early faith as to prophecy, led by men who
partook of the " spirit of the age," fixing the canon of
interpretation for Israel in Old Testament prediction,
and in the Apocalypse of John. No sooner was the
martyr-flame extinguished by the first imperial law of
toleration, and the Church protected by the State, than
laws most cruel were enacted against *Pagans, Heretics*,
and *Jews*. By the Church, which assumed to " *take
Israel's place in the Kingdom of God*," the Jews were consigned to an irreversible curse ; ostracised, hated, per-
secuted, their Synagogues burned to the ground.
Whatever cruelty the Inquisition and the Papal Empire
afterward practiced was begun here. It contributed
to make Julian " apostate," enlisted his favor for the
Jews, and roused him to dare the attempt of rebuilding
the Temple at Jerusalem and to seek to restore Paganism and Judaism alike.* Ambrose of Milan, good, great,
bold, and eloquent, and who moulded Augustine's view,

---

*Jortin. Eccl. Hist. II. 266. Du Pin, Eccl. Hist. II. 285. Basnage,
Hist. des Juifs vi:14. p. 1266. Baronius, Annal. iii:114. Alzog, Chh. Hist
i. 336, Sozomen, Eccl. Hist. 138, 240 Bohn's ed.

and cherished the spirit that formed the new canon of interpretation, was a zealot against the Jews, encouraging the conflagration of their synagogues, and rebuking Theodosius for insisting on restitution by the incendiaries. He wrote to the Emperor, saying : *"I declare that I would burn a Synagogue myself, lest a place should exist where Christ was denied,"** and avowed that he would have "set fire" to the synagogue at Milan, if God had not already applied the torch with His own hand! The *Globi Flammarum*, or balls of fire, that frustrated Julian's impious design to countervail the Oracle of Christ concerning the Temple, were deemed a divine invitation to consume all Jewish places of worship, for Christianity was now supreme! † In the heat of such hatred, the Church-Teachers of the 4th century, zealous for Christ, and robed in imperial toilet furnished at State expense, and believing the Millennial Age was born, and the Devil was bound, rejected the

---

* " *Declaro quod ego ipse synagogam incenderim, ne esset locus in quo Christus negaretur.*" Ambrose Epist. ad. Theod. Neander. ii:67-69.

† One would think that "when the Church began to heathenize" in the 4th century, and take to Roman philosophy and literature, she drank a full cup of the Roman spirit in reference to the *Jew*. How hated the Jew was, and how despised his religion, by the "Civilization" of the times, every classic student well knows. Even Cicero, the polished, had called their religion a *"barbara superstitio,"* (Orat. pro Flacco, 28) and Horace had sported his " *Credat Judæus Apella*" (Sat. I. 5. 100.) Tacitus calls them the *"odium humani generis"* (Hist. v:13) and Pliny, the elegant, declared their worship a *"contumelia deorum"* (Hist. Nat. xiii:9.) The Pagan implacability seemed to float everywhere, like a baleful contagion in the atmosphere of the christianized empire. The Church, just escaped from the flames, herself began to afflict and oppress both Pagan and Jew, for the sake of the glory of God ! And only by wrecking the true interpretation of "Israel" in the Apocalypse was the Apocalypse itself saved from the ban ! Guilty and blind indeed, was the Jew. Yet even under the curse, he kept up the old Maccabean shout, " *The Kingdom of God forever !* ἡ Βασιλεία τοῦ Θεοῦ εἰς τον ἀιῶνα !" just as the French say *Vive l' Empereur!* and the Germans " *Es leben König Wilhelm !*" Hence the hatred of the Jew. See Hilgenfeld, *Messia's Judæorum xvii*:33–36. Not till later times did the anger of Rome to the afflicted Israelite in any measure, abate, and only then as a matter of humanity; not because her interpretation was changed.

Chiliasm of the Ante-Nicene fathers and first apologists of Christianity, and formulating the new canon concerning "Israel," applied to themselves the Old Testament prophecies, and voted Israel nationally dead *forever!* It was the doctrine of the Middle-Age, and is Rome's doctrine to-day. The "*Church*" is the "Kingdom," and the "*Church*" is "Israel." In such times as these, *Post-Millennialism* came to the throne. The temporal splendor of the Church was the climate of the "First Resurrection," and the dining hall of Constantine yet unbaptized, was deemed by Eusebius possible to be the fulfilment of John's Apocalypse concerning the "New Jerusalem," and of Ezekiel's Vision concerning the "Holy Oblation!" The 1000 years had come! The Dry Bones in the Valley had stood up, an exceeding great Christian army, the adult population of the Roman Empire! A "feast of fat things" smoked on the Emperor's table, and Christian Bishops and Post-Nicene Fathers were experts to tell what was meant by "wines on the lees well refined!" It was a part of *pre-Advent Millennialism!* All the Apocalypses of both Testaments clearly foreshadowed, as Eusebius said, "*The Splendor of our Affairs!*" The sunlight of prosperity, and dream of the "Conversion of the Empire," intoxicated with brilliant delirium, the souls of men who had survived the Diocletian persecution. Under the edict of Licinius and Constantine, and again under the Code of Theodosius, which embodied the Ten Commandments, the New Song was sung, in Cathedral Chant, and the "*Visio Famossissima*," in Ezekiel, was read every Sabbath-Day to delighted hearers;—Ambrose, Eusebius, Licinius, Constantine, Augustine, Jerome, Theodosius, and the whole "Church" waltzing "in the splendor of our affairs," and being no

other than "*Israel*" restored to their fatherland, and
converted to Christ!*

But to return to Chapters xl–xlviii,—so long perplexing to so many,—the favorite retreat of post-
millennialists, and the ready refuge when pressed by
Chiliastic argument.   Intrenched here, they deem
themselves secure.   How interpret these Chapters?
Do they belong to the 1000 *years of John?   Are these also
a Millennial picture?* We answer, *Yes.*   They cannot
be literalized into the times of the Restoration under
Zerubbabel, nor spiritualized into the times of the New
Testament Church, nor celestialized into the heavenly
state, nor allegorized into the final New Heaven and
Earth, nor idealized into an oriental phantasmagorial
abstraction.   Whatever difficulties attend the interpretation which regards them simply as the expansion of
Chapter xxxviith, a picture of Israel's dwelling safely in
their own land glorified, with the temple shining on ·
exalted Zion, as the prophets have predicted it, more
and greater difficulties attend any other exposition.
Into a discussion of these it is impossible to enter here,
as every student knows.   It is enough, for our present
purpose, to state where we fully believe these Chapters

---

*Adverting to this great change of interpretation that came over the
Church, by her union to the State, Professor Orelli says : " The *national*
element in prophecy was more and more ignored, and everything received a
Christian coloring.   Israel is always now to be *spiritually* interpreted.
After the age of persecution was past, the attitude of the Church toward
prophecy was remarkably changed, *its fulfillment being no longer anxiously
looked for*. . Old Testament prophecy was regarded as finally fulfilled and
done with, and where the words of prophecy were not responded to, by
the actual history, all was *spiritualized*.   This spiritualistic interpretation
did not scruple to refer the promises pertaining to *Israel's* future, to the
Christian Church as the spiritual posterity of Abraham, according to Gal.
iii:7.   The view opened up by the same Apostle, viz.: That one day yet,
Israel, as a whole, will be converted, and the prophecies concerning Israel
be entirely fulfilled, Rom. xi:1-36, was allowed, by the Church, to fall to
he ground." Die alttest. Weissagung 75, 76.

belong, and their connection with the "first resurrection," even as John has briefly stated the connection of the 1000 years, in the same way. The organic unity of prophecy determines this, the analogy, the progress in development, the continuity, the relation of the parts, and the connection of the whole. The *locus* of the whole scene of the New Israel, in their New Land, redistributed and transfigured, their New Temple, New City, and New Cult, is *between* the Second Coming of Christ and the Last Judgment at the end of Ezekiel's "Many Days," xxxviii:8, Isaiah's "Multitude of Days," xxiv:22, Hosea's "Third Day," vi:2, and John's "1000 years," xx:1–7. That is the region where they belong. That *bloody sacrifices* seem a stumbling block, never can avail to dislodge the section from its place in prophecy or history. The picture is a picture of *restored Israel* from an Exile-point of view, when the Temple was destroyed, the City laid waste by the king of Babylon, Israel's instituted worship wrecked, and the prophet-priest, Ezekiel, was moved by "the hand of God" to comfort the exiles of the Gola!* It covers, perspectively, the *whole temporal future* of the people, and blends the Restoration, the Non-Restoration, the Abolition, the future Restitution, all in one. Isaiah had chiefly dwelt upon the *prophetic* side of the kingdom, in thrilling terms, Daniel dwells upon the *kingly* side and, to Ezekiel it is given to paint the *priestly* side

---

* Ezekiel, and the Aristocracy of Israel, lived in the Gola, during their exile, a locality in Tel Abib, by the river Chebar (*Cheboras*) iii:11, 15, 24; viii:1; xii:3, and near the plain, or *Valley* which is called, in his prophecy, the "Valley of Dry Bones," iii:22; xxxvii:1, 2. Ezekiel saw the Vision of the Temple and New Jerusalem, on the very day of the overthrow of Jerusalem, 14 years after the fall of the Temple. As to the dates of his prophecies, Chapters xxxvi–xxxix were B. C. 585. Chapters xl–xlviii were B. C. Oct. 572. To inspire the wretched survivors with Hope of a glorious future, in their own land, was the design of these predictions.

of it. And, as all the rest speak, so does he, in Old
Testament terms, and paints in Old Testament colors,
yet not without the most startling modifications of the
Mosaic worship ;—not legislating the " rudiments of
the Pentateuchal priest-code,"—as Kuenen and his
school would have it, but amending, abolishing, and
adding to it, changing it,—a sign of fading, not advancing, Mosaism. One thing we know, beyond dispute,
viz., that " *Israel*" of the Millennial Age, is a converted
people, " serving God in newness of the Spirit, and not
in the oldness of the letter." How much of Ezekiel's
typical picture will fade in the fulfilment, how much
brighten to intenser glory, we may not decide. Nor
does this impinge upon the doctrine of " exact accomplishment." It neither asserts nor denies. It
leaves, to the future, problems the future only can
solve. It refuses to reconcile apparent contradictions
by the adoption of a principle of interpretation which,
if logically carried out, would end in the denial of
Christianity itself. It waits. The early Jewish Christians adhered to their Jewish rites long after their
conversion on the day of Pentecost. They worshiped
still in the Temple. At any rate, the future will bring
the solution. We can agree with Van Oosterzee, that
" It is impossible to say with infallible certainty what
is *mere* imagery, and what is *more* than imagery,"* and
with Kahle, feel sure, that " it is not for us to determine *how much of these closing predictions of Ezekiel will
be literally fulfilled, how much not, when Israel has turned
to the Lord with all their heart*."† We may not go to
the length of Baumgarten and Hess who, perhaps,

* Person and Work of the Redeemer, 451.
† Kahle. Bibl. Eschatol. I. 156.

press the literal, in some respects, to the quick, but we may follow men of scholarship and greatness in the knowledge of God's word, like Crusius, Delitzsch, Nägelsbach, Hofmann, Neumann, and agree, even with Kuenen and Graf, in this, that " it is vain, either to *idealize*, or seek to *spiritualize*, the many and minute details of these Chapters," as Hengstenberg, Hävernick, Keil, and others do, and feel perfectly justified in saying, with Smend, that " *we have no right to distort into the spiritual, or pronounce fantastic, the hope of Israel's actual glorification in their land.*"* So speaks Orelli. " Clearly as the transformed physiognomy points to a new spiritual creation, yet *we ought not to spiritualize the facts, and least of all allegorize the particular traits,* so as to understand the ' fishers ' as fishers of men (Hengstenberg) or as angels (Kliefoth) or the 'trees' on the banks of the Temple-Stream, as of righteous men (Kliefoth). Rather the image stands before the eyes of the Seer *in concrete reality, apart from all interpretation.* The land of Israel, endowed of God, with altogether new forces of blessing, will be a very ' *Garden of God.*'"† And as to the *whole* picture, we shall, perhaps find it easy to agree with the same gifted and devout scholar when he asks and answers, " What picture is this in Ezekiel, Chapters xl–xlviii ? *Is it the Jerusalem of the Restoration* that has here presented itself to his prophetic vision, with historic fidelity? The form is too perfect for this. The relations described are too perfect to allow us to see in this picture a representation, beforehand, of the restored Church of Zerubbabel and Joshua, of Ezra and Nehemiah, such as was after-

---

* Smend. Der Prophet Ezekiel, 385.
† Orelli, Die alttest. Weissag. 421, 422.

ward realized historically. Or, *is it the consummated Jerusalem, the Eternal City of God?* For this, again, the relations are too limited, too specifically Jewish. And yet there are elements, even in the oracles of Ezekiel, that do not find expression in the architectural plan framed after the Mosaic pattern. The Temple is seen standing on a high mountain. This feature, and the Temple-River swelling as it goes, show that the whole is *more* than a new architectonic for the building of God's house, or a new revision of the Law, or the Restoration of the State. It is a prophetic vision in which the Church of God and the Temple, are presented in glorified form. And yet the detailed descriptions are of such a kind, the walls, the chambers, and the doors, that they yield a *real architectonic* of which a plan may be drawn, complete as that of the temple of Herod or Solomon. The Mosaic cultus here, is *typical prophecy*. Attempts have been made to crane up this picture, and its separate features, by artificial means, to the height of the New Testament revelation, *by putting a spiritual meaning into everything,* or an outward fulfilment has been claimed by which even the *bloody sacrifices* must be logically ascribed to converted Israel. Really neither the one nor the other view accords with New Testament teaching."*

The sublime picture, therefore, that Ezekiel has drawn in Chapters xl–xlviii, is a picture of the *Millennial Age.* Of that period many pictures abound in the Old Testament, *all perspectively covering, in front, the brighter glories of the Eternal State, and into which not a few rays from the splendor of the last and highest glorification are thrown forward and upon them.* We are not, however,

---

* Ibid, 418, 419.

to confound the two ages, because of this. If light from the final New Jerusalem shines in the Millennial picture, or if features common to the two ages are mingled in one, it is only because of that peculiar mode of the Spirit's unveiling, whereby we are enabled to *see one thing pictured in another,*—"*in re una cernere imaginem alterius,*"—and by a comparison of Scripture, and distinction of ages, attain to certainty in our interpretation. Hence the old maxim, "*Distingue tempora, et concordabit Scriptura,*"—"*Distinguish the times, and the Scriptures will agree.*" Each prophet, moreover, paints from his own standpoint, and at best gives only a partial view. It is Ezekiel's office to describe from a *priestly* point of view. Therefore he says nothing politically, or of the subject *nations outside* the Holy Land, as the other prophets do, but dwells on Israel, and Israel's land, and City alone. If the *Similarities* between his portrait of the "Many Days" of Israel in the Kingdom, and Israel's former Old Testament life, their ritual and laws are remarkable, still more remarkable are the vast and important *Differences* noted by Jews and Christians alike; differences so great as to make the former, at one time, almost extrude the book from the sacred canon, as uninspired. It is plain that these Differences imply an entire revolution from the Old order of things, and intimate strongly the "*vanishing away*" of the Law, to make room for the "*New Covenant*" he has elsewhere, like Jeremiah, Hosea, Isaiah, proclaimed with such spiritual force. There are *Changes* in the dimensions of the Temple so that it is neither the temple of Solomon, nor that of Zerubbabel, nor that of Herod; changes in the measures of the outer court, the gates, the walls, the grounds, and the locality of the temple itself, raised on a high mountain, and even separate from the City. The Holy Places have hardly anything like the furniture that stood in the Tabernacle of Moses, or the Temple of Solomon. There are *Subtractions* also. There is no Ark of the Covenant, no Pot of Manna, no Aaron's rod to bud, no Tables of the Law, no Cherubim, no Mercy-Seat, no Golden Candlestick, no Shew-bread, no Veil, no unapproachable Holy of Holies where the High-Priest alone might enter, nor is there any High-Priest to offer atonement to take away sin, or to make intercession for the people. None of this. The Levites have passed away as a sacred order. The priesthood is confined to the sons of Zadok, and only for a special purpose. There is no evening sacrifice. The measures of the Altar of Burnt-Offering differ from those of the Mosaic altar, and the offerings are themselves but barely named. The preparation for the Singers is different from what it was. The social, moral, and civil prescriptions enforced by Moses with such emphasis, are all wanting. The *Additions* too are wonderful. The entrance of the " Glory " into Ezekiel's temple to dwell there, forever; the Living Waters that flow, enlarging from beneath the Altar ; the Suburbs, the wonderful trees of healing, the new distribution of the land according to the 12 tribes, their equal portion therein, the re-adjustment of the tribes themselves, the Prince's portion and, the City's new name, " *Jehovah-Shammah*," all go to prove that New Israel restored is a converted people, worshiping God " in Spirit and in Truth." The laws and ordinances relating to the " *Prince*," all show that it is of a *priestly-kingdom* Ezekiel is speaking, and of which Israel is the center; the same kingdom Daniel speaks about, and that Chapters xl–xlviii are but the expansion of Chapter xxxviith. It is a development in which the Old passes out and the

New comes in, for the chosen people—a development that carries abolition along with it,—a development which began at the first Coming of Christ, and shall be completed at his Second Coming; one in which the Better Sacrifice of the Servant of Jehovah supplants the old sacrifices, and the sprinkling with clean water, by the Spirit, takes the place of vain ablutions. Zerubbabel never dreamed of erecting such a temple, nor receiving Ezekiel's " New Torah " as a "mandatory code for returning exiles." The prophets of the Exile and Restoration well knew that this wonderful picture was no " imperfect memory " of Solomon's dilapidated House, nor " model for the Restoration," nor "Utopia," nor " Platonic Scheme," nor " Fancy sketch," invented to beguile the weary hours of the *elite* in the Gola ; much less the " raw rudiment of the Pentateuchal priest-code," as the Graf-Wellhausen, and Colenso-Kuenen-Duhm, and Robertson Smith-School, upturningly teach. One thing was fixed as the " Hills of Olam," viz.: That Ezekiel's tableau of Israel's future could not be realized until the close of Daniel's 70th week, and that *this fulfilment was conditioned absolutely on Israel's repentance as a people, and the finishing of Israel's apostasy.* Ezek. xliv:7–12.

Once more. If, notwithstanding the *Similarities* between Ezekiel's picture and the Mosaic worship, the *Differences* are so great as to prove that Mosaism was then "waxing old"; and, furthermore, these *Differences* so great as also to prove that the picture was neither intended for, nor could be realized in, the times of the Restoration under Zerubbabel ; and, yet more, that the picture is not that of the New Testament Church drawn in Old Testament colors, since its realization could only occur after the close of Daniel's 70th week, still future; it is equally clear that, notwithstanding some *Similarities* between it and John's picture of the New Jerusalem, the *Differences* are so great as to prove that Ezekiel's vision of the Temple and Jerusalem does not belong to the final glorified New Earth, although it adumbrates the same. The Temple Ezekiel describes is that of the Millennial Age, " the 1000 years" of John; located in historic Palestine regenerate and reconstructed at Christ's Appearing. The transformation of the Holy Land is not the final new creation which extends to the entire Planet, but only the first step in the great cosmical process of renewal which culminates through a last catastrophe, in that remotest End. So Crusius, Lange, Christlieb, Rothe, Grau, Volck, Koch, Christiani, Ewald, Rinck, Karsten, Van Oosterzee, Delitzsch, Orelli, and many more. Strongly realistic, the prophet locates the realities *this side* the final glorified New Heaven and Earth. This is clear from the *geographical points* named in Chapters xlvii:10, 15, 19, 20 and xlviii:1, and from the references to the Dead " Sea," xlvii:8, the Mediterranean ".Sea," xlvii:10, 15–20, the "river Jordan" xlvii:18, the " Desert" xlvi:8, the " mountain," i. e. Zion xliv:12, and to the " borders of the land of Israel " given to the patriarchs in covenant, xl:2; xlv:4, 8; xlvii:13, 14. *Such designations find no place in John's picture of the glorified New Earth.* The marked *Differences* between the two pictures of Ezekiel and John show clearly that Ezekiel's vision is that of the kingdom of the 1000 years *this side* the final New Jerusalem. Ezekiel describes a Temple. John says, " I saw no Temple therein." Rev. xxi:22. Ezekiel's land is bounded by the " sea." In John's territory there is " no more sea," xxi:1. Ezekiel speaks of the "land of Israel." John speaks of a " New Earth," xxi:1. In

Ezekiel, the "Holy City" is built up from the ground
and "lifted high." In John, the "Holy City" is seen
"descending from God out of Heaven," xxi:2, 10, and
is the redeemed "Bride." Furthermore, the *measures*
in Ezekiel are insignificant, diminutive, compared with
the colossal magnitudes in John. In Ezekiel, the
"Glory" dwells in the Temple. In John it "lightens"
the whole City with its over-streaming splendor. Yet
more. The vision of the "living waters," in Ezekiel,
xlvii:1-12, is precisely that in Zechariah, xiv:8, and Joel
iii:18, realized at Messiah's Second Coming, and connected with the physical changes in the territory of
Judah, Zech. xiv:4-13; Jer. xxxii:38-40. They flow East
and West, summer and winter, out from Jerusalem elevated, and pass through the Acacia-Valley, Joel iii:18,
imparting life everywhere, and empty into the Dead
and Mediterranean seas. It is, evidently, the commencement of that cosmical regeneration and glorification of which Paul speaks, when "the creature itself is
freed from the bondage of corruption," and passes,
under the glorifying Spirit, "into the liberty of the glory
of the sons of God," Rom. viii:21, and embraces the
whole land of Palestine, and Judah especially, in whose
midst "the mountain of the Lord's house" stands "exalted," Isa. ii:2; Mic. iv:1; Zech. xiv.16. This, however, is not the universal regenesis of the Planet, but
the preparation of its theocratic middle-point for the
glorious kingdom of the 1000 years, in which Israel
stands pre-eminent. The moral process of development
has already passed over into the material, through the
resurrection from the dead, and where the children of
the resurrection are, there nature shares their liberty
and glory. Even the neighboring "Desert shall rejoice
and blossom as the rose," Isa. xxxv:1, and "be like Eden,

the Garden of the Lord," Isa. li:3, while above the City and "over all, the Glory shall be a covering," Isa. iv:5. But, entrancing as this vision is, it is *not* John's vision of the "Bride," the "Holy City" *after* the close of the 1000 years, but the vision of a state of things *before* that close, and in which the "Beloved City," Rev. xx:9, appears as the metropolis of an earthly kingdom whose overthrow is sought by Satan let loose, and by Gog and Magog, an expedition *impossible* on the final New Earth.

The argument, therefore, of the post millennialists, that because *Isaiah* introduces his picture of the Millennial Age with the announcement of a "New Heavens and Earth," Isa. lxv:17, *therefore*, his description following that *must be that of John's New Jerusalem, or else John's New Jerusalem must be that of the Millennial Age*, and Joel, Hosea, Isaiah, Micah, Daniel, Ezekiel, and John picture only *one* Age, the 1000 years being the time of the final New Heaven and Earth,— falls to the ground. *We cannot identify the* 1000 *years with the Eternal State.* This is set aside (1) By the manifold *Differences* between the pictures themselves; (2) *By the law of prophetic perspective;* (3) *By the common use of the same terms to express different stages of the one great development of the one Kingdom of God; and* in its different aspects, moral and material, spiritual and cosmical, down to the final consummation. All this, Hofmann, Delitzsch, Rothe, Luthardt, Lange, Volck, and Koch, have set forth in the most convincing manner. The Millennial Age, and the final New Heaven and Earth, are the *Two Great Phases* of the wide and *Total End*, as seen, far off, by the prophets, and undiscriminated, because blended in perspective, yet clearly out-rolled, and separated in John's Apocalypse, intimations of which are, however, already given, even in the prophets themselves, and in the Apostles. And thus the problem is resolved, and presented to faith and hope, precisely as the consummation will declare it. The *Order of the Eschata* is the same in both Ezekiel and John; (1) Israel in their land, sealed, and delivered from the rage of their last oppressor, Israel brought back from the sword. (2) The Resurrection from the dead. (3) The "Many Days," or 1000 years, of the priestly Kingdom. (4) Gog's destruction. And, if we supplement the *Eschata*, from Isaiah, we shall find the Order still the same, (1) Israel restored and Antichrist destroyed; (2) The Resurrection from the dead; (3) The Multitude of Days, or 1000 years; (4) Satan and his hosts let loose, for final Judgment; (5) The New Heaven and Earth, of which the Millennial Age was the mirror and the type transient and imperfect. On the basis of the *Similarities* John develops the final glorious picture of the New Jerusalem, and heightens it to special clearness and particularity, free from all temporal limitations.

The *"Symbolical* Interpretation" of Chapters xl–xlviii, and in fact of Ezekiel's whole Apocalypse, Chapters xxxvii–xlviii, is the name given, to their favorite mode of exposition, by the allegorizers and spiritualizers of these sections. As already said, these chapters are apocalyptic and eschatological, like the visions of Daniel, Zechariah, and Isaiah. They are a "Vision." But to assert that it is only a Symbol, and "One Vast Symbol of the *Church*," is simply to assume the "spiritualistic interpretation," and *beg the whole question*. Moreover, what a symbolical vision is, we know. It is like the vision of the 4 Beasts in Daniel, or of the Monarchy-Image Nebuchadnezzar saw in his dream. How, also, to interpret these we know. But what the "*symbolical inter-*

pretation of a symbol" is, what the *"figure of a figure"* is,
it might be interesting to inquire, if, the evaporation
did not too soon elude our grasp. It seems to be something "volatile and airy," like the idea of the "Absolute"
which has no "existence," but only "being," and gets
into being somehow, by its "self-becoming." At best
it is merely an abstraction, or *"quid ignotum"* which
Agnostics might admire, and reminds one seriously of
Cicero's famed definition of God, *"aliquid immensum
infinitumque!"* Such is ideal and symbolic Israel, their
Temple, City, and Land. It is something in which the
concrete real has disappeared. This view goes back to
the days of the platonizing Origen and Augustine, both
men of grandeur and renown, who, confounding the
"Church" with the "Kingdom," idealized Israel out of
his rights and place in future history. It became the
mediæval creed, and, naturally enough, influenced the
Reformers, not wholly escaped from Rome's traditions,
and lacking the time to study Eschatology, yet rebuking a false Chiliasm, and opening the door to the true.
It is held by many noble men who see in the "Psalms
of David" only the "Church" whenever "Israel,"
"Jacob," "Zion," or "Jerusalem" are named. Our
Christian Hymnology, so beautiful, also supports the
same exegesis as it stands on "Jordan's stormy banks."
The habit of allegorizing becomes a part of devotion,
and the result is that "Ideal Israel" emerges in the consciousness of believers as the only Israel known to faith
and prophecy! In addition to this, the Higher Criticism helps the same cogitation. The main thing in
prophecy is said to be "the inner thought," the "Idea
underneath"; not the words. There is no verbal inspiration. The words of God are human, the chaff to the
wheat, the waist-bands and ruffles, or the outer-cloth-

ing on the body, the "non-essential details," "generous expression," "Oriental figure," in short, the "rough rind of a sacred bulb," to be peeled and thrown away, or an "old bottle" into which "new wine," when poured — the wine of spiritual interpretation,— explodes the leathern flask. The only remark, necessary here, is this, viz.: That the whole trouble with this mode of interpretation is, that every interpreter fixes the amount of "details" to suit himself, either rejecting them as "mere form," or sublimating them into absurdities so grotesque as to destroy respect for both the interpreter and the interpretation, if not for the thing interpreted. It retains or remits, binds or looses, *ad libitum*, until most, if not all, of the vision has faded away.

In opposition to all this, the Bible speaks with a clear-ringing sound. Israel "abides" Israel, and the Millennial Kingdom, of which Israel restored is the sustaining center, and of which these Chapters of Ezekiel are a glowing picture, *follows* Israel's national and personal resurrection at the Second Coming of the Lord. To that glorious End the eyes of the exiles were directed, a Redemption they deemed due, indeed, at their return from Babylonian Exile, but which the prophet Daniel was assured could only accrue at the end of the 70th week. And in this we rest, our own eyes turned thither also. What Ezekiel did was to impress upon despairing Israel, scattered everywhere, and dead, like the bones in the valley, *the absolute certainty of God's omnipotence, faithfulness, and compassion, in the End of the Days, and that nothing could ever cause Him to forget His covenant, or alter the thing that had gone out of His lips.* Dead Israel shall yet awake. Broken Israel shall be reunited. Down-trodden Jerusalem shall yet arise. The Temple, laid in ruins, shall be rebuilt. The Outcasts shall be gathered to their home. The blindness shall be taken from their eyes, and reproach no more afflict their name. A new, a holy, royal, priestly, nation they shall be. As once Israel formed the nucleus of the "Church," so again Israel shall form the nucleus of the "Kingdom." In that kingdom, and its glory, we Gentiles shall have a share ; and, with Abraham and the patriarchs, Ezekiel and the prophets, David and the pious kings of Judah ; and yet more, with Christ and His Apostles, with Martyrs, Confessors, Reformers, and saints of all ages, enter in, recount the conflict and the victory, the danger and the faith, renew our study of God's word, hold converse with the Lord Himself, and, blended in one fellowship, unite to sing one song — the "*song of Moses and the Lamb.*" Does this appear too wonderful ? "*Neum Yehovah! It is the Utterance of Jehovah, Doer of these things!*"

Part 11
Our Present Age— The Christian State

Connected with the delusion of a Millennium in this present age, is the Idea of the so-called *"Christian-State"* —an idea gotten somewhere, but neither from the Prophets, Christ, or His Apostles. It is one of the false lures of the age. Forgetful of the law of deterioration in the march of empires, seen in the Monarchy-Colossus, and of the succession of the 4 Beasts, each later one inferior to the former, and of the continued *Beastly* and *Metallic* character of Gentile government, politics and power, till the Lord come, the admirers of human perfectibility, and priests of optimist progress, still boast of our " *Christianized civilization* " as the van-courier of millennial glory ready to burst over all the world. This is a part of the fine arts of " Satan transformed into an Angel of Light," teaching, as he first did, in the Garden, an improvement to man's condition by doubting the Word of God, then denying it,—a science of progress by means of Knowledge gained through transgression, and of Unbelief usurping the place of faith. " Yea, *hath* God said ?" " Ye shall be *as God !*" Gen. iii:1, 5. Subtle Beast,—he always
439

talks so! He dazzles and deceives. He seems righteous and philanthropic. *"Therefore it is no great thing
if his ministers also fashion themselves as ministers of
righteousness,"*—*" deceitful workers,"*—*" as apostles of
Christ,"* II Cor. xi:13–15. Professedly Christian men
shall do the Devil's work teaching this same method of
"progress," and women, too, shall assist to spread the
fascination. The very best thing God has given us,
His own Word, they will denounce as " Pessimism,"
teaching an " Optimism " born from its perversion.
*Corruptio optimi pessima; the Corruption of the best is the
worst corruption."* *"Habetur optima pessima; the worst is
esteemed the best."* It is the old story, from the Gates
of Eden downward, along with the curse, through all
history. A varnished lie is worse than naked poison.
" Great Babylon," bearing the Christian name, a
church at every corner, a preacher on every street, is
worse than the Chaldean City whose king was God's
rod to " destroy, and make a hissing, and desolation, of
Judah " the *Messianic State* of the old civilization. And
worse than Gold-headed Babylon was Iron-legged
Rome, though more *" advanced"* by 600 years. Men
seem oblivious of the fact that *it was at the very time of
the birth of the 4th Beast Christ was born ;* that it was
under the *"Empire"* of Rome, in its first imperial head,
claiming divine honors, *"Divus Augustus,"* and enrolling
Judea as a tributary province, that Messiah's manger
was made at Bethlehem, and that, down to the present
hour, Jerusalem still sits in the dust, trodden and
stamped by the Gentile power, the scepter departed
from Judah. They seem intent to forget, that though
this " Beast" has been christianized full 1500 years,
with a wound in its head, it still *"lives,"* and has poured
out the blood of God's saints, with more inexcusable

guilt than even in its old pagan condition, and that Christendom, to-day, is sinking beneath a weight of transgression unknown to heathen lands. They forget that the " Times of the Gentiles," in which we are living, our Church-Period, are the Times of the 4th Beast or Roman World-Power, divided into various kingdoms; a Beastly and Metallic power, whose essential character, in spite of Christianity, remains unchanged down to the time of its destruction; a materialistic civilization of iron force and will, yet with the weakness of clay in it, pervaded by a spirit of sensuality, and crowned with a false science, and false philosophy, over which Christianity has little or no control.

If we seek for the " *Christian State* " in Prophecy, we shall seek long, and travel far, before our quest is satisfied. It certainly will not appear in pre-Christian times; not in the Gold, the Silver, or Brass, of the Colossus; not in the Lion, Bear, Leopard, Ram, or He-Goat, among the Beasts. Shall we find it in the Iron and Clay, or in the 4th Beast, the anonymous monster? What prophet, what apostle, speaks to us about the " *Christian State ?* "

With just emphasis, Professor Kübel asks, " Where shall we find, in the Prophets, in Christ, in Paul, or in John, the idea of the *Christian State*, in this age, as that of the realization of the Kingdom of God ?"* With equal emphasis, Professor Bleek asserts that " nowhere in prophecy is the idea of a *Principatus Christianorum*, sprung from the Gentiles, known to the Times of the Gentiles." † And with what unanswerable power has

---

* Offenbaung, in Strack-Zöckler. pp. 453, 454.
† Erklasung d. drei erst. Evang. II. 372.

Auberlen shown that the "external Christianization of
the World-Power is only the temporary wound of the
Beast still unchanged in its heart, anti-christian still, notwithstanding its Christian order, culture, and civilization ; a civil structure accepting Christianity externally,
the Church accepting the World internally, both
parties meeting half-way, the Church and the World
making mutual concessions, the Beast Christianized, the
Church Bestialized, she the loser, it the gainer, the
Beast carrying the Harlot, the bestiality, proud intellectual culture, science, and wealth, of Christendom,
leading thousands away from, and preventing others
from coming to, the knowledge of Christ!"* How for-
cibly true those words which smite our idol of modern
Christian civilization! Herein consists the *gigantic lie
and narrow mindedness* of our generation, that our *civilization* is thought to be the highest thing, accepted as a
surrogate for grace, and for regeneration by the Spirit
of the living God. *"It is the idol of the modern world."*†
How true the words of Hahn, indorsed by Weber,
Gebhardt, Auberlen, Kliefoth, and how many more!
that, in the time of the so-called Christian State, " the
professing Christian Church becomes *Babylon*, (*Confusion*) the Harlot being not merely the City of Rome,
nor the Roman Church alone, but all Churches in
Christendom, without the Spirit and Life of our Lord
Jesus, apostate from moral righteousness, corrupt, life-
less, worldly, seeking the pleasures of the flesh, open to
the influence of all false spirits and false teachers, having a name to live, yet governed by the spirit, maxims,
policies, and principles, of nature and the world."‡

---

* Der Prophet Daniel 313–360.
† Ibid 234.
‡ Hahn. Briefe u. Leid. ub. d. Offenbar. Johan. Band v. §6. 1820.

" The time comes," says Professor Milligan, " when the Church *as a whole* will be more carnal than spiritual, more worldly than heavenly. The true members of Christ's flock will be fewer in number than the false. *The world will penetrate into the very sanctuary of God, and will not be rooted out until the Judge of all takes to Himself His great power, and reigns.* The longer the Church lasts as an outward institution in the world, the more does she naturally tend to realize the picture of 'Babylon' in the Apocalypse, 'that Great City,' the emblem of the degenerate Church. *Babylon is not the Church of Rome in particular.* Deeply, no doubt, that church has sinned, and because of this we interpret Babylon as Christian *Rome*. Yet, *the interpretation is false.* The Harlot is *wholly* what she seems. Christian Rome was never *wholly*, what, on *one side* of her character she was so largely. She has maintained the truth of Christ as against idolatry, and preferred poverty to splendor in a way Protestantism has never done, and nurtured the noblest types of devotion the world has ever seen. Above all, if at times, she has allied herself with kings, at other times she has the rather trampled kings beneath her feet, as when, in the interests of the poor and oppressed she has taught proud barons and imperial tyrants to quail before her. For deeds like these, her record is not with the Beast but with the Lamb. Babylon cannot be Christian Rome ; and nothing has been more injurious to Protestant Churches than the impression that the two were identical, and that, by withdrawing from communion with the Pope, they wholly freed themselves from alliance with the spiritual harlot. *Babylon embraces much more than Rome, and illustrations of what she is, lies nearer our own door.* Wherever professedly Christian men have thought the

world's favor better than its reproach, esteemed its
honors a more desirable possession than its shame,
courted ease rather than suffering, self-indulgence
rather than self-sacrifice, and substituted covetousness
in grasping for generosity in distributing what they
had, there the spirit of Babylon has been manifested.
In short, we have in the great Harlot-City, neither the
Church as a whole nor the Romish Church in particular,
but *all who profess to be Christ's flock and are not, denying in their lives the main characteristic by which they ought
to be distinguished,—viz., that they follow Christ.*"* Such
is Christendom apostate from Christ. Such the Church
under the so-called "*Christian State.*" Civil government is, indeed, an ordinance of God for the preservation of natural right and social order, and Paul made
use of it as such, counseling obedience to Cæsar and
the "Powers that be," when one was a Nero, both
pagan, and the "*Christian State*" unknown. The
"Christian Empire" of Constantine, and the "Holy
Roman Empire" of later times, are simply the "Beast"
with a wound in his head by means of Christianity, yet
alive, while still *seeming* to be slain. It is part of the
Colossus, and no part of the Kingdom of Christ. So is
it with the so-called "Christianized World-Power" everywhere, whether that of Kaiser, Czar, King, Queen, or
His Majesty, the "People." Its place is in the lower
part of the Iron-legs, and in the Clay and Iron Toes.
It is precisely where the Mountain-Stone will smite it
one day in order to clear the world of its presence,
and introduce the Kingdom of Christ. It belongs to
the "Ten Horns" out of which the Antichrist will come.
It lives and moves, and has its being, in the Interval

---

*Professor W. Milligan, D. D., University of Aberdeen. Revelation
of St. John, 179, 183, 184. (1886).

between the 69th and 70th Weeks of Daniel, and is doomed to destruction. It is that institution of Gentile Sovereignty which, in its most Christian pretension, refuses to recognize God in its Constitution, and glories in the fact that it stands *neutral and indifferent,* in law, toward the religion of Jesus Christ, protecting equally the most corrupt forms of Christianity and religious Heathenism, with the purest and the best; a State not daring to recognize Jesus Christ, by law, yet boasting of its peerless Christian institutions, licensing brothels, gambling dens, and saloons, by its Christian State Legislation as one of the prudent ways, approved by God, to " reform the world " and " promote the Kingdom of Christ,"— the *ad majorem gloriam Dei* doctrine which does evil that good may come, " whose damnation is just." In its most Christian portion, the United States, it spends the sum of $900,000,000 per annum, for *whisky* alone, chief staple in the national revenue, while, on the breast of Europe to-day, no less than 28,000,000 of woman-born, enrolled and armed to the teeth, stand ready to imbrue their hands in each other's blood;— officered, led, inspired, and paid by the " *Christian State.*"* The appalling corruption, venality, drunken-

---

*"Europe, to-day, is an *armed camp.* Over 28,000,000 of men, all in the prime of manhood, stand enrolled, to expose their lives in the next great war. The annual cost of this force exceeds 150,000,000 pounds sterling ($750,000,000). Since the Franco-Prussian war, seventeen years ago, 1,500,000 000 pounds sterling ($7,500,000,000) have been spent in preparation for the coming war. In one week, Germany can set 750.000 men in French territory, and France bring 850,000 to her frontier."—*London Daily News, Jan. 14, 1889.* "The British fleet, to-day, is inadequate for England's defense. France has everything to gain and nothing to lose in a war with Britain in the near future. I have no words strong enough to convey what I believe would be the judgment of the peoples of our magnificent Empire if we lost our great heritage, as we undoubtedly should, were we caught unprepared, through want of a sufficient navy." *Lord Charles Beresford in the Nineteenth Century, Jan.,* 1889. While thus preparing for war, 233 members of the British Parliament have memorialized the President of the United States, and Congress, to take steps to conclude a *treaty* with Great

ness, perjury, betting, pooling, purchase and sale of
votes, detraction, libel, and violence, seen in municipal,
state, and national elections, and in all Gentile politics ;
the base and degrading arts and devices employed by
Christian men to win office and power, with expectation of plunder besides ; the whole spirit and temper of
the times ; the proverbial dishonesty in all business and
all professions ; the lust for war in order to make
money ; the *Public Press* advertising every hole of vice
on earth, pouring out, as from a wide and stenchful
sewer, its endless stream of daily filth, into the bosom
of every home, and dumping, daily, at every man's
door, its endless car-loads of obscene incident and lewd
inuendo, scavengered up from all the highways, gutters,
slums and palaces, of all lands, until society wades
knee-deep in a cesspool of infamy whose atmosphere
asphyxiates its life ; the prodigious millions invested by
Christian men in Sabbath-breaking and crime-increasing
corporations ; the Titanic schemes of self-aggrandize-
ment; the oppression of the poor; the amounts spent in

Britain to settle, by a court of arbitration, all disputes *between the two
governments* which cannot be settled by diplomacy.   Fear alone dictates the
policy. Statesmen seem, however, not to know that, only after the last great
anti-christian conflict, such a thing is possible, and that the *first High Court
of Arbitration for National Differences, will be set up in Jerusalem,* bringing
universal peace, when men, weary of their sanguinary game, will flock to
Zion, for "*Light and Right,*" and "*learn war no more;*" a consummation to
be realized only at the "*End of the Days,*" when "*Christ Himself shall judge
among the Nations.*"   Isa. ii:2–4 ; Micah iv:1–3 ; Psa. xlvi:8–11.
    As a result chiefly due to the whisky Traffic, and licensing of Lust
by the " Christian State," is the appalling prostitution of the *marriage* relation.   February 20, 1889, Commissioner Carroll D. Wright, had reported to
Congress that, in 1867, the number of *Divorces* granted was 9.937 ; in 1886,
the number was 25,535, and for the periods between these dates 328,716.
The "*Christian Church*" has ceased to punish the guilty parties, or hold
responsible those who are instrumental in the destruction of the family and
the home. She retains in full communion, and in good standing, men and
women openly convicted by the State, of crimes against the laws of both God
and man. And she does this of set purpose : a "*respecter of persons*" in her
administration, making Christ and the Church the shield and minister of sin.

a gorgeous architecture, a luxurious living, and un-stinted pleasures; the heaping up of riches for the last times, and the rage and rush for more; all these have already made even the mention of the name of "*Chris-tian-State*," a theme for scurrility, scorn, and contempt. After 1800 years, in spite of all that is good, this is its latest physiognomy, and is but a meager feature of its unspeakable enormity.* No! Christendom is not a "*Christian-State*," albeit there are Christians in it. Its names in God's word, are "Babylon the Great," the "Mother-Harlot," and the "Dwellers on the Earth." Our "*politeuma*" is not here. Our "*civitas*" is one whose "Builder and Maker is God." We are "pilgrims and strangers," in this "Christian-State," if we are Christ's. Our one and only object in praying "for all in authority" is that we may be allowed to lead a godly life, resist the Devil wherever we find him, whether in Church or State, pay the penalty due to true fidelity, labor, suffer, and do God's Will, and "wait for His Son

---

*Crime Increasing. "The police authorities of more than 100 cities in the United States furnish statistics to the *New York* papers, as to the astounding increase of crime. These statistics show that Crime is more than keeping pace with the population, on the average. It is in advance of it, in spite of all legislation, moral influence, and punitive or reformatory measures. Burglaries, robberies, assassinations, the recklessness of human life, drunkenness, infanticides, prostitution, and the general corruption of young and old, male and female, have become alarming. Among women, left to provide for themselves, especially the young, the criminals, and de-bauchees are the worst. The sources of crime in our public play-houses, gilded saloons, private resorts of pleasure and places of amusement, the lax morals of our social life, and the example of many prominent in our com-munity, are making a Sodom and Gomorrah of the land. The picture is not an inviting one but full of material for grave consideration and anxious inquiry."—*New York Times, March* 21, 1889.
A dispatch from *London, March* 20, 1889, *to the New York Herald*, says, "The increase in *capital* crimes is attracting much attention. No less than 22 men and women, within a short period, are now under sentence of death in the United Kingdom, and will be executed within the next six weeks. This, however, is only what might be expected, for the chief cities of Christendom are reeking in crime."

from Heaven." Gigantic is the misconception, to dream that God has given the Church, unable to reform herself, to build the Christian State up to a Kingdom of Christ, or to reform the world. God's wisdom is not so foolish. Neither in the Times decreed upon the Gentiles, nor the Weeks decreed upon the Jews, is the idea of a "Christian State ' found anywhere in prophecy. What prophecy aims at is the Kingdom of Christ, first of all in the heart by the power of the Spirit, and next, the Kingdom of Christ as an outward Polity built upon the ruins of Gentile Sovereignty and Gentile Empire, at His Second Coming. Until then, the "*Beast*" lives! and what we are pleased to call the Christian State, is simply the *Christian-Beast*, either the *Horns* of the Beast, or the *Toes* of the Colossus!—a Beast whose power is *in check* for the present, but soon to be *unchecked** and drive Christianity back to the wall. Its wound will then be healed, in proportion as Christianity dies out of Christendom, and Heathenism revives.

The picture of the times of the Church and the State, whether independent of each other, or in union, and of the concurrent operations of the servants of Christ, and of Satan, is given us too vividly in God's

---

*Whatever the " *What withholdeth* " may be, whether the Civil Power, social order, the true church, the State or the Gospel, the " *He who now withholds*," II Thess ii: 6, 7, can only be the *Exalted Redeemer, Christ Himself*, to whom " all power " is given, not only to make the wrath of man praise Him, but "to restrain the remainder." Ps. lxxvi:10. The Antichrist will be revealed "*in his own time*." That time, we know, is the 70th Week of Daniel, Dan. ix:27, the last 1260 days of which are his persecuting supremacy, Dan. vii:25, xii.7, Rev. xiii:5. His *Parousia is obstructed, now, by the purpose of God and the ' Times of the Gentiles" in which the gospel goes to the Gentiles, between the 69th and 70th weeks.* Then, when the full number of God's elect is ·· *taken out*," and the gospel has been preached as a witness to all the world, the *Obstruction* will be "*taken out of the way*," the flood-tide of lawlessness inundate Christendom, and the " Man of Sin be revealed."

word to be misunderstood by any who care to know the truth. It is under the *Parable of the Sower*, the Missionary activity of the Church is represented, in this present age. It is under the *Parable of the Tares* the Missionary activity of the Devil, during the same period, is set forth ; and the Christian scholar who will give the world a treatise, with full statistics of the Devil's missions, and stations, their progress and expenditures, in the Christian-State, will do more to set the Word of God, concerning this present age, in its true light, than has yet been done by the one-sided views so constantly presented. It is under the *Parable of the Mustard Seed* we see the outward extension of the Church to a tree so large and overspreading that even the fowls of the air build convenient nests in its branches, and vultures make its forks their home. It is in the *Parable of the Leaven* we learn the inward corruption of the Church, by her own act, the Woman secreting false doctrine in the pure truth designed for the children's bread. It is in the *Parable of the Nobleman* we learn the attitude of the great majority who, during the time of the "Christian State," exult in rebellion against Christ, refusing to acknowledge Him. Wherever millennial glory is, it certainly is *not here, in this age!* The conversion of the world to Christ is *not in this present time!* Side by side, the servants of Christ and those of the Devil work on, every handful of wheat accompanied by a hundred handfuls of cockle sown even more widely. The statistics of 1,000,000 Christians, mean the statistics of 10,000,000 not Christians. A handful of wheat scattered on the earth, means three-fourths of it picked up by Satan himself, or scorched by the heat, or choked by the thorns. Tares everywhere, and so abundant and intermingled with the wheat, and so

resembling the wheat, that it is perilous to undertake a
separation.   Surprise indeed !   *"An Enemy hath done
this!"*   It is the Devil's sleepless missionary enterprise,
supported by trade, commerce, agriculture, distilleries,
breweries, railroads, politics, science, philosophy, art ;
a *Zizanian Christianity* interpreted to mean a *Millennial
Glory*, under the fostering care of the "Christian State!"
The picture of the Christian State, on its trading side,
is that of a Chamber of Commerce revolting against an
absent King.   On its agricultural side, it is that of a
Wheat Field crowded with cockle.   In both it is a vast
Area, the *"World,"* under the *"god of this world,"* filled
with growing grain, good and bad, in the midst of
which is a Colossus, and then a "Beast" having seven
heads and ten horns, stamping and goring everywhere,
a false prophet at his side preaching lies, the Devil
loose and roaring like a lion, ravening wolves prowling
for their prey, unclean spirits, "like frogs," repeating
their unending *croak*, the days of Lot and of Noah,
millions of men butchering each other, millions more
staggering drunk to the ground, palaces of lust and
temples of mammon, far as the eye can see, churches
also everywhere, and some preachers and pamphleteers
applauding the glories of the Millennium!   *No!*   The
rhetoric of a Millennium of righteousness and peace, in
this age, before Christ comes, is the eloquence of falsehood, pleasing to Satan, and offensive to God.   Down
to the "End," it shall be as it is, until *"all things that
offend,"* *"paṇta ta skaṅdala,"* the bundled crimes of the
Christian Church shall be removed, by judgment, from
the kingdom, and the polluted *"Christian State"* be
heard of no more!   The words of Christ are plain.
Upon the World-Acre stands, now, the seed of the
Kingdom of Heaven while, side by side, grow the

Devil's tares, numerous as they are surprising; nor
ever will the glory of the Kingdom come,— be the
Christian-State what it may,— until the sickles and the
angels have done their work! It is the double-work of
Church-missions, and Devil-missions, which, for a time,
procrastinates the Advent and the Harvest.

The Holy Spirit, as if anxious to guide us aright,
has multiplied pictures of our present age, and of the
condition of the Church and times of the Christian
State, together. Conquest, territorial acquisition, vast
commercial enterprises, immense riches suddenly
amassed, mammon-worship, harlotry, libertinism,
world philosophy, science, education, culture, iniquity,
formalism, love waxing cold, treacheries, infidelity,
apostasy, demonic spiritism, missions, revolutions,
blind Laodicean optimism, and final judgment. It is the
same elsewhere; "false teachers" " seducers, waxing
worse and worse," "Satan transformed into an angel of
light," "all seeking their own, and not the things that
are Christ's," "many walking who are enemies of the
cross of Christ, whose end is destruction, whose God
is their belly, who glory in their shame, who mind
earthly things," a "persecution" for the godly, "false
brethren," "brother betraying brother," intolerance of
"sound doctrine," "itching ears," "building, planting,
marrying and giving in marriage," "lies," "perjuries,"
"covenant-breaking," "thefts," "robberies" and "slan-
ders," "perilous times," "gangrene," moral "rottenness,"
"the wages of unrighteousness," "the way of Cain,"
"love of self," spiritual "decay," a "name to live yet
dead," love of " pre-eminence " in the church, "love
of the world," dominion of "the world, the flesh
and the devil," "the lust of the eye, of the flesh,
and the pride of life,"—while God's true saints, in the

"*Christian State*," are a jeweled "few" like to 7,000 out of 4,000,000, in Elijah's time, or the "remnant" in Isaiah's day, but for whom Israel had been " as Sodom and Gomorrah !"

Already, by hyperbole of expression, we say the gospel has gone to all lands, the Bible been translated into all tongues, and Christianity achieved a substantial victory over Satan's empire. Our vouchers for this, are Paris, London, Berlin, St. Petersburg, Vienna, Edinboro', Glasgow, Dublin, Boston, New York, Chicago, St. Louis, Cincinnati, New Orleans, Washington, etc., etc., the paragons of Christendom, like which, if the whole planet were, it would be ripe for the sickle of judgment ! *Blood-shedding, adulterous, intemperate and mammon-loving, Christendom! Sabbath-breaking too!* And this, after 18 centuries, the paraded boast of pre-advent Millennialism ! Blow the trumpet in Bethhaven ! What a phalanx of able and scholarly men challenge attention to the fact that, "*Not one nation yet, in its general mass, has accepted Christianity, but only individuals, and, relatively to the population, few!*" (Thiersch.) If we ask what the prophets looked for, what the Apostles expected, and what John saw in vision, in this state of things, there is but one answer, and that is, not the conversion of the *world*, but *the waxing of Anti-christianity to its height, in the very midst of Christendom, the crisis, the conversion of Israel, and Advent of the Lord to Judgment*. It is the one answer, everywhere. Only *after* Israel has become a *Christian Nation*, worthy of the name, not before, will the Nations, *as such*, become Christian. Rev. xv:4; Deut. xxxii:43. It is the one uniform doctrine in Moses, in the Prophets, in Jesus, in the Apostles. In manner, the most vivid, John distinguishes between those converted *before* the Advent, i. e.

individuals, Jews and Gentiles, and those converted *after* the Advent, i. e., *"Nations,"* Rev. iii:5, 8, 20; Rev. xv:4.

Most striking, in this respect, is the difference of representation in the 7 Epistles, from that in the later part of the Apocalypse; the difference between the Times of the Gentiles and the Times that follow Israel's conversion when Gentile Times are no more! How different the picture of the *"Churches"* from that of the *"Kingdom!"* In these Epistles, adumbrating the whole history of Christendom, or the Church-Period, between the 69th and 70th Weeks, we see, even in the first group of 3, Ephesus "fallen from her first love"; Smyrna alone unblamed because still faithful in the fire, and in the prison, Satan still raging, foes blaspheming, and Pergamos, though holding her faith, yet fellowshiping mammon-loving Balaamites, Nicolaitans, and dwelling "in Satan's seat." In the second group of 4, darker still is the scene: *The world has penetrated the Churches, all which have become secular.* In Thyatira, it is only a "remnant" we find maintaining the faith. The crowd still fellowship those who "seduce" the servants of Christ to heathenish ways. In Sardis a "few names" are worthy to walk in white. Philadelphia has only a "little power," and is urged to "hold fast." In Laodicea, the world is supreme. Surely, this is not a *Millennial* picture! And, when come to the 70th Week, it is *"Babylon"* we see, symbol of the false professing church, ripe for the judgments of God, as it will be when Christ shall come!

But how different the scene in the Age that follows the Advent! How different after Babylon's fall, and Antichrist's doom, and the passing away of Gentile supremacy over the Jew! It is Israel converted, now, all Nations acknowledging Christ, Jerusalem lifted to glory, the Saints awaked from their beds, the Kingdom come, and the Lord, Himself, enthroned over all! And what is made clear as the sun is the fact that this wondrous *Accession of the Nations, as such, is the result of the Conversion of Israel, as such, at the second coming of Christ.** And, herein, John is in perfect harmony with all other Scripture which affirms the same thing. It is when the "Set Time to favor Zion" has come, and Israel's sons, reclaimed to Christ, "take pleasure in her stones," and "pity her dust," and the Lord shall appear in His glory, "to build up Zion," that, then, "the *Nations shall fear the name of the Lord, and all Kings of the earth His glory,*" Ps. cii:13–18. It is when He "breaks in pieces the oppressor," at the close of the 70th Week, and "judges among the poor of the people," that, then, "*All Nations fall down and serve Him,*" Psa. lxxii:4–13. It is when His "Wondrous works" and "Mighty acts," are known, and His "arm made bare," that, then, "*All Nations shall come and worship before Him,*" Ps. lxxxvi:9. So sounds the harp of David.† Most emphatic is the form and the repetition of this testimony that the *Nations* of the Planet, as such shall never be Christian

---

* "*The entrance of the Nations into the Kingdom of God* FOLLOWS *Israel's conversion.* They are prepared for it by *judicial* displays of Jehovah's majesty in the destruction of the enemies of His Kingdom. Those who are spared are filled with fear and trembling at His presence. It is the *deliverance of Israel effected by these judgments, and the Messianic Salvation thus brought to her people, which first awake in the Nations the desire to belong to God whom they have thus learned to know as the only Helper.* There is a full recognition of the *equality* of the Gentiles with the Jews in their relation to Christ and the blessings of salvation, yet this does not exclude the idea that. without prejudice to this *equality,* Israel as a Nation may take a high position in the perfected Kingdom of Christ. The entry of the Nations in the Kingdom of God and their *natural* fellowship with Israel are realized *through Israel* as the special possessor of these blessings." —*Prof. Riehm. Mess. Proph.* pp. 208, 785.

† *Christendom embraces already the whole living civilization of the Globe. But, if the matter be carefully looked into it will be found that not seldom, when men speak about the spread of Christianity, God and His Christ have*

Nations in any true sense of the term, acknowledging Christ as their Lawgiver and their Prince,
until *after* Israel as a nation has done the same.
When Israel is a "nation born in a day," then "the Lord
will gather all Nations and they shall come and see His
glory in Jerusalem." Isa. lxvi:18-21. Then " Kings
shall be nursing fathers and Queens shall be nursing
mothers" to that people, and "all Nations shall say,
Come, let us go up to the mountain of the Lord, and
to the House of the God of Jacob, and He will
teach us His ways and we will walk in His paths,"
Isa. xlix:12-23 ; ii:1-4. It is when the Lord "brings
again Zion" that "all the ends of the earth shall
see the Salvation of God," and *"together,"* and "Nations
shall come to her light, and kings to her Sunrise," Isa.
xxxii:7-10 ; xl:4 ; lx:1. And all this only upon the destruction of the last Antichrist and the deliverance of
Israel, at the Coming of Israel's *Goel* to Zion at the end
of Gentile times. Isa. lix:19-21. It is precisely what
the *Cithara-Players on the Glassy Sea* tell us in Rev.
xv:4. The whole Bible from Moses to John is a unit

---

no place in their thoughts. It is the *natural growth* of a Reign of Justice
they are dreaming of, as if the Truth could prevail and conquer the world
apart altogether from the supernatural power and grace of Christ. The
progress of Christianity is the progress of *a Mighty Prince, who "having
girded His sword upon His thigh rides forth prosperously in behalf of truth,
and meekness and righteousness."* The conversion of *"the peoples"* is to be
accomplished by the "declaration of His *Mighty-Acts."* The *Presence of
Christ* is that alone which can secure the victory. *It is quite unwarrantable
to explain this by saying that the blessing is to be wrought out by the pacific
doctrine and institutions with which Christ endowed the Church eighteen centuries ago. * * * It is when He comes to judge the earth,* that, then, He
will, by some storm of controversy, or of revolution, sweep away the institutions in which injustice has entrenched itself, even when the storms that agi-
tate the Nations are the Chariot in which He rides to take possession of the
Earth and make it an abode of righteousness and peace. *Arise, O God,
judge the Earth; for thou shalt inherit All Nations! "Even so; Come Lord
Jesus! Come quickly!"*—Prof. Binnie, Aberdeen. *The Psalms,* pp. 314-
326.

on this question, every prophet, and apostle, and our
Lord Himself, denying, point-blank, any World-con-
version, or any Millennial Kingdom before the Second
Advent.   Paul's description and distribution of the
Dispensations in Romans IX–XI, viz., the *Patriarchal*,
before the distinction between Jew and Gentile existed,
the *Jewish*, then the *Pre-Millennial Christian*, during
which the Jewish people, as such, abide in their
unbelief, then the *Glorious Millennial Age* following Israel's Conversion and the Redeemer's coming
to Zion, refute this patent folly.   The *"Nations"* of
the Earth, whose *Register* was chronicled when
God chose Abraham to be the father of the Jewish
people, and "suffered the Gentiles to walk in their
own ways," cherishing Israel as his "first born" national
son, are now, by Abraham's Seed, reclaimed, and
"bless themselves" in the same.   Genesis, Chapters X–
XII.   To place this consummation in the present time is
to pervert God's word.   John, David, Moses, all the
Prophets and Apostles are in harmony here, and the
Apocalypse is the combined light of all.   The idea of
the conversion of the world to Christ, before the Lord's
appearing, is unknown to this great book which covers
the whole present as well as the future.   On the contrary, *the masses in this present age, reject the gospel. The
field is filled with tares.*   Even under divine judgments,
they only the more " blaspheme," and refuse to " repent," Rev. ix:20, 21 ; xvi:9, 11.   *And this in the "Christian State!"*   So-called "Culture" and "Civilization" are
powerless to teach even decent respect for God !   The
"Church" becomes a "savorless salt."   More and more,
the "Christian State" is a tool of Satan.   *"At the House
of God judgment must begin;"*—a house trampling the
divine ordinance of a godly discipline under foot and

preferring respect of persons, numbers, wealth, undisturbed social relations, outward prosperity, peace, business-thrift and corruption, to fidelity, suffering, trial, righteous contention, and loss. We need no Bradlaugh, nor Ingersoll, now, to tell us this. And what the *"End"* shall be of a *Christendom dechristianized*, we already know. An impenitent, world-loving Christian is worse than a Christless pagan, harlot, or publican. Gomorrah and Sodom were *"not half"* as guilty as the Jerusalem Nebuchadnezzar burned. Ezek. xvi:48–51. Ninevites, Tyre and Sidon, Chorazin, Bethsaida, shall meet a milder fate than *the "Christian State" which*, like Capernaum, *"exalted to heaven shall yet be thrust down to hell!"*

POSTSCRIPT

"With Augustine arose the idea that the *Church* is the *Kingdom*, and this, with the changed political condition, and the position of the Church, under Constantine, led to the downfall of the *Chiliastic* doctrine. The vigor of its life departed, as persecutions ceased, and when Christianity began to sway the Civil Power, this was regarded as the 'Victory' the Millennium had promised. The Middle Age perpetuated this great error." *Semisch. Herzog. Real-Encyc. I.* 659.

"The view that Christianity will expand in this age to a World-Religion, and bring the Golden Time, as the product of its historical development, is *fundamentally false*, and opposed to the Word of God. It rests upon a false ground, the identification of the inner life of the Church with her outward extension. Its consequences are the struggle after Secular Power, *National* Churches, *National* Creeds, *National* Confessions, *National* Patronage, *National* Legislation, *Propagandism*, and passion for *Union*, fatal to the true life and mission of the Church. We need only remember Constantine's time and the nominal conversion of the masses, mere *name-Christians*. The hope of a Christian-State ending in a Millennium is deceiving. According to the Word of God, the outcome of the development of the Chris-

tian Church, in this age, is a great apostasy through which Christianity itself
is forced back into the Great Tribulation." *Kliefoth. Christliche, Eschatologie*, 196, 197.

"Let us guard against the idea that it is either possible or destined, that
Christianity will Christianize, in a real spiritual sense, the world in this present age. The kingdoms of this world must first be destroyed. Then only
is it possible that, rising in a new form, they will become the Kingdom of
our Lord and His Christ. This view of the world, and of our times, is
founded on the Word of God." *Auberlen, Daniel*, 288.

"The Church may succeed in making a *worldly caricature* of the Kingdom, but let us never allow ourselves to dream that, by thus forming herself
according to her model in the midst of the world, the secret and continuing
increase of the World-Kingdom and power, with its fatal influence, is inter-
rupted. This interruption is effected, according to Scripture, in a totally
different way, even by the binding of Satan, and casting him into the Under-
world, at the Second Coming of Christ. Antichrist must first be destroyed,
and the Nations judged, before Christianity can ever become a World-
Religion." *Hofmann, Weisagg u. Erfull, II* 295.

"It is a real apostasy of which the Apostle speaks, and not a mere resem-
blance. Such is the future now impending, and whose beginnings are all
around us. Some resign themselves to a vain hope, and dream that Christianity will, more and more, become a power in human thought and action,
and finally complete itself in the synthesis of these two fields of natural and
Christian life, so becoming a World-Religion embracing in its bounds the
utmost barbarous tribes. On the contrary, *the future we go to meet is the
complete alienation of the masses from the Christian faith, and finally an
open apostasy from the same.* Not unity, but the sundering and separation
of the religious and natural consciousness; not the union but the disruption
of the Church and Civil Society, is the outcome before us. The Christ-
opposed consciousness of the age demands a *Leader* in whom it shall be
concentrated, and personally represented, and, in this sense, the Apostle
Paul connects with the last apostasy the '*Man of Sin.*'" *Luthardt Lehre.
v. d. letzten Dingen*, 150.

"The question before us is not a vain one. It forbids us making any alliance with State-Omnipotence, for this would be only worshiping the Beast.
Just as earnestly does it forbid what so many would exact of us, on all sides,
viz.: That we should stand shoulder to shoulder with the Great Harlot, in
order to contend the more energetically against the anti-christianity of modern culture, for this alliance with the Harlot would only be to hinder the
making of her 'naked and desolate by the Kings of the earth,' and the
'eating of her flesh with fire,' an event in which we should go hand in
hand with God. On the other side, it teaches us the right answer in refer-

ence to the appearing of the Antichrist in the last times, viz., that the sign of his presence is not to be expected first only at the Appearing of the Lord, but on the contrary, that *the signs of his presence are even now among us, whereby we know it is ' the last time.'"* Dr. *Ferdinand Philippi Lehie v. Antichr.* 79.

"It is decidedly and plainly foretold, in the Scriptures, that evil *must* attain to its supreme manifestation upon earth, before the Lord comes. In the last times, a great and *widespread apostasy* from Christianity will take place, and Christendom become a complete Babylon. The *Churches* will be in a state of corruption because false doctrines and unchristian government will have got the upper hand. Worldly luxury, combined with wealth, trade, and extensive commerce, will exercise a widespread dominion, and ungodliness and debauchery accompany it. But in ' one hour,' i. e., suddenly, Babylon will fall, a sudden catastrophe will ensue, and overthrow of the social condition of this whole world, culture and civilization, with its sham Christianity. *Then will the Antichrist and the anti-christian kingdom be manifested, even the climax of apostasy, the consummation of evil on the earth.* Then will great tribulation befal believers. *Antichrist will form a new religion, by ' strong delusion,'* into which the Lord will suffer all to fall who have not received ' the love of the truth,' a *Cæsaropapy* of the worst kind, a World-Religion which ends in the worship of the Image of the Beast, i. e., of the human spirit which has apostatized from God, a Beast whose boast is *Culture and Civilization*, more and more tending to *Bestiality*, to rude force, and carnal lust. And all who have any degree of skill in placing the ' Signs of the Times' in the light of God's Word, will not mistake the fact that those elements are more and more showing themselves from which the *False Prophet* is to be developed, atheistic and materialistic systems, denying God and the existence of spirit, and based upon a purely physical view of existence; an æsthetic literature which, by its poetry, fictions, and romances, diffuses the *Gospel of the Flesh* among the masses, and upsets all moral relations; a daily *Journalism* which is a prelude of what is predicted in Rev. xvi:13, viz., that, out of the mouth of the *Dragon*, and of the *False Prophet*, shall proceed three unclean spirits, ' *like frogs,'* creatures of the swamp, the morass, and the mire, whose croaking produces a sound that penetrates to a distance, *repeating the same thing, day after day*, and well adapted to delude men, such as they are, and bring them into the right disposition, or state of mind, for the service of Antichrist. Nor can the *Political State* of the times be misunderstood, especially *the prevailing tendency to banish Christianity from public life, to undermine all authority, to break with all historical tradition*, as furnishing elements from which Antichrist may, one day, emerge. No false Democracy, or Red Republic will be the last of historical events to precede the Coming of the Lord. *The last development will be Cæsarism, Absolute Despotism, a Scarlet Cæsarism, and Revolution,* the necessary pre supposition of the Antichrist. '*Here is the patience and faith of the saints.*'" *Bishop Martensen of Seeland; Christian Ethics,* 352–356.

" As the First Coming of Christ could only take place when the fulness of the time had come (the end of the 69th Week, Dan. ix:26) and the world, in its need of salvation had reached that point with which that salvation could, and must, connect itself, so also can the Second Coming of Christ, bringing judgment with it, only occur when the world has become ripe for judgment, and wickedness has increased to such a height as to draw down upon itself the judgment of God. *Apostolic prophecy expects, prior to the Second Coming, no Millennium, but the highest development of antichristianity. And this is before us.* The whole essence of New Testament prophecy is this, that it seeks, from the 'Signs of the Times,' to recognize the events of the antichristian development, and to stake off the remaining Stadia through which it has to run, then look for the inbreaking of the full salvation with the personal Appearing of Christ." *Dr. Weiss. Theol. Stud. u. Kritik.* 1869, *pp.* 8, 9.

AGES OF AGES.

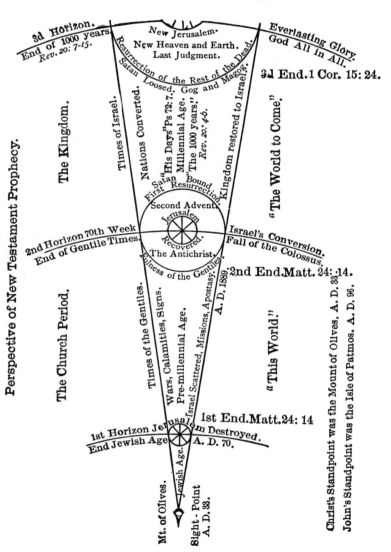

"What can be more absurd than to explain the prophecies, which foretell the calamity to befall the Jews, in a literal sense, and then those which bespeak their future felicity, in a mystic and spiritual sense."

DAVID LEVI.

"Who gives us the right by arbitrary exegesis, to refer the predictions made to Israel, to the Christian Church, when the judgments upon the same Israel evidently could not have been meant for the Church."

ISAAC DA COSTA.

"I hold it for a most infallible rule, that where a literal construction will stand, the farthest from the letter is commonly the worst. Nothing is more dangerous than this licentious deluding art which changes the meaning of words as Alchemy does, or would do, the substance of metals, makes of anything what it lists, and brings in the end all truth to nothing."

BISHOP HOOKER.

"We must never depart from the literal meaning of the subject mentioned, if all, or its principal, attributes square with the subject of the prophecy. The unalterable wisdom of God has shown itself in this, that the predictions of Scripture concerning the Jews are only in part fulfilled, the rest still waiting a future accomplishment."   VITRINGA.

"God has regulated the whole visible world according to number, measure, and weight, in the most perfect proportion and manner, applying Arithmetic and Geometry to inanimate things with infinite wisdom. What, then, must His government of rational creatures be, in their Times and Seasons, measured and numbered, according to His counsel, but one of complete order, a Divine Mathematics? Are not the prophetic numbers a part of divine economy? Are they merely *ideal, poetic, figurative, vague, high-flying* and *indefinite?* "   ROOS.

" About the time of the End, a body of men will be raised up who will turn their attention to the prophecies, and insist upon their literal interpretation in the midst of much clamor and opposition."

SIR ISAAC NEWTON.

APPENDICES

" The prophet promises a New Age in which the patriarchal measure of human life will return, in which death will no more break off the life that is just beginning to bloom, and in which the war of man with the animal world will be exchanged for peace without danger. *And when is all this to occur?* Certainly not in the blessed life beyond the grave, since these promises presuppose a mixture of sinners with the righteous, and only a limitation of the power of death, not its entire destruction. *When then?* This question ought to be answered by the antichiliasts,—the post-millennarians. They carry back the interpretation of prophecy to a time when commentators were in the habit of lowering the concrete substance of the prophecies into mere doctrinal '*Loci Communes*.' They take refuge behind the enigmatical character of the Apocalypse, without acknowledging that what the Apocalypse predicts under the definite form of 'the 1000 years' is the substance of all prophecy, and that no interpretation of prophecy, on sound principles, is any longer possible from the standpoint of antichiliasm, inasmuch as the antichiliasts twist the word in the mouths of the prophets, and, through their perversion of Scripture, shake the foundation of all doctrines, every one of which rests on the simple interpretation of the words of revelation. In the prophecies of the Old Testament, the eschatological idea of the New Cosmos does unquestionably *blend* with the Millennium. The Old Testament prophet was not yet able to distinguish from one another what the Apocalypse of John *separates* into distinct periods. It is in the New Testament this distinction is clearly made." FR. DELITZSCH.

EXTRACTS FROM EMINENT AUTHORS

Appendix 1

DOUBLE JURY OF SCHOLARS ON REVELATION 20:5, "THE FIRST RESURRECTION"

The spiritualizing, allegorizing, and idealizing, expositors seek to evade the doctrine of the pre-millennial Advent of Christ, by teaching that the *"First Resurrection,"* Rev. xx:5, is not a literal Resurrection of the Body, but means something else. In like manner, they seek also to evade the fact that the sublime scene of the Diademed Warrior on the White Horse, Rev. xix:11–16, is not that of the *Second Advent* itself, but means something else. Thus, the literal Resurrection denied here, the literal Second Advent is denied also. But if the "First Resurrection" is literal here, it must be coincident with the literal Second Coming of Christ. That the *"First Resurrection"* here announced *is* literal, the following testimony is adduced to prove. It might have been multiplied to a volume:

1.   *Volck.* "The view of Dr. Keil concerning the 'First Resurrection' is contrary to the Scriptures. The 'First Resurrection' is literal and occurs at the end of the present world-period, at the visible personal Advent of Christ. It is the same as that described by Paul, I Cor. xv:22, etc, and I Thess. iv:14, etc. *After* this are the 1000 years." *Volck, Der Chiliasmus,* 111-113.

2.   *Rinck.* "As to the Resurrection, it is two-fold; the general resurrection at the final judgment, and, previously to that, the 'First Resurrection' of Priests and Kings unto God, which finds place at the Advent of Christ *followed* by the 1000 years' kingdom." *Rinck. Zustand, etc.,* 223.

3.   *Füller.* "That a literal resurrection is here represented is evident from v. 5, which informs us that the 'Rest of the dead' lived not till the 1000 years were finished. This 'First Resurrection' is nothing new. It is only what Paul had already taught in I Cor. xv:23, and I Thess. iv:16." *Füller. Offenb. Johan.* 351.

4.   *De Wette.* "Paul's *Basilica* is here called the 1000 years' Kingdom, and is placed between the *Parousia* and the absolute *Telos* or End, named

465

in I Cor. xv:24. There is no contradiction between Paul and John, but perfect harmony. The 'End' in I Cor. xv:24 is not the End of this Age, but of the 1000 years." *Exegetisch. Handbuch on Rev. xx:*1–11.

5. *Lämmert.* "This is the First Resurrection in the true and proper sense of the word, as the preceding verse shows. What Paul in I Cor. xv: 23, calls the Resurrection of 'those who are Christ's,' is here called the 'First Resurrection.' The 'Rest of the dead' are not raised until the close of the earthly kingdom." *Lämmert. Offenb. Johan. Rev. xx:*1-4.

6. *Bengel.* "The 1000 years come in *between* Cap. xix:11-21, and Cap. xx:11-15. He must deny the perspicuity of the Scriptures, altogether, who persists in denying this, or seeks to refute it. The 'First Resurrection' is a corporeal one. The dead 'became alive' in that part in which they were dead or mortal, consequently in their body." *Bengel. Gnomon V, p.* 365.

7. *Kliefoth.* "The word 'Resurrection' must here not be explained by the word 'lived,' but the latter, by the former which is added by way of exposition. So Ewald and DeWette. It certainly means a return to life by a bodily resurrection. It is the same word as in Rev. ii:8. In the same way Christ Himself says He 'lived' again. This much is certain, that the 1000 years begin with the Visible Advent of Christ. Here all agree, Bengel, Ewald, DeWette, Düsterdieck, Hofmann, Ebrard, Luthardt, Auberlen, etc." *Kliefoth. Offenb. Johan.* 267.

8. *Christlieb.* "This is the 'First Resurrection.' See I Cor. xv:23; John v:25-29; Rev. xx:1-6. In the succeeding resurrection, Rev. xx:11-13, which introduces the great mundane catastrophe, and new heaven and earth, the grand process of the world's renewal has its fitting consummation." *Mod. Doubt,* 452.

9. *Lange.* "The Spirit of Glory is the Resurrection-Germ in the believer, Rom. viii:11; I Pet. iv:14. This Resurrection-Seed will become a Harvest in the 'First Resurrection,' I Cor. xv:23, which belongs to the beginning of the cosmical consummation. The 'End,' I Cor. xv:24, is the conclusion of the 'One Day' which is with the Lord 'as 1000 years.'" *Bremen Lectures, p.* 244

10. *Steffann* "The words 'they lived,' can mean nothing else than what is expressed in the explanatory clause, 'This is the First Resurrection;' the possession again of their bodily life in that glorification which the resurrection brings with it, to the saints. It is what Paul says in I Cor. xv:23, occurring at the Parousia of Christ. Either this 'First Resurrection' is a bodily one, or that of the 'Rest of the dead,' Rev. xx:11-15, is not a bodily resurrection, and the Apocalypse shows no resurrection of the dead at the close of our age, or of the world's history!' Whatever 'they lived' means in the one case, it means in the other." *Steffann. Das Ende,* 312.

11. *Rothe.* "The Apocalypse distinguishes a First and Second Res-

urrection. The 'First,' which ensues at the same time with the Advent, Rev. xix:11-21, is expressly described as the 'First' in Rev. xx:4-6. In it, the martyrs, and those who have remained pure from contamination of the world-power, have a share. Only these reign with Christ 1000 years, while the 'Rest of the dead' awake not to life. After the expiration of these years, and victory over Satan let loose, then the 'Rest of the dead' arise for Judgment." *Rothe. Dogmatik, Part II, p.* 77.

12. *Gebhardt.* "This resurrection is called the 'First, in distinction from the general resurrection of the dead to judgment, described in xx:12, 13. That the Seer means by it what Luke xiv:14 calls 'the resurrection of the just,' and what Paul speaks of as the 'resurrection from the dead,' Phil. iii:11; I Cor. xv:23; I Thess. iv:16, in which is included the change of the living, there can be no doubt. The remaining dead, remain dead, during the 1000 years' reign, until the general resurrection, the sleeping saints, or Christians 'live,' i. e., rise from the dead, and are glorified with Christ." *Gebhardt. Doct. of Apoc.* 280, 281.

13. *Gresswell.* "This resurrection is called the 'First,' and opposed to it is another, the second. A portion of the dead rise in that 'First,' the remainder in that Second. The subjects of these different resurrections, at two different times, are opposed as a part of a certain whole to the remainder of that whole. That whole is the aggregate or complex of the dead. On every principle of division, the parts must •be numerically distinct, and each exclude the other. Unless a *part* of the dead do actually rise on the former occasion, they must *all* rise on the second. But if they who rise on the second include those who rise on the first, *then one part includes the other, and the remainder is equal to the whole!* These are absurdities we cannot avoid, except by allowing, in the plain sense of the book itself, that part of the dead do actually rise on one and a former occasion, and the rest on another and later; which reconciles everything, and makes what is otherwise a flat contradiction and impossible, perfectly consistent and possible." *Gresswell on the Parables I,* 327.

14. *Elliott.* "The Resurrection spoken of *corresponds* in every case, to the Death out of which it was a revival. So constant and stringent is this rule that, in any doubtfully expressed case of Resurrection, there needs but to ascertain the *nature of the Death* revived from, to find an explanation of the Resurrection conformable thereto. In the present case the *Death* is that of those who had been beheaded for the witnessing of Christ; a form of expression which identifies them with those John had seen on the 5th Seal's opening—a literal bodily Death. The expression, the 'Rest of the dead,' absolutely and necessarily connects this *remainder of the dead*, later raised to life, with *the other dead*, just before said to have been earlier raised to life; as having been originally (i. e., prior to the abstraction of the dead first

taken; *part and parcel of the same community of the dead.* The Resurrection in both cases, therefore, is a literal one of the body, the death having been literal, the righteous dead, at the opening of the millennium, having then adjudged them an abundant entrance into Christ's kingdom; the wicked dead being excluded from it prior to their other and final judgment." *Elliott Horæ IV*, 140.

15. *Stuart.* " *They lived* means they revived, came to life, returned to a life like the former one, viz., a union of soul and body. So does the word mean in Rev. i:8, and in many other passages. Any other exegesis here would seem to be incongruous. ' *They lived* ' must mean, here, reviving, or rising from the dead. Thus the Saviour spoke of Himself in Rev. ii: 8 as being He who was ' dead and *alive again,*' after the death of the body. Thus too, it is said of the Beast, Rev. xiii:14, that had the deadly wound of the sword, that he ' *did live.*' Thus, in our context, also, it is said, the rest of the dead ' *lived not* ' until, etc. The point of antithesis, which decides the whole case, is the distinction of *order,* or *succession,* not of *kind.* The exigencies of the passage absolutely demand the sense of a bodily resurrection. Indeed, if this be not a position in the interpretation of Scripture, which is fully and fairly made out by philology, I should be at a loss to designate one which is." *Stuart Apoc. II*, 360, 475, *etc., etc.*

16. *Alford.* "If, in a passage where two resurrections are mentioned, —where certain souls lived, at first, and the ' *Rest of the dead* ' lived only at the end of a specified period, after that first,—the ' First Resurrection ' may be understood to mean a *spiritual* rising with Christ, while the second means a *literal* rising from the grave, then there is an end of all significance in language, and Scripture is wiped out as a definite testimony to anything. If the ' First Resurrection ' is *spiritual,* then so is the second,—which I suppose none will be hardy enough to maintain. But, if the second is *literal,* then so is the first, which, in common with the whole primitive church, and many of the best modern expositors, I do maintain, and receive as an article of faith and hope. * * I have ventured to speak strongly, because my conviction is strong, founded on the rules of fair and consistent interpretation. It is a strange sight, in these days, to see expositors who are among the first, in reverence of antiquity, complacently casting aside the most cogent instance of unanimity which primitive antiquity presents. * * I have again and again raised my earnest protest against evading the plain sense of the words, and *spiritualizing* in the midst of plain declarations of facts. That the Lord will come in person to this our earth; that His risen elect will reign with Him here, and judge; that, during that blessed reign the power of evil will be bound, and the glorious prophecies of peace and truth on earth find their accomplishment; this is my firm persuasion, and not mine alone, but that of multitudes of Christ's waiting people, as it was

that of His primitive apostolic Church, before controversy blinded the eyes of the fathers to the light of prophecy." *Alford. N. T. Vol. II, Part II*, 335, 336, 1088, 1089.

17.   *Starke.*   "The First Resurrection is a literal resurrection of the body; for, although John saw only '*souls*' yet this was for the reason that the souls which hitherto had been in a certain degree of heavenly joy, are now united with their bodies and are, by such union to be transplanted into still greater joy and glory.   Moreover, he does not say that the '*souls*' lived and reigned, but speaks of the *whole person*.   '*They*,' who were beheaded, and '*they*' who had not received the mark of the Beast, became alive by union of the soul with the body, and reigned with Christ 1000 years. That the word '*lived*' means they *came to life*, is clearly seen from Rev. ii:8, xiii:14, John v:25, Rom. viii:13.   Again, it is not said 'Blessed and Holy is the *soul* that has part in the First Resurrection,' but speaks of the *whole person*, (*He*) consisting of soul and body, which has part therein. For, if the First Resurrection and Reigning with Christ were to be understood of the *soul alone*, then John must have said, verse 5, the rest of the *souls* lived not again—which he does not.   As, moreover, he here speaks of the *whole person*, so in like manner, the 'rest of the *dead*' lived not again until the 1000 years were finished.   Therefore, we must explain the living and reigning with Christ, verse 4, of the *whole person*." *Starke. Synopsis. Vol. II* 182.

18.   *Birks.*   " We are told in the plainest terms that there are two resurrections which include all the dead;—that there is an interval of more than 1000 years between them; that all who rise in the first are blessed and holy; that the martyrs of earlier and later times have this privilege; and that every one whose name is not found in the 'book of life' appears and is judged in the second resurrection.   When *part* of the dead are raised it is self-evident that the 'Rest of the dead' remain unraised.   After the mention of those who live and reign with Christ 'in the First Resurrection,' we are told that the 'Rest of the dead' live not again till the 1000 years are finished.   After this negative statement, we naturally look for tidings of their later resurrection, under their own proper title,—'*the dead*.'   We find it in the exact place, where it might have been expected, from the order of the prophecy.   Four marks are given that the Millennium is *begun;* (1) the Binding of Satan; (2) the Cessation of His deceits; (3) the Reign of the saints; (4) the Delay in the Resurrection of the 'Rest of the dead.'   Four events are revealed in the very same order, to mark its *close;* (1) the Loosing of Satan; (2) the Deceiving of the nations; (3) the Compassing of the camp of the saints; (4) the Appearance of 'the dead,' small and great, before the Throne for judgment.   It is perfectly clear that this judgment corresponds, by strict parallelism, to the previous mention of the 'Rest of the dead'

whose resurrection was delayed till the 1000 years were finished. It is the judgment of the unfaithful dead, alone, and follows the Millennium." *Birks. Unfulfilled Prophecy.* 114, 174.

19. *Mede.* "The ' second *death*' is that of *bodies* not less than of *souls*, and, this conceded, it is sufficiently evident that the ' First Resurrection' is a corporeal one. Since the second Resurrection is a corporeal one, similarly so is the ' First ' as is proved by the adversative participle ' *but.*' John says, he saw ' the souls of those who were struck with the axe for the witness of Jesus, and for the word of God, and they lived and reigned with Christ 1000 years. BUT *the rest of the dead* lived not until the 1000 years were finished.' Who does not gather at once from this that both Resurrections are of *the same kind?* The use of the adversative requires this. And, as to the ' *souls*,' it is so well known as to need no proof that, in the Scriptures this word is used to denote not only *persons,* but *dead bodies; cadavera,* Psal. xvi:1. Acts ii:21. Ezek. xliv:25. Levit. xix:28. Apoc. vi 9, etc. All the righteous shall rise in the Millennial Kingdom, yet in a certain order, as the Apostle tells us, I Cor. xv:23; the Martyrs first, indeed, and at the beginning, Rev. xx:4–6; after that, the remaining righteous who have not borne the mark of the Beast; some sooner, some later, as shall seem good to Christ the Judge. And this is called the ' First Resurrection;' in Luke xiv:14, the ' Resurrection of the Just.' Then, 1000 years having passed away, the wicked also shall rise, and, at the same time, the last and universal Judgment be accomplished." *Mede. Works.* 572, 573.

20. *Hebart.* "The Aorist tense of the verb ' *lived*,' indicates one definite Act, a coming to life again, and finds its explanation in the added words, ' *This* is Resurrection the *First*,' so that by reason of the contrasted and corresponding Act, verses 5 and 12, it can only be a literal resurrection of the body that is meant, and no other. It can be understood here only in a literal sense, the sense ' they lived again.' If, by the ' Rest of the dead ' we understand Believers, who died either a natural or martyr death, the idea that ' *they*' should, first of all, come to a blessed life only after the 1000 years are expired, is contrary to Scripture. If we understand Unbelievers, the idea that ' *these*' should come to a blessed life, after the 1000 years, is equally contrary to Scripture. The same is the case if we take both at the same time, either way. It is, therefore, incorrect to hold that the words ' This is Resurrection the First' indicate any other resurrection than a proper and literal one. *Hebart. Zweite Zukunft.* pp. 188, 194.

21. *Van Oosterzee.* " The Scripture, in the dim distance, opens up the prospect of more than one resurrection ; first a partial one, and then an absolutely universal one. Of the former, not only does the Apocalypse speak, Rev. xx:4-6, but also the Lord, Luke xiv:14, and Paul, I Thess. iv:16, and

I Cor. xv:23, as compared with verse 26, without, however, its connection
with and difference from, the other one being more nearly indicated.   Thus
much is evident that the Gospel teaches a resurrection not only of the just
but of the unjust also." *Van Oosterzee. Dogmatik II* 786.

22. *Gill.* "It does not mean that they lived *spiritually*, for so they did
before, and whilst they bore their testimony to Christ and against Antichrist,
previous to their death ; nor *in their successors*, for it would not be just and
reasonable that *they* should be beheaded for their witness of Christ and His
word, and *others* live and reign in their stead.   Nor is this to be understood
of their living in their *souls*, for so they live in their separate state ; the soul
never dies.   But the sense is they *lived again*, as in verse 5,—they lived
corporeally, their souls lived again in their bodies, their bodies being raised
and reunited to their souls.   Their *whole persons* lived ; and this is called
the First Resurrection in the next verse." *Dr. John Gill, in ioca.*

23. *Seiss.* "My conviction is clear and positive that the resurrection
here spoken of is the resurrection of the saints from their *graves*, in the sense
of the Nicene Creed, where it is confessed, ' I look for the Resurrection of
the dead, and the life of the world to come.' The placing of it as the ' first ' in
a category of two resurrections, the *second* of which is specifically stated to be
the literal rising again of such as were *not* raised in the first, fixes the sense
to be a literal resurrection of the body.   It is a resurrection of saints only.
It is a resurrection from among the dead ones, necessarily *eclectic*, raising
some and leaving others, and so interposing a difference as to *time*, which
distinguishes the resurrection of the some in advance of the resurrection of
the rest.   The First Resurrection is one that takes place in different stages.
It is a resurrection which, *as a whole*, is nowhere pictorially described." *Dr.
Seiss. Lect. on Apoc. Vol. III., p.* 316, *etc.*

24. *Lechler.* " That this First Resurrection must be understood in the
literal sense is clear from the context, v. 5, where the ' Rest of the Dead '
live not until the 1000 years are expired.   We should do great violence to the
words if, with Hengstenberg, we interpreted the First Resurrection figuratively, and understood by it, the first step of a blessedness and rest in the
invisible world.   Independently of all other considerations, it would remain
inexplicable why this Resurrection, v. 5, must first begin with the beginning
of the 1000 years.   The word ' lived ' has the same sense, here, as in ii:8, i. e.
' came to life,' or as Bengel says, ' returned to life.'   The passage teaches,
as Lücke, Hofmann, Delitzsch, and others unanimously agree, a resurrection
of saints and martyrs from bodily death to the full enjoyment of dominion
with Christ, during the 1000 years ; a condition pictured, purely and grandly,
without any carnal traits whatever." *Lechler.   Apost. Zeitalter.* 203, 204.

Appendix 2

THE 1,000 YEARS IN THE APOCALYPSE
BY PROF. FREDERICK BLEEK, D.D.*

Chapters i–iii of the Apocalypse contain the Epistles to the 7 Asiatic Churches, while Chapters iv, v, are an Introduction to what follows.   In Chapters vi–xi, the Seals are successively loosed, and the Trumpets blown. In Chapter xi:7, the first mention is made of the "*Beast*" ascending from the Abyss, i. e. the Antichrist.   What now follows, from this point, is closely connected, the visions describing the Conflict with the powers of the world and of darkness, till the complete victory is won over Antichrist, and Satan is bound, Chapter xx:1, 2.   The final struggle of Satan, after his temporary release, is described in Chapter xx:7–10.   To this is annexed a description of the general resurrection, the last judgment, the everlasting glory of the faithful in a New Heaven and Earth.   Chapters xx:11–15,—xx:5.

We come now, specially to consider the Section Chapter xx:1-6.   The Seer beholds the Devil, bound for 1000 years, and thrown into the abyss and so deprived of his destructive influence over the Kingdom of God and its members.   Further, he sees that the souls of the faithful who suffered death in confessing their Lord, and did not give themselves up to the wicked one, live again, in order to reign 1000 years with Christ, whose victorious advent was already described in Chap. xix:11–21, to reign as priests of God and of Christ, and as such not to die any more.   Here, it is asked, (a) whether the 1000 years are meant as proper years, according to men's usual mode of reckoning, or merely as a symbolical way of counting, and in what sense, and (b) when the period begins.   Many interpreters, in opposition to millennarianism, have been of the opinion that, by the 1000 years' reign of Christ, none other can be understood than that which He established on earth at the time of His Incarnation, and which had already begun even before the Apocalypse was composed.   This is the view which has prevailed in the Catholic Church since the fourth century, and which is found in most Protestant interpreters, as well as in Bossuet, etc.   Others date the beginning of the 1000 years' kingdom later, but yet consider it as having not merely begun, long since, but as already expired.   Thus, Grotius and those who follow him, who reckon the 1000 years from Constantine the Great, on to the beginning of the fourteenth century ; and lately, Hengstenberg, who refers them to the time from the christianizing of the Germanic nations to the expiration of the German empire.   But here, first of all, the former assumption that the 1000

*From Bleek's Vorlesungen. ub. Offenbar. Johan. 75-82. 101-104. 328-356.

years begin with the Incarnation of Christ, is unmistakably against the meaning of our Book. A time of undisturbed peace belonging to the Kingdom of God is clearly represented, in opposition to the preceding one of affliction and conflict, a time when the Devil and his instruments would be powerless to exercise any disturbing influence over it, either in general or over individual members. Now, the time when the Book was written, whether early or late, could not well be described in such a way, in contrast with any earlier one. There can be no doubt that this 1000 years' kingdom alludes to a time which had not begun when the Book was written, and to one in which the Lord should *return* to unite His own people with Himself in His Kingdom. Accordingly, we find this hope almost in the whole Christian Church of the First Age, the hope that the Lord would return, and that soon, no longer in the lowly form of a servant which he had assumed at His first appearance on earth, but in the complete glory and majesty belonging to Him ; and that He would then join His own people to Himself in a Kingdom of peace and undisturbed happiness, giving them a share in His glory and power. It is grounded in the essence of the historical manifestation of Christ at His incarnation, that prophecy revived with new power in His Church, pointing to the fulfilment of the Kingdom of God and its complete victory over the world. Old Testament prophecy had already directed attention to this ; but as the Messianic salvation, expected at the First Coming of Christ upon earth, was not fully realized by His own ministry, or that of His disciples, Christian prophecy was directed, very soon, in a special manner, to a SECOND COMING of the Son of Man, to His glorious re-appearing. This is found even in the sayings of Christ Himself, as they were apprehended and communicated by the disciples, especially in the first three Gospels, chiefly in Matt. xxiv,. xxv. In like manner, the same hope is found in most of the New Testament writings, if not always expressly stated, yet clearly lying at the foundation.

The raising of the deceased or faithful dead, in order to participate in this Kingdom, beginning with the return of the Lord, *is not peculiar to the Apocalypse.* Already in Daniel xii:2, we meet with the promise that, at the time of Israel's redemption (the Messianic salvation) there would be a resurrection out from the dead. In the Jewish theology, this was developed with a two-fold resurrection (a) of the pious, the true people of God, at the appearing of the Messiah when they should be re-awaked to take part with Him in His Kingdom ; (b) of a later general one, at the last day, for universal judgment. The believers of the First Age seem to have adopted the distinction, and to put the "*First Resurrection,*" that of believers, at the time of Christ's glorious return. So we find it particularly in the Apostle Paul, I Thess. iv:14, and following verses, and in I Cor. xv:22, and following verses and verse 51, and following.

Paul, indeed, does not speak expressly of the *Second Resurrection*, the general one, since he had no particular motive for doing so according to the object he there pursues. Yet it is *implied unmistakably*. Here, in the Apocalypse, the idea occurs in a most definite shape, according to which true believers rise again that they may participate in the 1000 years' kingdom, and which is expressly designated as the "*first resurrection*," whilst the general judgment of the dead is placed after the expiration of the 1000 years. Accordingly, we find *a double resurrection*, that of believers at the return of the Lord, and the second general one at the last judgment, distinguished by different Church-teachers of the early centuries, particularly by Tertullian, Methodius, Lactantius, etc., etc.

As to the "1000 years," we find opinions about the duration of the Messianic kingdom among the later Jews very different. The idea that seems to have prevailed among some, at the time of Christ, was that it would be of eternal duration. Compare John xii:34, and Eisenmenger Entd. Judenthum, Königsberg 1711, 4, ii. pp. 813 segg. This idea might also have been founded on express utterances of the Bible. Yet other ideas prevailed also which made the Messiah subject to mortality, and assigned only a finite duration to his sovereignty, with all its splendor. These we find expressly in later times ; among others, that of a duration of 40 years, of 70 years, of 400 years, and also, definitely, of 1000 years. See Eisenmenger pp. 809 segg, and Wetstein ad Apoc. xx:2. It cannot indeed be maintained, certainly,* but it is not unlikely, that the idea, in this form, was known to the Jews even in the apostolic age, whence it was transferred, in the Christian Church, to the duration of the kingdom beginning with the return of the Lord. Yet it is also possible that it assumed this form in the Christian Church itself. The combination of that passage in the Psalms, Ps. xc:4, "A thousand years in Thy sight are but as yesterday," with the narrative of the creation of the world might have had some influence, from persons considering the latter as a type of the destinies of the world, and therefore concluding that, as God created the world in six days, and afterward rested the seventh day, so the world should be completed in six days, that is, in 6000 years ; and the seventh day, that is the seventh Millennium, should become a time of undisturbed rest and Messianic bliss. So Barnabas speaks, Epistles Chap. xxv. It is manifest that the same idea is found here, in substance, as in the Apocalypse, viz., that the kingdom of the Messiah should last 1000 years after the Second Advent of the Lord, and the renewal of the world be annexed to it. When this Epistle of Barnabas was written cannot with certainty be determined. In any case, it is later than the Apocalypse. Yet the relation of both writings upon this point is not of the kind that would

---

* This statement falls below the full truth of the case, as later critical investigations have shown —N. W.

make it probable that the author of that Epistle has borrowed his whole conception from the Apocalypse. The brief manner also in which it is stated in the Apocalypse, indicates that the idea is not one newly expressed, but such as the author found already, and not entirely unknown to his readers, whether, as already mentioned, it had first taken this shape in the Christian church itself, or had been found by the latter in the Jewish church.

As to the real significance of the 1000 years, it is most unlikely, from the probable form of the conception, that any other definite period of time could be meant than that denoted by the common use of language. Still, on the other hand, it may be that the number should not be too strictly pressed, in the sense of our Book, as a measured period of exactly 1000 solar or lunar years ; but certainly it must be assumed, especially since the idea was already developed, that the number here is retained as a general expression to denote a very long period of undisturbed repose and happiness for believers, beginning at the return of the Lord.

We ask, further, what does our Book teach about the time when the glorious appearing of the Lord will take place and the 1000 years' kingdom begin, as well as the relations under which this will happen ? what is to precede the catastrophe ? and how is the Apocalypse related to the other writings of the New Testament ? The Lord had expressly stated, Matt. xxiv.26 ; Mark xiii:32, and, according to Acts i:7, even referred to it after His resurrection, that to "know the times and the seasons," with regard to the coming of the kingdom, in its consummation, the Father had reserved to Himself. And, in Matt. xxiv:14, Mark xiii:10, the announcement of the gospel throughout the whole world is specified by Him as something which must precede. But, on the other hand, He exhorted the disciples to be always ready to receive Him worthily To this the apostles directed their attention, primarily, and sought to direct that of other believers, so that their looking forward to the Coming of the Lord might be of use to them all, as an ever living incentive, urging them to dedicate all their powers to the Lord and to the furtherance of His Kingdom, that they might be found faithful stewards of the talents He had intrusted to them. It cannot be denied that they generally cherished the hope that the glorious appearing of the Lord was near, so that they themselves, or many of their contemporaries, might perhaps live to see it. This may be recognized by the way in which several discourses of the Lord respecting the future, in the Synoptical Gospels, are reproduced and brought into connection with one another. We cannot but see that, with the apostle Paul, especially in some of his earliest Epistles, this point of time to his mind appeared quite near, so that he hoped to live to see the future advent of the Lord. See I Thess. iv:15–17 ; I Cor. xv:51, 52. Yet the expectation of his own survival seems to have receded into the background with him at a later period. In James v:7–11, also, the Coming of the Lord (Parousia) is specified as near.   So in the Epistles to the Hebrews, especially x:37.   The same hope may also be discerned in our Book, even in the first part of it.   For when the Lord Himself, Rev. iii:11, says to the Angel of the Church of Laodicea, "I come quickly," there can be no doubt, according to the New Testament usage, that this is meant of the glorious re-appearing of the Lord.   See also, i:17.   So, too, when it is said immediately at the beginning, i:3, "The time is at hand," there can be no doubt that this refers to the nearness of the time to which the hope of the believer was directed, when the complete inauguration of the Kingdom of God should begin, with the return of the Lord.   See Luke xxi: 8 ; Mark xiii:33 ; Rev. x:6, and following.

Our Book not merely specifies the catastrophe, in general, but endeavors to indicate in a still more definite manner, *the point of its commencement.* In what way this is done *depends upon the apprehension of the visions preceding the announcement of the* 1000 *years' reign.*   In general, especially in the closely connected visions (Chap. xii–xix) we find the sense easily discernible; that *before* the beginning of this reign, the adversaries of Christ and His Kingdom, the Devil and his associates, should be conquered by Christ and made powerless with respect to the continuance of that kingdom, deprived of all influence to disturb its peace and happiness, after they had previously made the most violent efforts against it.   *The general idea lying at the foundation and confirmed by the whole history is that an extreme effort of the opposing spirit of evil, falsehood, and darkness, precedes* EVERY *more important development of good, and of the Kingdom of Christ, the kingdom of truth, of light, of peace, and would, therefore, all the more precede the* COMPLETION *of Christ's Kingdom.*   Thus, we find already, in the prophets of the Old Testament, that the announcement of the Messianic salvation *is usually appended to the most lamentable condition of the people of God,* and their most violent oppression by their enemies.   The discourses of the Redeemer also, communicated in the Synoptical Gospels, make it obvious that his reappearing will not take place unless the greatest measure of suffering of all kinds for the people of God shall have previously been filled up.   But it may be asked, *in what manner, in what particular form, this general idea is individualized in the Apocalypse?*   Here, the determination mainly depends upon the view taken of the powers which are introduced as the adversaries and combatants of Messiah and of God's Kingdom. These powers are designated as different "*Beasts*" presented to the eye of the Seer, so that the question arises, "*For what are we to take these Beasts?*"

With reference to the 1000 *years' reign.*   This appears in the Apocalypse, *not as the ultimate completion of the kingdom of God,* which, according to our Book, takes place in the "New Jerusalem," *but as a preliminary close* of the conflicts of God's Kingdom with the world and its powers;—a period of time denoted as 1000 years, when the faithful and pious, particularly those who had fallen asleep before, and were awakened for that purpose, should *reign with Christ upon earth* in undisturbed peace and happiness, after the destruction of all earthly hostile powers and the binding of Satan. We may view every epoch of the Christian Church, in which an important progress of the Kingdom of God, with the conquest of hostile powers, takes place, as a partial fulfilment of the utterances of Scripture, especially those about the Lord's Coming; but in everything which the history of the Church presents, only a partial and preliminary fulfilment, not a complete one, is perceptible. As it is decidedly contrary to the meaning of the Apocalypse to make the 1000 years' kingdom begin with the Incarnation of Christ, so that the author considered the time already present; every view is inadmissible, according to the purport of our book, which supposes the 1000 years' kingdom as already expired or only begun. The interpretation of Hengstenberg, in modern times, belongs to this category, making it extend from the Christianizing of the Germanic nations to the end of the German empire. Thus, the times of the Middle Age, with the greatest splendor of the Papacy, and the Age of the Reformation, as well as that after the Reformation, are supposed, indiscriminately, to be the 1000 years' kingdom, including times when the most horrible deeds were perpetrated by the Romish Church, and other ruling powers, against the true confessors of the Lord, as in the wars against the Albigenses and Waldenses, against the Huguenots, in the Inquisition, and the night of St. Bartholomew, as well as many others. Auberlen (pp. 415 segg.) refers to these, very appropriately, against Hengstenberg. It is certain that we decide in accordance with the sense of the Book itself, when we consider the 1000 years' kingdom as a state of development belonging to the Church or the Kingdom of God which has not yet appeared, no more than has the glorious return of the Lord in close connection with it, and the first resurrection of believers awakened to participate in it. All this, according to the meaning of our book, must certainly be taken literally; not as Hengstenberg does, in relation to the happiness of believers beginning at their death.

With reference to Antichrist. In the past history of the Church, it may be pointed out that to every epoch, which reveals a special progress of the Kingdom of God, precedes a time in which the antichristian element comes forth with peculiar power; and every time of the kind may be considered as a partial and preliminary fulfilment of the prophecies of Scripture respecting destruction and mischief in the last time, and so respecting the appearance and activity of Antichrist. But, it may be said, on the other hand, that these prophecies have not yet found their complete fulfilment, and that the author of the Apocalypse himself would have seen in none of the phenomena, since the establishment of the Christian church an entire fulfilment of the visions in question. On the contrary, if we consider them according to their essential meaning, we are led to think of a person's appearance before the glorious coming of the Lord, armed as an instrument of Satan, with Satanic powers. We must think of a personal manifestation still future.

The Apocalypse considers and represents as quite near, both the glorious Coming of the Lord and the Coming of Antichrist. The thing is not peculiar to the Apocalypse. As already remarked, it cannot be denied that the Christians of the first time generally, and also the New Testament writers, cherished the hope that the glorious appearing of the Lord would not be very distant, would take place, perhaps, in their own lifetime. Such form of hope was necessary to believers of the time to sustain them against the manifold struggles and sorrows with which they had to contend both outwardly and inwardly; and we shall do well if, after their example we continually keep in mind that future as near; like them, finding in it an incentive to direct all our energies to this, viz., to be found by the Lord, watchful and true, any time He may come. Many exhortations of the Lord Himself, as well as of His disciples, refer us to it; and also the Apocalypse most certainly. This view of the nearness of the glorious appearing of the Lord supposes that the utmost exertions of the hostile powers, or coming of Antichrist, are impending.

The reference to the approach of the glorious Coming of the Lord, (Chap. xix) as Conqueror of the hostile powers, and for the inauguration of the kingdom of God upon earth, forms the central and leading point in the contents of the Apocalypse. Though the kingdom itself (Chap. xx) the 1000 years, is but briefly described, yet all that precedes only serves as a preparation for it, just as what follows appears its farther completion. In Chap. xix:1–10 voices of heaven resound, praising God for His righteous judgment on Great Babylon, and singing to Him because the marriage of the Lamb is come, the time of His union with His Church, and the complete inauguration of His Kingdom which is connected with the fall of anti-christian Babylon. In Chap. xix:11 to Chap. xx:1–3, the Appearing of Messiah, the Logos, is depicted in His triumphant glory; the defeat and destruction of all adversaries of the Kingdom of God, the casting of the Beast and False Prophet into the lake of fire, and the binding of Satan for 1000 years. Chap. xx:4–6, is the First Resurrection, or awaking of the believers who shall reign with Christ in the 1000 years' kingdom; verses 7–10 the final contest of Satan with the kingdom of God which issues in his complete destruction, he being thrust into hell forever after it. The prophecy in Ezekiel xxxviii, xxxix lies here at the foundation, where a Gog, the prince of Magog, is spoken of who, " *at the End of the days*," when Israel have strengthened themselves in their land after return from their last captivity, will march out against them with numerous hosts, but will meet with complete defeat. Then the time of the trial of the people of God will be properly at an end. They will inherit the land in perfect safety, forever, and forget all afflictions they suffered. So also, here, the subject is of a last struggle, which, even after the expiration of the 1000 years' kingdom, the people of God shall have to encounter * with the nations of the world which Satan will summon from the uttermost parts of the earth. Only, here, contrary to the manner in Ezekiel, Gog is treated in the same manner as Magog, as a collective designation of those who had their dwelling at the farthest extremities of the earth; nations outside the pale of Israel's kingdom.† Among the later Jews, also, Gog and Magog are mostly named together as nations who will march against Jerusalem, and the land of Israel, at the world's end, and shall then perish by the Messiah or by fire from heaven. *See Westein, ad loc.* The " camp of the saints," the place where the citizens of the 1000 years' kingdom were united is described as the " *Beloved City,*" beloved of God, a city to Him precious, namely "Jerusalem," as after its purification it is represented to be the seat of Christ, and His kingdom. In verses 11–15 is *the general resurrection of the dead, namely of all those who have not had part in the* 1000 *years' kingdom,* when all, who are not in the " Book of Life," are cast into hell, the lake of fire, after Death and Hades have been previously hurled into it, so that it is called the " second death." The Great White Throne is called " Great " in reference to the several "thrones" mentioned, verse 4. Chap. xxi:1 to xxii:5, describes, at large, the formation of the new world, and in it specially the New Jerusalem as the abode of believers and the blessed, in images which are borrowed mostly from, or follow, Old Testament representations, particularly the Mosaic description of Paradise, the Tabernacle of Testimony, and Ezekiel on the New Jerusalem, in Chapters xl, etc. But individual features must not all be pressed, according to the genius of our Book, neither in a literal nor an allegorical way. For representations of the New Jerusalem among the later Jews, see Eisenmenger's Entd. Judenthum II. 839, etc. The revelation of the future kingdom of God is now at an end. What follows forms only the conclusion to the book, in which the truth and reliability of these disclosures is especially affirmed, and it is repeatedly asserted that the time for the fulfilling of the Lord's coming is at hand. Meanwhile, until the glorious Advent of the Lord, each one may continue in his usual way of acting, corresponding to his inward character, " filthy " or " holy." The sinner is free to continue in his viciousness till then, as it is the part of the just and pious to increase in righteousness and

---

* No. It never comes to a battle! N. W.
† Designated by Kliefoth, as the " *peripheral nations.*" N. W.

holiness. " *The Lord comes quickly.*" He comes to reward every man in accordance with his entire conduct. " Blessed are they that do His commandments " (according to the Received Text, De Wette, Züllig, Tischendorf.) or " who wash their robes," i. e. " who are cleansed in the blood of the Lamb " (according to Lachman, Bentley, Mill, Ewald, A. 2 cursives, Eth. Arm. Vulg. Prim. Comment, and others).* The wicked and unclean shall find no access to the Holy City. The " Spirit " of Prophecy which had descended on John, and the " Bride," are saying, Come, O Lord, delay no longer Thy appearing. Each one who hears this call of the Spirit and the Bride, to the Lord, may join in it and make known his desire. Also, whoever has true longing for the treasures of the Lord,—let *him* come and take; the Lord will not withhold them from him. In reference to the entire prophetic contents of this Book, whoever makes additions to this prophecy, God will add to him the plagues that are written in this Book, and whoever subtracts aught God will subtract his part out of the Book of life, out of the Holy City, and the things written in this Book. The Lord, the Testifier, says, " *Surely, I come quickly!*" "*Amen; Come Lord Jesus!*"

Appendix 3

THE 1,000 YEARS IN THE APOCALYPSE

BY PROF. HEINRICH VON EWALD, D.D.†

The last 7 Visions of the Apocalypse disclose to the eye of the Seer an altogether new Outlook into the farther, and then farthest, future, which, endless as it is, must embrace events so much transcending all hitherto witnessed, that, just because of their remoteness, they can only be seen the more clearly when presented in mere outline. In this wide future, the glance of the Seer lingers with supreme satisfaction on the blessedness of *Two Great Ends* yet to be realized in history, the one at the Appearing of Christ in His glory, the other, more distant still, at the Ultimate Consummation of all things. For the Seer, these Ends were, from the very beginning, the most certain and blessed. For the purpose of filling up the wide and far spaces of the future, Old Testament prophecy offered itself to his hand. And just as the WHOLE *Messianic End* divides itself into *Three Great Ends of destruction and overthrow*, each succeeding greater than the one preced-

---

* The old Received Text is to my mind, beyond all question, the correct one. The " reward " is a reward of " Works," the reward of obedience the fruit of faith. It is measured by works all which have been wrought in us of God. Grace abounding to us, even in the Judgment Day! " *Well done!* " N. W.
† From Ewald's *Johan. Schrift.* or *Johannean Writings*, *II*, 321, etc.

ing, so does the *Whole Messianic Activity*, for re-establishment and glorification, divide itself into *Three ever higher Degrees* of advancement, of which the *Last Two* are certainly before us. It is of the very first importance to recognize this.

Indisputable is that most correct idea, viz., that the *End* of every great earthly Dispensation or Established Condition of things,—when, by its ever-increasing perversities and sins, its destruction becomes a divine necessity,— brings, only first of all, sad disaster and ruin, and enduringly so, were it not that the divine power of recovery, mightier still, has ever exerted itself to counteract the existing condition, and restrain, for the time, the ultimate consummation, hid in the will of God. Along with this truth, this other truth is coincident, viz., that, in the slow development of human things, this divine power of recovery, the more violently it is hemmed in, and resisted, by the wickedness brought to oppose it, rouses itself at times, the more powerfully, making a *New Condition* of things necessary out of the midst of the ruins of the Old, and by definite steps,—so that brief moments are obliged to still the long sighing of centuries,—yet such as let it be seen how, even for all the widest and farthest conceivable spaces in future times, a progress corresponding in ever-widening extension, and larger degree, has already been pledged, and revealed itself, even in the smaller and more unimportant relations of the past.* And thus it is, that the *One Great Complex Movement* is found in the divine word, to separate itself into *Three Individual Movements* at *Each Epoch* in the Great Development:

(1.) *The Approaching End*, with the dissolution of the previous Bad condition of things, though coming through many intermediate movements.

(2.) *The Last and Mightiest Struggle of Evil* to maintain itself against the Better incoming condition.

(3.) *The Complete Victory of the New and the Better*, on the ruins of the Old and Worse condition.

As, moreover, it is the Christian view and presentiment, in general, so is it especially that of our Seer, that *Christ only* can create a new world (or age) upon the ruins of the old, that He has done it already, that He will do it again, and in ever-widening extent and degree, until the last Consummation comes. And if we only observe how, on a large scale, all this moved onward before the eyes of the Seer, in definite outline, in reference as well to the past as the future, we shall also see the whole developing itself into *Three Great Stages*, according to what has been said. At the Dissolution and End of the Jewish Age or Old Covenant, Christ came (First Advent) in

---

* The Student of Modern History will not fail to see the working of these two great truths and laws, in the Times of the Reformation, the French Revolution, the American Revolution, the Slavery times in the United States, and now, once more in the Temperance movement in Christendom. We battle our Way to the End! N. W.

the restricted form of an earthly life and work, yet at the same time awaking
the *New* order of things in imperishable germ, and even then, by virtue of
His life and death, judging the world;—Nothing less than Christ as the
"*Crucified One*" introduced the victory, whereby He now rules, *at least
invisibly*, in His own.   If now *this first New order* of things is crushed, by
means of the Roman power, and only Rome's overthrow can introduce the
next great End, then only can Christ as the "*Glorified One*," reappearing
from heaven (Second Advent), and overcoming the Antichristian Trinity of
our time (Dragon, Beast, False Prophet), erect anew, upon the ruins, His
visible kingdom, and secure for His people a higher salvation.   Finally if
even this second New order of things, wide and glorious, is dissolved, at
length, again, by the irruption of the farthest and outside nations of the
earth (Gog and Magog), so introducing the *third* time, *another great End*,
then must also the re-establishment and glorification become, on this point,
the very greatest possible, so that nothing else can follow but the absolute
perfection of all things.   This is that which now becomes the widest and
ultimate outlook of our Seer; and thus it is that not only Dissolution but
Judgment also, and a Regenesis, step forth continually before his eyes, in
ever-widening circles, until, at last, all is attained that lay hid in the divine
purpose and will.

Of these great Ends in the development of Christianity, only the last two
are future ; yea, already their possibility is conceivable only after Rome's
overthrow.   In order to show how these remote spaces may be conceived of
as yet nearer, a special idea presented itself to our Seer which seemed to him
most appropriate to determine their wide extension according to a divine measure.   This is the idea of "the 1000 years" preceding the final consummation,
and which shall be more glorious and happy than our present period, but not
yet the period of the consummation itself.   The hope of such a Millennium is,
in itself, one that is most important, and if not too slavishly understood, preserves the correct view.   For it only represents, in a sensible manner, the
great truth that the ultimate perfection of all things cannot arrive as swiftly
as the glowing hope of man too oft desires it, and that, only from a better
beginning, attained in a future day, and never to be shaken, can this perfection come, and even gradually then.   It is, therefore, altogether good, and
fit, that this Hope of "the 1000 years" has been incorporated into the great
society of all other Christian Hopes, and woven into the web as closely as
possible.   When our Seer foresaw so certainly, the overthrow of Rome and
Rome's kingdom, and the victory of Christianity, it was only a proof of the
clearness of his glance into the future that he, nevertheless, saw the final
Consummation as not immediately following this, but, in view of the many
remote nations not yet brought into near contact with Christianity, referred
that Consummation to the still more distant future.   And yet, were we to

conclude that this Hope of Millennial Glory rose, first of all, on the mind of our Seer in the definite form in which he here beheld it, we should greatly mistake the fact. We do not, indeed, find as yet the fact quite so definitely expressed in any writing earlier than the Apocalypse, yet, even here, the 1000 years' Kingdom appears plainly enough as an already existing, previously established, and almost self-interpreting Hope,—a Hope in the highest degree peculiar and important, and which, by no possibility could, through mere chance have intruded itself, anywhere, into the circle of the Hopes cherished by the church. Had the Seer now received this special view of the 1000 years' Kingdom, only for the first time, like that concerning Rome and Christ, how much more prominently would he have put it forward, as something altogether newly revealed of God or Christ, to men, and have grounded, even still more deeply, its inner necessity ! But it appears, here, as something already given and well-known, something the mere mention of which is regarded as sufficient, and is only presented in Christian colors. The original vividness and holy longing of the universal Christian Hope are here. If we inquire more closely after the origin and meaning of "the 1000 years," we shall come to the same conclusion. For it was intended, originally, to denote that the Seventh Thousand of our present creation, is the last, when God will prepare a higher rest, in a Millennial Sabbath, for His people, inasmuch as the creative week was the model of the whole period of history, and because, according to Ps. xc:4, God could easily make a Sabbath "Day" to be a Sabbath of 1000 years. There is no reference, here, however, to this particular interpretation. The Sabbath itself, with all that depends upon it, was already lost. If we even do not know, accurately, in what production the representation of "the 1000 years" was first announced and diffused, still we must accept as most certain that, for a long time, it had already been firmly established, and that our Seer received it, and arrayed it in Christian colors and dress, and that, as appears from other intimations in the apostolic writings, it remained no stranger to primitive Christianity.

In the application to his own circle of hearers of the new anticipations, ' the 1000 years" become, for our Seer, the beautiful intermediate period, when, on the wide field of the Roman Empire, and on its final ruins, an earthly Kingdom of Christ shall rise and rule, with the restored earthly Jerusalem as its central-seat, and where under the strong protection of the returned and Glorified Messiah it shall begin, in narrower circumference, as a prelude, to the universal and eternal glorification of all things. Readily enough, to the eyes of the Seer, came the illustrations of this, from the Old Testament, running to meet him. Of a glorified earthly Jerusalem, even in the Old Testament, the discourse is most frequent. Pre-eminent, herein, is Ezekiel's vision of the Resurrection of Israel. As there, Israel rises anew, so only first, through the Messianic Judgment and Glorification, shall all true Christians, the dead as well as the living, and only such, first be glorified and gathered together, to reign with Christ, and so fulfill this part of the Old Testament Hope. From this it also results how closely the "Appearing" of Christ in His glory, which here stands as the beginning of all wider glorification, connects itself, backward, with all that went before it. This development is only the complete overcoming of the deepest spiritual devastation of former times, the conclusive judgment upon the whole former age, and strong grounding of a Better Order of things, victorious on the ruins of the past ;— the necessary complement, therefore, of the overthrow of Rome's power. It cannot, consequently be the last End, nor ground of the Consummation itself ; for Rome, more strictly taken, did not rule all the nations of the earth, and much of mankind still remains outside the circle of her power. But an enormous progress it is, from the destruction of Rome, nevertheless, as it is surely the beginning to every still wider glorification. It might, indeed, seem to come, of itself. But, rather, just as toward the end of the former manifestation of Christ, the Crucifixion was obliged to come, in order to introduce the full End of that time and the transition to our new period, precisely so there lies between Rome's destruction and the "Appearing" of Christ, as Conqueror over the Satanic Trinity and their friends, a great event of the most terrible character. It is impossible not to recognize it, and of it, there can be no doubt. Antichrist, with his allies from the East, will overthrow Rome, and think to have subjected the whole World-Power to his control in such degree, that he will now attempt to strike the stroke he has been harboring in his heart, from the very beginning of his career. His aim will be Jerusalem, not to destroy it, for already it has been laid waste, but, after the death of the "two witnesses" of Christ, to annihilate the Temple and all Christianity itself. Apoc. xi:1–13 ; xiv:14–20. And, when in this way, that is fulfilled which is spoken in Matt. xxiv: 15, and II Thess. ii:3–10, then is the supreme moment of the Epiphany of Christ in his glory !

Apoc. xix:1–10 is the Vision of Heaven's joy which the impending event —the final fulfilment of all the longing of God's servants both earthly and heavenly,—calls forth, just before the event itself steps up into visible history on earth ;—a high joy of redoubling "Allellujahs," the Marriage-Supper of the Lamb announced as at hand. Apoc. xix:11–16, is the Vision of the Visible Appearing of Christ, revealing the all-conquering King of Kings, Himself descending with His armies, from the "Opened Heaven." He is represented, now, not as a "Lamb" (which would be incongruous) but as a Warrior on His horse, Apoc. xix:17 to xx:15. Here enter — in the briefest manner,—the events and decisive issues of the most distant and longest period of the remaining development of divine human things. If, from a higher necessity it results that a two-fold judgment lies before us, these two judgments, because of their great significance, become the proper objects of the Seer's beholding, at the two sides of the great intermediate period of "the 1000 years" between these judgments, and before the final Consummation. Therefore, this whole section, xix:17—xx:15, falls, like the previous corresponding one, into three parts, viz.: (1) the Vision of the First Judgment and First Resurrection, and "the 1000 years," xix:17—xx:5 ; (2) the Vision of the End of the 1000 years' Kingdom, Gog and Magog ;—xx:7-10 ; (3) the Vision of the Universal Resurrection and Judgment, xx:11-15. The Two Grand Visions of the Consummation are (a) the Vision of the Glorification, xxi:1-8 ; and (b) the Vision of the New Jerusalem xxi:9 to xxii:5.

As to the Vision of the First Judgment, First Resurrection, and the 1000 years' kingdom, Satan is now bound, by an Angel who has the key of the Abyss, and is cast into the Abyss,— not yet into the Lake of Fire, xx:10— and carefully secured, as if under bar and bolt, that he should deceive the nations no more, as he had deceived the Roman world into hostility against Christianity. By this banishment to the Under-world there has happened to the Prince of Demons just what formerly happened to the individual demons themselves. After the 1000 years are expired, however, he shall, according to verse 2, be loosed for a brief period. Such a privilege has even Satan, before God, and the forelight of this is found in Isa. xxiv:22. The three Visions, viz.: xix:17, 18, xix:19-21, xx:1-3, taken together, form the ground of the last one. These three accomplished, then follows, xx:4-6, which, according to Luke xiv:14, is called the "Resurrection of the just," or what our Seer, verse 5, calls the "First Resurrection," set over in contrast with the yet more significant second one, in verse 13. That it is a real Judgment of God, in which the judges take their seats, solemnly, is already depicted in Dan. vii:9. Moreover, who these judges are is foreshadowed in Matt. xix:28, and from Apoc. iv:4. The power of these judges goes only to this extent, to summon true Christians to the new life, and, therefore, first of all, (1) those who have been beheaded with the axe,—a symbol referring to the well-known Roman mode of capital punishment, as Paul had experienced it, then (2) so many as had, in no one of the ways described, sworn allegiance to the "Beast." What number there shall be, of genuine Christians, actually living on the earth, at the time of these mightiest of all changes, is, in the glowing haste of these visions, not narrated, but we can clearly enough conclude it from what has been earlier said of John, in Apoc. xiv:1-5 : xix:14, 19. The risen saints, "caught up to meet the Lord in the air," according to Paul, just after the First Resurrection, II Thess. ii:1, I Thess. iv:17, appear here as fellow comrades with Christ, against the Antichristian host. The condition of the glorified in the Millennial Kingdom is only briefly pictured. "They shall be priests of God and of Christ." Then will first be fulfilled, completely, what was promised in Exodus xix:6, and in Isaiah lxi:6, 9, and they "shall reign with Christ," instead of sigh under Antichrist, as is so often promised in the Old Testament. The exalted station to which they have attained is expressed in these words, "Blessed and holy is he who hath part in the First Resurrection. Over such the Second Death has no power ; but they shall be priests of God and of Christ, and shall reign with Him 1000 years !" Rev. xx:6.

The prophecy of the 1000 years carries us swiftly over from the first Messianic judgment to the Final Judgment, without a full description of the Millennial Age which, in the purpose of the Seer, could only be impossible. Satan must yet be free, once more, because the old creation still exists. And, because he finds no opportunity to practice his favorite art among genuine Christians, he turns himself to seduce the nations in the four corners of the earth, Gog and Magog, dwelling outside the boundaries of the Kingdom of which Jerusalem, made better, is the middle point, and so he leads them against the "Beloved City." Rev. xx:7–9. Here, as Ezekiel's vision, in Chapter xxxvii, had swept before the Seer, in reference to the First Resurrection, so now Chapter xxxviii sweeps before him in reference to Gog and Magog, while the special reason for Gog's march, as given in Ezekiel, here falls away. The march of Gog's conglomerate hordes is the sign that the time for the Last and General Judgment has now come; this final assault upon the blameless City being the last and highest abomination of wickedness; the sign that *that* End, which brings eternal Victory over ever-increasing evil, and the full consummation of all the glorified, must now follow. Thus, Satan is foiled at every step. As the Crucifixion was, in the first of the Three Great Circles of ever-widening Glorifications, *that* out of which came Christ the Glorifier; and as secondly, the assault of Antichrist and the antichristian Roman World-Power upon Jerusalem made better, is *that*, out of which comes the Glorification of all Christians around the Glorified One, in the Kingdom of the 1000 years; so, now, in the third stage of development, Gog's assault, the last and highest abomination of wickedness, and Satanic enmity, is *that* out of which comes the final victory, and the last and highest consummation of glory for the Glorifier and the Glorified, in a Kingdom that has no end. In the first instance, the assault went only against "*The One Man*" that *He* might be put out of the way, and lo ! He is glorified! In the second instance. it goes against *All* those inwardly glorified, and *All* who, like Him, shall be glorified outwardly and lo! both He, and They that are His, are openly "glorified together," and on the earth! And, now, in the third instance, it goes against this sure and great beginning of the Kingdom of the Resurrection, in order to make all the previous steps of progress in the glorification amount to nothing. *Then*, must either "ALL THINGS" be annihilated and return to Chaos; absolute, or "ALL THINGS" must be glorified, and the longing after the Final Consummation be completely satisfied. The result is not doubtful. The End, the Final End, has come which brings with it the Final New Creation, the Final New Heaven and Earth, and Final New Jerusalem, a Glorified World, in which the Glorifier and the Glorified reign to all eternities, and the last outlook of all things is Glory Everlasting!

Appendix 4

DELITZSCH, ORELLI, AND LISTER, ON "EXALTED ZION"
DELITZSCH ON ISAIAH 2:2

"The expression the '*Last Days*,' i. e. the '*End of the Days*,' *Acharith Hayyamim*,' which does not occur anywhere else in Isaiah, is always used in an eschatological sense. It never refers to the course of history immediately following the time being, but invariably indicates the *farthest point* in the history of this life ;—the point that lies on the outermost limit of the speaker's horizon. This horizon was a very fluctuating one. The history of prophecy is just the history of the gradual extension of this horizon, and of the filling up of the intermediate spaces. In Jacob's blessing (Gen. xlix) the Conquest of Canaan stood in the foreground of the *Acharith Hayyamim* and the perspective was regulated accordingly. But, *here*, in Isaiah, the *Acharith* contained no such mixing together of events belonging to the more immediate and most distant future. It was, therefore, the *Last Time*, in its most literal and purest sense, commencing with the beginning of the New Testament Age, and terminating at its close. Compare Heb. i:1. I Pet. i:20. The prophet here predicted that the 'Mountain' which bore the temple of Jehovah, and therefore, was already *in dignity*, the most exalted of all mountains, would, one day, tower in *actual height* above all the high places of the land. The basaltic mountains of Bashan which rose up in bold peaks and columns might now indeed look down with scorn and contempt upon the small limestone hill which Jehovah had chosen (Ps. lxviii:16, 17), but this was an incongruity which the *Last Days* would remove, by making the outward correspond to the inward, the appearance to the reality and intrinsic worth. That this is the prophet's meaning is confirmed by Ezekiel xl:2, where the Temple-Mountain stands gigantic to the prophet, and also by Zechariah xiv:10, where *all Jerusalem* is described as towering above the country round about, which would, one day, become a plain. The question *how* this can possibly take place, *in time*, since it presupposes a complete subversion of the whole

of the existing order of the earth's surface, is easily answered.   The prophet
saw the New Jerusalem of the Last Days on this side, and the New Jerusalem
of the New Earth on the other side of the End, blended together, as it were,
in one.   Whilst, however, we thus avoid all unwarrantable spiritualizing, it
still remains a question *what meaning* the prophet attached to the word,
B'rosh,' 'at the Top.'   Did he mean that Moriah would one day stand
' *upon* the top' of the mountains that surrounded it (as in Ps. lxxii:16), or
that it would stand ' *at* the head' of them (as in I Kings xxi:9, 12. Amos
vi:7. Jer. xxxi:7)?   The former is Hofmann's view, who says ' the prophet
does not mean that the mountains would be piled up, one upon another, and
the temple mountain ' *upon the top*,' but that the temple mountain would
'*appear* to float upon the summit of the others.'   But inasmuch as the
expression ' will be *set*' does not favor this apparently romantic exaltation,
and since ' *B'rosh* ' occurs oftener in the sense of ' *at* the head' than of
' *upon* the top,' I decide, for my own part, in favor of the second view,*
although I agree with Hofmann so far, viz., That it is not merely an exaltation of the Temple Mountain in the *mere esteem* of the nations that is predicted, but a physical and external elevation also.   And when thus outwardly
exalted, the divinely chosen mountain would become the rendezvous and
center of unity for all nations.   They would ' flow unto it' as a river.   It
is Jehovah's Temple which, being thus rendered *visible to nations afar off*,
exerts such magnetic attraction, and with such success.   Just as, at a former
period, men had been separated and estranged from each other in the plains
of Shinar, and thus different nations had arisen, so, at a future period, would
the nations assemble together on the Mountain of the Lord's House, and
there, as members of one family, live together in unity again   Compare Isa.
xxv:6–9. xxiv:23. Isa. xl:4.'

Orelli on Isaiah 2:2

'" The question whether Isa. ii:2 is to be understood physically and
topographically, so that the territory itself and its relations shall undergo a
mighty transformation, in order that Zion, now encircled by mountains
higher than itself, may tower above them all,—or, whether it is meant only
in a spiritual sense —is an idle one.   The *Seer* actually *saw* Mount Zion,
the site of the Temple, standing higher than all the rest, just as he saw, in
fact, the nations journeying to this middle-point of the world under divine
rule, and beheld Zion over-decked with the fiery Glory-Cloud of God.   Isa.
iv:5, 6.   It was not his business to twist such concrete intuitions into
abstract thoughts.   Aware of the spiritual import which is the essential
thing according to our Christian consciousness, yet the Revelation of God

---

* So Orelli, Drechsler, Cheyne, Van Oosterzee, Caspari, Riehm, Hitzig, Nägelsbach,
etc., etc., "*at* the head."   N. W.

dwelling on Mount Zion *must* be acknowledged by all nations, and the world's whole physiognomy, even in its literal outward aspect, be transfigured into harmony with its subjection to Jehovah." *

LISTER ON ISAIAH 2:2

" In this passage, as in others,—Zech. xiv:3–5, 10; Jer. xxxi:38–40; Joel iii:18–21; Ezek. xlvii:1–12; Ps. xcvii:5; Isa. lxiv:3; Judges v:5; Exod. xix:18; Ps. cxiv:7; Isa. lxiv:1; Hagg. ii:6; Heb. xii·26, etc., there is nothing whatever to favor an allegorical interpretation, but everything to support a literal one. The prophet looks forward to the Last Days and points to great changes to be wrought in the land of Palestine, at the time of the Second Coming of the Lord. The events predicted in this, and other cognate passages are all *physical phenomena*. They may, indeed, for the most part be termed *geological phenomena*. They are matters with which Geologists are perfectly familiar. There is not a region on the globe in which they have not occurred again and again. They will consist in the *upheaval* of some parts of the land, and the *depression* and *dislocation* of others. There is nothing with which that science has made us acquainted that comes more frequently under our notice than phenomena of this kind. The terms, even, by which they are expressed have become as familiar as household words. Compare Isa. ii:2, with Zech. xiv:10. What we have here is called ' *Elevation,*' or an ' *Upheaval*' of the strata below, by some cosmic force. Every mountain, and mountain chain, throughout the world owe their origin to it. All lands and continents of the present day have been again and again subjected to an action of the kind, and also. on the other hand, to one of ' *Depression,*' or '*Subsidence,*' as they have successively become 'sea and dry land,' (Hagg. ii:6), which has been the case again and again. And the process is still going on. Instances of Elevation and Depression are perpetually occurring. Three times, in the course of the present century, 1822, 1835, 1837, the coast of Chili has been permanently elevated, the last time the bottom of the sea being raised more than 8 feet, the area over which the elevation extended being more than 100,000 square miles. In the destruction of Lisbon, 1755, we have a case of depression or subsidence, during the six minutes of whose action the new quay, built of marble, at enormous expense, sank beneath the waters, *one hundred fathoms.* These are cases of sudden and *convulsive* action. There are other cases of *gradual* action, such as the coast of Sweden raised *four feet* in the present century, and the coast of Greenland now sinking gradually, for a space of *more than* 600 *miles.* If we apply to the text referred to, the facts thus ascertained, there is not the slightest reason, from the nature of the case,

---

* Orelli Die alttest. Weisag. 287.

why the things foretold in them should not be literally fulfilled. What is predicted is neither impossible nor improbable. It is only what has occurred again and again. The Mount of Olives, and indeed the whole of Palestine have been already ' exalted,' and ' lifted up.' They consist, for the most part, of aqueous or stratified rocks, which were originally deposited at the bottom of the sea, and have since been raised to their present level. The phenomena have been those of ' *Elevation.*' Why, then, seeing that this has occurred before, should we think it strange, if told that it shall occur again ? Is it more improbable in the Future than it was in the Past? The process now going on is gradual, but it seems that when the things foretold occur, it will be *convulsive.* Still this is nothing new, for this also has occurred within our own time. Why should it not occur again ? All the passages referred to have the character of literality about them. We must, therefore, receive them as the Lord has set them before us   ' He hath said it, and shall He not bring it to pass ? '   ' The zeal of the Lord of Hosts will perform this.' "

The passage in Isa. ii:2, is a case of Elevation. In Zech. xiv:10 it is a case of both Elevation and Depression. In Zech. xiv:4, 5, it is a case of what is called ' Disruption," " Fissure," or " Fault." Without pretending to indicate the exact mode by which the Mount of Olives will be divided, and a Valley formed through the midst of it, it is enough to know that the phenomenon foretold is one that is fully understood as a fact of frequent occurrence in the history of our globe. We have cases innumerable of Elevation, Subsidence, and Lateral Pressure, the strata fractured in the process of the movement, and what is called a " Fault " has been produced. The disruption of the Mount of Olives may be produced by any of the above processes; and it would seem more than probable that by the " Mountains " in Isa. lxiv:1–4, and Mic. i:3, 4, Isa. xl:4, we are to understand those in the immediate neighborhood of Jerusalem, and the Mount of Olives, especially. This is rendered the more probable from a comparison of Mic. i:3, with verse 5, the latter being explanatory of the former. In verse 3 we read of the " High Places of the Land," and, in reference to these it is asked in verse 5, " What are the High Places of Judah ? Are they not Jerusalem ? " Again, verse 4, " the Valleys shall be cleft," pointing, no doubt, to the convulsion foretold by Zechariah, where lie the valleys of Jehoshaphat and Hinnom. "And, again, it must be remembered that Isa. ii:2, distinctly shows that a great disturbance and dislocation of the strata must necessarily take place in the immediate neighborhood of Jerusalem at this period, viz., the Second Advent. We have, therefore, good grounds for connecting *all* passages above referred to together, and for regarding them as all relating to the same period, and most of them, to the same locality. Isa. lxiv:1–3, and Mic. i:3, 4, are undoubtedly connected, and relate to the same great event, viz., the Descent of the Lord Jesus Christ to Earth at His Second Advent. In the former there is a prayer that He would do this; in the latter there is a prediction that he will do this."

It is clear, from a comparison of the Scripture passages, that the event predicted in Isa. ii:2, and Mic. iv:1, viz., the "Elevation" of Mount Zion, the Temple-Mountain, is the same event as that predicted in Zech. xiv:10. viz., the Depressions of the hills of Judah, and the "Elevation" of Jerusalem; and which Ezekiel sees accomplished, Ezek. xl:2; and with which the transformations in Jer. xxxi:38–40; Joel. iii:17, 18, Ezek. xlvii:1–12, are associated, viz., the Temple-Waters streaming through the Acacia-Vale, and emptying into the Mediterranean and Dead Seas; as also producing monthly fruit-bearing trees. It is utter folly to spiritualize this as Hengstenberg, Keil, Wright, Alexander, (W. L.) and others do. The objections to the literal interpretation, such as that "natural waters could not flow in all directions at once, from the same point," (R. W. Alexander) and "the whole land would be submerged by the waters of the Mediterranean, were such a depression literal," (Wright, C. H. H.) are misunderstandings of the text, and afford only too open a flank to keen critics like Kuenen and Graf. We hold with Hofmann, Smend, Neumann, Delitzsch, and many more, that the predictions will be literally accomplished, notwithstanding the unbelief of believers. What Isaiah says is that "Mount Zion shall be exalted above the hills." What Zechariah says is that "the whole *land* (not *earth*, but land of Judah. So Ewald, Umbreit, Hitzig, Kohler, Kliefoth, Pressel, and even R. W. Alexander and C. H. H. Wright) shall become as *a* Plain (not *the* plain, as Kliefoth, R. W. Alexander, etc.; but *a* plain, as Ewald, Bunsen, Wright, Maurer, Lange, Keil, notwithstanding Baer's retention of the definite article) from Geba to Rimmon, south of Jerusalem, and SHE (Jerusalem) SHALL BE LIFTED *high*, and shall abide in her place, from the gate of Benjamin to the place of the outermost gate, even the corner gate, and from the tower of Hananeel to the King's wine-presses." And all this in connection with the cleaving of "the Mount of Olives, which is before Jerusalem on the East." And what Joel and Ezekiel say is, that perennial waters shall flow, both sides, from the Temple Rock, and immortalize the land and sea together. Keil thinks this is "a figurative representation of the spiritual elevation and glory the City will receive by the gospel," and Hengstenberg imagines it means "the spiritual elevation and transformation of the church," while Wright is convinced that "high dignity" and "rivers of grace" are here signified. Others think the splitting of Olivet means spiritually, "a broken and contrite heart," which Bunyan keenly corrects by saying "The prophet saith that the mountain is 'before Jerusalem, on the East!'" Still others idealize the prophecy, counting out the "husk" as "mere external," and the "details" as "non-essential!"

Against such liberties, we hold to' the text, as it reads. What we are
told is that Palestine will be transfigured when the Lord comes. When He
renovates Israel for Himself, He renovates their City and their Land. *The
New-Born Tenant has a New-Built Home.* When the Daughter of Zion
is married to her Lord, it is not in the old ruin they keep house! Exalted
above the hills and crowned with the streaming light of the Glory-Cloud,
will be her special dwelling-place. The territory of Judah will become like
the "Arabah," or Ghor, which stretches from the slopes of Hermon or Sea
of Tiberias, to the Red Sea or Elanitic Gulf. It is a case of "Depression"
of the *mountains* and *hills*, an "Elevation" of the *valleys*, but not a sinking of the territory itself; certainly not of Jerusalem. The land is elevated
while yet its irregularities and inequalities are smoothed, and it becomes a
plain. The errors of the commentators here, are many. It is not said that
Judah's territory shall be depressed, but only that its mountainous region
shall be leveled like the Ghor, while the City and the Temple are exalted.
Isaiah has taught the same truth. "Every Valley shall be exalted, and
every mountain and hill be brought low, the crooked place be made straight
and the rough place plain and the *Glory of the Lord* shall be revealed and
all flesh shall see it together, for Jehovah's mouth hath spoken it." Isa. xl:
4. The delimitation of the boundary of the territory is sufficiently clear.
It is that of *the royal tribe and kingdom of Judah*, the central glory of millennial times. It is from Geba (old Gibeah, modern *Jeba*) in the territory of
Benjamin, the northern boundary line, to Rimmon (modern *Umer-Rumanim*)
the southern boundary line, i. e., "from Geba to Beersheba," the whole
extent of Judah's domain (II Kings xxiii:8). The entire hilly region shall
become like the "Great Plain," and "*Jerusalem shall be lifted high.*" The
total City shall be elevated. If we trace the delimitation of the City itself,
it is even more precise. From East to West, the boundary line runs from
Benjamin's Gate to the Corner Gate, while it stretches North and South,
from the Tower of Hananeel to the royal gardens at the junction of the valleys of Jehoshaphat and Hinnom. Zech. xiv:10; Jer. xxxi:38-40. This
particularity is intentional, on the part of the Spirit of Prophecy. But, it is
a false inference, from this, to conclude that *only this portion* of the Land of
Canaan is the subject of cosmical transformation. Dr. Robertson Smith's
sneer at the idea of "*the Kingdom of God reduced to the petty limits of the
erritory of Judah,*" rests upon his own ignorance of the prophetic word,
and is a sneer at the prophetic word itself. Elsewhere we read, clearly,—
and long ago, as Justin Martyr emphasized it,—that the entire land, and the
city, will be "*broadened, enlarged and adorned,*" according to the prophets.
It has been a misfortune that our English Version, like others equally defective, has obscured for us the sense in many passages. In the clearest manner, the prophet Isaiah, looking forward to Israel's glory accomplished at

Messiah's Coming, says, " Thou hast increased the nation, O Lord, thou art glorified; *thou hast extended wide the borders of the land*." Isa. xxvi:15. It is a prediction of increased population, both by restoration, and resurrection, and an enlargement of the limits of the land. So the promise is given, " Thine eyes shall see the King in His beauty, *and the land of breadths*," or " far-stretching land." The same is true as to the enlargement of the City, in future times. The magnificence of the Kingdom is elsewhere foretold in terms unmistakable. In the 72d Psalm, it is described as *"from Sea to Sea, and from the River to the ends of the Earth."* Ps. lxxii:7. Does all this seem too marvelous? *" Neum Yehovah!"* *" It is the utterance of Jehovah, Doer of these things!"* How blessed this Planet of ours one day will be, by reason of the Coming of the Lord from Heaven! How blessed the Holy Land! And Jerusalem lifted up! And Zion exalted! And Israel redeemed! And the Nations converted! And the holy sleepers waked into the image of Christ! How stupendous the change! What a different Age from ours! *Come, Lord Jesus!*